PRESS, POLITICS AND NATIONAL IDENTITIES IN CATALONIA

The Transformation of
La Vanguardia, 1881–1931

The Cañada Blanch / Sussex Academic Studies on Contemporary Spain

General Editor: Professor Paul Preston, London School of Economics

A list of all published titles in the series is available on the Press website. More recently published works are presented below.

Peter Anderson, *Friend or Foe?: Occupation, Collaboration and Selective Violence in the Spanish Civil War.*

Margaret Joan Anstee, *JB – An Unlikely Spanish Don: The Life and Times of Professor John Brande Trend.*

Richard Barker, *Skeletons in the Closet, Skeletons in the Ground: Repression, Victimization and Humiliation in a Small Andalusian Town – The Human Consequences of the Spanish Civil War.*

Germà Bel, *Infrastructure and the Political Economy of Nation Building in Spain, 1720–2010.*

Germà Bel, *Disdain, Distrust, and Dissolution: The Surge of Support for Independence in Catalonia.*

Carl-Henrik Bjerström, *Josep Renau and the Politics of Culture in Republican Spain, 1931–1939: Re-imagining the Nation.*

Kathryn Crameri, *'Goodbye, Spain?': The Question of Independence for Catalonia.*

Pol Dalmau, *Press, Politics and National Identities in Catalonia: The Transformation of La Vanguardia, 1881–1931.*

Mark Derby, *Petals and Bullets: Dorothy Morris – A New Zealand Nurse in the Spanish Civil War.*

Francisco Espinosa-Maestre, *Shoot the Messenger?: Spanish Democracy and the Crimes of Francoism – From the Pact of Silence to the Trial of Baltasar Garzón.*

María Jesús González, *Raymond Carr: The Curiosity of the Fox.*

Helen Graham, *The War and its Shadow: Spain's Civil War in Europe's Long Twentieth Century.*

Angela Jackson, *'For us it was Heaven': The Passion, Grief and Fortitude of Patience Darton – From the Spanish Civil War to Mao's China.*

Gabriel Jackson, *Juan Negrín: Physiologist, Socialist, and Spanish Republican War Leader.*

Nathan Jones, *The Adoption of a Pro-US Foreign Policy by Spain and the United Kingdom: José María Aznar and Tony Blair's Personal Motivations and their Global Impact.*

Xavier Moreno Juliá, *The Blue Division: Spanish Blood in Russia, 1941–1945.*

David Lethbridge, *Norman Bethune in Spain: Commitment, Crisis, and Conspiracy.*

Antonio Miguez Macho, *The Genocidal Genealogy of Francoism: Violence, Memory and Impunity.*

Carles Manera, *The Great Recession: A Subversive View.*

Nicholas Manganas, *Las dos Españas: Terror and Crisis in Contemporary Spain.*

Jorge Marco, *Guerrilleros and Neighbours in Arms: Identities and Cultures of Antifascist Resistance in Spain.*

Emily Mason, *Democracy, Deeds and Dilemmas: Support for the Spanish Republic within British Civil Society, 1936–1939.*

Soledad Fox Maura, *Jorge Semprún: The Spaniard who Survived the Nazis and Conquered Paris.*

Martin Minchom, *Spain's Martyred Cities: From the Battle of Madrid to Picasso's Guernica.*

Olivia Muñoz-Rojas, *Ashes and Granite: Destruction and Reconstruction in the Spanish Civil War and Its Aftermath.*

Linda Palfreeman, *Spain Bleeds: The Development of Battlefield Blood Transfusion during the Civil War.*

Isabelle Rohr, *The Spanish Right and the Jews, 1898–1945: Antisemitism and Opportunism.*

Rúben Serém, *Conspiracy, Coup d'état and Civil War in Seville, 1936–1939: History and Myth in Francoist Spain.*

Gareth Stockey, *Gibraltar: "A Dagger in the Spine of Spain?"*

Maria Thomas, *The Faith and the Fury: Popular Anticlerical Violence and Iconoclasm in Spain, 1931–1936.*

Dacia Viejo-Rose, *Reconstructing Spain: Cultural Heritage and Memory after Civil War.*

PRESS, POLITICS AND NATIONAL IDENTITIES IN CATALONIA

The Transformation of *La Vanguardia*, 1881–1931

POL DALMAU

sussex
ACADEMIC
PRESS

Brighton • Chicago • Toronto

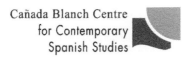

Cañada Blanch Centre
for Contemporary
Spanish Studies

CATALAN
OBSER
VATORY LSE

2 4 6 8 10 9 7 5 3 1

First published in Great Britain in 2017, reprinted in paperback 2019, by
SUSSEX ACADEMIC PRESS
PO Box 139, Eastbourne BN24 9BP

Distributed in North America by
SUSSEX ACADEMIC PRESS
Independent Publishers Group
814 N. Franklin Street, Chicago, IL 60610

Published in collaboration with the Cañada Blanch Centre for Contemporary Spanish Studies and
the Catalan Observatory, London School of Economics.

The European University Institute (EUI)

This book has been published with a financial subsidy from the European University Institute ("ouvrage
publié avec le concours de l'Institut Universitaire Européen"). This publication is a revised version
of an EUI PhD thesis, Department of History and Civilization, 2015.

British Library Cataloguing in Publication Data
A CIP catalogue record for this book is available from the British Library.

Library of Congress Cataloging-in-Publication Data
Names: Dalmau, Pol, author.
Title: Press, politics and national identity in Catalonia : the transformation of La Vanguardia,
1881–1939 / Pol Dalmau
Description: Portland, Oregon : Sussex Academic Press, 2017. | Series: The Cañada Blanch/Sussex
Academic Studies | Includes bibliographical references and index.
Identifiers: LCCN 2017034868 | ISBN 9781845198152 (hardback)
                                 | ISBN 9781789760033 (paperback)
Subjects: LCSH: Vanguardia (Barcelona, Spain : 1978). | God?o family. | Newspaper
publishing—Spain—Barcelona—History—20th century. | Press and politics—Spain—
Barcelona—History—20th century. | Newspaper publishing—Spain—Catalonia—History—
20th century. | Press and politics—Spain—Catalonia—History—20th century. | Journalism—
History—20th century—Catalonia (Principality) | Press—History—20th century—Catalonia
(Principality) | La Vanguardia (Firm)—History—20th century. | Catalonia (Principality)—
History—20th century—Political aspects. | BISAC: HISTORY / Modern / 20th Century. |
HISTORY / Europe / Spain & Portugal.
Classification: LCC PN1539.B32 D35 2017 | DDC 079.467/2—dc23
LC record available at https://lccn.loc.gov/2017034868

Typeset & designed by Sussex Academic Press, Brighton & Eastbourne.
Printed on acid-free paper by TJ International, Padstow, Cornwall.

Contents

The Cañada Blanch Centre for Contemporary Spanish Studies

In the 1960s, the most important initiative in the cultural and academic relations between Spain and the United Kingdom was launched by a Valencian fruit importer in London. The creation by Vicente Cañada Blanch of the Anglo-Spanish Cultural Foundation has subsequently benefited large numbers of Spanish and British scholars at various levels. Thanks to the generosity of Vicente Cañada Blanch, thousands of Spanish schoolchildren have been educated at the secondary school in West London that bears his name. At the same time, many British and Spanish university students have benefited from the exchange scholarships which fostered cultural and scientific exchanges between the two countries. Some of the most important historical, artistic and literary work on Spanish topics to be produced in Great Britain was initially made possible by Cañada Blanch scholarships.

Vicente Cañada Blanch was, by inclination, a conservative. When his Foundation was created, the Franco regime was still in the plenitude of its power. Nevertheless, the keynote of the Foundation's activities was always a complete open-mindedness on political issues. This was reflected in the diversity of research projects supported by the Foundation, many of which, in Francoist Spain, would have been regarded as subversive. When the Dictator died, Don Vicente was in his seventy-fifth year. In the two decades following the death of the Dictator, although apparently indestructible, Don Vicente was obliged to husband his energies. Increasingly, the work of the Foundation was carried forward by Miguel Dols whose tireless and imaginative work in London was matched in Spain by that of José María Coll Comín. They were united in the Foundation's spirit of open-minded commitment to fostering research of high quality in pursuit of better Anglo-Spanish cultural relations. Throughout the 1990s, thanks to them, the role of the Foundation grew considerably.

In 1994, in collaboration with the London School of Economics, the Foundation established the Príncipe de Asturias Chair of Contemporary Spanish History and the Cañada Blanch Centre for Contemporary Spanish Studies. It is the particular task of the Cañada Blanch Centre for Contemporary Spanish Studies to promote the understanding of twentieth- century Spain through research and teaching of contemporary Spanish history, politics, economy, sociology and culture. The Centre possesses a valuable library and archival centre for specialists in contemporary Spain. This work is carried on through the publications of the doctoral and post-doctoral researchers at the Centre itself and through the many seminars and lectures held at the London School of Economics. While the seminars are the province of the researchers, the lecture cycles have been the forum in which Spanish politicians have been able to address audiences in the United Kingdom.

Since 1998, the Cañada Blanch Centre has published a substantial number of books in collaboration with several different publishers on the subject of contemporary Spanish history and politics. An extremely fruitful partnership with Sussex Academic Press began in 2004. Full details and descriptions of the published works can be found on the Press website.

An ongoing interest of the series has been the relationship of Catalonia with the political establishment in Madrid. This has been reflected in the volumes by Ramon Tremosa on the Catalan economy, by Olivia Muñoz-Rojas on reconstruction after the Civil War, by Germà Bel both on the damage done to the Spanish economy by the country's dysfunctional transport and communications model and on the ever-intensifying problems of the dynamics of conflict between groups, their effects on the inter-territorial distrust, and their impact on the functioning of the state, and by Andrew Dowling and by Kathryn Crameri on the development of Catalan independence sentiment. The present volume looks at an earlier period in this complex relationship.

Whether under the corrupt politics of the Bourbon Restoration, the radical transformations of the Second Republic or the tragedy of the Spanish Civil War, *La Vanguardia* has remained Barcelona's indisputable journalistic benchmark. As Pol Dalmau explains, this success was primarily due to a twofold track of political engagement coupled with wide-ranging business interests in Spain and overseas. *La Vanguardia* still exerts considerable influence on Catalonian affairs and beyond, but the history of the paper's establishment and the intrigues of the Godó family dynasty has not hitherto been scrutinized. Dalmau's research is to be welcomed, for it sheds new light on how the media shaped Europe's birth of mass politics and Spain's uneven path to modernity.

PAUL PRESTON
London School of Economics

Preface by Guest Series Editor Angel Smith

This book by Pol Dalmau is destined to become required reading of all those seriously interested in modern Catalan and Spanish history. Furthermore, its location of events in Catalonia and Spain within a broad European context means that it will be of interest to academics as an important case study that challenges some of the broadly held assumptions with respect to the period covered. The centre of attention is how the Godó family, who rose to prominence in the town of Igualada after setting a large textile mill, joining the Liberal Party, and dominating the local political scene through clientalist links established with men of influence in the electoral district, adapted to changes in the political climate brought about by the growing politicisation of the electorate, the rise of mass parties and of a more professional class of politicians, most particularly after the "Disaster" of 1898. Key in this respect was the founding, by a branch of the family, of *La Vanguardia* in Barcelona in 1881 and its subsequent transformation, in two stages, into a commercial, mass circulation daily which, while conservative in outlook, did not overtly subscribe to any political party, and which offered succinct and wide-ranging information, most especially of events on the international stage.

This strategy turned *La Vanguardia* into Catalonia's best-selling newspaper by the late 1890s and one of Spain's major publications by the end of the second decade of the twentieth century. In the 1880s and 1890s it made its proprietors, Bartolomé and Carlos Godó, significant figures in the Catalan Liberal Party. The latter's son, Ramon Godó, who took over the paper in 1899, would then become a man of substantial political influence on the Catalan and, indeed, Spanish political stage. In undertaking this analysis the study provides new insights into the period at hand. Historians working on Catalonia have tended to focus on those political forces that challenged the Restoration Monarchy, the Catalanists, Republicans, and the anarcho-syndicalist trade union the CNT, rather than those families and organisations than came under pressure from their rise. And yet, Ramon Godó and *La Vanguardia* not only survived the fall of the regime in September 1923 but the newspaper remained Catalonia's major publication throughout the 1920s. Furthermore, there has been little work on the press per se, and the press is generally used to analyse the position of the various social and political actors. Dr Pol Dalmau's work shows the importance in studying the press as a historical actor in its own right; one that played a significant role in articulating a more globally inter-connected society and, in an era in which a mass circulation press was coming into being, attempted, with varying degrees of success, to set the political agenda.

The great strength of the book is the interconnection it establishes between the micro and macro levels of historical analysis. On the one hand, as indicated, Pol Dalmau provides us with a study of the strategy the Godó family pursued to achieve political dominance in their backyard of Igualada and wider political influence within Catalonia and Spain. This actually required the two branches of the family, located in Igualada and Barcelona, to pursue different political strategies. While the Igualada branch remained closely linked to the Liberal Party, Ramon Godó, from his base in Barcelona, affirmed that the regime needed reform and from 1906 drew close to the political figure of Antonio Maura, who proclaimed that the regime had to be transformed "from above" by undermining the power of the local power-brokers (the so-called *caciques*) and basing it on sound (that is conservative) public opinion. That is to say, Maura stated that he wanted to disempower people like the Godó family in Igualada (who Ramon, though breaking with the Liberal Party, in fact continued to back in their electoral campaigns). The relative success of these two strategies was also very different. While the Igualada branch eventually succumbed to the new political forces, Ramon Godó both upped his political and social profile, was given a noble title in 1916, and went on to play a significant role in the final crisis of the Restoration Monarchy between 1919 and 1923. While *La Vanguardia* was not a party-political broadsheet it did aim, in Ramon Godó's own words, to guide the "conservative masses". And when faced with the challenge of the Catalanists, who looked to pressure the king and parliament into granting Catalonia an autonomy statute in late 1919, it rallied in defence the king, order and stability, and, as against the Catalanist emphasis on Catalan iden-tity, proclaimed the Catalans dual Catalan/Spanish identity and their love for the Spanish motherland. Over the next three years *La Vanguardia* would play a key role in articulating these anti-Catalanist forces, helping to organise the ultra-conservative monarchist coalition, the Unión Monárquica Nacional (National Monarchist Union).

Dr Dalmau points to several major ways in which his work can inform more general European wide-analyses. First, he studies the interrelationship between events at a European level and those within Catalonia and Spain itself. With respect to the press, the rise of mass circulation dailies did not of course originate in Spain, and he notes that to a significant degree *The Times* was the module for the reform of *La Vanguardia* in 1888. Second, he indicates that it is mistaken to think that in western Europe liberal "nota-bles" were simply swept away by the new era of mass politics. The case of

Ramon Godó shows how they could ride the new wave. Finally, the example of *La Vanguardia* indicates that it is naïve to think that the commercial press became a neutral purveyor of objective news that held the political elite to account. While men like Ramon Godó were not officially behind a specific political party they had their own political agenda. This is a world that we know all too well today.

I would, however, add an additional point. While men like Ramon Godó may have started out as "notables" operating within liberal oligarchic regimes, their survival and, indeed, prosperity, meant that they might need to break with that world, and most particularly move in an authoritarian direction. As we have seen, Godó and *La Vanguardia* were between 1919 and 1923 behind a coalition of order and it is worth stressing that this coalition was opposed by the Liberals and the majority wing within the Conservative Party. And, as Pol Dalmau notes, the paper would back the coup by the captain general of Barcelona, Miguel Primo de Rivera, which sunk the regime in September 1923. And while at first Primo de Rivera declared he wanted to hand power back to parliament once he had cleansed the country of corrupt politicians, there was clearly a strong authoritarian thrust behind his movement. Fast forward a generation and Ramon Godó's son, Carlos Godó Valls, was to be found supporting the Franco Regime.

The study is given added piquancy by the fact that *La Vanguardia* is still Catalonia's highest selling newspaper, is still run by the Godó family, and, if subscriptions are taken into account, is the third highest selling newspaper in Spain. And some parallels can be drawn between the years 1919 and 1923 and the present day. In the earlier period, as Pol Dalmau points out, while *La Vanguardia* opposed Catalanism it had to tread carefully because many of its readers sympathised with the dominant conservative Catalanist party, the Lliga Regionalista. And what it did was try and peel away the Lliga's more conservative supporters by arguing that its radical actions were endangering stability and opening the door to social revolution. Today *La Vanguardia* opposes Catalan independence (though the occasional voice favourable to independence is permitted), but has to tread carefully because many of its readers vote for independentist parties, most notably the Partit Democràtic Europeu Català (Catalan European Democratic Party), the successor to the old party, Convergència Democràtica de Catalunya (Catalan Democratic Convergence), which used to back Catalan autonomy but became pro-independence in 2012. In this case, it plays on the impossibility of achieving independence, and the negative political and economic consequences that the movement in favour of independence has had in Catalonia. In both instances it is worth noting that the potential alienation of sections of its readership has not affected sales. Part of the answer at least lies in the fact that people will buy and read a quality newspaper even if it is not fully aligned with their political views. Here, it would seem, lies one reason for *La Vanguardia*'s success. Such readers may believe that they are not affected by its political line. Whether this is really the case is another matter.

ANGEL SMITH
University of Leeds

Acknowledgements

This book project took life with a doctoral thesis defended at the European University Institute (Florence, Italy) in September 2015. My first thanks must therefore go to my supervisor Bartolomé Yun-Casalilla. Throughout this period he was a continuous source of intellectual stimulus and constructive criticism. He transformed my approach to history and provided me with something that is fundamental for someone taking his first steps in the profession: trust. The members of the jury — professors Lucy Riall, Isabel Burdiel and Renato Camurri — are all historians whose work inspired crucial aspects of the thought embodied in this book. I would like to thank them for their generosity in agreeing to be part of the jury and, especially, for their valuable feedback.

My time in Florence was an incredible experience that I would not hesitate (if only I could!) to repeat. At the EUI, professors Antonella Romano, Steve Smith and Gerhard Haupt helped me improve my work, as did the inspiring seminars held at this institution. A generous grant from the Spanish Ministry of Education enabled me to conduct this long research, and I hope that the ongoing cuts in public funding will not prevent future researchers from benefiting from the same opportunities that I was able to enjoy. Although no place is perfect, the melting pot of intellectual traditions makes the EUI particularly special. Among the incredible people there are: Alan Granadino, Giorgio Potì and Romain Bonnet, the *Tre tenori* with whom I enjoyed many memorable moments. I must also mention the many good friends I made, such as Carolina Obradors, Brian Olesen, José Miguel Escribano, Miguel Palou, Kaarlo Havu, Daniel Knegt, to name a few. Our endless talks showed me the value of sharing views with colleagues working on different topics and periods in history.

I am particularly grateful to Paul Preston for offering me to participate in the Cañada Blanch/Sussex Academic Studies on Contemporary Spain series and opening the door to the Catalan Observatory at the London School of Economics to me. I am equally indebted to Angel Smith for his excellent Preface. I can only claim sole ownership of any mistakes contained in the book. Two research stays at other universities widened my intellectual scope. I would like to thank Edward Berenson and Andrew H. Lee for their warm welcome at New York University. My stay at Universitat Pompeu Fabra in Barcelona proved fundamental for improving the chapters on colonialism. I would particularly like to thank Josep Maria Fradera, Albert García Balañà, Stephen

Jacobson and Martín Rodrigo for their advice, and for the invitation to participate in their research seminar. Several chapters in this book have also benefited from the feedback of colleagues and professors in workshops and informal gatherings. Isabel Burdiel gave me the opportunity to participate in my first conference as a PhD researcher, and I am grateful for the support she has shown me ever since. My gratitude also goes to James Thomson, who has been supportive since my stay at Sussex University so long ago. At the Universitat Autònoma de Barcelona, Borja de Riquer and Maria Gemma Rubí provided valuable insights, as did Jordi Casassas at the Universitat de Barcelona. I have also been fortunate to share my thoughts, concerns and, above all, enjoy the company of several young and promising historians: Jorge Luengo, David Cao, Miguel Garau, Elisenda Loscos and Oriol Lujan.

The staff at different libraries and archives located in Barcelona, Vilanova, Igualada, Madrid, Bilbao, Pontevedra, London, Paris and Tangier were ever so helpful in locating the material for this book. At *La Vanguardia*, I would like to thank the current editor, Màrius Carol, and former archivist, Carles Salmurri, for giving me access to much valuable material. In Igualada, Marta Vives was vital in locating some of the most precious sources, and I also relied on the valuable advice of Teresa Miret and Pere Pascual. I would also like to thank Alfonso Pérez-Maura, at the *Fundación Antonio Maura* in Madrid; and Cecilia Fernández and Father Seijas, in the city of Tangier, in Morocco, for their guidance in archival research. Helen Aitchison meticulously edited my dissertation, while Bradley Hayes, James Yeoman and Matthew Ashcroft helped revise the book manuscript.

The last words go to my closest friends and family. Their support has been crucial and I don't even want to imagine what it would have been like to write this book without each and every one of them in my life. In Madrid my old Brightonian friends Paloma and Emi provided me with a *pied-à-terre* that made archival work much easier. And distance never dampened my friendship with Núria, with whom I shared the long and difficult journey that writing a thesis so often becomes. Raul, Sergi and Jordi are all exceptional cases of perpetually cheerful people and I feel fortunate for having them by my side. My parents Antoni and Montserrat, as well as my brothers Clara and Albert, encouraged me to leap into this research when I myself still harboured doubts. Sharing the thrill of *"Sapiens moments"* — as we called those instances when something valuable appeared in the archives — are among the best memories I have. Finally, as in the most memorable movies, the best comes at the end. Virginia has been by my side since we met in Brighton many years ago, and has stoically endured life with someone who spends so much of his time combing through the past. As I write these lines, our lives are being transformed by the blessing of the birth of our son Guillem. This book is dedicated to them.

POL DALMAU

List of Abbreviations

ABMVB	Arxiu-Biblioteca Museu Víctor Balaguer, Vilanova i la Geltrú
ACAN	Arxiu Comarcal de l'Anoia, Igualada
AMI	Arxiu Municipal d'Igualada
AFAM	Archivo Fundación Antonio Maura, Madrid
ACD	Archivo del Congreso de los Diputados, Madrid
AGP	Archivo General de Palacio, Madrid
AGA	Archivo General de la Administración, Madrid
AHCB	Arxiu Històric de la Ciutat de Barcelona
AHFB	Archivo Histórico Foral de Bizkaia, Bilbao
AHDB	Arxiu Històric de la Diputació de Barcelona
AHEB	Archivo Histórico Eclesiástico de Bizkaia, Bilbao
AHFTN	Arxiu Històric de Foment del Treball Nacional, Barcelona
AHPB	Arxiu Històric de Protocols de Barcelona
AHPM	Archivo Histórico de Protocolos de Madrid
ANI	Arxiu Notarial d'Igualada
GFA	Godó Family Archive (*Arxiu Família Godó*), Igualada
MP	Museo de Pontevedra, Archivo del Marqués de la Vega de Armijo
NA	The National Archives, London
ANF	Archives Nationales de France, Archives de l'Agence Havas, Paris
AMFT	Archivo de la Misión Franciscana en Marruecos, Tangier

List of Illustrations

Cover illustration
'News-stand on the Rambla in Barcelona', 1907, courtesy of Arxiu Fotogràfic de Barcelona.

The picture section (begins page xix)
1 First edition of *La Vanguardia* (1 Feburary 1881).
2 "Baptism of a Moor girl", the godchild of Carlos Godó and his wife.[1]
3 Supplement of *La Vanguardia* dedicated to the African War of 1859–1860.[2]
4 "The Customs of Moroccans".[3]
5 Ramón Godó Lallana (1864–1931), First Count of Godó.
6 Two generations of the Godó family (1915).[4]
7 Juan Godó Llucià laying the first foundation stone of a school in the town of Pierola (1914).[5]
8 Popular homage paid to the former deputy Juan Godó Llucià (1851–1935), and to his son and former mayor of Igualada Juan Godó Pelegrí (1876–1957) by the 32 districts of the constituency in recognition of their work (1914).[6]
9 Antonio Maura's portrait, with a dedication to Ramón Godó Lallana, reproduced in *La Vanguardia*.
10 Front page of *La Vanguardia*, 14 April 1931.[7]

Sources
1 "Bautizo de una mora" ("Baptizing of a Moor girl"), *La Vanguardia*, 28/10/1893, p. 5.
2 *La Vanguardia*, 12/10/1893, p. 1.
3 *La Vanguardia*, 13/10/1893, p. 8. The drawing on the top left is of Father Lerchundi, the man who contributed so decisively to promoting Godó's plans in Morocco.
4 Godó Family Archive (GFA). Picture taken on June 24th 1915 to celebrate the centenary of the building of the Godó's family home. **Ramón Godó Lallana** (owner of *La Vanguardia* and First Count of Godó) is the first man from the left in the second row. The woman on his right is his wife Rosa Valls i Valls. His mother Antonia Lallana Aspe is the second woman from the left in the front row wearing a black dress. The man next

AÑO I.   MIÉRCOLES 2 DE FEBRERO DE 1881.   NÚM. 2.

LA VANGUARDIA.

DIARIO POLITICO Y DE AVISOS Y NOTICIAS

ÓRGANO DEL PARTIDO CONSTITUCIONAL DE LA PROVINCIA.

REDACCION Y ADMINISTRACION: calle de las Euras, núm. 8 y 10, (entre la Plaza Real y la calle de Raurich.)

PRECIOS DE SUSCRICION: En Barcelona, un mes, 6 rs.—Fuera, un trimestre, 20 rs.—Ultramar: 40 rs.—Extranjero: 60 rs.—ANUNCIOS Y REMITIDOS, à precios convencionales.

AFECCIONES METEOROLÓGICAS dadas por el óptico aleman D. ALBERTO BURCKHART

Dia.	Horas.	Termómetro		Barom Aneroi	Higro. Saus	Vientos.		Atm.ª y obs. notables.	Sol.		Luna.	
		Reau.	Centig			Flojo	Rec.		Sale.	Pone	Sale.	Pone
31	10 n.	7'	8°7	756	77		NO	Sereno.				
1.°	7 m.	8'	10'	757	79		NO	Claro.	7'11	5'18	9'40	8 41
»	2 t.	12'	15'	757	70		NO	Claro.				

SANTO DE HOY.—La Purificacion de Ntra- Sra., San Cornelio Centurion y San Firmo.— SANTO DE MAÑANA. —San Blas, el beato Nicolás de Longabardo y Santa Celerina. — CUAR NTA HORAS. —Iglesia de Santa Basílica. — CORTE DE MARIA.—Nuestra Señóra de los Angeles en su propia iglesia, o Nuestra Señóra de las Gracias, en San Pedro.

REUMA, HERPES, (brians), VENÉREO.

Si se sospecha que existe en la sangre alguno de estos humores, causa de la mayor parte de enfermedades, depurarla con las *Grajeas Universales*, segun fórmula del Dr. Salvat.
Este precioso depurativo obra sin irritar ni debilitar las fuerzas, y no hay mal sostenido por algun virus que se resista á tan poderosa medicacion. Frasco, 1 peseta Depósitos principales: Farmacias de Montserrat, Rambla esquina Puerta-ferrisa; de Aguilar, Rambla del Centro, 37; de Botta, Platería, 48, y de Marqués, Hospital, 108.

INYECCION SALVAT
El mejor especifico para la curacion de toda clase de flujos, así en el hombre como en la mujer.
Véndese: Farmacias de Aguilar, Rambla del Centro, 37; de Montserrat, Rambla. esquina Puerta-ferrisa y de Botta, Plateria, 48.

VENEREO
El Dr. Salvat, seis veces premiado en públicas oposiciones por esta Facultad de Medicina, asegura la curacion pronta y radical sin uso de mercurio. Recibe de 11 á 1 y de 6 á 8.—Puertaferrisa, 11, 1.°
SIFILIS

ESPECTÁCULOS.

TEATRO PRINCIPAL.—Funciones para hoy miércoles.—Tarde: 4 rs. A las tres.—La aplaudida opereta I Briganti y el gran baile mímico-fantástico de espectáculo Clorinda.
Noche.—33 de abono.—Impar.—La nueva opereta en 3 actos La Fronda y el gran baile de espectáculo Clorinda.—Entrada 4 rs.—A las ocho.
GRAN TEATRO DEL LICEO.—Hoy 2.—10 de abono.—Par.—Por la tarde, á las tres:—A 2 rs.—Los Miserables. —Por la noche.—La ópera de espectáculo Mefistófeles.—A las 8.—A 6 rs.—5.° piso, 4 rs.
TEATRO DEL CIRCO.—Funciones para hoy.—Tarde.—A las 3.—El tributo de las cien doncellas y El lucero del alba.'
Noche.—1.ª representacion de la preciosa zarzuela del malogrado Bartrina, La dama de las camelias cuyos primeros papeles desempeñarán la distinguida tiple Sra. Peset y el reputado tenor Sr. Prats.—Entrada 2 rs.—A las ocho.

CRÓNICA LOCAL.

Nuestro primer artículo nos ha valido una inundacion de *El Diluvio*. Nos atribuye conceptos equivocados con el propósito, sin duda, de proporcionarse el placer de comentar lo que no hemos dicho. Lea mejor nuestro colega el artículo á qué se refiere y se conven-

1 First edition of *La Vanguardia* (1 February 1881).

Bautizo de una mora

Cuando las hordas rifeñas lanzan el grito de guerra contra los *perros cristianos* á pretexto de defender una endeble mezquita y un cementerio de supuestas y problemáticas profanaciones; cuando en los montes y valles del Riff se predica la guerra santa, la guerra de exterminio y de venganza, consuela ver espectáculos como el que anteayer tuvieron ocasión de presenciar los que por devoción ó por curiosidad asistieron á la solemne é imponente ceremonia del bautizo de una niña, hasta entonces mora y hoy discípula fervorosa de la religión de Cristo.

Esta hermosa conquista en favor de la religión cristiana es debida á las Religiosas franciscanas establecidas en Tánger. Parece que los padres de la niña Fatma Ben Ansor, que así se llamaba, deseaban desprenderse de ella, por lo cual las religiosas de Tánger se apresuraron á recogerla, con el objeto de ampararla y ganar un alma más para el cielo.

Las hermanas de Tánger tuvieron por espacio de dos meses en su compañía á la niña Fatma, colmándola de solícitos cuidados y preparándola convenientemente para ser bautizada.

Hace unos seis meses llegó la niña mora á Barcelona, continuando su catequización las religiosas franciscanas, que con tanta habilidad y celo la han llevado á cabo, que Fatma era desde hace ya tiempo una fervorosa y amantísima devota de Cristo y de la Virgen María.

La ceremonia de anteayer ha completado la obra de las celosas franciscanas.

Se verificó dicha ceremonia en la iglesia

parroquial de Santa Madrona. La administró el santo sacramento del bautismo el Muy Ilustre Canónigo Estalella y la apadrinaron el diputado á Cortes por Igualada don Carlos Godó y la señora doña Antonia Llana de Godó.

El acto resultó imponente y conmovedor por las ceremonias litúrgicas, por el candoroso fervor de la catecúmena y por el escogido y numeroso acompañamiento que llevaban los padrinos.

La niña que, como hemos dicho, se llamaba Fatma ben Ansor, en la religión de Cristo ha recibido el nombre de María Luisa, indudablemente más hermoso y más dulce que el primero.

Los padres de la niña, se llaman Mahomet y Fatma.

Si por un momento prescindimos de los bienes espirituales, puramente del orden religioso, que con el ingreso en la fé de Cristo haya podido adquirir la preciosa niña, cuyo retrato acompañamos por partida doble, para que nuestros lectores la puedan ver con la veste mora y con la veste de cristiana, si prescindimos de los bienes religiosos que haya podido alcanzar, repetimos, y sólo nos fijamos por un momento en los terrenales, en los materiales, ¡cuánto no ha ganado la pequeña Fatma, escapando á la miseria presente, á la esclavitud tutora, al embrutecimiento y á la abyección en que los mahometanos suelen tener á sus mujeres, y viniendo á vivir en un pueblo libre, en donde por lo menos encontrará consideración y respeto, si ella es bastante virtuosa para hacerse respetar, que sí lo será, siendo educada por religiosas tan hábiles y tan celosas como las religiosas franciscanas deesta ciudad!

2 "Baptism of the Moor girl", the godchild of Carlos Godó and his wife.

LA VANGUARDIA

SUPLEMENTO

al número 3752 correspondiente al dia 12 de Octubre de 1893

PRECIO DE ESTE SUPLEMENTO:

A los suscritores de «La Vanguardia». . . . . Gratis.
Al público: Número suelto. . . . . 10 céntimos. 25 números 1'25 Ptas.

LA GUERRA DE ÁFRICA DE 1859-60

El presente Suplemento

No tiene otro objeto que el de tributar desde las columnas de LA VANGUARDIA un recuerdo de admiración y de agradecimiento á los héroes de la guerra del 60. La mayor parte, casi todos los caudillos españoles de aquella campaña legendaria han muerto ya; sus nombres, idolatrados por la generación que presenció los hechos, suenan en los oidos de la generación presente como rumor de gloria para la patria, pero como rumor lejano cuyos acentos no pueden precisar las generaciones que nacieron luego; la leyenda: Prim, O'Donnell, el cabo Muz, Tetuán, Castillejo, Vad Ras, cien nombres y cien hechos de armas, orgullo de la patria, van de oido en oido, pero á girones, incompletos, sin que la muchedumbre pública, ante la cual ha de cumplir su misión de vulgarización la prensa, pueda adquirir idea aproximada de lo que fué aquella epopeya nacional que conquistó para España el respeto de los indiferentes y el temor de sus adversarios. Precisar en lo posible aquellos hechos y aquellos nombres, en tributo de admiración, es nuestro propósito, creyendo que lo han de ver con gusto todos nuestros lectores, los cuales nos perdonarán estos recuerdos evocados en su alma los días de la juventud y pueden sentir el renovado cosfortante del fuego que les animaba, la gente moza porque acaso que en la historia de sus antepasados tienen altos ejemplos y nobles virtudes que imitar, para ser á su vez ejemplos de las generaciones que vengan.

No estamos ahora al del sentimiento creemos que no hay disparidad alguna de opiniones ni en el gobierno, ni en el público, ni en la prensa que es su eco y su guia.

Existen, es verdad, distintas opiniones y diversos temperamentos al hacer aplicaciones prácticas de esos sentimientos, al apreciar las ocasiones en que se puede y se debe franquearlos, al elegir los medios contingentes de darles satisfacción satisfaciendo el decoro y el interés de la nación; pero nosotros no damos mucha importancia al hecho de que había de diversidad de apreciaciones. No sólo naturalmente inevitable, sino necesario nos parece que exista el movimiento impulsivo de unos y el reflexivo de otros: de su casamiento y harmonía puede resultar la fuerza consciente; en relación con estas ideas, y mirando al fondo de las cosas, tan respetable nos parece por noble y útil la manifestación del que dice francamente que quiere herir sangre de moros, por ejemplo, como tal de que lo diga con sinceridad, con toda su alma, y esté dispuesto á sancionarle con su prestación personal, como la del que públicamente en la forma y en el tondo, como corresponde á su mayor cultura y su clarividente intelligencia, examena los peligros de una acción popular irreflexiva: sinceridad es lo que ha de avalorar una y otra manifestación, para que no den esas fuerzas legítimas y respetables de la patria.

No queremos ahora discutir hasta donde debe llegar la acción de España, en cosa que fórmulas y medios debe ejecutarse, ante tan problema histórico de Marruecos. Et tema es socorrido, y pasando la hebra en tono de polémica pronto degeneraría en fastidio y enfadoso. No queremos más que marcar un hecho, un hecho que reconocen propio y extraños, viejos y jóvenes, políticos y particulares, ignoros y tranquilos, pueblo y notabilidad. España tiene necesidad absoluta de construir sus fuertes de Melilla y de mandar como diseño básico en su territorio. ¿Imentarán los moros impedírselo?... Pues contra los moros. Sobre son los dos términos de la cuestión.

El primero no suscita divergencias, porque es conocido. El segundo les susita por que es vago, y como todo lo vago, temido; pero nos parece que con vaguedad no desaparecen con artículos de periódicos, ni con previsiones de política, porque es tan contingente como los hechos no nacidos. A España no se le puede pedir más que la declaración ideal y sincera de que no piensa en conquistas, sino en construir sus fuertes territoriales y en castigar á los cabilas que se opongan á ésta necesidad nacional. Hablar ahora de otra cosa, yo sin con su cuenta, es adelantar á los sucesos. Que el fuerte quede construido, y allí termine toda... ¡quera Dios que así suceda!... Que sean más grandes y más insuperables las dificultades para construirlo, y ahora nadie sabe en donde debe acabar la acción de España.

Las páginas en que hemos escrito este recuerdo á la guerra de África y á sus hombres son de todo punto incompletas, pero ni el tiempo ni nuestra deficiencia nos han permitido otra cosa. Una relativa á la masa de soldados y de oficiales, tantos buenos hijos de España en los cuales yacerán tantos héroes anónimos, pero quedó suplida con este recuerdo de su memoria... Los datos y grabados proceden unos del Diario de un testigo de la guerra de África, de Alarcón; otros de Corona de laurel, de Ros Olano; otros de impresiones y recuerdos personales de nuestros redactores y colaboradores.

Deficiente y todo como es este número, guerenos que sea expresión de nuestro cariño á España y de atención á nuestros lectores.

Don Leopoldo O'Donnell

Descendiente de una familia irlandesa de régia estirpe, que á consecuencia de la subvación de los protestantes contra los caudillos de Irlanda, huyó de su patria y vino á España, allá por los años 1691 ó 1691, era don Leopoldo O'Donell y Jorei, natural de Santa Cruz de Tenerife, en cuya ciudad vió la luz primera el día 12 de Enero de 1809.

Su padre, el teniente general don Carlos O'Donell, distinguióse mucho durante la guerra de la independencia y el primer que tomó á su hijo Leopoldo en el difícil arte de la guerra. Ingresó en el ejército por gracia especial de clase de subtenientes cuando no había cumplido aún los doce años. En el año 1823 y como consecuencia de la campaña para restaurar al gobierno absoluto, fué ascendido á teniente. Destinado cuatro años más tarde al regimiento de granaderos de la Guardia Real, se encontró en la expedición que hizo Fernando VII á Cataluña para sofocar la insurrección carlista, ascendiendo entonces á capitán.

Al estallar, á la muerte de Fernando VII el alzamiento carlista, tomó partido toda la familia O'Donell por el pretendiente, excepto don Leopoldo, que se declaró por della del II.

La acción de Lumbrel, dió ocasión al capitán O'Donell de ganarse en el campo de batalla el grado de coronel de infantería. Poco tiempo después su heróico comportamiento en la acción de Eraca, valióle la cruz laureada de San Fernando de segunda clase. Herido en un combate tuvo que alejarse del campo de la lucha cerca de un año, reincorporándose al ejército con el empleo de segundo comandante de la Guardia.

El 16 de Julio de 1833, tuvo lugar la célebre batalla de Mendigorría, en la cual se distinguió O'Donell, que obtuvo por su comportamiento heróico el empleo de teniente coronel efectivo.

A fines de Noviembre del mismo año fué destinado el regimiento á que pertenecía á pasar á Madrid. Avido de gloria O'Donell, abandonó entonces el regimiento permaneciendo en el ejército del Norte. Al mes y medio después de consumar este rasgo de entusiasmo, fué nombrado coronel de infantería. Si rápida fué la carrera de este bizarro militar desde su ingreso en filas hasta obtener el empleo de Coronel, no lo fué menos á partir de esta época.

A los tres meses de su ascenso á coronel,

ó sea el 16 de mayo de 1836, nombrósele Brigadier. Por su comportamiento en la acción de Miñano Mayor, obtuvo la cruz de San Fernando de tercera clase, y más tarde la Gran Cruz de Isabel la Católica.

Subióras por el brigadier O'Donell la insurrección de las tropas del ejército del Norte, fué nombrado interinamente Comandante general del cuarto derigerán de la costa de Cantabria y el 19 de diciembre de 1837 proponíalo Espartero para el empleo de Mariscal de Campo, Jefe de Estado Mayor del ejército de operaciones, gestó por sus merecimientos la gran cruz de San Fernando.

A medida que se agranda la figura militar de don Leopoldo O'Donell, hácese más difícil reseñar los principales hechos de su vida, fuerza es en poco espacio, así es que nos limitaremos á recordar los diferentes cargos que ocupó, siempre debidos á su gran inteligencia militar y valor personal.

En el año 1839 y poco atejar los pasos al jefe carlista don Ramón Cabrera, fué nombrado O'Donell General en jefe del ejército del Centro y Capitán general de los reinos de Aragón, Valencia y Murcia.

Después de distinguirse extraordinariamente en el sitio de Luchan nombrándole teniente general y después General segundo en jefe de los ejércitos reunidos hasta la terminación de la guerra civil.

Terminada la revolución de 1854, por real decreto de 9 de julio fué ascendido á Capitán general.

La influencia é intervención de O'Donell en las intestinas luchas políticas de nuestro país, no es de esos casos estariñas, basta decir, como círcunstancia de una brillante hoja militar, algo referente á la gloriosísima campaña de África, el hecho más culminante de su vida.

Declarada la guerra á Marruecos por el Congreso español el 22 de octubre de 1859, el General en jefe del ejército y Presidente del Consejo despidióse de los Reyes el 7 de noviembre, desembarcando en Ceuta el 19 y con el segundo cuerpo de ejército. Establecido O'Donell el cuartel general en las alturas del Otero y desde entonces puede decirse que empezó con gran vigor la campaña que había de inmortalizar el nombre de España y el de su caudillo.

Relatar los hechos heróicos, la suprema previsión, la incomparable táctica del general O'Donell en aquella ocasión, sería elevar como tantos monumentos ó holocausto del político, del gran militar, del gran caudillo. Sería necesario relatar una por una las diversas acciones libradas casi á diario con los marroquíes y seguir paso á paso las cuatro grandes batallas que coronaron de gloria á nuestras tropas.

La arrogante figura del general en jefe, sintetizara el deseo nacional de llevar con sangre marroquí la ofensa recibida, y á su vista sentíanse transportado de entusiasmo todo el ejército, por cuyo medio confiasa cogía en los talontos de su general restos seguro de alcanzar la victoria.

En Castillejos vióse la radiante de entusiasmo alentar á sus soldados con frases oportunas y patrióticas, no escatimando á su persona los peligros de la batalla. En el paso de Cabo Negro pudo todo el ejército admirar sus grandes dotes estratégicas salvando enorme dificultad con excesísimas pérdidas. En la batalla de Guad-el-Jelú, hízose patente la previsión, el certero golpe de vista del gran caudillo, cualidades particularísimas esteriorizadas con mayor intensidad aun en la gran batalla de Tetuán, librada el 4 de febrero de 1860. Todo salió aquel día glorioso tal y como lo había dispuesto O'Donell; la batalla más importante de aquella guerra, la que nos abrió las puertas de Tetuán dos días después, fué para el general español el triunfo mayor de su vida militar; la jornada más gloriosa para España.

¿Y qué decir de la permanencia de las tropas en Tetuán? ¿Y qué de la jornada de Wad-Ras? Cada paso desde que aquel valiente ejército en suerra página de gloria para la historia patria. La ofensa inferida á nuestra bandera quedaba lavada con sangre, al contemplar el hermoso espectáculo de los Campos de Wad-Ras al terminar la batalla que nos aseguraba la llave de Tánger, el temido Fondak.

O'Donell, entonces, recordando los nombres de patriota, cumplido ya el propósito que había llevado las tropas al África. La figura del general entró su paso al de Isabel de 1860. Con la paz de Tetuán terminaron los días de gloria para España. La ilustre perso-

Don Rafael Echagüe
(Jefe del primer cuerpo de ejército de África).

¿Quién no recuerda el nombre de Echagüe, el general que por primera vez hizo vibrar en África el entusiasmo nacional?

En las alturas del Serrallo obtuvo Echagüe la primera victoria. Esta es una gloria que nadie podrá disputarle.

Militar distinguido, como lo probó en la guerra carlista en las acciones de Alaimi, Assun, Gorriti, Oñaz, Arenzazu, Ormáiztegui, Villarreal, Arlabán y otras otras más tarde la terminación de la guerra, fué designado como comandante general del primer cuerpo del ejército que pasó al África. Al frente de estas tropas dirigió las acciones del 20 de noviembre, del 22 y 23, logrando en todas ellas obtener la victoria, esto todo y cuyo exceso fuerzas. Las escuadrillas de la guerra obligaron al general Echagüe á permanecer en Ceuta, mientras el resto del ejército continuaba su marcha hacia Tetuán. Incorporóse con tal ejército en esta última ciudad con 6 batallones, la caballería y artillería del primer cuerpo.

En su marcha, siguiendo el camino que antes había recorrido el grueso del ejército, tuvo que sostener continuos combates con los moros que se cebaban en hostilizarle. Pudo llegar no obstante á Tetuán y tomar parte en la batalla de Wad Ras, celebándose la honra de formar con su cuerpo de ejército á la vanguardia de las tropas que principiaron la batalla. Firmada la paz, regresó á Ceuta, donde, junto con los comisionados marroquíes, procedió el general Echagüe á la demarcación de los límites de esta plaza española.

El general Ros de Olano
(Jefe del tercer cuerpo del ejército de África)

General y poeta, lo mismo manejó la pluma que la espada. Como Garcilaso y Cervantes, el general Ros dedicó los ocios momentos que le dejaban libres las faenas de la guerra en escribir páginas bellísimas, exqui

El Padre Lerchundi.

Es uno de los hombres más conocedores del imperio de Marruecos y que más servicios han prestado á la causa de España. El Padre José, como familiarmente le llaman sus amigos, y le son toda la colonia de Tánger y cuantos le han tratado alguna vez, al frente de las misiones franciscanas de Marruecos, ha hecho más por el prestigio é influencia de España que todos los diplomáticos juntos. Misionero infatigable, ha establecido escuelas españolas en las principales ciudades de la costa con sólo los escasísimos recursos que el gobierno destina á estas atenciones, sentando con ellas otros tantos jalones de españolismo.

El sultán le distingue extraordinariamente y tanto los moros como los cristianos lo veneran. En Tánger, es el Padre José, para los menesterosos la providencia, para los caídos el consuelo, para los fuertes el consejero más autorizado.

Residente desde muchos años en el Mogreb, ha realizado notabilísimos estudios acerca de la lengua schelog, considerándosele por sus trabajos como un arabista distinguido. Su gramática de árabe vulgar, el que hoy se habla en Marruecos, es de gran utilidad.

En las escuelas de la misión, reciben esmerada educación los hijos de los españoles y de los extranjeros, que de otro modo vendrían obligados á concurrir á las de los hebreos. Enseñando el árabe á los alumnos de sus escuelas, crea por ese medio un plantel de agentes de comercio de inapreciable valor y que con el tiempo pueden hibernos de la tutela á que hoy venimos sujetos al tener que recurrir á los judíos como intermediarios en las relaciones mercantiles.

Debido á la poderosa iniciativa del P. Lerchundi, se ha montado en la casa-misión una imprenta hispano-arábiga. Con los alumnos de las clases de música se ha organizado una pequeña banda, que irá aumentando á medida que sean más numerosos los alumnos de aquellas clases, y en fin, si los propósitos de este español meritísimo se llevaran á cabo tendríamos en Tánger una escuela de artes y oficios y un instituto de segunda enseñanza, y en Alcázar y Fez casa misión-hospedería, donde encontrarían los viajeros sitio en que guarecerse.

La abnegación y actividad del P. Lerchundi han hecho verdaderos milagros en bien de la religión y de la patria, es estableciendo escuelas dónde se dá enseñanza gratuita á todo el que lo solicita, ya construyendo una barriada de casetas para los pobres residentes en Tánger y realizando, por último, toda suerte de obras benéficas, que lo mismo son alabadas de los moros y hebreos, como por los cristianos, cualquiera que sea su nacionalidad.

En esta continua labor y luchando á brazo partido con el gran número de obstáculos que en el transcurso de su vida ha tenido que vencer, destácase venerable y simpática la personalidad del P. Lerchundi, uno de los hombres que más han trabajado por el bienestar de los españoles y el prestigio de la patria en el imperio de los Scheriffes.

El poeta marroquí Chorbi

El escritor Chorbi, uno de los pocos hombres ilustrados de su tierra, le conoció Alarcón en su propia casa, situada en un extremo de Tetuán, en el barrio más tranquilo, sosegado y pavoroso.

Chorbi era un moro de faz triste, rica boudadosa, ojos grandes y expresivos, barba escasa y de unos cuarenta años. Sabía de memoria el Koran y cien libres de comentarios sobre el mismo; conocía la historia de la dominación árabe en España, mucha geografía, estaba al corriente de la política universal y escribía versos.

La poesía de los moros estaba ya entonces en completa decadencia, conservando de la antigua poesía árabe, generalmente sensual pero expositivas y fresca, sólo algunos rasgos, pues el estado de decrepitud del imperio, las costumbres casi salvajes de sus habitantes y la brutal depravación, han infuido grandemente sobre la imaginación y sentimiento de los moros, academizando á los pocos sabios que en aquel imperio se dedican á la contemplación y á la versicultura.

El padre Sabater

Curando á los heridos, asistiendo á los moribundos, en el campo de batalla y en la ciudad, veros la noble figura del padre Sabater derramando á manos llenas los tesoros albergados en su corazón magnánimo. Sus servicios son de aquellos que serán recordados con admiración siempre que las circunstancias pongan sobre el tapete los mil actos meritorios verificados por españoles en tierra de África.

Muley-el-Abbas

Era de los príncipes que se baten, de aquellos que con su sola presencia entusiasman á las tropas. Popular Muley-el-Abbas como el que más en el imperio, nadie como él podía, en los días de peligro, mandar las huestes marroquíes. Por esto, su hermano el Emperador encomendóle la misión de destruir á los ejércitos cristianos. No pudo el príncipe cumplir con su intento, y sus acciones de guerra fueron otras tantas derrotas.

Las relaciones que con los generales españoles contrajo en aquella guerra, desarrolla con en Muley-el-Abbas vivísimas simpatías por España, de cuya nación fué todo el resto de su vida un leal amigo.

Dotado de un carácter leal y caballeresco ne quiso, al morir su hermano, disputar la corona á su sobrino el actual Sultán, á lo que le inclinaban sus partidarios. Muley el-Abbas mereció por sus virtudes todo el cariño y simpatía que le profesaron después de la campaña todos los generales del ejército de África.

Hermana de la Caridad

¡La hermana de la caridad! Esa, sí, que es la nota más delicada, más tierna, más conmovedora, más sublime de la guerra de África, como de todas las guerras á que ella acude con su toca blanca, su modesto vestido azul, su alma humilde, su corazón inflamado en puro amor.

No había, no, exageración en las hermosas palabras del gran tribuno español, cuando de decía que la Hermana de la Caridad es más pura y más sublime que los ángeles, porque si los ángeles moran en el cielo, las hermanas de la caridad llevan al cielo al seno de la miseria y de la muerte.

Tamo

Era ésta la mujer más hermosa de Tetuán, cuando la guerra de África. La que arrancó á Alarcón frases encomiásticas, no es hoy ni sombra de lo que fué. Tamo sabe lo que se dijo de ella en aquella ocasión, y guarda como en un paño el libro de Alarcón. El que eso escribe tuvo ocasión de verla no há mucho tiempo. Está muy gruesa y es difícil adivinar lo que sería, cuando el paso de las tropas por Tetuán.

Dícese de que Alarcón echara á su marido veinte años más de los que tiene.

—¿Por mí salud? mírelo usted, y diga si es posible lo que dice Alarcón.

Gusta mucho de hablar con los españoles, y al presentar á su bellísima hija, adivinase su mirada el orgullo mal disimulado con que mira á su hija, refi-jada la hermosura que en ella admiraron los de su generación.

Tamo es aún hoy objeto de gran curiosidad por parte de los españoles que visitan á Tetuán, debido á la magistral descripción que de su persona hizo el inolvidable Alarcón.

Ben-Abu

General de caballería, intérprete de los primeros enviados de Muley-el-Abbas

— Moro simpático y bullicioso, era Ben-Abu un soldado rudo, á cuyo mando estaban las grandes masas de caballería que con tanto denuedo cargaron en las batallas de los Castillejos y 31 de enero. Hablaba el español, y debido á esta circunstancia intervino como intérprete en las negociaciones de la paz.

Labrador moro

La principal ocupación del moro en el ejercicio de las armas y el cultivo de las tierras. Estas son tan fértiles, que, aun cultivadas rudimentariamente, dan grandes cosechas, especialmente de cereales. Como se ve por el grabado, usan todavía los moros el antiquísimo arado formado por un trozo de madera encorvado de una sola pieza.

Victoriano Sugrañes, Comandante de los voluntarios de Cataluña

Obtuvo la señalada distinción el comandante Sugrañes, de mandar en África á los valientes voluntarios de Cataluña.

Las frases de Prim, al recibirlo en los campos de Tetuán, y que el otro día publicamos, quedarían sin duda grabadas en su mente. «Catalanes, nuestra responsabilidad es inmensa» había dicho Prim, y Sugrañes cuyo pecho adornaban tres cruces de San Fernando, como testimonio elocuente de su valor, sentiríase enardecido al pensar en la parte principalísima que en aquello responsabilidad le cabía.

En la batalla de Tetuán, á la vanguardia del ejército y al frente de sus voluntarios, murió Sugrañes como bueno, á las veinte horas de desembarcar en África.

Hazaña del cabo de húsares Pedro Mur

Entre los varios rasgos de valor y actos de heroísmo que dieron nuestras tropas en África, merece mención aparte el realizado por el cabo de húsares Pedro Mur.

Formando parte de los escuadrones de húsares que en la batalla de los Castillejos dieron tan brillantes cargas á la caballería marroquí persiguiendo á los dispersos moros hasta su propio campamento, el cabo Mur, cuando ya su compañeros emprendían la retirada, batióse denodadamente con un jinete marroquí que, con iracundia una bandera, defendíase valientemente del soldado español alejándolo cada vez más de sus compañeros de armas; Mur, que con un valor extraordinario persiguió á su enemigo sitiándola al fin y luchando desesperadamente, derribó al moro de una estocada, y arrebatóle su crispada manos el estandarte que tremolaba. Con tan precioso trofeo dirigióse el osé Mur buscando al regimiento, en medio de un diluvio de balas de que escapó casi milagrosamente.

La hazaña del cabo Mur es de aquellas que pasan á la historia y su nombre de los que se graban en letras de oro.

El Alcaid Ahmet-et-Batin.

segundo de Muley-el-Abbas

Era el segundo de Muley-el-Abbas, durante la campaña y ocupaba el importante cargo de gobernador de Tánger cuando estalló la guerra. Al lado del príncipe marroquí combatió con más ardor cuanto dos fortuna Ahmet-et-Batin, hasta la terminación de la guerra.

5 Ramón Godó Lallana (1864–1927), First Count of Godó.

6 Two generations of the Godó family.

7 Juan Godó Llucià laying the first foundation stone of a school in the town of Pierola (1914).

8 Popular homage paid to the former deputy Juan Godó Llucià (1851–1935), and to his son and former mayor of Igualada Juan Godó Pelegrí (1876–1957), by the 32 districts of the constituency in recognition of their work (1914).

9 Antonio Maura's portrait, with a dedication to Ramón Godó Lallana, reproduced in *La Vanguardia*.

SUSCRIPCION
Barcelona, un mes ... 2'— Ptas
Provincias ... 7'50 »
Portugal, trimestre 8'50 »
América ... 8'50 »
Demás países ... 25'— »

Dirección telegráfica
VANGUARDIA-BARCELONA
Anuncios, esquelas, remitidos y reclamos
a precios según tarifa
No se devuelven los originales

LA VANGUARDIA

OFICINAS: Calle Pelayo, 28. - Teléfono 14135

La vuelta al mundo en 80 minutos

Tabla redonda

[columnas de texto]

LUIS DE ZULUETA

Libros de investigación

Geografía y orígenes del primer arte románico

II

BUENAVENTURA BASSEGODA

Marruecos franco-español

El caso de Ain-Harruda

10 Front page of *La Vanguardia*, 14 April 1931.

Introduction

Press Barons and Liberal Politics

"Examine the current psychology of the Spanish people, penetrate into the recesses of its brain, and it will appear to you for a moment that we find ourselves in the days of Charles II, except he who is possessed, he who is bewitched is not the king, but the nation itself. By whom? By the daily press."

JOAQUÍN COSTA, *Oligarquía y caciquismo*[1]

One of the key intellectuals of Modern Spain, Joaquín Costa (1846–1911), wrote this bitter observation shortly after his country had lost the remnants of its empire in a war against the United States, in 1898. In Costa's view, Spain's loss of the colonies culminated a process of national decay that had a clear explanation: the country was in the hands of a small but powerful "oligarchy" that controlled public office for their exclusive self-benefit. As well as blaming the ruling classes, Costa also blamed the so-called "press oligarchy" ("*oligarquía periodística*") for the state of decay. Drawing on the popular currency of Social Darwinism to measure the strength of nations, Costa metaphorically compared Spain's situation with the reign of Charles II (1661–1700). The physical condition of this king had been so poor that it prevented him from ruling well and plunged the country into a harsh struggle over the succession to the throne. While Charles' physical state was said to be the result of a curse, Costa considered that in 1898 the Spanish had also been bewitched, this time by the influence of the press. According to Costa, this influence was so pernicious that even the fullest renewal of the political class would not suffice to achieve the nation's recovery: the replacement of the *press oligarchy* was indispensable for Spain to regain its greatness.[2]

This book will focus on the "press oligarchy" to which Costa referred during Europe's crisis of liberal politics. The years prior to the First World War (1914–1918) have traditionally been considered to be a turning point in the history of the Continent. In the political field, two elements started challenging the socially restrictive politics of liberalism. First, the growing demands to expand democracy (by establishing universal manhood suffrage, in countries that did not have it, and by making elections transparent, in countries where clientelism was widespread); and second, the emergence of new professional politicians and large-scale organisations with the capacity to mobilise thousands of supporters through new forms of action (e.g. political rallies, new spaces of sociability, direct political affiliation, etc.). This new era also entailed a substantial change in the composition of elites, often described as the "end of the notables" and the emergence of a new professional class of politicians.[3]

Recent comparative analysis has revealed that in most European countries the social composition of elected representatives started changing in the 1880s.[4] The common trend was a declining presence of the traditional upper classes (the so-called notables), whose sources of authority originated from advantageous positions in society (such as a well-off background, title of nobility or patronage networks), and its replacement by a new "class" of professional politicians, whose election was more dependent on political organisations than on privileged status.[5] The characteristics and chronology in the turnover of elites varied noticeably according to the specificities of each country, and in most cases was not consolidated until the destabilising experience of the First World War.[6]

However, far from being a top-down process or a pre-determined process of change, the democratisation of politics implied new competition for the sources of political legitimacy. In the Mediterranean area this competition was characterised by the efforts of new political movements (like the Republicans, Socialists and Nationalists) to overthrow the political system and undermine the privileged position of liberal elites. Whether in the form of clientelist practices (in the case of Italy, Portugal and Spain) or in the disclosure of successive scandals (in the case of France's Third Republic), accusations of corruption became part of the political struggle and contributed to discrediting the parliamentary system.[7] In parallel, these countries experienced a series of setbacks in their plans for colonial expansion that intensified the feeling of national decay. A new intellectual discourse influenced by biological terminology fostered public concerns about the nation's future, and was often referred to as the decadence of the Latin race and the rising dominance of the "Anglo-Saxons".[8]

In this regard, what makes Joaquín Costa's remarks particularly valuable is that he considered newspaper editors to be both to blame for Spain's decay *and* its potential saviours. Costa's testimony evoked the impression that the newspaper editors were decisive actors in directing public affairs. That perception – which was shared by contemporaries in other countries – was influenced by the transformation of the press into the main form of mass communication. From the second half of the 19th century, the press underwent a series of deep transformations across Europe, epitomised in the expansion of the consumer market, the growing circulation of commercial newspapers and the rise of new ethics codes in the journalistic profession (such as impartial reporting and a public service vocation). However, although 19th-century commentators often observed that newspaper editors had a powerful influence over public affairs, scholars today have rarely bothered to test those observations in any depth. One explanation for this is that the study of elites has tended to concentrate on a limited range of prominent figures, such as ministers, intellectuals, military officers and businessmen. Journalists, in contrast, are rarely regarded as *political actors*.[9] Another reason is that the growing specialisation of academia has often resulted in a lack of interdisciplinary work between fields of research. Thus, while political historians mostly use the press as a historical source, but rarely see it as an *agent of change*, media scholars rarely bother to integrate press transformations into the broader history of politics.[10] The result is two separate narratives that focus on different aspects of the same picture but fail to provide an interwoven account.

This book will focus on one of the most prominent dynasties of press proprietors in modern Spain, the Godó family, in order to reconsider the way historians have interpreted the crisis of the liberal state in Europe. In 1881, two members of this family established a newspaper in Barcelona and called it *La Vanguardia* ("*the Vanguard*"). Over the years, and thanks to the efforts of successive generations, and notwithstanding numerous setbacks, this newspaper became one of the most influential papers in the country. *La Vanguardia* is still in print today, in fact it is Barcelona's leading paper, and ranks third in the country in total print sales. Moreover, the value of examining this newspaper is due not only to its condition as one of the oldest (still active) dailies in Spain, but also to its historical significance. To put it bluntly, *La Vanguardia* represents one of the most enduring emblems of modern Catalonia.[11] Throughout its long trajectory it has established a deep emotional connection with large segments of Catalan society, probably to an extent that no other newspaper has matched. Contemporaries were the first to notice the wide social impact *La Vanguardia* had come to achieve. As one of them commented:

> "Every day, at sunrise, it entered in the sacristies as well as in the Masonic lodges, in the cloistered convents as well as in the brothels; it was read by both the financial director and the anarchist, by the citizen and by the farmer, in the heart of Barcelona and in the lost corners of the Pyrenees, from the French border to the marshlands at the Ebro Delta."[12]

While *La Vanguardia* is one of the great emblems of civil society in Catalonia, its influence has traditionally reached beyond the region. Since its foundation in 1881, this newspaper actively engaged in debates that possessed a broader Spanish dimension. As in most of nineteenth-century

Europe, the consolidation of the liberal state in Spain was not a linear process. Rather, it took place in the context of heated, multidimensional tension (that included armed resistance by the most reactionary sectors) that would determine the characteristics of the new society. The organization of the state, the role of religion in public life and the limits of political participation were distinct issues that hardened in the process of shaping liberal institutions.[13] Catalonia was an integral part of Spain's state-building process, to which it brought a number of distinctive features – above all, its industrialisation and pronounced regional identity. The expansion of the cotton industry in the late eighteenth century had transformed Catalonia into Spain's only major industrial centre. Contemporaries were the first to notice this economic transformation, to the point that already in 1770 one observer would refer to the region as "a little England in the heart of Spain."[14] This development led to repeated attempts from Catalan elites to shape the liberal state according to their interests and concerns, and explains their deep concern for the social and labour tensions affecting Catalan society. Alongside – and in combination with – the consequences of industrialisation was the emergence of regional consciousness. In contrast to the centralised state model that Moderate liberals had implemented since the 1840s, partly in imitation of the French model, cultural elites in Catalonia insistently argued in favour of a more plural and diverse understanding of the Spanish nation.[15] From the late 1880s onwards, this regional consciousness was transformed into an explicit nationalist ideology.[16]

As a newspaper printed in Barcelona, *La Vanguardia* not only recorded the tensions that characterized Spanish liberal politics, but also *actively* intervened in an effort to influence them. It became one of the most important mouthpieces for Catalan interests in the rest of Spain while remaining one of the main bulwarks of liberalism in Barcelona. Its prominent role in public affairs led one contemporary to venture the opinion that *La Vanguardia* had gained greater influence than the most important organisations of the Catalan bourgeoisie put together.[17]

If this was truly the case, it was because as well as taking an active stand in politics, *La Vanguardia* came to embody one of the finest ideals for quality press in the country. Its high calibre journalism was characterized, amongst many other ways, by the attention paid to foreign news. Every day, thousands of readers would turn to its pages to learn about events in the rest of the world. This thirst for distant news implied heavy investments in foreign correspondents and new communication technologies, such as the telegraph and news agencies, to such an extent that *La Vanguardia* came to enjoy an international reputation for its strong informative character. In 1916, for instance, the English newspaper *The Times*, considered that:

"(...) in size, seriousness, and circulation, as well as in completeness of organisation, [it] is the most important paper in Catalonia, one might almost say in the whole of Spain. (....) Its neutrality, like its independence of party, is not only a name but a fact, and appears to be the result of a considered policy and a strong sense of responsibility."[18]

Paradoxically, the high reputation of *La Vanguardia* is in sharp contrast with the scarcity of studies about its origins and trajectory. In fact, and contrary to other big dailies in Europe that have a long-standing presence, such as *The Times* (UK), *Le Figaro* (France) or *Il Corriere della Sera* (Italy), to mention but a few, there are no scholarly studies about the Catalan newspaper's origins and the family who founded it.[19] What are the reasons, we might then wonder, for this lack of studies on what is today Barcelona's top-selling newspaper? This was precisely the question that the scholar Daniel Jones posed in 2006, during the 125th anniversary of *La Vanguardia*'s founding, and he offered two theories in answer.[20] The first regarded the influence the political agenda arguably had for the interests of Catalan scholars. According to Jones, the majority of the research had been conducted from a "nationalistic and ethnocentric perspective" which led to prioritising the study of newspapers that were published in Catalan, to the detriment of those published in Spanish, like *La Vanguardia*. The second hypothesis is that the long ownership of the newspaper impeded historians' access to the necessary sources. Since its foundation in 1881, and to this very day, *La Vanguardia* has remained the exclusive property of the Godó family. Only during the period of the Spanish Civil War (1936–1939) did the newspaper briefly escape their control, and it is currently managed by the fourth generation of the same family. The difficulty of access to the owner's private archives represents, according to Jones, the second reason for the lack of scholarly research on the newspaper.[21]

Drawing on hitherto unused sources, including a wide range of archival material,[22] this book sets out to examine the trajectory of the Godó family, between 1881 and 1931. This chronology starts at the foundation of the newspaper and ends with the passing of the second generation of its owners. During this period, *La Vanguardia* underwent a series of drastic transformations that radically altered its character. From being a small partisan newspaper with an early circulation of 1,400 copies, by 1931 it had reached a circulation of 200,000 copies and was one of the most admired exponents of quality journalism in Spain. This transformation was not accidental – it echoed a widespread phenomenon in both Europe and the United States where the partisan press model changed into a commercial and politically independent one.[23]

Still, none of the family members ever saw journalism as a vocation (not one of them ever published a single article in *La Vanguardia*), but rather as a tool to promote their private interests in a wide range of fields, such as politics, business and colonialism. Indeed, the case of the Godós is evocative of the new European elites that emerged in the mid nineteenth century, amidst the consequences of industrialisation and the consolidation of the liberal state, elites that saw politics as the best way of advancing their private agenda.[24] For more than two generations, the ownership of the newspaper allowed the Godó family to promote their interests in all of these fields and to navigate through the country's turbulent 20th century. Whether under the corrupt politics of the Bourbon Restoration (1874–1923), the pretorian takeover of Primo de Rivera' dictatorship (1923–1930) or the radical transformations of the Second Republic (1931–1939), the members of this family managed to stay afloat despite the drastic changes that took place in the political scenario. As the first in-depth study of the most renowned newspaper in Catalonia and one of the most influential ones in Spanish history, this book will use the history of the Godó family to examine how the changing relations between press and politics became entwined in the crisis of the liberal state, and at the same time explore the strategies that traditional elites developed in order to adapt to the changing political scenario.

Since the last quarter of the 19th century, the Mediterranean area saw the consolidation of a centralised liberal-state model and a progressive – though complex and very limited – process of democratisation. Despite the particularities of each country, the exercise of "politics without democracy" became a common practice in all of them. The fear of the liberal parties over widening the social bases of the political system led to a strong restriction of suffrage (only around 2% to 5% of the population) and the establishment of clientelist procedures (*sistema del turno*, in Spain; *rotativismo*, in Portugal; *trasformismo*, in Italy) for the rigging of elections. By means of these procedures public office remained concentrated in the hands of liberal parties and the vast majority of the population was excluded from it.[25]

As a result, instead of holding elections to choose the ruling party, the liberal parties in all these countries controlled the government. In the case of Portugal and Spain, this occurred through the alternation in power of two liberal parties,[26] whereas in Italy clientelism took the form of broad government coalitions. Despite the differences in the methods, in all these countries elections became a formality, designed to confirm the results the liberal parties had agreed upon beforehand.[27] Crucial for the working of these mechanisms was the role of local bosses or "notables", who acted as intermediaries between the liberal parties and the local communities. Therefore, the countries in this area had parliamentary systems but not democratic ones, because they were based on the systematic rigging of elections. The rest of the political parties (e.g. Republicans, Socialists and Catholics) were systematically excluded from power.[28]

Criticism of the liberals' monopoly of public office was raised. Particularly at the turn of the 19th century, the climate of national introspection became common to Southern European countries and gave place to a rich literature that denounced the clientelism on which the liberal politicians based their monopoly of government.[29] Historians, however, have often assumed the views of these contemporaries (such as Joaquín Costa or Antonio Gramsci), as well as their interpretative framework. A clear example is the definition that the Spanish dictionary gave of the word "cacique" (local boss) in the 1970s, when it defined a *cacique* as "someone of a town or region who exerts an excessive influence on political and administrative matters".[30] This definition does not just fail to define the term on the basis of this individual's main source of power (namely, his role of intermediary between the centre and the periphery), but contained an implicit moral judgment: the cacique's influence was considered to be "excessive". Something similar happened with the term "notable", which despite its differing connotations from country to country, was used to refer to an "old way" of doing politics before the birth of mass politics.[31]

Indeed, the majority of historians writing in the 1960s and 1970s considered clientelism (to which they referred as *caciquismo*) to be a distinctive feature of backward societies, in which a powerful "oligarchy" used the system as an instrument to maintain a privileged position and subjugate the majority of the population. This socio-economic interpretation, inspired by historical materialism, presented clientelism as a sign of "failure" in historical development: first in the 1970s, from a paradigm of *bourgeoisie revolution* (*rivoluzione mancata*, in the Italian case), and later in the 1980s from a paradigm of *failed modernisation*. Clientelism was thus interpreted as a feature of rural and underdeveloped countries that differed from the rest of Europe because of the weakness of their middle classes and the consequent failure this caused in the transition to democracy.[32]

Such an understanding of European democratisation, however, was based on ideal models of development.[33] While the early extension of the franchise, in countries like France and England, was portrayed as a process inexorably leading towards the full democratisation of politics, the presence of patron–client relationships in Mediterranean countries was regarded as a sign of backwardness. Something similar happened in countries like Germany, where the role that corporate representation played in elections was regarded as a "special path" in historical development (*Sonderweg*). This perspective fostered a fruitful controversy in the 1980s and 1990s about the role of the "bourgeoisie" (and about the meanings and limitations of using this term) in European societies.[34]

In the meantime, an alternative historiographical trend (the so-called functionalist perspective), which did not escape from the idealised models of

democratisation either, started explaining clientelism as an essentially political and administrative phenomenon. This trend focused mostly on elections,
with the aim of providing an explanation for the mechanisms that liberal
parties implemented to control public office.[35] The scholars attached to this
trend – here presented from a broad perspective, even though they adopted a
national perspective – shared a basic conception of clientelism as a form of
patronage, in which the control (or privatisation) of public office was considered to be the mechanism to control a vast network of supporters.[36] Indeed,
and as a new stream of works published in the 1990s explained with further
precision, the liberal parties' monopoly of public office did not necessarily
mean that the political systems of the Mediterranean area were entirely
disconnected from society, because larger numbers of people besides the local
bosses also benefited from it.

As a result of this new interest in delineating the social roots of clientelism,
a crucial step was made in the redefining of the terminology used for the
social actors who benefited from clientelistic practices. While local bosses
were firstly referred to (in the Spanish case) as a "block of power" or as an
"oligarchy", two expressions that implied a closed social group who monopolised both economic and political power, scholars subsequently started referring to them as "bourgeois", and later on as "elites". The latter expression was
used for the first time in Spain in the late 1960s and in Italy in the 1970s and
has arguably remained the more common term until nowadays.[37] Although
the decision to use the term *elites* is often justified on the grounds of using a
less politically connoted terminology, historians have often noted that this
term is also deeply entrenched in the liberal tradition of Italian sociology, as
Pedro Carasa has discussed.[38]

More recently, some scholars have started revisiting the period known as
the "end of the notables". While this expression was popularised by the work
of the French historian Daniel Halévy,[39] the main argument lying behind it
is indebted to Max Weber. In Weber's theory, the bureaucratisation of the
state and the professionalisation of politics were presented as two steps
towards the democratisation of society and the birth of mass politics. The
most visible consequence of this process was a deep transformation in the figure of the politician, often evoked through Weber's famous differentiation
between men who lived "for" politics from those who lived "off" politics.[40]
Since then, a high number of scholars have devoted their attention to examining the ways in which the democratisation of the political system was also
translated into the democratisation of elected representatives. It has been
shown, for instance, that the European aristocracy that Arno Mayer presented
as a "feudal vestige" was, in reality, a social group whose internal composition had been thoroughly redefined after the French and the Industrial
revolutions of the 18th century.[41]

Recent research has also made attempts at comparative analyses of liberal elites at a European scale. This has been the case, among others, of the work coordinated by Heinrich Best and Maurizio Cotta.[42] The great merit of this work is that by building on a long tradition of studies about continuity and rupture in the composition of elites, it has provided a broad overview of the crisis of liberal elites at a continental scale.[43] Indeed, by means of large set of cross-checked data from different countries, these authors have delineated the chronology and the changes in the social composition of Europe's elected representatives. They have concluded that the period spanning between the 1880s and the 1920s was characterised "by the decline of the traditional components of the social and political establishment, that is, of privileged social status (particularly aristocratic background), land-ownership, state offi-cialdom, and university education".[44] Rather than disappearing as if in an earthquake, traditional elites (landowners, notables, state officials) remained important until the First World War, thus confirming some of the hypothe-ses of Arno Mayer.[45]

However, in giving priority to quantitative analysis (prosopography), scholars have nurtured a narrative of *decline* and *rise* to explain the social composition of Europe's elected representatives. As a result, liberal elites tend to be presented as a static group that was doomed to disappear with the advent of democratisation – the only question open to debate has been *when* and *why* this happened in each country.[46] Or to put it another way, scholars have been more concerned with illustrating the "end of the notables" rather than with testing the heuristic value of this narrative for our understanding of the past.

The notables' strategies of adaptation and the public dimension of power

This book, in contrast, will argue that Europe's crisis of liberal politics was far more complex than a simple substitution of one social group by another. Liberal elites were not a static group who watched the democratisation of politics with their arms folded, nor did they simply oppose it through "auto-cratic means", but often sought to adapt to this new scenario by re-designing their power strategies.[47] This capacity of elites to adapt to a changing polit-ical scenario will be examined through the Godós, the dynasty of Catalan politicians, manufacturers and newspaper proprietors who established what would become Barcelona's top-selling newspaper: *La Vanguardia*.

Hence, this work will examine the press as one of the strategies that liberal elites (or *notables*)[48] used to build their legitimacy in public and widen their spheres of influence. In so doing, I will argue against the theories of modernisation that picture the notables as the embodiment of an "old way" of doing politics, depicting them as social actors that were disconnected from society. Being well-off was certainly indispensable to run for office in liberal politics, but the legitimacy that elites could not obtain from the elections – since they were based on fraud – would have been cultivated in public. In other words, the public sphere became an alternative dimension for the notables to invest in different forms of reputation (symbolic capital) and build their image as the natural representatives of local interests, as well as a space to promote their private interests.[49]

Family often acted as the primary unit through which the elites managed to concentrate power in all its diverse forms – economic and political, but also symbolic – across time and space. This implied the promotion of strategies on a collective basis, both from a synchronic perspective – different members of the same family acting through common aims, benefiting each member of the family; as well as from a diachronic perspective – since the family name, memory and tradition were transmitted between generations. Particularly in local communities, the continuous presence of the same surname across time reinforced the public legitimation of successive members of the same family.

However, the public sphere did not only constitute the space where liberal elites sought to reproduce their pre-eminent position in society. It was also a space open to contest from other social actors aspiring to dispute the "legitimate discourse".[50] Indeed, and as Hilda Sábato has argued, the low participation in elections does not necessarily imply the complete demobilisation of society.[51] Besides the institutional framework (like elections and representative bodies), other channels of political participation existed, like the press. Especially since the last quarter of the 19th century, newspapers experienced exponential growth – both in terms of circulation and number of publications – that ran parallel to an expansion of the reading market (fall of illiteracy levels and new reading practices). This situation reached the point that every political party and organisation of any type had its own mouthpiece. In the case of heavily populated cities, with very active labour organisations, and, ultimately, better connected to current thinking in Europe, the goal of maintaining a parliamentary system that marginalised large sections of the population became much more difficult to achieve.

The main objective of the chapters to follow will thus consist in exploring the function of the press in the process of self-perpetuation of traditional elites and as an instrument that other actors used to undermine the sources of authority of liberal institutions. This implies an understanding of public opinion that is not socially limited to Habermas' bourgeois sphere; and where communication is not understood as a top-down process, but rather as a multidirectional one.[52] Thus, the focus will be on the Godó family for the period between 1881 and 1931. This chronology embraces two generations of the family, and provides the opportunity to study their trajectory over a long span: from their process of upward mobility in the mid-19th century to the crisis of liberal politics in the aftermath of the First World War (1914–1918).

In so doing, the case of the Godó family will provide the opportunity to tackle the narrative about the *end of the notables* from a qualitative and dynamic perspective, which is absent in prosopographic studies. Rather than testing to what extent the career of this family fits or does not fit into the wider picture drawn by quantitative research, a "thick description" based on micro-analysis will be used to allow a rich understanding of the crisis of liberalism, and to examine the role that newspapers played in this process. Accordingly, the Godós will *not* be studied for the sake of representativeness, but rather to concentrate on the "exceptionally normal" and, in so doing, to challenge grand narratives about the birth of modernity in Europe.[53] Indeed, the case of this family raises a series of questions about this period that have barely attracted attention. For instance: what function did public opinion play in the legitimation of elites, in those societies where power was structured according to patron–client relationships? What role did the press play in the competition between different elites to act as the interlocutors between central government and local communities? Furthermore, and in relation to the crisis of liberal politics: in which ways did the changes in the press contribute to discrediting clientelism in public? How did liberal elites seek to adapt to changes in society once politics became more competitive and clientelism started to become difficult to manage? Providing an answer to all these questions represents a dual attempt: first, to meet the calls of historians to renovate the studies of liberal elites from the cultural perspective of power; and second, to adopt an interdisciplinary perspective where media studies and historical analysis is merged.

The Foundation of *La Vanguardia* and the Transnational Origins of Modern Journalism

On November 1915 a correspondent of *La Vanguardia* named Agustí Calvet was in Athens, where he had arranged an interview with renowned Prime Minister General Venizelos. As Europe was tearing itself apart in the First World War, Greece had unexpectedly become a crucial piece on the chessboard. The interview on the future plans of the Greek Prime Minister was therefore of great interest for any of the big dailies in Europe, and that included the case of *La Vanguardia*, by then Barcelona's top-selling newspaper and a benchmark of independent journalism in Spain. Yet to Venizelos, the name "*La Vanguardia*" ("*the Vanguard*", in English) sounded suspicious. Calvet would evoke in his memories the tough time he experienced when the Greek statesman started asking inquisitively about the ideological connotations that lay behind the title of his newspaper:

> "*The newspaper you represent must be Socialist, isn't it?*". No, I said. "*Then it must be* – Venizelos insisted – *radical, of the extreme left?*". Once again I shook my head. "*Or Republican, at least?*" And as I felt helpless, unable to answer the flood of questions, Venizelos exclaimed, visibly shaken: "*Will you please do the favour of telling me what does the name of your newspaper actually mean?*"[1]

Calvet escaped from the situation as best as he could, unable to find a straight answer. He would recall finding himself trapped in the same embarrassing situation dozens of times. Every time he visited a new country, his interviewers always met him with the same suspicious attitude about the revolutionary-sounding name of the newspaper he represented. "*La Vanguardia*" was, as he put it, "a name that always made me look foolish".[2] Calvet's anecdote reveals the blurred and often misleading meanings that *La Vanguardia*'s title carried. Venizelos was right to suspect that this was a Socialist or at least a left-wing newspaper: there were in fact several newspapers belonging to this political leaning that were equally entitled, both in

Spain and in other Spanish-speaking countries. But what were the origins of a newspaper that rather than for its revolutionary orientation, would be widely acclaimed (as well as harshly criticized) for its liberal and conservative standing? How can we explain that the origins of what is Barcelona's leading newspaper today, as well as one of the most respected voices in the Spain's political agenda, still remain unknown?

To some scholars, these questions are of little importance: "La Vanguardia" was simply an empty name. The same newspaper could have been equally been named "The Sun", "the Moon" or "the World".[3] The following pages, in contrast, will argue that the name of this newspaper had a very good reason to be chosen, and that explaining it provides new insights into the ways power was exercised in modern Europe. Indeed, explaining the origins of *La Vanguardia* implies examining the life story of a family who established this newspaper more than 130 years ago, for the sake of a political cause. Between the last quarter of the 18th century and first half of the 19th century, Europe underwent a series of structural transformations (demographic growth, urbanisation and the industrial revolution) that radically transformed the patterns that had characterised society during the early modern era. This transformation went hand in hand with drastic changes – triggered by the Napoleonic Wars and the new liberal-state model – in the way power was structured in societies. The Godó family became an example of the new social class of traders and manufacturers who emerged from these transformations, and who saw in politics the best way of securing their interests. The first part of this chapter will examine in which ways the founding of *La Vanguardia* allowed the Godós to promote their political careers in a period characterized by uncertainty and social turmoil.

The second part will focus on the radical turnaround that *La Vanguardia* experienced in 1888. During that year, which also saw Barcelona host its first World Fair, the family suddenly put an end to the partisan affiliation of *La Vanguardia* and decided to transform it into a politically independent newspaper. The case of this newspaper will thus allow examining a broader process which took place in Europe and the United States in the second half of the 19th century: namely, the birth of an incipient mass media culture.[4] However, while historians have traditionally examined this transformation from a state-centred perspective, this chapter will show that the transition from the partisan press model towards a commercial and politically independent one was a hybrid process powered by cultural transfers across national borders. Thus, in their attempt to renew *La Vanguardia* the Godó family took the English newspaper *The Times* as their source of inspiration. The examination of this Catalan newspaper will therefore provide a unique perspective on the beginning of modern journalism from a transnational approach.

The beginning of it all

The remote origins of the Godó family are to be found in an industrial town of inner Catalonia named Igualada, located 60 km northwest of Barcelona. The links of the family with this town go back in time, and specifically to the 20th of January 1716. On that date a young man named Oleguer Godó, from the neighbouring town of Esparraguera, moved to Igualada and married Caterina Gomà in the local church of Santa Maria.[5] The wedding seems to have been rooted in a commercial strategy: like Oleguer, Caterina's father worked as a *"paraire"* – as the various procedures involved in the spinning of wool were referred to in Catalan at the time. The wool industry was, in fact, the town's most important industry and attracted numerous migrants at the time. Only few of them, however, managed to enter into what was a corporate form of trade, organized according to the strict codes and norms that, though waning, still structured most European societies in the early eighteenth century. Marriage is presumably what opened the doors for Godó's entry into the guild: two years after he passed the examination of the wool's guild and joined it under the name initials *"GO"*.[6] From that moment on the successive generations of the Godó family maintained and reinforced their link with Igualada. Their activities, whether in the world of commerce, family, or politics, cannot be fully understood without taking into account the importance that *localism* played in the decisions of the family members. The peculiar way in which this town experienced industrialization in the 19th century directly affected the lives of the Godó family and conditioned their future strategies – including the very same foundation of *La Vanguardia*.

Catalonia became an early exponent of the industrialisation process that Europe went through in the 18th century. The cotton textile industry played a central role in this process, and was to remain the region's most important economic activity in the century to follow.[7] The town where Oleguer Godó settled down illustrates some of the most basic features that characteristed this transformation: throughout the 18th century growing numbers of *"paraires"* in Igualada started to spin cotton outside the control of the guild, by relying on the putting-out system and the introduction of foreign manual spinning machines.[8] The result was the growing specialisation of this town in the cotton textile industry – built upon its long tradition in wool manufacturing – and the mushrooming of new small-scale factories. By 1841 Igualada had as many as 413 workshops dedicated to the cotton industry, making it the second most important textile centre in Catalonia, both for the spinning process and in total volume of wages paid. Only Barcelona fared better in both cases.[9]

The Godós became active players in the expansion of Igualada's cotton industry. Ramón Godó Llucià (1801–1862), the father of *La Vanguardia*'s future founders, was a textile manufacturer who inherited a set of spinning machines that were installed in the same building in which he and his family lived – number 10 on the street called "Rambla Nova".[10] Ramón's workshop had been founded in 1808 and was the third oldest in town. His business consisted in weaving calicoes, a new commodity that started spreading across Europe in the early 18th century and which, as its Catalan name indicates (*"indianes"*), came originally from India and the Middle East. Ramón was the kind of small manufacturer who directly benefitted from the growing popularity that this commodity, tainted with vivid colours and beautiful artworks, was considered at the time. Thus, by 1845 he had relocated his factory to a new and larger building and employed as many as 120 people.[11] Annual production amounted to 75,000 pesetas and made of him the sixth largest manufacturer in town.[12]

The future founders of *La Vanguardia* – Carlos and Bartolomé Godó Pié – were born in this context of family prosperity, in 1834 and 1839. They did so in the house where the first family's workshop had been installed, in the street called Rambla Nova, and lived in that house together with eight other people: their parents, the above-mentioned textile manufacturer Ramón Godó Llucià (48 years old) and his wife Rita Pié Perramon (47); three older brothers, named Josep (18), Antoni (21) and Ramón (24); the wife of the latter, named Bonaventura Llucià Grifell (19) and their newborn child; and a bachelor uncle called Magí Godó Llucià (35).[13] A total of ten people belonging to three different family generations were consequently sharing the same roof. The time that fathers, sons and nieces spent together everyday created strong ties of affection and shared memories between them, and contributed to imprint a collective understanding of the world (or *habitus*) between the different generations. The household thus symbolised the continuity of the family lineage across time, as well as the place where different generations lived side by side. These kinship ties, woven in the warmth of the household, were to play a fundamental role in future political careers.

In the short term, however, the fact that Carlos and Bartolomé were the youngest brothers in the family explains why they decided to leave Igualada and move to the Basque Country, first, and later on to Barcelona. The main reason is because in Catalonia, in contrast to most parts of Spain, family was structured according to a primogeniture system. Accordingly, the first-born son (called *"hereu"*) was bestowed with the lion's share of the inheritance (around eighty per cent of the total), while the younger sons and daughters (named *"cabalers"*), in contrast, only received the remaining twenty per cent (which was divided into equal parts).[14] The fundamental purpose of this uneven system of inheritance was to prevent the dispersal of family assets and to maintain the economic status, and was institutionalized in many ways. Child-naming customs was one of them. Thus, the oldest son of the Godó family was named Ramón after his father, and indicated his position as future family heir. Differences between children did not stop in child-naming customs and affected their upbringing too. Thus, it is said that the young Ramón had chocolate for breakfast everyday, carefully prepared by his mother, while the rest of his siblings went without this luxury.[15] Further evidence of such preferential treatment is demonstrated by the fact that Ramón, together with his wife (Bonaventura Llucià) and their son, were allowed to live in the family home. In contrast, Carlos and Bartolomé only received the dowry that corresponded to younger siblings. According to the will their father signed in 1851, this dowry consisted of 1,500 *lliures* each.[16]

The prevailing of an impartible inheritance system in 19th-century Catalonia placed the two future founders of *La Vanguardia* in a favourable position to abandon Igualada. The immediate reason that triggered the departure of the two brothers, however, was a violent episode involving their family. The context behind this tragic incident was the strike of July 1855 – the first general strike in Spanish history. One year earlier a military coup d'état led by general O'Donnell had brought the most advanced sectors of Spanish liberalism into power and prompted the short-lived political system called *"Bieno Progresista"* (1854–1856).[17] In this context Barcelona became the epicentre of the workers' mobilisation in defence of the freedom of association and the protests for the growing mechanisation of the textile industry. Riots and demonstrations spread quickly to the main cities in Catalonia (where the strike became circumscribed, given that almost all the industry in Spain was concentrated in this region). Textile workers in Igualada took advantage of the general strike to present their demands, consisting in limiting the workday to 12 hours, increasing the salaries, and abolishing arbitrary dismissal. However, while all the businessmen eventually came to accept some of the workers' demands, Ramón Godó Llucià remained the only manufacturer to reject them.[18] In fact, Godó's singular stance had to do with his traditional opposition to the workers' claims, an attitude for which he was already well known and earned him the nickname of "bourgeois number one".[19] Amidst this atmosphere of entrenched positions, the situation reached a tipping point:

"When the workers of Mr D. Ramón Godó's factory presented him with the new production tariffs that they said must take the place of those previously agreed upon, the factory workers drew a knife that befell Mr. Godó at the very moment of having denied his compliance, leaving him lying in his office bathed in a sea of blood. The workers then entered the room of Mrs. Godó, who they stabbed eleven times in the chest and back and, at the same time, others shot and wounded the landlord of the fabric mill."[20]

The assault left Ramón and his wife Rita on the brink of death. The young family heir, who at the time of the attack was on the way back home, escaped by hiding in a neighbouring house. Although some other sources present different versions of the assault, and claim for instance that it was Godó's wife who provoked the workers, this episode reveals the context of extreme social tension in which Igualada was immersed at the time.[21] If this town had once exemplified the great thrust that industrialisation experienced in Catalonia, the aggression to the Godós evidenced the downside of this process and the growing social tensions it implied. In fact, Igualada's lack of water resources became an insurmountable obstacle for the mechanisation of the industry and forced local businessmen to rely on the so-called *"bergadana"* – a by then old-fashioned manual spinning machine. The immediate outcome of this failure to adopt to the mechanisation of the textile industry was a traumatic process of de-industrialisation that carried profound social consequences. Igualada went from a population of 14,000 in 1857 to 11,900 in 1860 and 10,200 by 1887, and working conditions deteriorated sharply: the working day in the textile industry lasted between 13 and 16 hours and the vast majority of the workforce was formed by women and children so as to keep salaries as low as possible.[22] The consequences of this very localized economic crisis (other neighbouring towns like Manresa and Mataró did not suffer the same lack of water resources) were the exacerbation of social conflict, of which the assault to Godó's house became one of the clearest symptoms. In fact, the aggression to the family members had a great echo and was recorded in the press of Barcelona and Madrid.[23] The reaction of the authorities, however, did little to bring peace. In the trial that followed, where the Godó's heir testified, six workers were condemned to more than two years of imprisonment. In practice, however, only two workers eventually returned, while the other six disappeared during their confinement.

The news about the disappearance of these eight workers created the black legend of the Godó family in Igualada. For the working class in this town, this incident equated the Godó name to despotic rule and labour exploitation. In 1918, that is to say 67 years after the incidents took place, the Republicans celebrated the end of the Godó family's political career right in front of their house. Asked for the reasons behind this animosity, people noted that the grievances against this family dated back to 1855.[24] These incidents are crucial to understanding the context in which the political career of the Godó family would develop in the future, and evoke the importance that memory played in the highly localised dynamics that characterised liberal politics in Europe.[25] Newspapers were a way of keeping these memories alive, but also a device for those interested in counteracting them.

It was amidst the economic and social crisis into which Igualada fell in the mid-19th century that the two future founders of *La Vanguardia* emigrated in 1856 to Bilbao. By then Carlos and Bartolomé Godó Pié were still young (Carlos was 21 and Bartolomé was only 16 years old) and were seemingly in a precarious situation. The few sources that have been preserved speak of two men of humble origins who made a fortune thanks to their effort and persistence, despite the difficult circumstances they encountered.[26] As one of these sources explained:

> "It was he (Carlos) who, like his brother Don Bartolomé, became one the most splendidly charitable men ever known in Catalonia. He came from Igualada to Barcelona from a humble background with little more means than normal. He learned to do business in a Commission House in Bilbao side-by-side with his older brother. He later opened up the same business in Barcelona, and afterwards became a factory owner and an affluent man, with great effort and without much more than his own natural gifts."[27]

Some of these testimonies, however, need to be interpreted with caution because they were written as obituaries that celebrated the image of the "bourgeois self-made man". In the case of Bartolomé, for instance, his obituaries stressed his initiative, honesty, and love of work. These were portrayed as commendable social qualities. In fact, Bartolomé himself apparently "liked to boast, when he was among friends, about the innumerable pieces of cloth that he had loaded on his robust shoulders during his youth".[28] The praise of such values, which placed the emphasis on the right to control one's own destiny, exemplified the growing criticism that the Catalan inheritance system began to undergo during the second half of the 19th century. Meritocracy, rather than birthright, started to be presented as the guiding pattern in the life of an individual. Obituaries thus constituted one of the rituals where the Catalan bourgeoisie constructed and redefined public values as a social class. As part of this meritocratic discourse, the departure of the younger sons was presented as a sign of determination to control one's future, as the case of the Godó brothers illustrates.[29]

In fact, the understanding of migration as an emblem of individualism has also been evident in the work of scholars. Historians of the European family have often interpreted the departure of junior siblings as ruptures in the bonds of kinship. According to this view, departure was the result of an individual choice where younger siblings sought to escape the control of the family and seek a better future. In other cases, departure was regarded as a mechanism to regulate demography, for instance the overpopulation of given societies.[30] In both explanations, migration is seen as part of a process of "modernisation" taking place in Western Europe since the late 18th century: the rise of the nuclear family.[31] However, and contrary to the assumptions above, the settlement of the Godó brothers in Bilbao did not imply the breaking of kinship ties. The situation was rather the opposite: the two brothers maintained a strong link with their family in Igualada and collaborated in the family business. In fact, the departure of Carlos and Bartolomé was part of the family's commercial strategy. The first evidence of this dates back to 1856, when the municipal census of Bilbao indicates that Carlos was sharing an apartment with an older brother Josep Godó Pié, at number 47 on the street named "Ronda". Apparently, Josep had moved to Bilbao two years earlier, in 1854, and worked as a textile tradesman.[32] That Carlos settled in Bilbao, following the same path and doing the same work as his brother, suggests that the Godó family operated following a "migration chain" pattern.[33] Hence, and in contrast to spontaneous mobility, the family marked the route of the siblings leaving Igualada.

The second evidence of a collective family strategy was sibling cooperation. On December 1864 the two brothers established a new business in Bilbao called "*Godó hermanos*" ("Godó brothers") with the declared purpose of selling and distributing all types of textiles.[34] In practice, however, the company seemed to give preference to Catalan goods. This is shown by the company's stated purpose of establishing a new branch in Catalonia and the opening of a new shop in Bilbao called "*Ciudad Condal*" (as Barcelona is also referred).[35] All this suggests that the migration of Carlos and Bartolomé Godó brothers to the Basque Country was part of a family strategy, consisting in the distribution and selling of the family's production from Igualada and complemented with the selling of other manufactures, mostly from Barcelona. In short, everything indicates that the Godó brothers were a typical example of "Catalan mercantile diaspora", as the small communities of Catalan merchants that scattered across Spain since the 18th century is commonly referred to.[36] Moreover, shortly after moving to Bilbao (by then a city of 20,000 people) Carlos and Bartolomé both married. They did so in the same year (1860) – within a few months of each other, and in the same church ("Basilica de Santiago el Mayor"); and both married Basque women. But most importantly, marriage is what allowed the Godó brothers to expand their company's sphere of action to Spain's colonies in the Caribbean. In fact, two of Bartolomé's wives (he married as many as three times) came from families with business interests in Cuba.[37] This island was one of the few colonies that were left of Spain's former empire (after the independence of the South-American dominions in the 1820s and 1830s) and also the most valuable one. Marriage proved decisive to establish commercial alliances to export Catalan cotton fabrics to Cuba. Hence, Bartolomé's first brother-in-law (a man named Felipe Belaunzarán) became the legal representative of "*Godó hermanos*" in Cuba. The strong commercial alliance that marriage provided is revealed by the fact that these alliances continued after the death of the married couple. As late as 1897 (more than thirty years after the settlement in Bilbao) the

Godó descendants still relied on the Belaunzarán family to represent their interests in Cuba.[38]

In the case of Carlos Godó, his wedding provided alternative (though complementary) benefits to those of his brother Bartolomé. Carlos married Antonia Lallana Azpe (1836–1924) on June 30 1860.[39] Antonia was originally from the Basque city of Vitoria and had moved with her family to Bilbao two years before the wedding. According to contemporaries, Antonia was a woman with a strong character. She had a very close bond with her son, the future owner of *La Vanguardia* (Ramón Godó Lallana), to the point that upon her request the newspaper stopped publishing reports on bullfighting (which she abhorred) despite it being the most popular sport in Spain at the time.[40] Another example of Antonia's imprint and influence on the Godó family is that after the marriage the family started using Spanish as its customary language – not just in Bilbao, but also when the couple moved to Barcelona.[41] The adoption of Spanish (instead of Catalan) in the private sphere became a common practice among the Catalan bourgeoisie, and was a marker of "social distinction".[42]

Clientelist methods in competitive politics

Despite having got married in Bilbao, in 1864 Bartolomé Godó moved back to Barcelona. His return followed a new business agreement the two brothers had established: Carlos would be in charge of the Bilbao office and Bartolomé would be responsible for the new Barcelona branch.[43] This task consisted in purchasing all the fabrics that Bilbao's branch required, as well as taking charge of all company matters. For this work Bartolomé received an annual salary of 12,000 *reales*, plus a two per cent commission. The "Godó brothers" business seemed to be going well: in 1864 the company reported a profit of 329,470 *reales*.[44] Besides running business from Barcelona, Bartolomé also began a political career in this city, during the so-called "Democratic Sexennium" (1868–1874). This new political system, founded after the overthrow of Queen Isabella, replaced the liberal-conservative model that had dominated the construction of the nation-state in Spain since 1843.[45] A coalition of liberal-progressive and democratic elites seized power and put an end to the monopoly of power that one single party (the "Moderados") had exercised until then. Despite holding very different projects, the link that brought this wide array of political forces together was the desire to put an end to the state of moral decay that characterized Queen Isabella's reign; and the wish to imprint a more progressive character to the political system. Many of these revolutionaries were open admirers of the Italian Risorgimento and saw in this political revolution the mixture of constitutional liberties, national unity and popular participation that Spain's moral recovery needed.[46] The outcome was the introduction during the *Sexenio* of the most advanced legislation in Spain's recent history: i.e. the establishing of a democratic monarchy under a new foreign dynasty (not by chance, the Italian house of Savoy), and the granting of extensive individual rights (like freedom of religion, education, assembly and press).

In addition to the progressive legislation it introduced, the *Sexenio* also represented a novelty for the popular expectations it awoke, especially in Barcelona. The revolution of 1868 was warmly welcomed in this city and led to some of the traditional demands of the working classes being satisfied, like the end to indirect tax on good's consumption and the city's duties of entry.[47] In parallel, the *Sexenio* renewed the political system in this city and opened decision-making positions to the most progressive elites. For the first time the Republicans won control of Barcelona's city council and obtained their best electoral results. Moreover, as much as 75% of the new elected officials had never held public office before, and they came from a much more varied social background compared to the politicians of Queen Isabella's era. Thus, the vast majority of the new ruling elites in Barcelona continued to be businessmen and liberal professionals, but as much as the 11% were manual workers and 6% were workers and clerks, a percentage never seen before in the city. Likewise, the majority of local officers were of Republican ascription (62%).[48]

The case of Bartolomé Godó is illustrative of the new generation who first entered into politics during the Sexennium. According to some contemporaries, he was a man of "strong political convictions" and "independent character", who always remained faithful to the Liberal Party.[49] This organization was also known at the time as the "Constitutional Party" ("Partido Constitucional") in reference to the document comprising their ideological principles: the Constitution of 1869. This document was one of the landmarks of the period and established the following principles: the constitutional monarchy was the base of Spanish sovereignty; the franchise was based on universal manhood suffrage; and wide individual rights (freedom of assembly, freedom of press and popular juries) were granted. Still, the advocacy of popular sovereignty did not prevent the Constitutional Party from distrusting the mobilisation of popular classes, which both the Democrats and the Republicans sought; and considered that freedom was inseparable from political order. In parallel to this, the Constitutionals defended the right of private property, the preservation of good relations with the Church and a limited administrative decentralisation.[50] For all these reasons, the Constitutionals were among the most conservative movements of the *Sexenio*.

It was in defence of the ideals of this party that Bartolomé Godó held his first political office, as alderman in Barcelona's city council in 1869. This appointment marked the beginning of a more ambitious political career that would take him to gain national pre-eminence. Thus, soon after receiving his position of alderman, Bartolomé was elected deputy in Barcelona's provincial body ("*diputación provincial*"), a position that he held between 1871 and 1878; and later on, in 1881, he was elected deputy in the Spanish Congress, in Madrid.

However, Bartolomé's political promotion was not a smooth path. It would be misleading to see his career as that of a "*bourgeois conquérant*" who climbed the state's ladders with ease, namely, because liberal elites were neither a unified class nor a "block of power".[51] The vast majority shared a well-off background, but their private interests were not always comparable and they often held different views on state issues, like foreign and economic policies.[52] Moreover, the political career of Bartolomé was not an ascending path but was suddenly interrupted in 1874, when a new political system ("the Bourbon Restoration") replaced the Democratic Sexennium. The case of Bartolomé thus provides a valuable opportunity to examine the strategies that the new urban elites designed to advance their interests in a context of political turmoil, and to shed light on how the founding of *La Vanguardia* became a valuable device to adapt to a changing political scenario.

Bartolomé's career during the *Sexenio* relied primarily on political clientelism. In other words, his political promotion was not so much dependent on the voters' support, but rather on his capacity to rig elections in his favour. Indeed, despite the fact the *Sexenio* was born with the aim of breaking the monopoly of power that one single party had enjoyed during Isabella's reign (1833–1868), the establishing of universal suffrage in 1868 did not imply the full democratisation of politics. This became clear for instance in the attitude that the Constitutionals held in the face of the elections. Although they were fierce defenders of the principle of popular sovereignty, in practice they often subjugated it to the need of assuring the existing social order. In their view, voting was a social responsibility – rather than an individual right – that consequently required certain conditions to be exerted. According to the "discourse of capacity", gender, wealth and education were the conditions distinguishing those who were suitable to enjoy political rights ("active citizens") from those who were not. This restrictive understanding of citizenship went often together with the submission of political rights to broader conceptual entities (like the "nation" and the "general interest"), and is what ultimately justified the rigging of elections – a principle that was morally defended at the time as the "legitimate influence" of the government in elections.[53]

Even the Republicans and the Democrats, who argued for a more egalitarian model of political representation than the Constitutionals and who defended voting as an individual right, sometimes rigged elections too.[54] The reason is that clientelism also became a way of coping with political instability. In its five-year existence the *Sexenio* had countless governments and saw the state model changed on repeated occasions.[55] In parallel, the political system was confronted with the armed opposition of Catholic fundamentalists (1872) and a separatist insurrection in Cuba (the "Ten Years War", 1868–1878). These circumstances explain why all parties – even the most advanced, like the Republicans and the Democrats – saw the rigging of elections as a way to control public office in times of political instability.

The extended presence that political clientelism had in Spain, however, should not be regarded as a sign of backwardness in historical development. In fact, when compared to most European countries, the *Sexenio* had one of the most progressive systems of political representation at the time. While the curtailing of political rights according to the "discourse of capacity" was a common trend across most of the Continent at the time,[56] Spain was the only country – other than France and the German Empire – in which universal suffrage existed.[57] Furthermore, clientelism was also a widely extended practice in France. The literature usually neglects the case of this country because it is regarded as an ideal model of democratisation. However, the fact is that clientelism proved to be a deeply-rooted practice in this country too – even if it mutated under successive political systems. Instead of the traditional manipulation of elections based on the arbitrary use of electoral rules that characterised clientelism under France's Restoration (1815–30) and the July Monarchy (1830–48), the introduction of universal suffrage in 1848 transformed clientelism through a practice aimed at influencing the voters' behaviour. This was done through different methods and combined the use of incentives (like the buying of votes and the concession of privileges) with the use of coercive measures.[58]

The case of Bartolomé Godó exemplifies how in Spain too the routes to public office often relied on the use of clientelist procedures, despite the introduction of universal suffrage. The fact that he was able to take advantage of clientelism was based upon two factors. The first one was the control of local politics: Bartolomé always ran for Igualada's constituency, where the Godó family lived and had numerous supporters. The second source of influence was the personal acquaintances he had in various institutions, especially with the leaders of the Constitutional Party. These acquaintances allowed Bartolomé to intercede in far-flung places like Madrid, where the most important decisions were taken.[59]

In local politics, Igualada became the first source of influence for Bartolomé Godó. The prominent position the Godó family held in this town allowed him to mobilise a network of friends, relatives and supporters – this being a form of social capital that was of prime importance to manipulate elections. Second, Igualada had a series of administrative features that made it a valuable gateway to various political posts. Under the Democratic Sexennium, this city was the head of a judicial district in charge of electing one representative for Barcelona's Provincial Deputation and one for the Spanish Congress.[60] These two elements – local supporters and Igualada's administrative position – explain why the Godó family sought to turn Igualada's constituency into its personal political domain. In fact, in the long-lasting political trajectory of the Godó family (spanning from 1869 to 1914) none of their members would ever run for any other constituency. Localism became the first and most important source of political power of the Godó family.

Indeed, the desire to protect the family's interests in Igualada was a major reason for Bartolomé to stand for this constituency, even though he now lived in Barcelona. At a time when Igualada was suffering a major economic downturn – as evidenced in the aggression that his family suffered in 1855 – Bartolomé's career became a way for the Godó family to cope with the industrial crisis. The case of Bartolomé thus illustrates a common trend among the European petite bourgeoisie: namely, the entry into municipal government to protect private interests. Still, and as Geoffrey Crossick and Gerhard Haupt have rightly noted, the entry into local politics was also "an expression of their social and cultural, as much as of their economic, concerns".[61] In other words, the elites' entry into municipal politics was not limited to a defensive strategy, but was part of a highly localised identity.

However, while some European elites could rely on the municipal government to defend their private interests (in the case of Prussia, for instance, where municipal governments enjoyed wide autonomy), this was not the case of Spain, as a highly centralised state-model was implemented during Queen Isabella's reign (1833–1868).[62] Since 1833 the "Moderados" established a new territorial organisation inspired by the French-model that was based on three levels: municipal, provincial and central. The outcome was a highly centralised model where the president of the Provincial Deputations (the so-called "*Jefe político*" or "political boss") concentrated all the attributions of municipal government. In fact, the "political boss" had a tight grip over the elections, to the point that this figure became the backbone of political clientelism during Isabella's reign: he was "in control of the process of voter registration, the creation of voting lists, the nominations of those who would supervise the polling locations on election day, and the validation of the electoral rules".[63] This control of electoral procedures by state officials, coupled with an extremely limited franchise (limited to one per cent of the total population) explains how clientelism worked during Queen Isabella's reign (1833–1868).

Under the Sexennium, by contrast, progressive elites like Bartolomé Godó saw the Provincial Deputation as a new way of promoting their private concerns. Indeed, while these institutions had a very restricted room for manoeuvre during Isabella's reign, during the Sexennium they gained new importance. In line with the liberal-progressive decentralised state-model, Provincial Deputations were entrusted with the administration of public funds and gained new executive functions, mostly concerned with education, charity, and infrastructure. Additionally, deputies started to be elected on the basis of a universal suffrage, including the position of president.[64] As a result of these new attributions, Provincial Deputations became one of the key institutions where local elites sought to defend their respective interests. This was the case of Bartolomé Godó, who devoted most of his time in Barcelona's Provincial Deputation (between 1870 and 1874) to fulfilling some of Igualada's most urgent needs. These needs consisted, above all, in the lack of overland connections, which were vital for the economic recovery of this city. The archives of Barcelona's Provincial Deputation reveal that he always opted to be part of the commission in charge of promoting new infrastructures.[65] In September 1874, for instance, he was part of a commission that went to Madrid to solve various issues concerning the province. The outcome of that visit was the approval of a new road between Igualada and the neighbouring town of Santa Coloma de Queralt – a connection that Igualada had long requested.[66]

Together with the local support, the adscription to the Constitutional Party was Bartolomé's second source of influence in politics. Still, this kind of influence did not manifest so much through party organization, but rather through the friendship that Bartolomé held with one of the party leaders: Víctor Balaguer (1824–1901). Balaguer was a renowned writer and historian, and one of the main leaders of the Progressives in this region. During the *Sexenio* Balaguer started holding important political posts in Catalonia (among which, the presidency of Barcelona's Provincial Deputation) and in 1869 he settled in Madrid, where he held important government positions and became the main representative of Catalan economic interests.[67] During his time in Madrid, Bartolomé Godó was one of the contacts Balaguer used to stay abreast of the political situation in Catalonia. The relation between the two men, however, was not a relation between equals but operated on a patronage basis. This can be seen for instance in the letter Godó wrote to Balaguer on 7 October 1871. The aim was to inform Balaguer about the divisions existing between the Constitutionals of Barcelona. As the letter went:

"My good sir and friend (...) I assume that you know, from the letters you have received from here [Barcelona], that we the political friends are divided, some in favour of Sagasta and the others in favour of Zorrilla [;] [the latter] treat Sagasta and his friends in very harsh terms [...], to the point that the committee might become divided, but we are some friends who will sustain unity whatever it takes, and sooner or later I am convinced that justice will be done (...). I can imagine the bad moments that what can be called family disputes have caused on you, but I can assure you that the majority are prudent and they are on your side (...). We will fight and I hope we shall win. If I can be a resource for you in this or in any other matter please command me, and I shall serve you with pleasure."[68]

This letter is the clearest testimony to Godó's political commitment and reveals the way political parties worked at the time – this being a crucial element to understand the reasons behind the founding of *La Vanguardia*. Although Godó introduced himself as a "sincere friend" ("*verdaderos amigos*") the letter was not written in an informal way, but has a tenor of reverence. This is because Godó's purpose was to reaffirm his commitment to Balaguer in the face of the division among the Constitutionals. Indeed, in 1871 the Constitutional Party became divided on a national scale into two opposing camps: the group of Mateo Práxedes Sagasta and the group of Manuel Ruiz Zorrilla. Two factors explain this division: the lack of a clear leadership, especially after the murder of General Prim (the leader of the liberal progressives); and the different understandings of the Constitution of 1869 held by the two aspiring leaders (Sagasta and Zorrilla).[69] When this division was echoed in Barcelona's branch, Godó hurried to reassure his allegiance to Balaguer.[70] This loyalty was expressed in the letter quoted and implicitly linked Godó with the candidate that Balaguer supported at a national scale: Sagasta.

This evidence reveals how parties functioned at the time: through personal allegiance, instead of regular membership. In fact, Godó referred to the division of the Constitutionals in Barcelona as a "family dispute" ("*disgustos de familia*") and referred to the other party members as "political friends" ("*amigos políticos*"), this being a type of language that evokes a political culture where the holding of public office was still the concern of a social minority. Indeed, the personal bonds that Godó held with the leaders of the Constitutional Party is a revealing example of "cadre parties" (also-called "notable parties"), the party organisation that prevailed in Europe during most of the 19th century.[71] The socially restricted levels that official politics had during most of the century, coupled with the liberal's political culture of limited suffrage, left public office in the hands of a tiny minority. For the people who belonged to this minority, like Bartolomé Godó, public office was not a professional career, but represented a secondary activity. Or, to put it in Max Weber's famous quote, politicians at that time "did not live from politics but for politics".[72] Consequently, "cadre parties" had a low number of supporters and instead of having a regular membership they were structured around patronage networks.

An example of the importance that political friendship had in the building of political careers is exemplified by the provincial elections of 1871. On this occasion, a letter was circulated around all the towns of the district in which the state's provincial representative (the Civil Governor) "recommended" to vote for Godó, and threatened the people who refused to do so. More precisely, the letter announced the state's future rejection of any local requests in case Godó was not elected. According to some witnesses, this threat made a great impression on the "common people", most of whom preferred to follow the official recommendation rather than face the consequences.[73] This incident shows to what extent the state's prerogatives were used at the time to satisfy partisan goals, and how the parties of the *Sexenio* did not hesitate to make use of the state machinery for their own profit. Moreover, the coercion that state officials exerted on voters shows that, like the case of France, in Spain too the existence of clientelism was not limited to rigging of elections; but also implied coerciive measures on the voter's decisions.

The case of Bartolomé Godó thus sheds light on how patronage networks worked at the time. In his condition as party member he provided Balaguer with the support that reasserted his leadership in the Catalan branch of the Constitutional Party; while Balaguer, in turn, assisted Godó to win the elections and gave him access to a series of public resources in Madrid. These resources were linked to the trade with Cuba, especially after Balaguer's appointment as "Minister of Ultramar" (the ministry in charge of the Spanish colonies) in 1871. Indeed, Cuba started gaining importance for the Godó family business (as Chapter 3 will explain in more detail) and politics became a way of interceding in Madrid to secure the family's interests in the island.

At the "vanguard" of the Constitutional Party

The instalment of the Bourbon Restoration in 1875, however, suddenly toppled the channels of influence that Bartolomé Godó had patiently built during the *Sexenio Democrático*. A military coup d'état in the Valencian town of Sagunt put an end to the *Sexenio* and brought back the Bourbon dynasty to Spain. The immediate outcome was a swift change of political system, as well as a shift in the way patronage networks were structured. In this new political scenario the Constitutional Party fell on the losing side, and so did Bartolomé Godó. Hence, the day after the military coup proclaimed Alfonso de Borbón as Spain's new king, Godó resigned from the Provincial Deputation together with the other Constitutionals.[74] In the blink of an eye, Godó went from being one of the *Sexenio*'s representatives in provincial government to being a declared adversary of the new political order.

Indeed, the Bourboun Restoration was in line with the conservative reaction that took place in Europe after the Paris Commune (1871). The man responsible for organising the Restoration was Antonio Cánovas del Castillo

(1828–1897), a liberal-conservative politician. Since 1873 Cánovas had been the leader of Madrid's *"Partido Alfonsino"*, a movement in support of the Bourbon dynasty that gained popularity in the last years of the *Sexenio*, especially among the aristocracy and the army.[75] Taking the British system of representation as a reference model, Cánovas prepared the return of the Bourbon dynasty in 1875, in the shape of Isabella's son (Alfonso XII), and based the new political system upon the joint sovereignty between the Crown and the parliament (divided into Congress and Senate).[76] If Cánovas was the intellectual architect of the Restoration, the new Constitution of 1876 reasserted the new political system. For the most part, this constitution represented a substantial step backward in relation to the *Sexenio Democrático*. The new constitution granted basic individual rights but made them subject to different restrictions. In practice, this meant that basic rights like freedom of expression, association and union became restricted. For instance, censorship was imposed on newspapers, and Catholicism became the only religion that could be practiced in public. In the field of political representation, the passing of a new electoral law in 1878 limited the franchise drastically. From this moment onwards only 5% of the population had the right to vote. Additionally, the King was granted a series of important attributions, like the capacity to appoint the mayor of cities with over 30,000 inhabitants.

In this way, the Constitution of 1876 and the electoral law of 1878 became the two legislative pillars of a new political system, which was far more restrictive than the *Sexenio*. However, the Restoration did not imply a return to Queen Isabella's political model. Although some of the new laws were inspired in this period,[77] Cánovas was aware that the monopoly of power by one single party had been the main reason behind the downfall of Isabella II in 1868. To avoid the same mistake, Cánovas wished to integrate the most conservative parties of the *Sexenio* into the new Restoration. His aim was to establish a two-party system similar to the English model, where the *"Partido Alfonsino"* would play the role of the Liberal-conservative party, and the most conservative members of the *Sexenio* would form the party on the left (or Liberals). In this way, Cánovas aspired to consolidate a new political system based on the alternation in power between two liberal parties, where the King would play a stabilising role through the wide political attributions that the Constitution granted to the Crown. Ideally, this formula would assure the stability of the Restoration, while excluding the most radical parties both on the left (Republicans and Democrats) and on the right (the Moderates and the Carlists).

This aspiration to create a two-party system, however, did not materialize immediately. During the first years of the Restoration Cánovas sought to content the most conservative sectors of Spanish society with the hope of underpinning the new situation and dividing his rivals on the right. The passing of additional policies, such as the abolition of civil marriage, or the restriction of academic freedom in universities, was a further step directed at reasserting this new conservative shift.[78] In the face of this situation the Constitutionals became deeply divided on how to react to the new situation. For the most progressive sector of the party, headed by Víctor Balaguer, accepting the Restoration was a betrayal of the democratic principles that had inspired the *Sexenio*. The shared sovereignty between the Crown and the parliament of the Restoration went against the principle of popular sovereignty that the Constitutionals defended. Likewise, the new political system did not assure the political rights (freedom of expression, press, and assembly) that were the banner of the Constitutionals. For all these reasons, Víctor Balaguer stood at the head of those Constitutionals who rejected both the integration in the Restoration and the need to create a new Liberal Party.[79]

In the short term, Balaguer's refusal to join the new political system had pernicious consequences for the Godó brothers. The refusal to cooperate also implied a self-exclusion from holding public office, a position that the Godós seemed not prepared to accept. Indeed, the commercial interests they had started developing in Cuba (see Chapter 3) made access to policy-making decisions crucial for their business, and in a centralized state model like Spain's, these decisions were taken in Madrid. Against this background, Bartolomé Godó decided to ignore the official position of the Constitutional Party and run for the elections in Congress without the party support. Immediately, both Balaguer and Sagasta (the main leaders of the Constitutionals in Catalonia and Spain, respectively) wrote to Godó and urged him to abstain from standing.[80] Godó, however, showed his stubborn character and ignored the recommendations of the party leaders. Apparently, he was confident that his supporters in Igualada would suffice to win the elections. To this end, he also hired new people to manipulate elections in his favour.[81]

However, the elections of 1876 proved to be a stark lesson for Bartolomé Godó. Contrary to what he expected, his resources of influence proved to be insufficient to win. Prior to the elections, the state' provincial officer (Mr. Villalba) removed the city mayors of Igualada's constituency and replaced them with new mayors that were favourable to the government's candidate. As a result, the same clientelistic methods that Godó had used to build his career during the *Sexenio* were now used against him.[82] The elections of 1876 thus demonstrated that having a network of local supporters was important but not sufficient to fight against the state's intervention in elections. The Restoration had redefined the functioning of patron–client networks, and in this new scenario Godó could no longer rely on the state's support. The last evidences of this were the next elections of 1880, when once again, Godó ran to the elections without party support. His eagerness to gain power was such that he even considered the possibility of running in the elections for another constituency (Manresa) and in representation of another party. According to the Republican newspaper *La Montaña*, Godó made contact with various political forces (including the Carlists and the Democrats) about the possibility of running for this constituency.[83] If this decision casts doubts about Godó's supposed blind support to the ideals of the Constitutional Party, it also reveals the difficulties of winning the elections without the support of a wider patronage network.

In the face of this second failure, founding a newspaper became an alternative stratagem to exert influence. Indeed, the founding of *La Vanguardia* was a move from the Godó brothers aimed at creating a new platform of influence now they could not rely on clientelist procedures. This move went in line with the changes that were taking place at a national level, especially when an alternative branch of the Constitutional Party showed readiness to join the Restoration. At the head of this position there was Práxedes Mateo Sagasta, one of the main leaders of the liberal progressives during the *Sexenio*. Since 1875 he had publically accepted the new political situation and had been the main inspirer, in 1880, of a new party called *"Partido Liberal Fusionista"* (in its abbreviated name, "Liberal Party"). This new organization sought to bring all the liberal-progressives forces together with the aim of defending the *Sexenio*'s main landmarks in the Restoration. The two-party system that Cánovas had in mind thus appeared as a real possibility, which finally materialized on 8 February 1881: on that date the King called Sagasta's Liberal Party into power. When this took place, Sagasta counted on the support of a new journal that had been created in Barcelona just one week before: *La Vanguardia*.

Indeed, it is not by coincidence that *La Vanguardia* was founded seven days before the new Liberal Party reached power for the first time in the Restoration. Rumours had spread since the end of 1880 about the possibility that the former Constitutionals could reach power. In the event of this possibility, the Godó brothers reacted to take advantage of the new situation by establishing a newspaper. This agenda became clear since the newspaper's first issue. Following an extended practice at the time, *La Vanguardia* announced its future editorial line the first day it was published:

"(...) Our programme is clear and concise. In the last years of conservative governments, a new parenthesis has been opened to public freedom (...) Amidst this shipwreck and widespread uncertainty [e.g. end of the Democratic Sexennium], only one party and one man have managed to stay afloat; (...) the Constitutional Party, gathered closely around its leader [Sagasta] did not abandon the fight for a moment, and did not budge one inch without fighting this bloody battle, and in six years of relentless struggle (...) the party has reconquered public opinion. (...) This leader we shall follow and to this party we belong. (...) We come to the field of the press, therefore, to defend the principles of the Constitutional Party in line with the fusion this has allowed [e.g. creation of the new Liberal Fusionist Party]. From our position we are committed to combatting the government as ruthlessly as it seeks to combat us. (...) We shall do so by opposing the government through our love and enthusiasm for liberty, which shall never desist no matter the threat or the danger at stake (...)."[84]

Thus with this bellicose editorial did *La Vanguardia* make its appearance on the streets of Barcelona. The Liberal Party was about to reach power for the first time under the Restoration (a situation that did not materialize until February 8, that is seven days later) and the newspaper was ready to endorse the new situation. Indeed, six years had passed since the end of the *Sexenio*, during which the Constitutionals had been relegated to the opposition, but this "bloody battle" (as *La Vanguardia* called it) seemed to come to an end. A new period was to begin in Spanish politics and a brand-new journal had appeared to bear the banner of the Constitutional Party. Though the organization no longer existed, as it had formally been merged into the new Liberal Party, this was not an impediment for the newspaper to vindicate its name. In fact, for many years *La Vanguardia* would be published under the heading of "Spokesman of the Constitutional Party of the Province". The Constitution of 1869 was to be the beacon for the progressive forces in the Restoration, and *La Vanguardia* was there to proclaim it in public.

Still, what evidence do we have that the Godó brothers were really behind the foundation of this newspaper? Why did the former Constitutionals from Barcelona need a new spokesman, if they already had one called *"La Crónica de Cataluña"*? Why did *La Vanguardia* praise Sagasta in such laudatory terms, to the point of presenting him almost as a war hero? And from a broader European perspective, what can the founding of this newspaper tell us about the functioning of cadre parties?

Despite historically being one of the oldest and most influential newspapers in Spain – and it remains so today – the origins of *La Vanguardia* remain controversial. According to the official account, the brothers Carlos and Bartolomé Godó founded the newspaper in February 1881. This point, however, has never been empirically demonstrated. In fact, there is an alternative account arguing that the Godó brothers did not in fact establish the newspaper, but rather purchased it in 1887.[85] Unfortunately, the historical document that could resolve this controversy – the registry of foundation – has been lost.[86] As a result, the origins of Catalonia's top-selling newspaper today have remained lost in the mists of time.

One of the sources that can solve this enigma and shed new light on the origins of *La Vanguardia* is an article that *La Correspondencia de España* – a Madrid newspaper – published in November 1880. The value of this document is that that it mentions *La Vanguardia* three-months before it was even founded. More precisely, the article in *La Correspondencia* referred to an intra-party struggle in which the Constitutionals in Barcelona were immersed at the time. The leader of this party branch was Francesc de Paula Rius i Taulet (1833–1899), a man with flamboyant sideburns whose name has gone down in history as Barcelona's most important mayor in the modern era. During his long political career Rius always disregarded all the offers he received from high politics and put Barcelona first. As mayor of this city (a position he already held during the *Sexenio*, between 1871 and 1872) he became one of the promoters of Barcelona's radical urban transformation, especially through the World Fair of 1888. None of this, however, saved Rius from a group of rebels who constantly challenged his position as leader of the Constitutionals' branch in Barcelona. At the head of this faction was a man called Pedro Collaso Gil (?–1887), a rich landowner born in La Habana (Cuba), who had contributed financially to the "Glorious Revolution" of 1868 and who aspired to be the new party leader. In such attempt Collaso counted with the invaluable support of two close friends: the brothers Carlos and Bartolomé Godó. Together, they would be the main responsible for the perennial instability that characterized the first years of the Liberal Party in Catalonia. It was in this context that in November 1880 *La Correspondencia* reported on the latest new about the intra-party struggle:

> "The political harmony is so far from reigning over the constitutionals of Barcelona that (…) according to a letter from that city published in *La Correspondencia*, the friends of Mr. Collaso Gil are thinking of establishing a newspaper that will be called *La Vanguardia*, that will oppose *La Crónica de Cataluña*, which is well-known to represent the faction of Mr. Rius Taulet. Two important circumstances must be noted in the news that follows: firstly, that the launching of the newspaper – which will be soon, as the necessary funds have already been collected – will be accompanied by a banquet in Tivoli, which will not be attended by neither Mr. Balaguer nor the friends of Mr. Rius Taulet; and secondly that the editorial direction of said newspaper will be ordered by the deputy from Tarragona, D. Pedro Antonio Torres (…)."[87]

The information given in *La Correspondencia* was predicting what was going to happen three months later, on 2 February 1881: the appearance of *La Vanguardia* as the hobbyhorse of Collaso's faction to challenge the leadership of Rius. As part of this enterprise, Bartolomé Godó became the owner (and therefore the founding partner) of *La Vanguardia*. There are at least three pieces of evidence to support this statement. The first is Bartolomé's obituary, in which *La Vanguardia* referred to him as the sole founder.[88] The other, but most important piece of evidence, comes from the *Semanario de Igualada* – the newspaper published by the political rivals of the Godó family in Igualada. As this newspaper once noted, "(...) *La Vanguardia* is a newspaper that is also published in Barcelona, and it is the mouthpiece of Mr. Bartolomé Godó Pié, who covers its expenses". Further evidence, with even more details about Godó's aims, is another article from the same newspaper, according to which "One day, with the aim of climbing the ladders of power, Godó founded *La Vanguardia* in Barcelona (...) to create an atmosphere and present himself to the people as big as Rigoletto".[89]

All this seems to confirm that Bartolomé Godó became both the owner and founding partner of *La Vanguardia*. The name of his brother, Carlos Godó, in contrast, does not appear anywhere. From a broader European perspective, what makes the founding of this newspaper interesting is that it reveals the role the press played as an instrument to both legitimise and dispute the "authorized discourse" of cadre parties.[90] The weak organisational structure of cadre parties implied that besides an electoral committee, these organizations usually lacked a permanent structure. This is illustrated by the case of the Constitutional Party in Barcelona. When this local branch was created in January 1871, it made a public call for the creation of a cohesive party structure. In practice, however, it failed to do so and the local branch became limited to a small electoral committee. As their political enemies rightly pointed out, the Constitutionals of Barcelona were a group of dispersed people with vague political principles.[91] Within this weak organizational structure, their only permanent organ was a newspaper called *La Crónica de Cataluña*. This newspaper acted as the party's mouthpiece and reaffirmed its principles against the attacks of its adversaries. The press thus acted as a channel of communication between the members of a political community and gave it a vital sense of group cohesion. No matter where the reader lived, the act of buying the party' spokesman demonstrated the reader's predisposition towards a certain vision of the world; and it reinforced the notion of political community. Moreover, party organs were charged with the vital task of publicising the party's official discourse. Thus, *La Crónica de Cataluña* was the official voice of the Constitutionals in Barcelona, this being a function that also implied the task of publishing the official list of candidates. The control of *La Crónica de Cataluña* was, in consequence, the "source of delegated power" (to use the terminology of Pierre Bourdieu) that made Rius the official representative of the party in the city.[92]

La Vanguardia was founded with the ambition of disrupting the leadership of Rius. For the rebel faction led by Pedro Collaso and the Godó brothers, establishing a newspaper became a way of gaining visibility and to challenge monopoly of representation that *La Crónica de Cataluña* possessed in Barcelona. This intention was made clear in the name chosen for the new journal: *"La Vanguardia. Spokesman of the Constitutional Party of the Province"*. Therefore, and in contrast to what some other scholars have argued, the name "La Vanguardia" ("the Vanguard", in English) was not random: in the context of an intra-party struggle, typical of the weak structure that cadre parties had in Europe, the newspaper was created to fight for the leadership of the party and to gain public visibility. All this explains why *La Vanguardia* always carried – and continues to do so today – a revolutionary-sounding name.

"As big as Rigoletto": the partisan function of the press

Still, equally as important as the strategy used to dispute the "authorized discourse" was the audience to whom this discourse was addressed. The first copy of *La Vanguardia* reveals, in this respect, how extremely modest the origins of this newspaper were. At a cost of 5 cents, *La Vanguardia* had a circulation of only 1,400 copies. The newspapers were printed with a Marinoni rotating machine and the newsroom was housed in a dark and narrow apartment, number 8–10, on the street called Les Heures in Barcelona. From a European perspective, the characteristics of *La Vanguardia* in its early stage were in line with the presses in other Mediterranean countries, like Italy and Portugal. These characteristics consisted in a very small number of copies, limited circulation – usually restricted to the local or to the provincial sphere – and strongly partisan-oriented content.[93] These very modest characteristics hardly made of *La Vanguardia* a profitable business. In fact, there is evidence suggesting that this newspaper became a longstanding source of economic loss for the Godó brothers.[94]

However, it would be misleading to interpret the paper's financial losses as a failed investment. The reason for this is that in the beginning of *La Vanguardia*, partisan goals prevailed over commercial ones. When Bartolomé Godó invested in the founding of this journal his ambition was neither to reach a massive audience, nor to make profits, but rather to present himself as "big as Rigoletto" – that is to say, to gain public notoriety.[95] This strategy was also referred at the time with the expression of "creating an atmosphere" (*"crear atmosfera"*) and consisted in gaining the attention of a target audience. And this audience was not the public of Barcelona, but the directors of the Constitutional Party in Madrid, headed by Sagasta. The calling into power of Liberal party had signalled the beginning of a new era, in which the former Constitutionals could continue to defend its political agenda in the new Restoration system. The strategy behind the founding *La Vanguardia* was, in the face of this new scenario, to stop Collaso's faction being regarded as a small rebel faction and to become the legitimate interlocutor of Sagasta in Barcelona.

In fact, the benefits of founding *La Vanguardia* became evident very early, when in February 1881 Sagasta received the two warring parties in Madrid. As one newspaper from the capital commented, "Two distinct commissions of the constitutionals of Barcelona have come to Madrid, one presided by Mr. Rius Taulet, and another by Mr. Torres. Both have pertained to represent the majority opinion of members of the Constitutional Party of the province, and the second has ordered some newspapers to report that it was not entirely correct that Mr Sagasta recognised the leadership of his friends Mr. Rius Taulet in the province of Barcelona."[96] The fact that Sagasta received the two commissions showed the immediate benefits that founding *La Vanguardia* had brought for Collaso's group: they were not seen anymore as rebels, but Sagasta acknowledged them as one of the party representatives in Barcelona. At the head of the Collaso delegation was Pere Antoni Torres Jordi (1844–1901), the first editor in the history of *La Vanguardia*.[97] The case of Torres illustrates how closely interlinked politics and journalism were at the time. In fact, it can be said that he was recruited as the first editor of *La Vanguardia* because of his political affiliation. His political career spanned back to the Democratic Sexennium, when he founded various newspapers in his home-town of Tarragona to support the Constitutional Party.[98] The activism in the press provided him with political contacts, among which his close friendship with Sagasta, as well as public positions like that of civil governor in Girona, Malaga, and Granada. The case of Torres thus reveals that political affiliation, rather than professional value, was the guiding pattern in the recruitment of journalists. This is further proved by the fact that the first four editors in the history of *La Vanguardia* were all members of the Liberal Party.[99] The case of this newspaper shows the lack of autonomy that journalism had in relation to politics; and its lack of differentiation as a distinctive professional field.

The first consequence of the close links between press and politics was that journalism often acted as a platform into politics. Due to the extremely low circulation of partisan papers and the lack of professional recognition, the salaries of journalists were very low forcing most of them to take on other jobs to complement their incomes. These precarious working conditions meant that journalism was not regarded as a profession in itself, but as a springboard into public office. For men of humble origins, journalism became a way to attain seats in parliaments, provincial administrations, and city halls, and governments took advantage of this situation by bribing jour-nalists through the so-called "reptile funds". In fact, many journalists were on the payroll of the ministry of interior (under various guises – even as street cleaners), while others made their way into public positions thanks to their political contacts.[100]

The second characteristic that journalism had in Spain, besides the lack of autonomy from politics, was a strong literary profile. This was also a distinguishing feature of journalism in Italy, Portugal, and France.[101] The entry into the newsroom allowed many men to satisfy their literary vocation, this being a tendency that was favoured by the strong commentary-oriented tradition that journalism had in the mentioned countries. As a result of this tradition, journalists often combined the writing of aggressive political editorials with the writing of literary works – sometimes published in the same newspaper. The first editor in the history of *La Vanguardia* (Torres) was the paramount example of this combination of self-education, literary vocation, and political ambition. Besides his affiliation to the Liberal Party, Torres was also a renowned poet and playwright. And he soon abandoned his position as editor of *La Vanguardia* for a new appointment, in 1882, as *"Director General de Beneficiencia and Sanidad"*, which he combined with his role of deputy in the Congress.[102] His case reveals to what extent journalism was regarded as a temporary stepping-stone to higher political positions.

Bartolomé Godó did not take long either to see the returns from his investment in *La Vanguardia*. In the days following the creation of the newspaper his position within the Liberal Party improved rapidly. On the 2nd of February 1881 (that is to say, the day after *La Vanguardia* appeared on the newsstands) Godó was elected as vice-president of Barcelona's Local committee, and soon after he was made vice-president of the party's Provincial Committee.[103] The crowning moment of his ascendant career took place in August 1881, when he was finally elected as deputy to the Congress. If he finally reached the position he had sought so relentlessly (he had failed to do so in the elections of 1876 and 1880) it was because *La Vanguardia* had placed him in a favourable position to reap the benefits of the Liberal Party's first seizing of power. Thus, Godó made use of the same clientelist methods that he had already used in previous elections (such as adding the names of dead people to the polling box), but the difference is that he now counted with the state's support to win them.[104]

The victory in the elections of 1881 marked the beginning of Godó's long-lasting career. From this moment onwards, and thanks to influence obtained through *La Vanguardia*, he (and his relatives after him) managed to gain a seat in the Spanish Congress, in Madrid. More precisely, Godó's career became dependent on the rotation system that the two main parties established at a national scale. Hence, the Liberal Party soon became one of the central pillars of the Restoration, and in 1885 Sagasta reached an agreement with Cánovas (the so-called *"Pacto del Pardo"*) according to which their respective parties would alternate in power successively. According to this agreement, reached under critical circumstances,[105] instead of holding elections to choose the ruling party the two liberal parties would decide –

Table 1.1. *Electoral results of the Godó family during the period 1879–1897*

Year	Date of the elections	Party in power	Winning candidate	Other candidates	Electoral turnout	Percentage of votes obtained
1879–1880	20/04/1879	Conservative	Manuel Camacho (C)	Josep Mª Rius Badia	—	63.60%
1881–1883	20/08/1881	Liberal	**Bartolomé Godó Pié (L)**	Manuel Camacho (C)	—	—
1884–1885	27/04/1884	Conservative	Francesc Gumà Ferran (C)	**Bartolomé Godó Pié (L)**	—	76.80%
1886–1890	04/04/1886	Liberal	**Bartolomé Godó Pié (L)**	Vicente Romero Baldrich (L)	—	—
1891–1892	01/02/1891	Conservative	Josep Mª Rius Badia (C)	**Carlos Godó Pié (L)** and Josep d'España (Carlist)	—	—
1893–1895	05/03/1893	Liberal	**Carlos Godó Pié (L)**	Josep d'España (Carlist) and Nicolau Estévanez	42.35%	62.45%
1896–1897	12/04/1896	Conservative	**Carlos Godó Pié (L)**	Josep d'España (Carlist)	33.72%	52.43%

with the decisive intervention of the King – when power was to be transferred between them.

The *"Pacto del Pardo"* set out the procedure through which the two liberal parties would monopolise public office during the Restoration period (1874–1923), while excluding from it the rest of the parties. In consequence, elections in Restoration Spain became a pure formality aimed at confirming the results the two parties had agreed beforehand; to the point that until the crisis of 1913, the two liberal parties managed to alternate in power without much difficulty.[106] *Caciquismo* became the method the two parties used to impose electoral results, as well as the procedure to distribute public office to all the local bosses ("clients") they had across the Spanish territory. It has been estimated that between 1,000 and 5,000 administrative positions (in institutions ranging from city councils to judiciary courts, as well as other positions in public bodies) changed hands after each election.[107] In this way, in 1885 the Restoration implemented a procedure that was similar to that of Portugal: two parties agreed to rotate in power and secured this agreement through the rigging of elections. In Italy too, clientelism was the procedure liberal parties used to monopolise government, even though the procedure was slightly different: in this case, it consisted in the building of intra-party coalitions ("*trasformismo*") rather than in party rotation.[108]

Bartolomé Godó was an example of one of those local bosses (or "caciques") who benefited from the two parties' monopoly over public office. His election to the Spanish Congress for Igualada's constituency became dependent on the alternation in power between the Conservatives and the Liberals. Thus, only when the Liberal Party seized power was Bartolomé elected as deputy, as Table 1.1 (page 37) illustrates. It was not until more than a decade later that the political influence of the Godó family became powerful enough to impose its own candidate against the will of the government. From a broader perspective, the case of Bartolomé reveals the importance that the press played in liberal politics. If he managed to overcome the downfall of the *Sexenio* it was because the founding of a newspaper – as part of a broader collective project headed by Collaso – allowed him to return at the centre of provincial politics. Therefore, it can be concluded that *La Vanguardia* was not born from a literary vocation, nor to make money – rather, its primary mission was, first and foremost, to serve a political agenda.

Transnational encounters: "The Times" as a model in the reform of *La Vanguardia*

If Godó's paper was born with the ambition of acting as the mouthpiece (or "Vanguard") of the Liberal Party in Barcelona, in 1888 it suddenly left this ambition aside. On January 1st, and without prior notice, *La Vanguardia* announced the beginning of a series of drastic reforms that were to transform it into a politically independent newspaper. This drastic change of editorial line was announced on its front page, in an article addressed "To our readers" ("*A nuestros lectores*"). As *La Vanguardia* explained:

> "One of the clearest signs of culture in every people is its periodical press. (...) Any one who sees *The Times* does not need to know that it is printed in London to know that this is the newspaper of a rich, powerful and wise nation. The rich life of England in modern history is reflected in this great newspaper, through its select writing, which is always varied and entertaining, as well as accurately made in its material and typographical dimension. Every newspaper

is the loudspeaker (...) of legitimate interests; every reader must find in it its own sentence and concept, and in this way the newspaper will come to be the exact portrait of the society where it is published. We do not pretend to emulate *The Times*, for this would be a vain pretension, but we do want to make of our newspaper, together with our distinguished colleagues in this city, to reflect as exactly as possible the life of Barcelona, then Catalonia and finally Spain, for these constitute the three raison d'être of our existence. (...) We are convinced that the press only provides a public service when it is inspired in high ideals and the principles of severe criticism. These shall be, therefore, our guiding patterns. Impartiality and severity. (...) This aim appears to be diffi-cult to us, for at the end as all the men we too have our passion; but our will is to overcome human petty miseries for the sake of the general interest (...) A warm greeting to all the press in Barcelona from LA VANGUARDIA and shall our readers support us in this task to which we are now committed for their service."[109]

This new editorial line stood in clear contrast to the bellicose tone the newspaper had used until then. The audience *La Vanguardia* now addressed was neither Sagasta nor Rius but was generally referred to as "the readers". Consequently, for the first time *La Vanguardia* did not define its readership according to political affiliation, but as a notion surpassing the frontiers of opinion. As the newspaper put it, every "class" and "every reader" should now be capable of finding their own concept in *La Vanguardia*. Instead of the Liberal Party, three elements now justified the raison d'être of this newspa-per: Barcelona, Catalonia, and Spain.

La Vanguardia's statements did not go unnoticed among the Liberals of Barcelona. Some of Collaso's supporters viewed these statements with disdain; some others were deeply disappointed by them. Still, the general impression was scepticism about the capacity of the newspaper to move away from its partisan origins.[110] At this point we should ask: what was really behind this drastic transformation in the editorial line of Godó's newspaper? There are at least two reasons that explain this decision. The death of Pedro Collaso, in 1887, was one of them. Until that year, *La Vanguardia* never got tired of drumming that it would always back the leadership of Sagasta but that it would never accept the authority of Rius.[111] The result had been a long period of heated struggles between the two factions that did not spare personal attacks, to the point that Rius even sued *La Vanguardia* for slander.[112] By 1888, however, it was clear that Rius had won the contest: he continued to be the leader of the Liberals in Barcelona and even ruled as mayor of this city between 1885 and 1889. The death of Collaso further aggravated the situation and left the rebel faction (amongst whom, Bartolomé Godó) without their mean leader. The second reason that explains

La Vanguardia's sudden change of line were the changes taking place in Barcelona. The redesigning of Godó's newspaper coincided with a turning point in the history of this city, the moment when it abandoned its provincial status and started having a new international vocation. The symbol of this transformation was the World Fair of 1888. Although public opinion was initially sceptical about the capacity of Barcelona to organise an event with international standing, the ultimate success and the massive audience that the fair attracted (around 400,000 on the first day) opened eyes about the city's potential. The dimensions of the fair were undoubtedly modest compared to those of London and Paris, but they announced Barcelona's potential to become a cosmopolitan and dynamic urban centre.[113]

Indeed, the World Fair coincided with a new period of economic prosperity and great urban transformations in Barcelona. In the mid-19th century the walls that had prevented the city's enlargement since medieval times were pulled down and a new process of urban expansion started, reaching the highest point in the 1870s with the construction of Ildefons Cerdà's new district (the so-called "*Eixample*"). The World Fair continued this trend and filled the city with new architectural ideas and iconic buildings. As many as 30,000 workers were recruited for the construction of the fair, most of which were migrants from rural Catalonia that kept arriving in Barcelona and caused the city to swell from 400,000 inhabitants in 1887 to 587,000 in 1910.[114] The World Fair thus symbolised the emergence of an incipient mass society in Barcelona and gave it a new international projection. For a new generation of intellectuals, this event opened their eyes to Europe and created the ambition of turning Barcelona into the "Paris of the Mediterranean".[115]

In the light of these events, the redesign of *La Vanguardia* was an attempt to match the great expectations the World Fair had created in Barcelona. When the 1888 editorial of *La Vanguardia* spoke about the necessity to mirror the society in which it was published, the newspaper was trying to harmonise itself with the changes Barcelona was living at the time. The city was entering a period of rapid change and remaining the spokesman of the Liberal Party was not the way to face these transformations – all the more if Rius was the mayor of Barcelona and the main promoter of the World Fair.[116] The wise move of the Godó brothers consisted, in this regard, in understanding the transformations that Barcelona was undergoing at the time and in developing *La Vanguardia* accordingly. The main architect of this transformation was a young journalist named Modesto Sánchez Ortiz (1858–1937), who was born in the Andalusian town of Aljarque (Huelva), in 1858, to a well-off peasant's family. Like many other men from rural Spain, he migrated to Madrid to become a journalist. He started publishing comedies to make a living (this being another pattern of the journalists' literary vocation) and in the meantime he acquired an education in an autodidactic way:

he showed an interest in literature and the arts, and also learned English and French. In 1881 he joined the Liberal paper *El Correo de Madrid* and seven years later, at the age of 30, was appointed as the new editor of *La Vanguardia* shortly before the reforms started taking place. As he himself would explain, he was hired with a very specific purpose: "the Godó brothers (...) commissioned me with the task of regenerating or remaking the newspaper of their property, *La Vanguardia*, and to such purpose they entrusted me with the position of editor, their capital and most valuable of all, with their trust".[117] To fulfill the task he was commissioned, Sánchez Ortiz initiated a new plan of reforms by taking a foreign model as inspiration: the English newspaper *The Times*.

In this regard *La Vanguardia* represents an opportunity to examine the birth of the mass press from a fresh perspective. Instead of focusing on the new mass press that emerged in Europe to evaluate the Spanish case in terms of "failure" or "success" – as scholars have usually done – the case of *La Vanguardia* allows examination of the importance that *cultural transfers* played in the making of modern journalism.[118] This approach implies moving from the national perspective, as well as challenging the ideal-types that still permeate communication studies. Emphasis will be placed on the importance of the exchange of ideas as a crucial element to understand the emergence of new journalistic codes, as well as the interest that Barcelona's elites showed to find reference-models of "modernity" in foreign countries.

If *The Times* influenced the change of *La Vanguardia* it is because this newspaper was the oldest still-active newspaper in Europe and arguably the most reputable one.[119] It was established in 1785 by John Walter (1739–1812) as *The Daily Universal Register* and rechristened as *The Times* in 1788. Walter's son (John Walter II, 1776–1847) was responsible for turning the newspaper into London's top selling paper during the period 1815–1840. The principal reason for this success was Walter II's advocacy of an editorial line based on independence – this being understood as the need to avoid the interference of political parties in news. As *The Times* stated, its objective was "not the prying into private life (...) but the full and fearless investigation of all public acts of public men". The second ambition of this newspaper was to record – or to "register", as its original name suggested – all the news and commercial transactions that might be of interest for the widest audience possible.[120] When Sánchez argued that the new goal of *La Vanguardia* was to mirror three elements (namely, Barcelona, Catalonia and Spain) he was following *The Times'* principle of acting as a "mirror of society". Indeed, although Sánchez believed that it would be naive to imitate the model of the British newspaper,[121] as the characteristics of *La Vanguardia* were too modest, he gave further evidence that *The Times* was the model he had in mind. Proof of this is that in February 1890, two years after the programme of reforms started, Sánchez published an editorial called

"*Doctrina profesional*" ("professional doctrine") where he mentioned, again, the principles that would guide the newspaper in the future. Sánchez referred one more time to the idea that newspapers should be "an exact portrait of society", and referred, again, to *The Times* as the best example of this. The reason he chose the British newspaper is because he saw many points of coincidence between England and Catalonia. As he put it:

> "Simply two words in what concerns our professional doctrine; namely, that the newspaper must hold an intimate relation with the country where it is published. This is not mere rhetoric, but an observation: the best newspaper will be the one that shall better reflect the country where it is published. *The Times* – to put but an example – reveals from the head to the bottom (and that is both its strength and beauty) the English culure. The newsprint and the typography, chosen among the best, to the text, always reflexive, juicy, ency-clopedic; to the moral sense, selfish as it is the interest of the motherland, every part of England is in *The Times*. England the patriot, the powerful, the hard-working. When we read the beautiful pages of this newspaper, our love to Catalonia and to journalism merge together, and this will for progress is encap-sulated in the following formula: that LA VANGUARDIA shall reflect Catalonia; that it is not necessary to read the date in LA VANGUARDIA to know that this is Barcelona's daughter (...)."[122]

The text above quoted reveals the way Sánchez imagined Catalonia's future. In his view Catalan identity should be based on the industrial character of this region and the values associated with it (like "hard-labour" and "prosperity"), coupled with a proud sense of regional identity based on a series of "distin-guishing features" ("*rasgos propios*"). Surprisingly, Sánchez did not consider language to be one of the distinguishing features of Catalan identity; or at least he did not apply language to his understanding of journalism as a "plant rooted in the earth" (since *La Vanguardia* continued to be published in Spanish, like most of Barcelona's press). Besides, there is another element worth noticing in Sánchez's writing: in his view Catalan culture should be "European". This kind of aspiration was not unique to Sánchez, but evoked a broader aspiration of the Catalan bourgeoisie. The way this social group reacted to the consequences of industrialisation was by "constructing" a regional identity. This construction was based on two pillars: the vindication of Catalonia's past (through its lan-guage, history and tradition of special civil law), and since the 1880s on the aspiration of emulating Europe (and Paris especially) in the fields of art and architecture, as the emergence of "Modernisme" – "Art Nouveau" in France – illustrates.[123]

Consequently, the case of Barcelona's urban elites can be seen as an example of those "second cities" which had a similar size to the capitals of their respective countries, but sought foreign reference-models to reaffirm a distinctive identity.[124] Indeed, Barcelona possessed a series of characteristics that distinguished it from Madrid (namely, an expanding manufacturing industry, a large working class, a different language, the defence of protectionist policies, the claim for administrative de-centralization, etc.) and gave it a modern look – even to the eyes of some Madrid's observers.[125]

Sánchez's achievement consisted in turning *La Vanguardia* into the favourite newspaper of Barcelona's Modernist bourgeoisie. Sánchez was well connected with the intellectual milieus (like the *"Ateneu Barcelonès"*, where *La Vanguardia* had its own cultural gathering)[126] and recruited some of the city's most talented intellectuals. Thus, in the editorial of 1890 Sánchez announced the list of nineteen artists, writers and painters who would contribute to *La Vanguardia* on a regular basis. The list included prestigious figures like Santiago Rusiñol, Ramón Casas, Josep Lluís Pellicer and Joan Sardà, among others.[127] *La Vanguardia* also started distinguishing itself from other Barcelona newspapers for the space it devoted to European culture; and culture, in fin-de-siècle Europe, was a synonym of Paris. *La Vanguardia* began including different sections about the French capital (entitled *"Bosquejos parisines"* and *"De Barcelona a París"*), and avidly followed the careers of Catalan painters who had migrated to the French city (like Rusiñol and Ramon Casas).[128] Moreover, the newspaper dedicated the entire front page to the Paris World Fair of 1889. The reason for this, the newspaper argued, was that "the people of Catalonia and especially from Barcelona hold a close link with Paris".[129]

The second "ideal" that *La Vanguardia* arguably imported from *The Times*, besides the need to mirror the taste of the society where it was published, was the relation between the press and politics. *La Vanguardia* did not regret its partisan past (and even accepted it as part of its history) but announced that it would no longer be at the service of a political cause. Instead, two principles would now guide the editorial line of *La Vanguardia*: "impartiality and severity". Sánchez believed that the press should hold "high ideals" and should judge "deeds, but not the people who do them".[130] That statement was reminiscent of the famous principle of *The Times* (quoted earlier): "not the prying into private life (...) but the full and fearless investigation of all public acts of public men". Accountability earned *The Times* the nickname of the "Thunderer" and the resolution of men like Sánchez to behave as "ruthless censors" (*"despiadados censores"*), while respecting personal honour, evoked the same ideal. The ascription to these principles implied that *La Vanguardia* stopped being the organ of the Liberal Party (at least formally), and abandoned all personal attacks against Rius. The newspaper would now be at the service of "the common good", and to do so it should focus on providing raw information (*"facts, facts, and facts"*) for the reader's judgement.[131]

The emphasis that Sánchez put on providing information was a plea for political neutrality. Supplying "facts" to the public was not an easy task (as Sánchez acknowledged), but it revealed a new professional ethos of public service. This ideal implied that news needed to be gathered as fast as possible and with the highest possible accuracy, to let every reader make his or her own judgement. As Chapter 7 will show, *La Vanguardia* became one of best providers of international coverage of the Spanish press. What needs to be stressed, at this point, is that the emphasis Sánchez put on public service presented similarities, once more, to the journalism model of *The Times*.[132] The formula of this newspaper was, as one of its editors put it, "to obtain the earliest and most correct intelligence of the events of the time and instantly, by disclosing them, to make them the common property of mankind."[133]

La Vanguardia's new vocation of public service implied that journalists should work accordingly. Instead of publicising the views of the Liberal Party, journalists should now focus on providing raw information to the public. This change of philosophy reveals the emergence of a new occupational ethic for journalists, one of the great obsessions in Sánchez's career. In the book entitled *El Periodismo* (the first theoretical work ever published in Catalonia about journalism)[134] Sánchez expressed his concern about the tight links between politics and the press. In his view journalism should not be a pathway into public office, but an independent profession; or, to use his own words, journalism should be both "priesthood and magisterium" ("*sacerdocio y magisterio*"). These two concepts, which Sánchez borrowed from Catholicism, expressed his understanding of journalism as a profession that required discipline and rectitude, and was aimed at fostering the "good" and the "truth" in society.[135] Accordingly, Sánchez criticised the press that took advantage of dramatic events, like murders and gossip, to sell more copies. In his view, journalists should stay above the kind of reporting that fuelled the "lower passions" of society; they should adopt, instead, a calm state and a moderate tone so as to serve society in a rightful manner.[136]

Besides the highly moralistic tone that Sánchez's thoughts contained, they present a certain similitude to the type of reporting that characterised *The Times*. As some scholars have noted, this newspaper abstained from using morbid events as a strategy to increase sales; this being a professional attitude that stood in contrast to the strategy used by the – increasingly successful – sensationalist press.[137] Despite the differences between the two newspapers, what *The Times* and the new *Vanguardia* had in common was not just the emphasis placed on "news", but also the emphasis they placed on the need to balance it. In other words, journalism should not simply consist in providing the public with the latest and most abundant news, it should also be done in a "responsible" manner. This philosophy – certainly not exempt from an educative and even condescending view of society – reveals the emergence of a new ethic based on public service, a key element in the professionalisation of journalism in Europe.[138]

Still, the fact that Sánchez took *The Times* as a reference model was not an obvious choice. In the 1880s *The Times* had lost its position as London's leading newspaper. The once prestigious and top-selling newspaper had entered a period of decay in the last quarter of the century, to the point that it was losing money and its very survival was in peril.[139] One of the reasons behind the decay of *The Times* was the emergence of the "New Journalism". This expression makes reference to a new model of journalism that emerged in the second half of the 19th century with the aim of targeting a more popular audience (sometimes including women) through a lower selling price and an emphasis on non-political content, like gossip, fashion and the serialised story. The New Journalism represented a completely new way of organising language, content and format in the press, and symbolised a new form of mass consumption characterised by a less politicised and more entertainment-oriented content. Advertisement revenues compensated for the low price of this popular press, known in France as *"presse au bon marché"* and as the "penny press" in England. In late 19th-century Europe, the top-selling newspapers were exponents of this new journalism: *Le Petit Journal* (1863), in France, sold 600,000 copies daily; and England's *Daily Mail* (established in 1896) sold 540,000 copies daily. *The Times*, in contrast, had a circulation of "only" 100,000 copies in 1882.[140]

At this point we should ask: why Sánchez chose to use *The Times* as a model when by 1888 the paper was on the brink of bankruptcy and remained the exponent of the "Old Journalism"?[141] Moreover, if Barcelona's reading public was so interested in Paris, why did Sánchez not choose the example of ascending French newspapers, such as *Le Petit Journal*? The answer is that Sánchez aspired to turn *La Vanguardia* into a quality journal, of which the "Old Journalism" of *The Times* remained – regardless the newspaper's state of decay – the international benchmark.

Indeed, although Sánchez claimed to serve the "broadest public possible", in reality this newspaper was targeting, as *The Times* did, an educated upper-middle class market, including the members of the petite bourgeoisie. Two elements prove this. First, in 1890 *La Vanguardia* started to sell for 0.10 *pesetas*. This price doubled that of the vast majority of newspapers in Barcelona.[142] Moreover, if compared with the average wage in Barcelona (3.75 pesetas a day in 1904) the price of *La Vanguardia* (0.10 pesetas) was quite expensive for the popular classes, but not for the well-off groups.[143] Second, although Paris was Barcelona's icon of modernity, this was particularly the case among the bourgeoisie but not among the working classes. Indeed, the majority of the leisure activities in this city continued to be highly provincial. In other words, *zarzuelas* and bullfighting awoke far more enthusiasm in fin-de-siècle Barcelona than the arrival of a foreign artist, as some observers lamented.[144]

It was to the relatively narrow – but expanding – elite market that Sánchez was targeting the future expansion of *La Vanguardia*. Evoking the prestige of *The Times* was a way of doing so, to the point that Sánchez's references to the British newspaper can also be regarded as a strategy of self-publicity aimed at building an image of a new and respectable newspaper. The fact that *The Times* was in a period of decline was not an obstacle for this strategy. Proof of this is the fact that in Italy too, the newspaper *Il Corriere della Sera* started a plan of reforms that was also inspired by the British newspaper. Established in Milan in 1875 by Eugenio Torelli and Riccardo Pavesi, *Il Corriere della Sera* eventually became, together with its competitor *Il Secolo*, the main organ of Milan's bourgeoisie.[145] Initially, *Il Corriere* had a modest circulation (less than 10,000 copies in 1880) and supported the Moderate policies of Cavour and was directly opposed to Giolitti's. At the turn of the century the newspaper underwent a process of renovation in the hands of Luigi Albertini, a young journalist who spent six months in London and gained first-hand knowledge of *The Times*.[146] The outcome was the drastic reorientation of the editorial line according to a series of principles: a politically neutral standpoint; an emphasis on news content; the hiring of prestigious intellectuals; and a profit-oriented business based on advertisement revenues.[147] The case of *Il Corriere* and *La Vanguardia* thus reveal that the "Old Journalism" of *The Times* was still an esteemed ideal for those newspapers targeting an educated upper-middle class readership.

Last but not least, it is interesting to note that although Sánchez and Albertini took the same reference model, *La Vanguardia* also imported some features from the French popular press. Proof of this was the serial novels this newspaper introduced in 1888. These novels were written mostly by French and English authors and were published on a regular basis (a few pages at a time). They were displayed at the bottom of the page (the so-called "*rez-de-chaussée*", in French), so that readers could combine the different excerpts into a collectable book.[148] Although this type of novel had been published in literary journals for a long time, its introduction in the popular press in the 1830s has been considered a breaking point in the history of the press, and as the "beginning of the cultural democratization of French society".[149] Indeed, while most of the newspapers traditionally had a strong political content, the serial novel ("*roman-feuilleton*") represented a new type of entertainment that attracted the interest of social groups traditionally marginalised in the "quality press", like the working classes and women. Thus, some French popular newspapers like *Le Petit Journal* started to recognise women as potential consumers as early as the 1860s. The introduction of the serial novel became central in this strategy, as Jane Chapman has recently shown.[150]

The introduction of the serial novel in *La Vanguardia* was probably a strategy aimed at targeting a female upper-class readership. The high selling price of *La Vanguardia* excluded the working classes (not to mention illiteracy rates, which were particularly high among working-class women), but not the educated female readership.[151] There are different testimonies that mention the popularity of European (and especially French) literature among Barcelona's bourgeoisie women.[152] The presence of advertisements targeting female consumers provides further evidence that *La Vanguardia* also had female readers.[153] The serial novel thus exemplifies the last point that needs to be stressed about the transformation of *La Vanguardia*: the goal was to turn this newspaper into a profitable business.

Adopting a commercial orientation represented a radical change in the way the Godó brothers had managed the newspaper until then. While political payoffs were traditionally expected to compensate the loss of money, the Godó brothers now aspired to make a profitable business of *La Vanguardia*. The way to achieve this consisted in increasing the number of readers and in making advertisements the main source of income. To this end *La Vanguardia*'s page layout was completely redefined in 1888. The page size increased substantially (from 16 pages on 15 x 10 cm format; to 8 pages in two daily editions, each 21.5 x 31.5 cm format) and a new typeface was introduced. The political motto was deleted from the heading and the new heading only bore the newspaper's title, coupled with the name of the place where it was published (Barcelona) and the day edition (morning or afternoon). The single-column format of 1881 was replaced with a new distribution of content in four columns. Although *La Vanguardia* traditionally dedicated the front page to advertisements, the changes made to the content layout in 1888 reveal a new awareness about the economic value of space. Moreover, *La Vanguardia* increased its invitations to companies to insert advertisements on the grounds of a (supposed) growing circulation and the serial novel.[154] All these efforts to reach the broadest audience possible reveal the Godó's new aspiration to make this newspaper a profitable venture.

Summary

While official accounts attribute the foundation of *La Vanguardia* to Carlos and Bartolomé Godó, this chapter has shown that the origins of this newspaper were more complex. Rather than being founded as a family enterprise, *La Vanguardia* was the project of a political faction aspiring to become the new spokesman (or "the vanguard") of Barcelona's Constitutional Party. As part of this struggle to control the party leadership, Bartolomé Godó became the founding partner of the new journal and consequently became its proprietor.

That Godó, a man of humble origins, decided to finance such an enterprise is revealing of the strategies that local elites developed to advance their private interests in a centralised state-model. At a time when the most vital decisions concerning local interests were taken in Madrid, and public office was distributed according to patronage-networks, the founding of a newspaper became a way of gaining public influence and visibility.

However, coinciding with Barcelona's World Fair of 1888, the Godó brothers implemented a radical turnaround in *La Vanguardia*. The great ascendance that this newspaper experienced in the next two decades, to the point of becoming one of Spain's top-selling newspapers, can only be understood from the decision adopted in 1888 to abandon the links with the Liberal Party and become a commercial newspaper. That this move was inspired in *The Times* and also included French features (such as the serial novel or the great attention paid to Paris) reveals the importance of cultural transfers in the making of modern journalism. In contrast to the nation-centred approaches that are still predominant among historians, this chapter has shown that the circulation of practices across national borders became fundamental in the birth of new journalistic genres. This does not imply, however, that the new journalism was exclusive to England. *El Imparcial* and *El Diario de Barcelona* are two examples of Spanish newspapers that also had a non-partisan adscription and targeted a broad audience. And yet, the case of *La Vanguardia* reveals that provincial elites sometimes preferred to look abroad when they searched for models of modernity. This decision had probably to do with the personal preferences of the new editor Modesto Sánchez Ortiz. In his work *El Periodismo*, Sánchez did not hide his personal admiration for *The Times*, to which he referred as "the most illustrious newspaper in London, the terror and hope of all governments, and the crystallisation of English civilisation: the most complete, in my judgement, of modern times."[155] The glance paid at the Italian newspaper *Il Corriere della Sera* provides further evidence that *The Times* remained, despite its clear state of decay, the best international benchmark of quality press.

Still, the transition from a partisan towards an independent and commercially oriented-press model was not a lineal story of progress. Proclaiming that *La Vanguardia* now was an independent newspaper was one thing, but the practice often proved to be much harder. Examining the tensions that arose out of the new professional principles *La Vanguardia* started asserting in 1888, particularly in relation to the Godó brothers's political career and the business interests they developed in the Spanish colonies, will constitute the main questions at stake in the next chapters.

2

"Our future lies in Africa": Newspapers and Colonial Ambitions in Morocco

The 1870s have traditionally been considered a turning point in the history of European colonialism in Africa.[1] From this date onwards, the continent that lay beyond Gibraltar became the land where the main European powers sought to fulfil their expansionist ambitions. The literature on colonialism has traditionally regarded Spain as a minor actor in this "scramble for Africa". At the time, Spain was a second-rate country in the international arena that only possessed the scattered remnants of her former Empire (Cuba, Puerto Rico, the Philippines and few islands in the Pacific), and some small possessions in Africa (Ceuta, Melilla, Western Sahara and Equatorial Guinea). Two decades later, the defeat in the Spanish–American War of 1898 put an end to Spain's empire and turned the country into one of the "dying nations", as Lord Salisbury called them. However, the image of Spain's weakness in the aftermath of 1898 has prevented historians from noticing the efforts that some elites made to intervene in Europe's scramble for Africa of the 1880s. While Spanish expansionism on this continent is often associated with the outcome of the Spanish–American War, and is therefore regarded as a response to the loss of the empire, less is known about the colonial endeavours made before this time. This chapter will examine one example of such an endeavour by focusing on the Godó family's involvement with a group of elites who actively promoted colonialism in Spain: the so-called "Africanist lobby".

In the 1870s Carlos and Bartolomé Godó entered the textile industry and became interested in exporting to colonial markets. This interest was not limited to the Spanish colonies in the Caribbean (Cuba and Puerto Rico), but also embraced the possibilities of future colonial expansion in North Africa. At a time when the main imperial powers were competing to impose their control over African territories, the Godó brothers joined an influential group of Catalan businessmen determined to increase Spain's presence in Morocco. *La Vanguardia* actively contributed to this lobby's wish to turn what was still the concern of a small circle of elites (that is, Spanish expansion in the north of Africa) into a new issue on the national agenda. In so doing, the Godó brothers constitute a case study to address one of the most recurrent questions in colonial studies, namely, the popular dimension of European colonialism. The point at stake in this field is the assumption that imperialism was not just the work of a few elites, nor a top-down process, but rather a phenomenon that required a minimum level of consent from society. While the works of John Mackenzie were seminal in raising interest on this topic,[2] a new stream of research dedicated to studying how colonial rule was perceived in Metropolitan societies has emerged in the last decade. These works have aimed to break the artificial division between metropolis and empire, and constitute an attempt to insert the transnational dimension into the writing of national histories. The outcome has been a rich analysis of how the idea of Empire was lived out at home, sometimes in unsuspected daily practices and contexts (such as the church or the school), and of how it influenced the shaping of national identities.[3] The importance of certain media in disseminating visions of empire – like monuments, imperial exhibitions, and music – has been stressed in these studies.[4]

The case of *La Vanguardia* will serve to explore the role of the press as an active political agent in transforming public understandings of issues such as colonialism and national identity. While Benedict Anderson stressed the importance the press played in building the "nation",[5] less is known about how newspapers contributed to this process in their role of intermediaries between colonial contexts and domestic audiences. To shed light on these issues this chapter will be structured in three parts. The first part will explain how interest in Africa arose from a voyage of exploration that Carlos Godó undertook in 1889. This trip gave birth to an ambitious plan to spread Spanish influence in Morocco, consisting in a wish to build a brand-new neighbourhood in the city of Tangier. And *La Vanguardia* became a tool for this family to draw public attention to Morocco.

The second part will provide further insights into how the Godó brothers used the press to promote colonialism by focusing on the War of Melilla (1893) – a three-month conflict that saw Spanish military intervention used to defend its possessions in the north of Africa. During this war newspapers portrayed Moroccans as Spain's eternal enemy and fabricated an image of the "other" against which Spanish identity was defined. At a time when a regional identity started gaining momentum in Catalonia, the war in Morocco will provide an opportunity to examine how Spanish patriotism was lived in this region, and to examine how *La Vanguardia* positioned itself in the face of identity issues.

Finally, the third part of this chapter will examine the role that commercial newspapers played in popularising an orientalist discourse about Morocco. This will illustrate the new commercial orientation *La Vanguardia* adopted in 1888, and how this implied changes in terms of management, marketing, and content, which reveals the ambition to turn the newspaper into a profitable business while simultaneously promoting the Godó private agenda to new audiences.

The private interests of the Godó family in the Moroccan Empire

During the last quarter of the 19th century Africa became one of the most important lands in the plans for expansion of European countries. The Madrid Conference of 1880 represented the first attempt to bring some order to the competing interests of European powers in this continent. Later, the Berlin Conference of 1885 marked out the scramble for Africa in areas of influence, mainly between Great Britain, France, and Germany. In the case of Spain, its influence in the north of Morocco was formally acknowledged due to the possessions it had there (Ceuta and Melilla) and to its strategic position in the Mediterranean.[6] Yet the fact was that Spain was little more than an observer in all these conferences.

The difficulties the Restoration was facing at the time – above all, a chronic budget deficit – led to an official policy of "retreat" ("*recogimiento*") and neutrality in international relations. This position did not mean that certain parties had no ambitions for new colonies (especially in the case of the Conservative Party of Cánovas del Castillo). Rather, it meant that there was a general agreement that such initiatives should be postponed for the future, and that maintaining what was left of the Spanish Empire should be the priority, not to mention the modernisation of Spain itself. Consequently, caution in international relations became the leading strategy of Restoration Spain – a strategy that was symbolised particularly well by the influence of Castelar's "*Doctrina de la Comodidad*". According to the policy coined by this Republican politician, Spain's geographical position was the best guarantee to maintain the country's sovereignty at a time of avid imperialism.[7]

However, this policy started to be increasingly contested by the partisans of the Spanish colonialist project. Officially known as "Africanistas" ("*Africanists*"), they argued that the best way to modernise Spain was by actively promoting an expansionist policy in Africa. According to Sebastian Balfour, two different conceptions were present in this highly heterogeneous movement.[8] First there was a "neo-colonialist lobby", composed by a myriad of different vested interests, mainly those of businessmen, traders, and industrialists. All of these parties had high expectations about the benefits that Morocco could provide in the future. The main strategy defended by this lobby was that of a "peaceful penetration" in Morocco. Influenced by positivism's then-current popularity, they thought that "civilization" would follow trade, thus benefiting both Spaniards and Moroccans alike. The second trend within the Spanish Africanist lobby was composed, according to Balfour, by two different tendencies. First, the "traditionalist" movement formed of Carlists and Catholics, which defended proselytising as an additional mission of colonialism in Africa; and, second, a nationalistic and conservative trend. Their social base was hazy, and included a wide social spectrum: from people who considered Morocco as an exclusively Spanish possession; to those whose objective was the creation of a new Spanish empire in Morocco.[9]

Balfour's remarks represent a valuable step forward in our understanding of Spanish Africanism, but they still need further research to be confirmed, as Martín Corrales has recently noted.[10] I believe that the case of the Godó family might shed some light here, demonstrating that the dividing lines within the Africanist movement were actually more blurred than Balfour has suggested. Thus, the plans of the family in Africa will reveal a commercial strategy that did not refuse Catholic proselytism, but actually made it the cornerstone of a strategy with clear colonial ends. Emphasis will be placed on the importance of the press in promoting this private enterprise, as part of a broader attempt to raise public awareness about the benefits Africa could provide for Spain.

The Godó family's interests in Morocco went back to 1889. By then, certain members of the Spanish elites regarded the Moroccan Empire as a potential new market for their products. A former intervention in this territory (the so-called "Guerra de África", 1859–1860) resulted in a contract of free trade with the Sultan that included a special mention for Spain as "the friendliest country". However, the fact was that the economic transactions of the majority of the European powers (especially England and France) with Morocco were much higher than those of Spain.[11] To reverse this situation, and with the added goal of promoting geographical exploration, the main employer organisation of the Catalan bourgeoisie, the *"Fomento del Trabajo Nacional"*, started promoting exploration missions to the Moroccan market. It was precisely from one of these missions that the Godó family's interest in Africa would arise.

It is important to note that these kinds of missions were not new, but rather relied on a long tradition of Spanish expeditions to Africa. Numerous explorers, diplomats, businessmen and even tourists had long been traveling to African territories.[12] Furthermore, the initiative of the *"Fomento"* exemplifies the popularity of geographic explorations in Europe at the time: between 1871 and 1890, almost one hundred new geographic societies were founded around the world.[13] The creation of these types of entities intensified as the rivalry between countries to seize new territories increased. In Spain, too, the fear of falling behind in the European scramble for Africa prompted the gathering of explorers, intellectuals, and businessmen alike in these geographical (and often openly colonialist) associations, for example the "*Sociedad Geográfica de Madrid*" (1876) and the "*Sociedad de Africanistas y Colonialistas españoles*" (1883).[14] It must be highlighted, in this regard, that the "*Fomento del Trabajo Nacional*" was an employer's association, not a geographic society. This entity shared the perception that Africa could bring remarkable benefits for Spanish commerce, but mistrusted the free trade policies the majority of geographic societies promoted.[15] This discrepancy on economic policies is an important point, because the support for protectionist policies (one of the traditional demands of Catalan elites) would re-emerge in 1893, during the War of Melilla. Therefore, the fact that the Godó brothers chose to use the *Fomento* as their route into Morocco, rather than through another institution, is an issue that needs to be borne in mind.

While the exploratory mission of the *Fomento* exemplified the interest of Catalan economic elites in Morocco, the brothers became interested in it due to their new textile business. Having initially moved from their hometown of Igualada to Bilbao, in the 1870s the brothers Carlos (1834–1894) and Bartolomé Godó Pié (1839–1897) had established themselves in Barcelona as textile manufacturers. As Chapter 3 will explain in detail, the business of the two brothers consisted in the manufacture of jute sacks, which was a type of manufacture that Spain's overseas colonies needed in great quantities to store raw materials (like sugar, tobacco and coffee). Each day the Godó brothers' factory produced 12,000 jute sacks that were exported to Cuba and Puerto Rico alone. This pace of production, however, did not seem to satisfy them and they soon set their sights on the Moroccan market.

Indeed, by the 1880s the brothers appeared to have an interest in opening new markets for their business. The journals of the Africanist movement tirelessly repeated the abundant opportunities the Moroccan Empire offered for businessmen daring enough to explore these territories. The same journals stressed that low-quality manufactured goods were the ones that would fit the Moroccan market better. Jute sacks, which were an extremely cheap and resistant commodity, consequently appeared to be the perfect product to satisfy "the taste of the indigenous people".[16] With this goal in mind, Carlos Godó joined a mission promoted by the *Fomento del Trabajo Nacional* and travelled to Morocco in March 1889.[17] He did not make this voyage alone, however, but was accompanied by two men: his close friend Enrique Collaso, and the journalist and Arabist Josep Boada Romeu. Although there is little information about Enrique Collaso, his brother José Collaso (1857–1926) was one of the most prominent figures of the Liberal Party in Barcelona and also the colleague with whom Bartolomé Godó had established *La Vanguardia* in 1881.[18] In the case of Boada, he was a famous expert on Morocco and would be the first correspondent in the history of *La Vanguardia*, precisely during the War of Melilla (1893).

In March 1899 the three men (Godó, Collaso and Boada) embarked on an exploratory journey that took them to the main Moroccan cities. Boada included a vivid account of this tour in his book *Allende el Estrecho*, one of the classic works of 19th-century Spanish travel literature. As this book explains, the trip had a clear commercial motive: "With the sole goal of opening new markets to Spanish manufactures, Mr. Carlos Godó, one of the most renowned manufacturers of Catalonia and a man with great initiative, did not hesitate to undertake this trip despite his advanced years".[19] Although the initial plan was to visit the interior of Morocco (from Fez to Meknes and then back to Tangier through Tétouan and Ceuta) the problems they encountered on the road to Alcazar forced them to change their route. The expedition then headed towards the West coast, where the travellers visited some of the main commercial cities of the Empire (Asilah, Larache, Salé, Rabat, Meknès, Fez, Ksar el Kebir and Tangier). Some Moroccan newspapers, like *Al-moghreb al-Aksa*, provided constant updates about the journey of the three men.[20] Boada penned a rich description of the various cities they visited, and stressed the opportunities the country offered for Spanish goods. Numerous details about the cloths consumed by Moroccans, as well as the fibres they were made of, were included in such descriptions. Boada often compared Spanish manufac-tured goods with those of other countries (particularly of England and France) and stressed Spain's secondary position in the trade with Morocco.[21]

Having come across certain difficulties, the expedition finally arrived at Tangier in late April 1889. The journey turned out to have been a worth-while endeavour and stirred numerous ideas that soon materialised: thus, one month after the trip Godó and his colleagues founded a new company in Tangier, called *"Sociedad Hispano-Marroquí"*. This company had a very specific purpose: building a whole new neighbourhood, the *"Nueva España"* ("New Spain"), with the aim of fostering the settlement of new Spanish immi-grants.[22] Although this goal was very different from the Godó's initial purpose of selling jute commodities, Tangier appeared to be a highly prom-ising market for the building industry. Indeed, this city was undergoing a profound process of expansion. Tangier's traditional lack of buildings and the great affluence of foreigners radically increased the price of property, to the point that its value multiplied twenty times.[23] The international community was traditionally very significant and was led by Spanish citizens, whose number grew from 664 individuals in 1876 to 1,412 in 1888. The majority of these Spaniards were of humble origins and came from the provinces of Cadiz and Málaga.[24]

The considerable number of Spaniards that abandoned the country each year became an issue of concern for the Africanist movement, especially because many of these migrants chose to settle in French possessions (especially in Algeria), rather than Spanish ones.[25] *La Vanguardia* contributed to raise public awareness about this population flow, and referred to it as "an open artery where the blood of the nation is shedding". This newspaper considered that positive benefit could be obtained for Spanish interests if these migratory flows were properly redirected from French Algeria to Morocco.[26] The agenda this newspaper was promoting was clear: migratory flows could be turned into a profitable way to increase the Spanish presence in Morocco, provided they were coordinated. These kinds of articles reveal how the Godó's used the press to create a favourable atmosphere to endorse their business interests in the region, especially at a time of high imperialism. Tangier was the most dynamic port in the country, and its strategic position in the Strait of Gibraltar attracted the interests of the main powers, especially England. In fact, the British consul in Morocco (Edward Meakin) was well aware about the plans to build a Spanish neighbourhood and carefully reported all their movements to the British Prime Minister, Lord Salisbury.[27]

Moreover, in a move aimed at thwarting Spanish influence in the region, the Godó's plans were even disclosed in public. As the English newspaper the *Western Morning News* informed in an article entitled "Spain and Morocco", "At present moment the [Spanish] Government is exerting influence at the Sultan's Court in favour of Senor Godo, a well-known and wealthy manufacturer, who seeks for a concession to build a complete Spanish quarter at Tangier. The scheme, which is backed by a powerful syndicate of Catalonian manufacturers, includes the construction endowment of a teaching college, a bank, and a building for the Spanish Legation, the Consulate, and Military Mission."[28] The British concern explains why Godó's plans were kept secret, and that the memorandum of the *Sociedad Hispano-Marroquí* declared that this company had been founded "by the patriotic desire to promote Spanish interests in Morocco and to contribute as much as possible to the increasing of Spanish influence in the Moroccan Empire". As a result of this, foreigners were forbidden from participating in this company, and its capital (200,000 *pesetas*) remained in the hands of the five partners, among whom the Godó brothers controlled the largest share (40%).[29]

While the Godó brothers showed a serious interest in Morocco, and used the press to secure their economic interests in the country, they were not planning to do so on their own. Since the very beginning, the project of building the neighbourhood of *"Nueva España"* was designed as part of a broader plan, in which other agents interested in promoting Spanish colonialism in Morocco participated. One of these agents was the Catholic Franciscan Mission in north Africa. Although this religious order had had a presence in Tangier since the 13th century, its presence was favoured by the liberty of movements granted by the peace treaty of 1861.[30] A network of Catholic missions was subsequently established in the main cities of the Empire, and included the running of hospitals and primary schools, as was the case of Tangier. At the head of this Franciscan Mission was father José Lerchundi (1836–1896). Besides being a renowned Arabist, Lerchundi enjoyed a close acquaintance with the Sultan Hasan I, to the point that he had been the main promoter of the Sultan's visit to the Vatican in 1884, and also acted as the Sultan's translator during his official visit to Spain in 1885. For all these reasons Lerchundy was arguably the most influential Spanish individual in Morocco.[31]

Carlos Godó established a close friendship with this Franciscan priest during his stay in Morocco, and this personal acquaintance became an invaluable path to obtaining the support of the Monarchy for his projects. Spain's Queen Regent María Cristina de Habsburgo (1858–1929) was in close correspondence with Father Lerchundi's Franciscan Mission through her honorary presidency of the so-called "*Asociación de Señoras españolas bajo los auspicios de María Inmaculada*". This association was founded in 1887 with the purpose of supporting the mission of the Franciscans in Africa. Among its members were some of the wealthiest ladies of Madrid and Barcelona, such as María Gayón, the wife of the second Marquis of Comillas, Claudio López Bru (1853–1925), one of the leading businessmen involved in the programme to increase Spain's commercial influence in Morocco.[32] Through his acquaintance with Lerchundi, Godó was received in an audience with the Queen Regent in the summer of 1889, after which he obtained the Crown's support for the building of a Spanish neighbourhood in Tangier.[33]

For the reasons mentioned above, the plans of Carlos Godó proved to be part of a much broader initiative, which brought together people like the Queen Regent, Father Lerchundi and the Marquis of Comillas. What all these individuals shared in common was the belief that Spain's influence in Morocco should be strengthened, and that the spreading of the Catholic religion should play a central role in achieving this. Therefore, the objective of this group was not simply based on the positivist conception that civilization would follow trade (although this certainly played a part), but was based on the conviction that a moral duty was also at stake. The spreading of Catholicism was crucial for such an endeavour as it was deemed to contain a set of values that would contribute to the moral improvement of the Moroccans. The importance of the press in promoting a religious dimension in Spanish colonialism became evident at a public event that was held on 27 October 1893. On this day, a public ceremony was celebrated in Santa Madrona's Church, in Barcelona, to celebrate a triumph of the Franciscan Mission in Tangier: the religious conversion of a Moroccan girl to Catholicism. The Franciscan sisters had picked up a Moroccan girl (Fatma Ben Ansor) and saw this as a priceless opportunity to convert her to Catholicism. The culmination of this religious endeavour took place when

Fatma was baptized in public with the new name of "María Luisa". And amidst the great excitement that this ritual represented for Barcelona's most fervent Catholics, Carlos Godó and his wife Antonia Lallana attended as the new god-parents of the Moroccan girl. Moreover, Godó used *La Vanguardia* to give wide coverage to this event. The newspaper published an article that described the baptism with enthusiasm and included two illustrations that compared the previous Moroccan Fatma with her new Christian incarnation – María Luisa (see Illustration 1). As *La Vanguardia* reported enthusiastically:

> "If we leave aside for a moment the spiritual goods that the girl – portrayed in our picture first with Moorish clothes and then with new Christian ones – might have obtained; and we simply pay attention for a moment to the worldly goods she has obtained, ¡how lucky little Fatma is! Since she has escaped from the misery and future slavery, from the degradation into which the Moors usually hold their women; and has come to live with a free people, where at least she might gain everyone's respect and consideration if she behaves virtu-ously; and we are sure she will, ¡since she has been educated for such skilful and zealous Franciscan nuns like the ones of this city!"[34]

Events like the one described above demonstrate Godó's close commit-ment to the task of "bringing civilization" to Morocco, as well as his efforts to convince the public about the central role religion should play in this. If Godó felt that this was an element that deserved more publicity it was because proselytising was not part of the colonial strategy the Liberal govern-ment had promoted at the time. On various occasions Godó met with the foreign minister and with the Spanish consulate in Morocco, who officially granted him the state's support. In private, however, diplomats saw the use of religion as a rather old-fashioned method to foster Spanish colonialism. In the view of these state diplomats, Morocco needed "doctors and business-men", rather than the preaching of the Franciscans.[35] In fact, state officials proved to be greatly concerned about the Missionaries' growing involvement in Spain's plans for expansion in Morocco, because this religious order was subject to a foreign authority (the Vatican).[36] This suspicion from state offi-cials reveals to what extent a plurality of projects existed on how to promote Spain's expansion in Morocco, and explains the importance Godó gave to public opinion to reform foreign policy. A few years later, the beginning of a new war presented a new opportunity for Godó to publicise his views on foreign policy.

Popular imperialism and the press: The War of Melilla (1893)

By the 1890s, Melilla was little more than a speck on the Mediterranean coast of the Moroccan Empire. Although its origins as a Spanish possession went back to the late fifteen-century, Melilla was no more than a fortified town where a small community of 2,000 people lived – basically soldiers, together with a prison population. The territorial limits of Melilla were not entirely clear, but were about 3 km. At the time the hinterland of Melilla was the site of frequent skirmishes between Spanish soldiers and the Amazic tribes that lived in the area known as the Riff. These local tribes were formally bound to the religious authority of the Sultan. However, the truth was that by the last decade of the nineteenth century the Moroccan empire was undergoing a deep internal crisis that would bring it close to dissolution. Vast parts of the territory were detached from the authority of the Sultan, particularly in the interior and south of Morocco, and it was only the intense competition between the European powers that ultimately guaranteed – and greatly benefited from – the fragile equilibrium of the Empire.[37] The Spanish press frequently protested about the Sultan's weakness. The Treaty of Wad Ras (1860) formally obliged the Sultan to protect the Spanish possessions from the attacks of the Riffians, but this obligation was rarely enforced. The majority of the Spanish press neither believed in the will nor the capacity of the Sultan to fulfil such agreements. The only solution, the newspapers claimed, was to "repel the aggressions with weapons, since no other plan is possible in Melilla to protect the sacred lives of those who live there".[38] In consequence, wide segments of printed opinion started calling for military action as the only way to guarantee security in Melilla. In October 1893 another incident between the Spanish troops and the *kabilas* of the Riff triggered the beginning of a new conflict, the so-called "War of Melilla".[39]

Although this war only lasted three months, it revealed the popularity colonial wars enjoyed among wide segments of Spanish society. Even though the country had recently experienced sporadic eruptions of patriotism,[40] no other international episode generated such public consensus – either politically or sociologically – as the War of Melilla. With very few exceptions all political leaders demanded an exemplary punishment of Moroccan tribes.[41] This included the conservatives of Cánovas del Castillo and the republicans of Emilio Castelar, who severely criticised the management of the crisis by the Liberal government of Sagasta and called for prompt military intervention. The same line was followed by the parties at the margins of the political spectrum, such as other minor republican parties, the Carlists and the Catalan nationalists. Broad consensus therefore existed among the majority of political parties in favour of a new intervention in Morocco. This consensus was remarkable, since the Restoration's foreign policy had been characterised, until then, by a reluctance to take part in foreign adventures (as discussed earlier). The majority of parties threw this caution aside in October 1893.

The decisive contribution of the press in fostering popular imperialism became evident as growing segments of Spanish society mobilised in favour of an intervention in Morocco. As news about the first skirmishes arrived, a wave of patriotism and outrage rapidly spread to various Spanish cities. Newspapers described the behaviour of Spanish troops in heroic terms and presented the soldier's bravery as the only thing that prevented a massacre from occurring.[42] Patriotic demonstrations were organised in cities like Granada, Madrid, Seville, Barcelona, Valladolid, Zaragoza and Valencia, where some 10,000 people ran through the streets to protest against the attack perpetrated by the Riffians.[43] Other cities sent telegrams to the government to make "the popular dissent against the moors" known and to offer assistance, while city councils promoted public subscriptions to buy weapons and groceries.[44] Large numbers of civilians of different social origins publically volunteered to sign up for combat; private entities, like the Red Cross, offered their help to the government; and many declared themselves to be ready to "shed their blood for the motherland". The Church joined this collective fervour and blessed the wounded soldiers of Melilla and praised their deeds.[45]

All these public demonstrations, which the press reported and helped to promote, were characterised by widespread enthusiasm. Spanish flags were hoisted and demonstrators constantly cheered the names of Spain, the king, and the army. Some contemporaries saw in these demonstrations an opportunity to overcome Spain's worst problems, among which the emergence of a nationalist movement in Catalonia. Indeed, the 1890s saw the growth of an identity-based movement that proposed an alternative conception of the Spanish state to the centralist model of the Restoration. Although a sense of regional identity had long existed in Catalonia, the 1890s were a key moment in the politicisation of these feelings. A new platform called *"Unió Catalanista"* (Catalanist Union) brought together different entities that opposed the liberal's plan to implement a common civil law system in all of Spain. This plan revealed the liberal's ambition to underpin a uniform and centralist state-model, but started facing growing opposition from the periphery. This became evident in 1892 when the *Unió Catalanista* approved the first political manifesto (commonly known as the Manresa Principles) in which autonomy for Catalonia was explicitly requested.[46] In the face of these demands for self-government, some journalists saw the War of Melilla as an opportunity to transcend domestic politics. As Madrid's newspaper *El Imparcial* commented with unconcealed joy:

"What a remarkable event! Now that the honour of Spain is at stake, everything has been put aside: the regional particularities, religious controversies,
class conflicts, selfish interests, etc. The small fatherlands have disappeared
and only the greatest one has remained. No one thinks anymore about being
Galician, from Navarra, Castilian nor Catalan: in this moment everyone is a
Spaniard. Nothing bad comes without being followed by something good and
the savage Riffians (...) have been the best proof that despite all the miseries
of our public life, the Spanish character remains in all its vigorous strength."[47]

Indeed, the press repeatedly portrayed the war against the Moroccans –
referred to in Spanish as *"moros"* – as a "national movement". In a political
system like the Restoration, where the institutional channels for mass participation were manipulated by the strong presence of clientelist practices, and
where the political system showed little capacity to mobilise the population,
the euphoria that a potential war in Morocco generated in most of Spanish
society was remarkable. The press became decisive in fostering this euphoria.
The "war against the Moor" had numerous precedents in Spanish history,[48]
but newspapers greatly contributed to popularising them. Newspapers repeatedly referred to previous military interventions in Morocco, particularly the
War of Africa (1859–1860), and made the public familiar with them. Such
was the case, for instance, of the Catalan Volunteers (*"Voluntarios Catalanes"*),
a corps of 500 volunteers (mainly from the popular and Republican classes of
Barcelona) who fought in Morocco in 1859.[49] During the War of Melilla the
press in Barcelona repeatedly evoked the deeds of this corps as an example of
an alleged tradition in fighting against the "Moors". A whole mythology about
the Catalan Volunteers (including songs, poems and plays) re-emerged, and
several proposals were made to regroup this corps. Similarly, though to a lesser
extent, the press remembered the myth of the Spanish *Reconquista*, which had
ended in 1492.[50] Newspapers consequently depicted Moroccans as the eternal
enemy of Spain, and the term "Christian" was often used as a synonym for the
Spanish troops in opposition to "the Moors".

These historical evocations in the press were combined with a discourse
that reinforced a stereotypical image of Moroccans, who were depicted as
savage, religious fanatics. In so doing, newspapers contributed to building a
sense of Spanish identity based on moral superiority and heroic virtues.
Indeed, newspapers contributed to creating a general mistrust towards the
Moroccans and portrayed them as a bellicose and anarchic people driven by
primary instincts. Thus the majority of newspapers presented the Spaniards
as being morally superior and this served to pave the way for the conquest of
territories in Morocco. In such an enterprise, violence was considered the only
language that the local population could possibly understand.[51] The violent
language employed towards the Moroccans was, in fact, another ingredient in

the construction of an "other" against which Spanish identity was defined. The press of the time is full of examples in which aggression was used as a sign of Spanish patriotism. For instance, the liberal newspaper of Madrid *El Imparcial* recounted, in an article entitled "We are going to eat Moors!" ("*¡Comeremos moros!*"), the case of a Spanish soldier who declared that "Spain may not have money to buy ovens to bake bread in Melilla, but we must go there and if there's no bread, we will eat Moors". According to the same newspaper, "Several officers that were there (...) burst into enthusiastic applause, feeling the same way".[52] This hostile vocabulary, however, was not exclusive to pro-government newspapers like *El Imparcial*. The Republican press in Barcelona, which mainly addressed the popular and urban classes, shared a similar stereotyped image of Moroccans. The Republican and satirical newspaper *L'Esquella de la Torratxa*, for instance, had a daily section entitled "Against the Moor". Another satirical and Republican newspaper from Barcelona, *La Campana de Gràcia*, published an illustration in which the head of a Moroccan was shown spiked on a bayonet and called it "the only national solution".[53]

Still, the case of the Republican press in Barcelona provides evidence that jingoism also became an opportunity to carry messages with a domestic content. Looking closely at the content of the patriotic discourse that Republican newspapers published reveals that jingoism contained a multifaceted dimension. While supporting the deeds of the Spanish army, some Republican newspapers also started drawing parallels between the "savage" Moroccans and the liberal politicians in Spain.[54] These newspapers argued that liberal politicians were as "uncivilized" as Moroccans because they represented the same type of obstacle to progress; to the point of considering that Spain's political system was worse than that of Morocco, because its politicians were never held accountable.[55] Moreover, the same newspapers repeatedly referred to liberal politicians as the "moors of Madrid" ("*moros de Madrit*"). This type of satire was not used as mere entertainment, but contained a clear political strategy aimed at making readers aware of Spain's political situation. The newspaper *La Campana de Gràcia*, for instance, rhetorically asked: "Reader, think about it, and tell me if you are served properly: Where are the real Moors: In Melilla or in Madrid?".[56] As well as this use of patriotism to criticise liberal politics, other Republican newspapers like *El Diluvio* started echoing the impression that the soldiers sent to Melilla came from the lower classes; and that the ultimate purpose of the military intervention was to defend the economic interests of a few elites.[57] In other parts of Spain, the Socialist press manifested similar views and portrayed the intervention in Melilla as a "bourgeois war", as Rafael Núñez Florencio has noted.[58]

At this point we may ask how the readers in Barcelona responded to the bellicose stance that most of the press had adopted. One way of answering

this question consists in examining some of the apparently casual observations that the newspapers made about society. The Barcelona newspaper *El
Diluvio*, for instance, noted the lack of enthusiasm among a theatre audience
applauding the names of Spain and Catalonia at the beginning of a play.[59]
Even though this newspaper did not pass on the chance to take political
advantage of this event, the fact that the journalist was surprised by the
public's cold reaction reveals that the "war against the Moor" was not as
unanimously supported as the newspapers suggested. Further evidence that
reveals the reader's autonomy in the face of jingoist propaganda was the failed
attempt to reunite the Catalan corps of volunteers. During the War of Africa
of 1859 this corps of civilians became a symbol of Republican pride among
Barcelona's popular classes.[60] In their attempt to foster popular imperialism,
during the War of Melilla liberal politicians made repeated calls to regroup
the same corps of volunteers. Many pro-war newspapers endorsed this endeavour, but the fact is that the initiative provoked little enthusiasm and the
corps of volunteers was never recovered. This was because, in contrast to the
war of 1859, during the War of Melilla there was a wide perception among
the Republicans that the same authorities they opposed (the "Moors in
Madrid") were trying to appropriate the myth of the Catalan Volunteers for
their own advantage.[61] The scepticism of the Republican press provides
evidence that popular imperialism was not a top-down process, rather, it
contained a multifaceted dimension. Thus, the publishing of racial stereotypes about Moroccans in the Republican press coexisted with alternative
forms of patriotism. In this respect, the multifaceted attitude of the
Republican press has the value of setting a context against which we may
contrast the attitude of *La Vanguardia*. Hence, comparing the stance of this
newspaper with that of the Republican press will serve to shed some light on
certain aspects of the Godó's intentions that would otherwise go unnoticed.

On 2 October 1893, *La Vanguardia* first reported the earliest incidents in
Melilla. From that day on, and until around mid-1894, news from Morocco
appeared on a daily basis. *La Vanguardia* used an aggressive tone to describe
the events, and it criticised Sagasta's Liberal government for being too
cautious. In opposition to the government's attitude, the newspaper argued
for a more energetic response against the Riff tribes:

> "¡Diplomacy was the useless method that was implemented in the past, and
> also the one that is used now, to respond against the brutal attacks against our
> nation and our security! (...) It will not be until the day that our government
> changes its way of thinking, and until it decides to repel any aggressions with
> the weapons, that something important will be done in Melilla. (...)
> Meanwhile, diplomacy only means to put at risk the lives of those dwelling
> there. (...) The immediate future should prove it."[62]

Although many other newspapers argued along the same lines, events would demonstrate that *La Vanguardia* had succeeded in distinguishing itself as a pro-war newspaper. Hence, on the night of 7 October 1893 a public discussion was held in one of the bars of Barcelona's city centre about Spain's future in Melilla. Although this public discussion explicitly forbade any form of partisan speeches, as the debate went on the audience became so passionate that it incited a spontaneous demonstration through the streets of Barcelona. The crowd went down *La Rambla* (Barcelona's high street) cheering Spain and the army. As the crowd reached *La Vanguardia*'s editorial office in La Rambla, "the demonstrators suddenly went in, where they were welcomed by the staff of this newspaper; a commission of the demonstrators explained to the staff what had happened in the bar (...) and both parties enjoyed a long and pleasant chat. Later on, the demonstrators abandoned the office and continued their march down *La Rambla.*"[63] Events like this demonstration reveal that *La Vanguardia* was identified in Barcelona as a newspaper in favour of Spanish patriotism. In terms of domestic politics, this was not a minor issue, especially at a time when Catalan nationalism was gaining momentum. These connotations, however, did not seem to worry *La Vanguardia*, but rather the contrary: the following day this newspaper reported the jingoistic demonstrations in *La Rambla* in very positive terms.[64] Moreover, *La Vanguardia* actively sought to promote Spanish patriotism by promoting a public drive to collect groceries for the soldiers in Melilla. This effort turned out to be a great success: in less than a week more than 50,000 *pesetas* had been collected, a considerable amount at the time.[65] The case of *La Vanguardia* thus reveals that Spanish patriotism enjoyed considerable support in Barcelona, despite of the growing presence that regional issues had gained in recent years.

Moreover, if *La Vanguardia* showed a clear commitment to Spanish patriotism, the mobilisation generated in domestic opinion also became an opportunity for Godó to promote his own views in favour of a more active policy in Morocco. Thus, as the first troops were sent to Melilla (in October 14th), *La Vanguardia* published an article with an illustrative title: "Our Mission in Morocco".

"The events in Melilla, which have provoked so much outrage in the whole country to the point of awakening its patriotism, have contributed, more than anything else, in directing public attention towards some [Spanish] possessions that have certain potential as well as handicaps that have often been ignored. [...] Amongst us, there are still people who think, with little perspective, that our mission in Morocco consists purely in the conquering of the territory. No. It is important to correct such erroneous thoughts. *Our duty is to bring our civilization to Africa*, and to look for positive compensations to this generous effort by intensifying our trade and *by assuring a market for our products*. [...] Therefore, once we have fortified our possessions [e.g.

Melilla]; once we have taken revenge for what the savage Riffians did to our fellow countrymen; and once we have obtained a fair compensation in a treaty of peace [...], we must make sure that our trade flourishes and that no one, including the Sultan, shall interrupt this. Otherwise, we will spend money and blood totally in vain, (...) and that would present us as a country that is neither provident nor practical."[66]

As this article put in clear terms, *La Vanguardia* wanted Spain's intervention to be more than a flash in the pan, and instead the first step towards a bolder and longer-term intervention in Morocco. These kinds of articles reveal the importance that the press had in the Godó family's attempt to secure their private agenda. At the time, both Carlos and Bartolomé Godó were members of the Liberal Party, as well as deputies in Congress and in the Provincial council, respectively. The affiliation to this party, however, was not an impediment for the Godó brothers to pressure the Liberal Party over adopting a bolder policy in Morocco. The reason for this is because since 1888 *La Vanguardia* had formally abandoned its official position as Sagasta's Liberal Party mouthpiece in Barcelona. *La Vanguardia*'s new editorial independence allowed the Godó family to publicise their private agenda to a broader audience, and at the same time to criticise the official policies of their own party. Throughout October, *La Vanguardia* published further articles that revealed an ambition to use their newspaper to turn Morocco into a new issue of the national agenda. The euphoria generated by the War of Melilla became a precious opportunity to disseminate these demands to new segments of society. Instead of presenting the "civilizing mission" as the demand of the Africanist lobby, *La Vanguardia* presented it as a demand coming from the "whole nation", and used this argument to exert pressure on the Liberal government:

"On various occasions, LA VANGUARDIA has portrayed the deep emotion that the events in Melilla have provoked in all of Spain, including Barcelona. All the social classes have offered their moral and material help to the Government to help it maintain (...) the Spanish honour. (...) However, today we do not pretend to insist on the qualities of this national movement. Rather, we only want to remind the Government that it should pay attention to not becoming separated from this national movement, because this movement is capable of overthrowing the Government itself in a matter of hours. (...) We still have recent memories that suggest that the Government, despite its patriotism and good intentions, does not seem to be very willing to give appropriate solutions to future events that may come from Melilla (...)."[67]

But who authored these articles? Despite the large editorial staff of *La*

Vanguardia, when Morocco was the issue at stake the articles were usually signed by some of the most conspicuous members of Catalan Africanism, like Josep Ricart, Josep Roca and Josep Boada.[68] In contrast to the majority of players in the Africanist movement, however, Catalan Africanists differed from their counterparts when it came to the economic policy colonialism was to follow. In opposition to Spain's Foreign Office Minister, Segismundo Moret (who supported a peaceful penetration in Morocco by promoting free trade policies), the Catalan economic elites conceived of the colonies as a protected market for their products.[69] Consequently, during the War of Melilla *La Vanguardia* acted as the mouthpiece of a network of interests and entities of Catalan Africanism, like the *"Fomento del Trabajo Nacional"* and the *"Sociedad Geográfica de Barcelona"*. This point can be clearly seen in the newspaper's fierce advocacy of a colonialist project that had protectionism as one of its key points, in contrast to free trade advocates. Josep Ricart i Giralt, together with other writers like the Republican J. Roca i Roca (director of the newspaper *La Campana de Gràcia*), and Josep Boada i Romeu (a close friend of Carlos Godó and expert journalist in Morocco) were the main writers that defended the colonial project of the Catalan bourgeoisie through the pages of *La Vanguardia* – with the explicit support of the Godó family.

Orientalism as a new commodity for readers

If the War of Melilla revealed the attempts of the Catalan Africanist lobby to condition Spain's foreign policy, this war also became an illustrative example of the new commercial orientation *La Vanguardia* adopted in 1888, especially in terms of management, marketing and content. In comparison to the majority of Barcelona's press, *La Vanguardia* stood out for the amount of information it provided and for the way this information was presented. Thus, *La Vanguardia* did not just provide the latest news and bellicose editorials against the Riff tribes, but combined them with all sorts of extra information for a growing number of readers who were eager to learn more about Morocco. The articles in *La Vanguardia* during the conflict of Melilla displayed a deep interest in the customs, language, and traditions of Moroccan tribes. Even if that interest was influenced by a deeply stereotyped image of "the Moor", an interest in *orientalism* proved to be popular among the urban classes of Barcelona.[70] "Orientalism" had already been fostered in Spain by the burgeoning field of travel literature. Although this was by no means a new genre, since the mid-nineteenth century travel literature had become a growing genre following the new wave of European colonialism in Africa and Asia. Like the emergence of tourism, the great popularity enjoyed by the works of certain adventurers, explorers and scientists created a new market of consumers interested in distant cultures and places. In the case of the Moroccan Empire, numerous Spanish travellers had already been there since the 1850s. Their work decisively contributed to the re-discovery of north Africa. However, the travel literature had a limited audience, since its potential readership was usually restricted to the upper classes. Books on travel became a sign of distinction of this social group. The knowledge of certain classic works and authors – such as David Livingstone, Henry Stanley and Gustav Flaubert – became a cultural background for the elites, and constituted a set of symbols in the *habitus* of this social group. Travel books thus turned out to be the kind of knowledge that developed together with new forms of elite consumption.[71]

In contrast to travel literature, the information *La Vanguardia* provided about the War of Melilla contributed to popularising an orientalist discourse about Morocco that had been restricted until then to the upper classes. And this was possible because in wide segments of Spanish society the "war against the Moor" showed a capacity to attract bigger audiences. This also became an opportunity for newspapers to increase their profits. Madrid's newspaper *El Imparcial*, for instance, had an estimated circulation of 80,000 copies. When the conflict in Morocco started, sales rose to 100,000 copies, and reached 124,000 copies during the hot moment of the war.[72] In other words, the War of Melilla and the resulting explosion of patriotism generated the interest for a new public to learn more about Morocco: the war "against the other" also proved to be a great market for newspapers.

In fact, and contrary to its long tradition of partisan orientation (see Chapter 1), the European newspaper industry of the late nineteenth century was adopting a stronger commercial orientation. Editors began to be concerned not only with potential readership but also with potential advertisers, who provided the biggest revenues for the newspaper. As Gerald J. Baldasty has explained, in order to attract advertisers, the editors also had to redefine the way news was presented in order to attract bigger audiences.[73] In fact, the 1890s were the moment when "sensationalism" emerged as a new journalist practice that Spanish newspapers started adopting to make news more attractive.[74] The increasing attention that newspapers devoted to reporting crimes illustrates this change in the content of the press. Therefore, the gradual transformation from a politically to a commercially based press led to a substantial shift in the way in which news was presented. News became a new commodity and, like any other commodity, its profitability was directly related to its capacity to attract more consumers. The way *La Vanguardia* reported the War of Melilla is a good example of this process. For the price of 10 cents (0.10 Spanish' *pesetas*) per copy, the reader of *La Vanguardia* gained access to a completely new world of information about Morocco. Together with pictures *La Vanguardia* included extensive descriptions about the habits and character of the Riff tribes, their religious practices, and their military capacities. For instance, on 12 October (the National day), *La Vanguardia* published an extra supplement, together with the ordinary copy, dedicated to the War of Africa of 1859–1860 (see Illustration 2). The aim of the supplement (free to subscribers) was to recall the deeds of the Catalan corps of volunteers, because *La Vanguardia* considered this to be something that "will please all our readers: the old ones because these memories will evoke their past days of youth and the inner fire that animated them; the young ones because they will discover that in the history of their ancestors they have high values to imitate, and they will certainly constitute an example for the generations to follow".[75] As Illustration 2 shows, the supplement included numerous illustrations of the most famous soldiers that had participated in the war of 1859–1860 (such as generals Leopoldo O'Donnell and Joan Prim) with a description of their family origins, military careers and deeds in Africa. The supplement also included an extensive description of the customs of Moroccans (Illustration 3) and included a range of other characters and entries: a description of Father Lerchundi and a sister of the charity; an article about a "Moorish farmworker"; an article about the "differences between the Spaniard and the Berber" – which included a 50-point list; and even a collection of "Moroccan popular songs" provided by Father Lerchundi. Such supplements reveal that as well as the racial and caricaturised image of Moroccans, there stood another one that revealed a curiosity to learn more about north Africa. This point is of special importance, because it provides further evidence of the contradictory (or "disoriented" image, to use the words of Susan Martin-Márquez) that Spaniards had about Morocco, which they both hated and admired.[76]

Besides these supplements, the newspaper of the Godó family promoted other initiatives aimed at popularising interest in Morocco. Thus, in November 1893 *La Vanguardia* opened an art gallery in the offices that the newspaper had in *La Rambla*. In this gallery, the public could contemplate, for free, up to 30 pictures and photographs dedicated to the customs, cities and ways of living in Morocco and Algeria.[77]

Summary

The War of Melilla ended, finally, at the beginning of 1894. Despite the repeated attempts of the Spanish army to turn the confrontation with the Riff tribes into an open war against the Moroccan Empire, this did not ultimately take place. Besides the bellicose tone that characterized this conflict, the peace treaty with the Moroccan Empire brought little benefit to Spain. In fact, the conflict represented a very high cost: the economic outlay went up to 35 million *pesetas*, while the Spanish army suffered 123 fatalities and 165 wounded soldiers. Yet the worst consequence was for Spain's international prestige and, as had already happened in the War of Africa (1859–1860), the peace treaty signed in 1894 did little to help foster Spanish colonialism in Morocco.

However, the newspaper of the Godó brothers made a positive assessment of the War of Melilla. First of all, the war against the tribes of the Riff had generated an explosion of Spanish patriotism. Like many other pro-governmental newspapers, *La Vanguardia* welcomed this sociological phenomenon as a way of transcending class boundaries. Second, the incidents in Melilla contributed to fostering colonialism among Spain's public opinion, one of the traditional claims of the Africanist movement. *La Vanguardia*, which gave proof of acting as the voice of these demands, took clear advantage of the conflict. The journalist, and Godó's companion on the trip to Morocco, explained:

> "Even if what we have finally received from the Moors will not compensate all the expenses, it does not necessarily mean that that the campaign in Melilla has not been worthy. Thanks to this campaign, we have achieved, at least, to direct the attention of our statesmen to the matters in Morocco. In fact, these matters in Morocco are of great interest, because they affect our nationality and because in a future that is not so distant, they might contribute to give more splendour and glory to our motherland."[78]

Thus Josep Boada, on behalf of the Godó family, used the newspaper to exert pressure in favour of a more active presence of Spain in Morocco. Although their initial purpose of building a new quarter seemingly failed to materialize,[79] their commitment to fostering Spain's influence in the region remained absolute throughout the campaign. The public subscription promoted by *La Vanguardia* and the wide coverage that the newspaper gave to the conflict, are clear examples of this position. Moreover, the War of Melilla proved to be an illustrative example of the new commercial orientation *La Vanguardia* had adopted since 1888. If the newspaper was to attract new readers and advertisers, then reflecting the new tastes of society was crucial. An example of how these changes were implemented were the distribution of supplements during the war. The great number of illustrations and anecdotes that these supplements contained reveal an attempt to move beyond the strict description of military events to provide extra information aimed at satisfying the curiosity of readers. The mission of the commercial newspaper was not limited to informing about providing the latest news, but also about satisfying the curiosity that a broad audience was feeling at the time about Morocco. These changes in consumption modes reveal the contours of an incipient mass society, as well as the great appeal that a stereotyped image of the "Moor" had for a mass of consumers.

In this regard, the growing impetus that regional identity was gaining in

Catalonia at the time, as evidenced by the approval of the first manifesto for political autonomy (the so-called "Manresa Principles"), did not seem to make a difference in the way the events of Melilla were portrayed in this region. This colonial episode proved to be very popular in Catalonia, just as it was in other parts of Spain. That said, the consequences of this popular enthusiasm should not be misunderstood: the great excitement of the war did not necessarily imply that the ordinary people identified with the imperial projects of the Africanist movement. Likewise, even though the press contributed to popularising an understanding of Spanish identity based on the opposition against Moroccans, we might wonder to what extent this understanding of identity was actually consolidated – especially if we take into account the short duration of the war.

All these questions uncover some epistemological problems about using the press to measure popular attitudes. Examples of these are the common tendency among historians to confuse the opinions of newspapers with those of the people. The case of the Republican press provides evidence that readers were not passive actors, and that below the surface of bellicose editorials there were certain segments of society who were indifferent to the war mongering. Moreover, for the Republicans the War of Melilla became an opportunity to criticise the Liberal government in public and to use the case of Morocco as a metaphor to justify Spain's need of rejuvenation. The case of the Republicans therefore reveals that patriotism was a multi-layered phenomenon that could be instrumentalized to promote a political agenda. This strategy was not only present among the opponents of the political system, but also became present in *La Vanguardia*. On repeated occasions the newspaper warned the government of the perils of "distancing itself from the nation". These types of calls reveal the widening gap between the "official" and the "real country", this being a form of critique to liberal politics that would intensify in the years to follow; especially after the Cuban War of Independence (1895–1898).[80]

Although the Godó brothers were closely involved in liberal politics, the editorial independence of *La Vanguardia* allowed to distance themselves from this criticism and to take advantage of the situation. Thus, and in contrast to the partisan press, which was obliged to stick to line of their respective party, *La Vanguardia*'s editorial independence allowed the Godó brothers to promote their particular views – especially in those cases where these views were against the official position of the Liberal Party. The need of a more long-term commitment towards Morocco and the defence of protectionist policies were two examples of this.

Overall, despite the fact that the War of Melilla was a minor conflict that barely lasted three months, the conduct of *La Vanguardia* during this campaign has the value of showing the important changes newspapers were undergoing in the 1890s: above all, the transition from a partisan press towards a business orientation; and the important consequences that this evolution had both in terms of content and the way news was presented. This transition was to change journalism's traditional *raison d'être*: it was about attracting new readers and making profits, but also about endorsing private interests while doing so.

3

Between Barcelona and Cuba: Colonial Business and the Mechanisms of Influence

The hegemony of liberal elites in Southern Europe is often associated with the mechanisms they used to monopolise power, like electoral legislation and clientelism. The liberal parties in fin-de-siècle Italy showed little interest in extending the franchise, while in Portugal their counterparts responded to the mobilisation of new social actors (above all, the Republicans) through franchise restriction.[1] These reforms in electoral legislation – as well as the lack of them – reveal the liberal's desire to retain exclusive hold over public office. Even in the case of Spain, where electoral legislation took a different direction and universal manhood suffrage was introduced in 1890, the rigging of elections continued to be the norm.[2] Consequently, it can be argued that in all of these countries liberal elites showed little interest in integrating wider segments of society into the political system. Clientelism remained the main channel used by these elites to distribute public office among their network of supporters.

Nevertheless, the integration into patron–client networks did not always suffice to secure the private agendas of local elites. Liberal parties did not always share consensus on state issues, like foreign and economic policies. This lack of consensus implied that in order to secure their interests, local elites often developed alternative mechanisms besides – and in combination with – clientelism to exert pressure on central government. Thus the mechanisms that local elites designed to exert influence in centralised political systems constitute a major historiographical concern of the liberal period in Europe.[3]

This chapter will focus on the mechanisms of influence that the brothers Carlos and Bartolomé Godó used to secure their business in the Spanish colonies of Cuba and Puerto Rico. The first part will explain the process by which the Godó brothers expanded their interests to these Spanish possessions in the Caribbean and examine how this made them very dependent on the orientation of economic policies. The outcome was the design of different strategies, sometimes in collaboration with other elites, aimed at exerting pressure on central government. As part of these strategies, *La Vanguardia* became immersed in the identity controversies that began to appear in Spanish politics and was obliged to position itself in the face of them.

The second part will focus on the Cuban War of Independence (1895), a separatist insurrection that threatened Spain's centuries-long presence in the Antilles. Among the different measures addressed at pacifying Cuba, changing the commercial laws became a possibility that successive governments started considering. In parallel, a growing proportion of Spanish society started to show a reluctance to contribute to the war effort. It was in the face of this double threat (the change of commercial laws and the opposition to the war) that the Godó brothers saw public opinion as a way to reverse the situation. By examining the ways in which they sought to do so, light will be shed on the growing importance of public opinion in the competition between different elites to impose their views in policy-making.

Finally, the last part of this chapter will focus on the demise of the Spanish empire. The immediate reason behind this demise was the entry of the United States into what had been until then a separatist insurrection against colonial rule. This section will examine the role of the press in creating a public state of mind that was favourable to the war by popularising an imaginary of the nation based on jingoism. All these elements will be fundamental to address, in subsequent chapters of this book, the reasons that led many contemporaries to hold the press responsible for the loss of the empire and for the discredit of the liberal institutions.

The Godó family business and the "Pearl of the Antilles"

As previous chapters have described, the brothers Carlos (1834–1897) and Bartolomé Godó Pié (1837–1895) were textile traders during their youth in Bilbao and Barcelona. However, it was not until the 1870s that the two brothers established as manufacturers and built their fortune. The secret behind this fortune consisted in specialising in a manufacture that the colonies of Cuba and Puerto Rico needed in great quantity, but which had little tradition in Spain: namely, the manufacturing of jute bags. Well until the first half of the 19th century, jute was a little known fibre in most of industrialised Europe. The special climatic conditions that jute requires to be cultivated concentrated its production in the region of Bengal, in British India. Unlike cotton, jute's sturdy composition had long prevented its use in the textile industry. However, things started changing during the Crimean War (1853–1856), when the shortage of Russian flax produced by the conflict generated new interest in the possibilities that jute could offer, particularly as a substitute for flax bags. Sugar, coffee, wheat and corn were all raw materials that were being consumed on a mass scale by that time and needed to be carried around the world in cheap but resistant containers. By the 1860s, the first jute mills were established in Germany, France and other countries in Europe, and in the United States too.[4] In contrast to these countries, in the last quarter of the 19th century jute manufacturing was still a minor industry in Spain. The factories that used this raw material were few and were mostly located in Bilbao, Valencia, and Barcelona – all of which had a tradition in the manufacturing of esparto grass. Nonetheless, even in Catalonia where 84% of the Spanish textile industry was concentrated, jute manufacturing represented a very small sector. Of the estimated 106,000 workers that lived off the Catalan textile industry in 1890, only 8,000 of them worked in the industries that used flax, hemp, or jute (alone or combined) as their prime raw material.[5] As these figures demonstrate, the manufacturing of jute was still a very modest activity in Spain.

In Barcelona the Godó brothers came up with a new business strategy that sought to use jute to address the specific needs of Spain's colonies in the Caribbean. Cuba and Puerto required huge amounts of packaging material to store the enormous production of sugar and coffee that the plantation-based economy of these two islands produced each year. This production had traditionally been carried in wood packaging but since the 1870s started being replaced with the cheaper and more resistant jute bags. For the Godó brothers, the export of jute bags to the Spanish colonies in the Antilles consequently appeared as an untapped market with a great potential; all the more so when one considers that Cuba was one of the world's leading producers of cane sugar at the time. To supply this market the Godó brothers established a new business alliance with a man named Pere Milà Pi (1838–1880). Milà was a wealthy textile manufacturer from Barcelona, whose name became famous when his son commissioned the architect Antoni Gaudí to build the famous Modernist building *Casa Milà* (best know as *"La Pedrera"*), in Barcelona. The outcome of this new alliance was the establishing of a new textile company, called *"Godó hermanos, Milà y Compañía"*, and the setting of a new factory in Barcelona's neighbour city of Sant Martí de Provençals. The factory was popularly known as *"Els Sachs"* ("Bags", in English), in reference to the activity to which it was dedicated. Although the lack of documentation makes it difficult to follow the factory's trajectory in detail, there is evidence suggesting that it was a mill of big proportions (its surface covered 9,000 square meters) and that the Godós and their associate paid 1,939 *pesetas* in real estate taxes in 1886.[6] This sum represented the 20th highest contribution of all the industries in Sant Martí de Provençals, by then known as the "Catalan Manchester" for the high number of industries this city contained. There is further evidence suggesting that the Godó's business grew rapidly. By 1880 their factory produced between 10,000 and 12,000 jute bags every single day, to be exported exclusively to the Spanish colonies in the Antilles.[7] To meet this large pace of production the factory employed 2,000 workers (most of them women) who worked in a multiple-shift system.

For the Godó's plans to expand their business in the jute industry, politics became decisive. The reason for this is that while the export of jute bags to the colonies depended on a series of duty tariffs charging foreign production, liberal parties did not share an agreement on the need to maintain these tariffs. In fact, the confrontation between the supporters of free-trade policies and those in favour of protectionism became one of the major political controversies throughout the 19th century. Although this was a widespread debate in Europe, which scholars have explained as a response to globalization,[8] in Spain this debate became very heated. The reason for this is that the two main parties, the Conservatives and the Liberals, could not agree on a common and long-lasting economic policy. While the Conservatives of Cánovas del Castillo embraced protectionism, the Liberals of Sagasta were quicker to defend free trade (albeit with a few exceptions, like the politician Germán Gamazo).[9] In contrast to the divisions between the Conservatives and Liberals, the importance of the textile industry in Catalonia created a wide consensus among the politicians of this region on the need to defend protectionism. This consensus among Catalan representatives went beyond partisan adscription and made room for a collective lobbying strategy known as "*diputació catalana*". This strategy had a long tradition that went back, at least, to the period known as "*Trienio Liberal*" (1820–1823), and consisted in a corporate strategy in politics. Thus, every time a debate over tariffs was at stake, Catalan deputies gathered together to defend protectionism in Congress, regardless of their political affiliation or the position of their respective party.[10]

Still, it would be misleading to consider that the wide consensus that protectionism enjoyed in Catalonia was limited to a contest between this region and the rest of Spain. In fact, some historians have seen the heated debates on economic policies as one of the clearest signs of the Spanish state's alleged incapacity to integrate the demands coming from the periphery – thus providing fertile ground for the emergence of Catalan nationalism.[11] However, a closer look at the period reveals that the situation was more complex than a mere territorial dispute. Protectionism certainly enjoyed the widest consensus among Catalan economic elites, but it is equally certain that other minority groups in this region saw free-trade policies as the most profitable for their business. The plainest example is the case of Laureano Figuerola (1816–1903), a Catalan who served as new Minister of *Hacienda* and who was the intellectual factotum behind the free-trade reforms that were implemented during the Democratic Sexennium (1868–1874). Likewise, Catalonia was not a region tightly grouped around protectionism, but was – alike any other industrial society in Europe – deeply riddled with domestic conflicts. In fact, in the early 1880s Catalan industrialists did not only devote great energies to debating against the promoters of free-trade policies, but were also immersed in a tight domestic quarrel against labour unions. Catalan businessmen showed a systematic opposition against any proposal for social reforms and refused to take part in proposals for collective bargaining.[12] Therefore, the strong tensions that were to characterize the relation between liberal governments and Catalan elites should not be reduced to a dispute between centre and periphery, but should be understood as part of a broader set of tensions that industrialisation provoked, and which were felt with particular intensity in Catalonia.

Because the business of the Godó brothers in Cuba was dependent upon maintaining duty tariffs, they participated in the actions of Catalan elites aimed at lobbying the government about policy-making on several occasions. In this regard, the case of the Godó brothers provides a valuable opportunity to examine a crucial element of liberal politics in Europe – namely, the mechanisms local elites used to exert pressure on central government. The following pages will examine two different – though complementary – strategies that the Godó brothers implemented to secure their colonial business. These strategies consisted, on the one hand, in the adscription to the Liberal Party; and, on the other, on business associativism. These two strategies were eventually reinforced by a third one: the founding of *La Vanguardia*, in 1881.

The first mechanism the Godó brothers used to defend their economic interests in the colonies were the patron–client networks of the Liberal Party. The private correspondence of Víctor Balaguer (the leader of the party in Catalonia, and the Minister of Ultramar in the government of Sagasta during the *Sexenio*) contains several requests from Bartolomé Godó. The majority of these requests were written in the 1870s and touched upon the same issue: the tariffs concerning the trade between Spain and the colonies of Cuba and Puerto Rico. For example, in May 1870 Godó wrote to Balaguer under the following terms:

"Dear Sir, I am taking the liberty to write to you at present with regards to whether the new customs duties formed in the Intendence of the island of Cuba have arrived at the Foreign Ministry. In this case, a commission of industrialists and businessmen will set out with the objective of making the government aware of what would hurt the national industry since it imposes the right to many goods while others on that island pay nothing of the current tariff. Better still, something that could affect the interests of said island. I apologise for disturbing the attention of V. but I believe that you will be assured of the good intentions of my guidance. I gratefully await your reply and I am at your service. Sincerely (...)."[13]

As Chapter 1 showed, Bartolomé Godó traditionally displayed an attitude of allegiance towards Balaguer in the party's leadership. The letter above quoted reveals that in return for this personal allegiance, Godó obtained first-hand information on colonial tariffs. The links of personal deference ("political friendship"), upon which cadre parties were structured, were thus crucial in connecting the interests of elites on the periphery with the decision-making process in central government. Moreover, besides promoting his private interests Godó also acted as an intermediary of the broader economic interests. The personal acquaintance he held with Balaguer became the channel through which regional concerns about economic policies related to Cuba were expressed; both in the form of job recommendations and concerns about economic policies.[14] The case of Godó reveals to what extent patron–client relationships were an important channel to connect regional elites with Madrid, and to secure group interests in the colonies.

The second strategy the Godó brothers used to secure their business in Cuba resided in their membership of the *"Fomento de la Producción Nacional"*. As the most important association of economic elites in Catalonia, with up to 1,800 members, the *Fomento*'s main goal was advocating protectionist policies. Bartolomé Godó was one the founding members of this institution, created in 1869, and his brother Carlos joined soon afterwards.[15] Within the different sections that the *Fomento* comprised the Godó brothers turned its Section number 5, which was in charge of controlling the tariffs concerning "flax, hemp, and jute", into the family's personal domain. Hence, Carlos Godó was first appointed as vice-president of this section in 1880, and his brother Bartolomé followed him shortly after.[16] Later on, the second generation of the family inherited the same position in the *Fomento*. The reasons for the Godó's interest in controlling this section were twofold: first, through this section they obtained direct information on tariffs concerning the jute industry; and, second, they were placed in a favourable position to exert pressure on tariff policy. This reveals that in addition to patron–client relationships, business associativism was also central for elites to secure their private interests.

Protectionism and national identity

The establishing of *La Vanguardia*, in 1881, can be considered a further step forward in the Godós' attempt to secure protectionist policies. Their position on economic policy went against the mainstream of the Liberal Party, which mostly stood for free-trade policies.[17] It was in their attempt to make this dissent in economic policy visible that the Godó brothers used the press. Hence, in the very first edition of *La Vanguardia*, the newspaper's total commitment to Sagasta's Liberal Party was proclaimed, but it was also stated in very clear terms that this would not prevent it from supporting protectionism at all costs:

> "Now that we have expressed our opinion in the political order, it is our duty to express in the clearest terms our ideas about the most important of all economic issues. We are going to fight tirelessly for the protection of the national industry. We do not belong to those who stay for free trade, for this would turn us into slaves of other nations; and we have independence to such a high degree that we do not want to be subject to the greed of modern Carthaginians. (...) dignity and patriotism require us to hoist the banner of protection, which is the best warranty for the most precious interests."[18]

The fact that the newspaper's editorial line was expressed in such clear terms reveals that as well as the aspiration of challenging the leadership of the Liberal Party in Barcelona, *La Vanguardia* was established to oppose the party's official free-trade policies. This position became particularly clear when Sagasta's Liberal party reached power for the first time in the Restoration, on February 1881, and started considering the possibility of lowering protection tariffs. By then the Spanish economy suffered a series of difficulties (above all, a crisis in agriculture) and Sagasta, who already stood for free-trade policies in the *Sexenio*, saw in these policies a solution to the economic situation.[19] The fear that the reduction of tariffs on foreign imports might harm the Catalan industry resulted in several demonstrations in this region and paved the way for another corporate mobilisation in defence of protectionism. The Godó brothers actively contributed to this form of collective action through the pages of their recently founded newspaper. Hence, in an article entitled "Warning", *La Vanguardia* urged Catalan manufacturers to respond rapidly against the new campaign that free-traders were organizing in support of the Liberal government.

> "Yes, it is necessary that our industrialists be very concerned about the work being done by the enemies of national labour protection. It is necessary that they redouble their efforts so as to paralyse those who have proposed the triumphs of their utopias to the detriment of the ruin of the country (...) Not a day goes by when, as if it were obeying a motto, a plan skilfully planned and with persistent tenacity, the newspapers of Madrid bring us news of new projects, of new mediums of propaganda aimed at creating tension, to stir unrest as well as putting pressure on the cabinet, as if they were trying to prove that the whole of Spain (is) by its side and that these apostles are the mouthpiece that speaks for all of the country."[20]

The scaremongering of *La Vanguardia* is revealing of the great tension that debates on economic policy provoked in Catalonia, and the crucial role that the press played as a means to stir political mobilisation. In the eyes of the newspaper Catalan industrialists were not sufficiently aware of the risks that were at stake, and called them to commit more actively in defence of protectionism. Moreover, the article even urged this social group to have the leading voice in the protests against the new economic reform. If this call is revealing of the kind of audience that *La Vanguardia* was trying to mobilise, it is equally revealing to whom the attacks of this newspaper were addressed. Thus, and despite the fact that free trade was a widely extended position in Spain, particularly in those regions with an export-oriented economy,[21] *La Vanguardia* did not hesitate to present Madrid's press as the root of the problem. Still, the problem was not limited to a difference in economic criteria, but had a deeper, underlying cause; namely, the disrespect that Madrid's press showed towards Catalan demands. As the Godó newspaper bitterly protested:

> "We are tired of hearing talk from Madrid of Catalanism as well as provincialism. For those of Madrid, all noble and lofty aspirations of Catalonia are provincialism; every complaint, every cry of anguish is Catalanism. When the former Principality asked for protection of its industries: 'It is Catalanism', was the reply; the call for the suspension of a tariff reform, the terms of which could not be more disastrous: this is Catalanism. Enamoured with its ancient liberties and franchises, remembering those times in which it was an example for the Mediterranean nations with its laws and conduct: this is provincialism. Thus, we repeat, there is no aspiration, wish, tendency, complaint or cry of anguish in memory that is not decreed with a chorus of 'Catalanism'. Nevertheless, nothing could benefit Madrid – and Spain as a whole – more than having a region like Catalonia. No sense of individual aspiration can be found in any other region than that which created the great works and colossal business that have formed within the enterprising business spirit of the Catalans. And if so, tell us which province, which region, has achieved, with its own resources, without assistance from outside forces, the great works achieved by Catalonia. If this is Catalanism, then blessed be the nickname that they give us, but the term has an air of disdain and underestimation that can only have been inspired by the complete ignorance of our country."[22]

The article quoted above, which was published under the title "Catalanism", reveals how in the early 1880s the debate on economic policies became intertwined with identitary issues. In fact, the years previous to the founding of *La Vanguardia* had seen the development of an incipient Catalanist movement. Since the second half of the century a literary movement known as *La Renaixença* ("Rebirth") had fostered the recovery of Catalan language in culture, but this movement had not developed into a political claim.[23] This situation started changing in 1880, when the Federal Republican Valentí Almirall (1841–1904) called for a Catalanist Congress to be held.[24] The purpose of this congress was to unite the different strands that had promoted the recovery of Catalan language into a single organization and to debate the possible orientation of this movement towards embracing a political standpoint. The congress, however, soon revealed the numerous factions that existed within Catalanism and how different the understandings of this movement actually were. The attempt of the congress' promoter (Almirall) to claim a federalist understanding of the Spanish state and defend autonomous rule for Catalonia clashed with the positioning of the rest of groups. Some of them, like the one grouped around the newspaper *La Reinaxensa*, were opposed to the politicizing of what had been until then a Romantic, literary-oriented movement; while Catholic and conservative groups feared the progressive and secular vision of Almirall, and even boycotted the congress. At the end, the congress achieved some modest successes (it gathered around 1,200 delegates and created the first academy in charge of uniting Catalan grammar), but ultimately revealed the great internal dispersion that characterized the incipient Catalanist movement.

The bitter observations that *La Vanguardia* made about Madrid's press reveal that no matter how diverged and unripe Catalanism was, it was becoming a heated issue in Spanish politics. Yet for *La Vanguardia* the problem was not Catalanism in itself, but rather that all the demands coming from Catalonia were misunderstood in Madrid as selfish demands. No matter all the efforts that were made to explain and justify the need for protective tariffs, *La Vanguardia* lamented that all the explanations were repeatedly rejected in Spain's capital under the pretext of being a shortsighted claim from the periphery ("*provincialismo*"). These accusations were all the more regrettable given that, in the view of *La Vanguardia*, Catalanism was a blurred movement that did not deserve much consideration. As this journal bluntly stated, "Catalanism does not exist, but it is imprudently fed by those who deny Spanish protectionism and who consider this word as the expression of Catalan selfishness"; and concluded that "No one really knows what Catalanism is really about (...) but it is the duty of every government to prevent things to go down this road".[25] Besides the inherent contradictions that these statements contained (e.g. the newspaper denied the existence of Catalanism but at the same time feared its growth), they reveal a trait that was to characterize the political debate in the following decades; namely, the recurring practice of associating Catalanism with separatism. It must be clarified, in this regard, that none of the different tendencies that integrated the Catalanist movement in the 1880s claimed for independence. At most, and only in the case of the most progressive factions, did they stand for a decentralizing or federal understanding of the Spanish state, but none of them envisaged the partition of the country as a desirable possibility. Therefore, the accusations that some of Madrid's newspapers made of separatism should be seen, above all, as a strategy aimed at discrediting protectionist demands, rather than as a reality.

Likewise, when *La Vanguardia* spoke of a "national market" or of the "national industry" it was not referring to Catalonia, but to Spain. Despite the fact that this newspaper responded to the comments of Madrid's press with disdain, and had displayed a visible sense of pride for Catalonia's economic achievements since medieval times, the nation to which *La Vanguardia* appealed was – and would always be – Spain. This position became visible when in subsequent articles, the newspaper proclaimed its position in the face of identitary issues:

> "(...) Those journalists who incite outrage instead of advising prudence and justice will find out (...) that today's Catalan generation is no less virile and dignified than those generations past and that, with good reason, we consider ourselves to be at such a higher level of civil virtue and patriotism than the rest of the provinces that make up this disgraced noble nation. *We consider ourselves as the children of Spain with such courage and dignity as our brothers*, whose harmony of interests we long for. We do not try to exploit our own advantages, according to our detractors' understanding."[26]

Indeed, pride in Catalonia's achievements and the entrenched positions that flavoured the political debate did not prevent the Godó newspaper from identifying itself as a Spanish patriot. One reason for this is because *La Vanguardia* exemplified what the historian Josep M. Fradera has called the "dual patriotism" that permeated wide segments of Catalan society.[27] This newspaper combined the esteem for regional identity with the attachment to the Spanish liberal project. In line with this argument, the need for protection against foreign imports was not presented as a demand exclusive to Catalonia, but as a demand that would yield benefits to the whole of Spain. Furthermore, the Godó newspaper would distinguish itself from other newspapers for the repeated efforts it made to act as a bridge for the better understanding between Catalonia and the rest of Spain. As the newspaper explained, "every time that we see some newspaper from the Court [Madrid] rising up in defense of Catalonia, we cannot but be pleased and applaud the honesty and independent character that is needed to oppose to the flood of unfounded allegations".[28] This kind of statement shed light on the positioning that *La Vanguardia* adopted in the face of identity politics, and the role of mediator that this journal sought to embody between Barcelona and Madrid.

Still, the good intentions of *La Vanguardia* did not prevent the newspaper's owner to actively participate in the mobilisation in defense of protectionism. In his condition of deputy for Igualada's constituency, Bartolomé Godó became an active member of the collective strategy of lobbying known as *"diputació catalana"*.[29] Thus, he participated in different demonstrations that were organised to protest against the plans of the Liberal government, and later on he joined other Catalan politicians in Congress to vote against the signing of the new commercial treaty with France, in 1882.[30] During the parliamentary session Godó openly opposed the discourses of his own party, and later on he held a "long conversation" with Prime Minister Sagasta on the need to maintain duty tariffs on French imports.[31] The behaviour of Godó illustrates to what extent personal interests went before the discipline of cadre parties. It was in the face of this situation, when private interests clashed with the party's official position, that the press became a valuable instrument to publicise dissent. *La Vanguardia* thus became a platform for the Barcelona members of the Liberal Party to express their opposition to the party's official position in economic policy. This provides further evidence that in addition to patron–client relationships, the press became another instrument the elites used to secure their private interests; especially when there was a desire to make the dissent visible in public.

Public opinion and economic policy in Cuba's War of Independence (1895–1898)

If the editorials of the early days of *La Vanguardia* were addressed at pressuring the leaders of the Liberal Party, the Cuban War of Independence (1895–1898) revealed interest in conveying the same demands to a broader audience. With the aim of reaching an audience beyond the members of the political community, adopting an independent editorial line in 1888 became decisive (see Chapter 1). As the last section of this chapter will show, addressing new readers implied adopting a series of new journalistic practices to make the newspaper's content more accessible. All these strategies were aimed at increasing readership, while at the same time contained the aspiration of guiding public opinion.

The Cuban War of Independence symbolically started on February 1895, when an insurrection took place in the Cuban town of Baire. This insurrection initially raised little attention in Spain. The number of insurgents was small, the Spanish newspapers said, and the killing and arrest of some of its leaders indicated that the events in Cuba were mostly under control.[32] In the case of Barcelona, far more attention was paid to a different issue, also related to Cuba: namely, the new attempt of Sagasta's Liberal Government to change the commercial laws concerning Spain and the Antilles.[33] Although the Catalan elites traditionally showed great concern about maintaining tariff duties, in 1895 the situation reached a critical point. As news arrived from Madrid about a meeting between the Liberal minister Romero Robledo and the Cuban deputies to reform the commercial laws, unrest spread rapidly among the Catalan elites. The senators and deputies of this region were summoned to the headquarters of the *Fomento del Trabajo Nacional* to discuss the situation. The conclusion they reached was put in clear terms: any reform to the existing commercial laws between Spain and Cuba would endanger the prosperity of the Catalan industry.[34]

The economic ties between the Catalan industry and Cuba had a long tradition, reaching back to the 18th century, but had intensified enormously in the late 19th century. Especially in 1882, a series of tariffs were established that greatly benefited the trade with the colonies: while foreign products entering the Spanish colonies were subject to heavy duties (of around 40%), Spanish exports to the colonies, by contrast, incurred far lower duties (between 11–12%). All these measures clearly favoured Spanish exports and decisively contributed to turning the colonies of Cuba, Puerto Rico, and the Philippines into a fabulous market for Spanish manufacturers. In fact, in all of Europe only England exported more to her colonies than Spain did to her own.[35] The economic dependency of exports on the colonial market became acute in the country's most industrialised region, Catalonia. For manufacturers in this region, who faced serious difficulties to compete with foreign production, the protected market of Spanish overseas colonies became a great gateway for their manufactures. Thus, while the trade with the colonies had traditionally been particularly fruitful, the passing of new protective tariffs in 1886 multiplied by five times the volume of exports of cotton manufactures to the colonies in the following decade.[36] Cuba was undoubtedly the chief market for these exports, and this earned the island the meaningful nickname of the "pearl of the Antilles".

It is no surprise, in consequence, that when rumours spread in 1895 about the new intention of the Liberal government to change the commercial laws between Spain and its colonies that Catalan politicians were rapidly summoned to the *Fomento del Trabajo Nacional*. Among the people who attended this meeting was Carlos Godó (1834–1897). Carlos officially attended the meeting as deputy of the Liberal Party in Congress. He had been elected in 1893, in replacement of his brother Bartolomé, who suffered a disease that confined him to bed for many years. The fact that Carlos replaced his brother as deputy reveals to what extent the constituency of Igualada remained concentrated in the hands of the Godó family. Rather than a personal merit, the position of deputy was a position of influence in Madrid that this family was determined to keep in its exclusive hands. And the way of doing so was, as in the times of Bartolomé, through the systematic rigging of elections.

Still, when Carlos Godó attended the meeting at *Fomento* he did so not only in his condition of deputy in Congress, but also as a businessman with direct interests in Cuba. At the time Carlos was running the jute factory he had established together with his brother Bartolomé and their business associate Pere Milà in the 1870s. According to the description in a commercial guide of 1895, it was the most important factory in the country dedicated to the manufacturing of jute bags for the Spanish Antilles.[37] Because of the great importance of the colonial market for his business, Godó participated actively in the various meetings that business associations dedicated to examining the events in Cuba.[38]

Godó's commitment to defending protectionist policies, however, was not limited to business associativism, but also extended to the field of journalism. *La Vanguardia* gave wide coverage to all the protests of the Catalan manufac- turers and portrayed the Cuban insurrection as an action aimed at pressuring the Spanish government to change the commercial laws. This understanding of the Cuban insurrection was influenced by the official accounts of the Liberal government, who initially hoped to hide the extent of the separatist insurrec- tion by presenting it as an act of banditry. In the face of the events, *La Vanguardia* condemned the insurrection as being motivated by selfish inter- ests, and urged the government not to yield to them.[39] Yet, the need to publicise the reasons for opposing any changes in the commercial laws to new publics was as important as pressuring the government. As the separatist insurrection grew in intensity, *La Vanguardia* started publishing a series of articles under the title of "*La Información cubana*" ("Information on Cuba"). As the newspaper explained to its readers on the first day these articles started being published:

> "We have thought it was convenient, now that a debate has started on such an important and complex issue like the commercial laws that shall be introduced between the provinces of Ultramar and the Peninsula, to dedicate to it a column of *popular* information, so the problem can be studied in detail and be given a fair solution."[40]

As this paragraph illustrates, *La Vanguardia* was concerned that the public became aware of the debate that was taking place. The newspaper did not limit itself to providing the latest news about the political debate (on the page it dedicated daily to publishing the telegraphs arriving from Madrid and La Habana), but also made an effort to attract the interest of a popular audience to this topic. Every article of "*La Información cubana*" was conducted as an interview with businessmen holding commercial relations with the

Antilles, who explained the characteristics of their business. An example of these articles was the interview with a businessman called Mr. Baldés, who was in the shirt industry. Before commencing the interview, the journalist of *La Vanguardia* set the tone by stressing *"the importance that shirt production has in this country, not just because it has successfully rejected the entry of foreign production, but also because it has conquered our own markets in Ultramar and some in South America"*.[41] Mr. Baldés then expressed his opinion on the economic debate affecting the Antilles in very clear terms: "The withdrawal of the commercial laws between Spain and the provinces of Ultramar would truly be a disaster for Spain and especially for Catalonia, as far as the manufacture of shirts is concerned. The number of families that live on the jobs our industry provides is incalculable."[42] As the interview with Mr. Baldés illustrates, the people interviewed in *La Vanguardia* were mostly small entrepreneurs who were dedicated to the textile industry (tailors of cloths, ties, hats, etc.) who conducted business with Cuba. These were the kinds of businesses that many readers of *La Vanguardia* could identify with, especially given the fact that the majority of readers of this newspaper belonged to the diverse ranks of the Catalan bourgeoisie. As this newspaper confessed, on repeated occasions, the goal of the articles published under the title *"La Información cubana"* was:

> "(...) to open a [section] of popular information, not so much to instruct the tariff commission on the Antilles, but to bring *public opinion* to the conviction that for the sake of the general interests, both from the Peninsula and the Antilles, it is convenient that the nature of the current system of commercial laws should be maintained (...)."[43]

In consequence, the mission of *La Vanguardia* was no longer limited to pressuring the government – even though this remained central – but was combined with the ambition to address wider segments of opinion. While this ambition had started becoming evident since *La Vanguardia's* transformation of 1888 when it became an independent newspaper, both the War of Melilla (1893) and the Cuban War of Independence (1895) revealed the introduction of new journalistic practices to achieve this goal. This new interest in targeting a broader segment of society revealed that *La Vanguardia's* function as an independent newspaper was not limited to delivering neutral information to their readers (*"facts, facts and facts"*, as the newspaper proclaimed in 1888), but also included the ambition of guiding public opinion. In other words, the Cuban War of Independence provided further evidence that *La Vanguardia's* mission was not limited to mirroring the interests of its readers; it also consisted in waking the interest of those readers on certain issues and influencing the opinion they should have about them.

The two paragraphs quoted above on "*La información cubana*" exemplify how opinion formation and the search for new publics were combined. The use of an accessible language (the interview) and an informal format (personal stories) were two journalistic techniques aimed at making the content of the newspaper easier to read for a wider public. The case of *La Vanguardia* consequently reveals that despite the fact that large sections of the population were excluded from politics by means of clientelism, and illiteracy rates were still high (48% in Barcelona in 1900),[44] businessmen like the Godó brothers were sensitive to the role that public opinion played in political debates. The press thus constituted a key mechanism used by economic elites to publicise their agenda to broader segments of society; and, in parallel, they used the calls to an imaginary public opinion as a pretext to pressure the government.

As it began to become evident that the insurrection in Cuba was more serious than a simple act of banditry, the Godó brothers made great efforts to appeal to the broadest public possible to secure their business interests. Despite the initial attempts of the Liberal government to play down the scope of the insurrection, in March 1895 the call to war was officially announced in Spain. The first troops were sent to fight the Cuban insurrection and the Congress approved a special budget to cover the war expenditure. As the Prime Minister declared, Spain "was ready to spend the last peseta and the last drop of blood of her sons in defence of her rights and of her territory".[45] The explanation for such strong sentiments was that Cuba was a sensitive part of Spain's public imaginary. Rather than a colony, the island was regarded as an integral part of the Spanish territory that belonged to the so-called "provinces of Ultramar".[46]

At this point the danger was not limited to the possible reduction of protective tariffs, but to the loss of Cuba from the Spanish empire. In the face of this situation *La Vanguardia* did not hesitate in fully supporting the action of the Spanish army to maintain Cuba at all costs. As this newspaper asserted, "Catalonia and Barcelona are the most concerned of all the peninsular regions in that the national flag shall always wave in the biggest [island] of the Antilles, a precious reminder of our vast American empire". Still, for the Godós the war was not something to be proud of. In the view of their newspaper the majority of the Spanish people did not want to go to war because it stemmed from a misunderstanding between two parts of the same nation. Indeed, the apprehension about a war in what was considered to be part of the Spanish territory is what led *La Vanguardia* to present the conflict as something that was particularly painful, but nonetheless necessary. This "unpleasant necessity", as the newspaper called it, became manifest in the comparisons that *La Vanguardia* drew with the recent War of Melilla of 1893. The memories of this conflict (studied in Chapter 2) inevitably came back in 1895. As soldiers were in Barcelona's harbour boarding the ships that would take them to Cuba, *La Vanguardia* noted how distressing this scene was; and compared it with the recent war in Morocco:

> "On Friday morning Barcelona witnessed the boarding of two batallions to Cuba, where again has echoed the cry of rebellion against the motherland. Going to Melilla to fight against the infidel, the traditional enemy of Spain was not as unpleasant as going to Cuba to fight against the *ill-advised brother* who, at a moment of obfuscation, forgets its duties towards the generous nation who at the peach of its glories sacrificed to give birth to a new world. As long as one atom of gratitude exists, Cuba will remain Spanish. The sending of troops to the African coast gave place to great moments of enthusiasm, to noisy demonstrations of public passion, to cheers and shouts. For these soldiers embodied one of the most long standings aspirations of the Spanish nation. In contrast, the boarding of the two battalions to Cuba was seen with some regret, but neither because someone thinks that the rebellion should not be fought; nor because there is one single Spanish soldier who is not ready to the biggest sacrifice to assure the integrity of the national patrimony, but simply because it hurts and it is always sad any fight between brothers, any bloody collision between the sons of the same mother."[47]

The article above is enlightening about how newspapers were central in fostering patriotic behaviour, but also in hiding possible forms of opposition to the war. Different scholars have shown that wide segments of the popular classes were opposed to the Cuban war of 1895, especially due to the uneven system of military recruitment.[48] Carlos Godó, however, sought to conceal this popular opposition in *La Vanguardia* because it ran contrary to his economic interests in Cuba. Hence, the little enthusiasm that the departure of troops drew in Barcelona was not presented in *La Vanguardia* as an indication of a certain reluctance about going to war, but was justified for the "unpleasant" character that the people – arguably – considered this war had. In contrast to the war against the "Moors", which *La Vanguardia* presented as a reasonable conflict (since combating the Moroccans constituted "one of the more lasting and vivid aspirations of the Spanish nation"), the newspaper presented the war in Cuba as a regrettable misunderstanding between brothers. For Cubans were "ill-advised brothers", yet brothers nevertheless. This case illustrates that the power of newspaper editors as *political actors* consisted in their capacity to select which issues were given public visibility and which others were silenced, according to their private agenda.

Carlos Godó had indeed good reasons to use the press to publicise the war effort in favourable terms. In contrast to the majority of Catalan textiles exports to Cuba, which remained steady during the war,[49] the separatist insurrection was having very negative effects on the jute sack market. The Cuban separatists had adopted a strategy of economic warfare that drastically reduced sugar production, upon which the jute bags industry was highly dependent. As a result, and as one commercial report on Barcelona's industry noted, "Since 1895, owing to the destruction of the sugar crops in the island, the export of empty jute sacks to Cuba has suffered heavily".[50] If we take into account that "Godó brothers and Company" was the leading company in the export of jute bags to the Spanish colonies, it is clear that the rebellion was having a negative impact on their economic interests.

In fact, the Godós' resolute commitment to securing the integrity of the Spanish empire also became noticeable in their public behaviour. On August 1895 Carlos Godó contacted the Minister of War to offer one *peseta* per soldier, 1.50 *pesetas* per corporal, and 2 *pesetas* per sergeant departing from Barcelona to Cuba.[51] Godó also offered one daily *peseta* to every deprived family of Igualada's district that had a son fighting in the army. These donations amounted to thousands of *pesetas* (the district included 32 villages) and became the first of the successive donations he made throughout the war. The press rapidly welcomed these donations and presented Godó as an example to follow.[52] Moreover, on April 1896 Godó was awarded the "Grand Cross for Military Merit" for his support of the war effort, and he travelled to Madrid to personally thank the Queen Regent for the decoration he received.[53] The award given to Carlos Godó reveals the public status he had reached in society and his total commitment to Spanish patriotism. Although he had already obtained the support of the Queen Regent for his business plans in Morocco, the award he received in 1896 provided further evidence of the excellent relations Godó held with the monarchy. From a different perspective, the donations Godó made reveal the extremely delicate situation in which his business was positioned, and how the support to the Spanish army (both through the press and through public gestures) were an attempt to reverse the situation.

Colonial conflicts and the press: The entry of the United States into the war (1898)

The last episode of the Cuban War took place in 1898, when the United States joined the conflict. What had been until then a domestic confrontation was consequently turned into an open war between an emerging power, the United States, and a country desperate to hold on to the remnants of its empire, Spain. In fact, since the beginning of the war in Cuba the majority of the Spanish press showed a clear mistrust towards the United States. If the new foreign policy under the motto "Keeping America for the Americans" (the Monroe doctrine of 1895) already created uneasiness among the Spanish press,[54] the collision of interests between the two countries increased in

1896, when the United States' Senate recognised the status of belligerent government to the Cuban insurgency. Despite the attempts of Spain's Prime Minister Antonio Cánovas del Castillo to minimise the importance of this declaration, Spanish newspapers took an aggressive stance. The Madrid newspaper *El Imparcial*, for instance, argued that "Spain shall succumb before tolerating the offence of foreign intervention in its own matters".[55] Other newspapers from Madrid, like *El Heraldo*, responded vehemently to the US declaration, while *La Correspondencia de España* took a more moderate tone, albeit considering the situation "extremely serious".[56] In the case of *La Vanguardia* the declaration of the US Senate was presented as a direct attack on Spain's honour. The newspaper referred to the United States as a "perfidious and greedy nation", since Spain had already "sacrificed a great part of its sovereignty and its interests to the American postulates", in reference to the change of the tariffs that were implemented in 1895 to promote American trade with Cuba.[57]

The crucial role of the press in increasing public concern about the possibility of a future war against the United States became all the more evident on 15 February 1898. On that day a diplomatic incident between Spain and the United States took place: a US ship located in Santiago de Cuba was accidentally sunk. The outcome of this incident was the declaration by US President McKinley of a possible military intervention in Cuba. Although war was not a certainty, only a possibility, the newspapers contributed to spreading the idea that it was indeed imminent. Newspapers published President McKinley's statements and encouraged the demonstrations that took place throughout the Spanish territory. In Barcelona, for instance, a play held at the Liceo theatre turned into an impromptu demonstration that *La Vanguardia* warmly welcomed and presented as a sign of the patriotic atmosphere that dominated the city.[58] Similar demonstrations took place in the Godó's hometown of Igualada, where a play in the local theatre led the audience to request, with much enthusiasm, that the national anthem be played. Afterwards, "An individual jumped onto the stage and burned an American flag. The crowd started shouting 'death to the United States and long live Spain'. A demonstration was soon improvised and 3,000 people marched through the streets playing music and carrying Spanish flags".[59] This event in Igualada highlights that the excitement about a war against the United States was not a phenomenon that was restricted to the big cities like Madrid or Barcelona, but generated great enthusiasm in all corners of the Spanish territory. Newspapers became central in fostering this kind of patriotic behaviour, as well as in hiding possible forms of opposition (or indifference) to the war. The writer Miguel de Unamuno, for instance, recalled having seen great indifference to the war among a group of farmers in Castile.[60] In a largely rural country such as Spain, where 27.5% of the population lived in rural communities of less than 2,000 people in 1900, similar careless attitudes were probably very widespread. Likewise, numerous soldiers avoided conscription or deserted the army in different parts of the country.[61]

However, resistance or antipathy towards the war left only a small trace in the press. With the exception of the Socialist and the Anarchist press, which saw the war as an opportunity to attack the political system, the vast majority of the press highlighted events that reflected – and encouraged – patriotic behaviour. To give an example of this, the event that took place in Igualada's theatre (described above) was reported by various national newspapers, like Spain's top-selling newspaper (*El Imparcial*) and Madrid's *La Época*, which referred to the events in Igualada as a "patriotic movement".[62] As could be expected, in Barcelona too *La Vanguardia* published positive reports of the same event, and contributed to fostering jingoism by arguing that "another thousand events like this will follow tomorrow, in which our residents will renew their bravery as they have done every time the Spanish fatherland has required the efforts and abnegation of their children".[63] This capacity of editors to be selective in their reporting became particularly clear in the case of commercial newspapers. Madrid's newspaper *El Imparcial*, for instance, abandoned the criticism it usually directed against the government and joined the patriotic discourse without hesitation. Something similar happened in other cities, like Barcelona and Seville, where the press that did not have a partisan leaning largely supported the war.[64] In fact, if the war-like stance was an easy attitude for newspapers to follow, editors also saw it as an opportunity to increase sales, especially in the case of profit-oriented newspapers, because large numbers of readers chose to buy newspapers that were in favour of the war. The militaristic newspaper *El Imparcial*, for instance, saw its circulation increase from 70,000 copies to 120,000 during the war.[65]

In contrast to the commercial press, partisan newspapers seemed to have fewer difficulties in opposing the war (when they chose to do so). The reason for this is because partisan newspapers privileged opinion formation over selling copies. This was the case, for instance, of a Catalanist newspaper named *La Renaixença*, whose sympathy towards the Cuban insurrection made it an opponent of the war. Despite Catalanists initially supported the war effort, mainly to protect the interests of the Catalan industry, later on they argued in favour of conceding autonomy to Cuba as the best way to solve the situation. Opposing the war, however, was a decision that carried commercial consequences. As the editor of *La Renaixença* later declared, "during the madness unleashed by the war against the United States" his decision of opposing the war became "*disastrous*" in commercial terms.[66] This illustrates to what extent the war became popular among significant number of readers. In the eyes of *La Renaixença*, the eagerness of the press to meet these expectations could have a pernicious influence for the country's future:

"little more can be said to the people in the city that are waiting impatiently for the outbreak of the war against the United States. Influenced by newspapers that are more concerned with selling copies than in being Spanish, they cannot wait for the news arriving to Madrid or Washington (...). They want the war: let's have it then. They shall regret it (...)."[67]

The words of this newspaper reveal the perception that in their eagerness to reflect the wishes of the public, and consequently to increase their sales, commercial newspapers were failing in the moral duty of looking for the general interest. Still, some exceptions existed in the generalised pro-war behaviour of the commercial press. This was the case, for instance, of *El Diario de Barcelona* – one of the most representative newspapers of conservative opinion in Barcelona. The opinions of its editor (Joan Mañé Flaquer) and those of its leading figures were highly respected. Unlike the newspaper of the Godó family, *El Diario de Barcelona* became a resolute opponent of war, this being an attitude that became clear in the much more moderate tone it adopted to speak about the United States.[68] However, the patriotic pressure that imbued public life became so heated that it was difficult to stand, not just for the liberal politicians, who felt the pressure of going into war to save the political system,[69] but also for the moderate opinion-minded newspapers like *El Diario de Barcelona*. One of the most reputed writers for this newspaper, Joan Maragall, reflected on the oppressive atmosphere the press contributed to create in an article called "*la obsesión*" ("the obsession"):

"The war! The war against the United States! There is no way to talk about anything else. (...) the obsession has reached the point when it is a necessity, almost a phisiologhic one (sic), to get rid of it in whatever way: the moment has been reached when everyone wants this to be ended no matter how it goes. There is nobody in favour of peace, no matter his commitment, who is not wishing the breaking of war if this, with all its catastrophes, shall put an end to uncertainty."[70]

Summary

Although the fear of a war against the United States was a possibility that the Spanish press had contributed to broadcast since the very beginning of the Cuban insurrection of 1895, when the war finally did break out in April 1898 it was a short-lived affair. Spain suffered a series of rapid defeats on the battlefield and the war was concluded in little more than three months. This conflict put an end to the Spanish empire and to the centuries-long presence of Spain in the Antilles. Neither of the two Godó brothers, however, lived to see this. Bartolomé passed away in 1895, after a long illness, and Carlos died in 1897 during a sojourn in his country house.[71]

In many ways, Cuba was central to the strategies of the two Godó brothers. As this chapter has shown, securing protection for Spanish exports to the Antilles became a recurring theme in the Godó's activities in the fields of business, politics, and journalism. The case of these two brothers exemplifies, in fact, why Barcelona has been referred to as "Spain's business centre in the trade with the colonies".[72] The importance of the colonial market for the Catalan economy traditionally led the elites of this region to give great importance to protectionist policies. This need became all the more important in the last quarter of the 19th century, when the lack of consensus between the two liberal parties implied that economic policy could be changed at any time. Catalan elites were certainly not the only ones that were concerned about protectionism. In other parts of Spain, like Castile and Andalusia, the securing of protectionist policies also became an important concern of local elites.[73]

Indeed, if the question of how local interests were represented in central government was a fundamental question in Europe during the liberal period, the Godó brothers constitute a case study that illuminates how the mechanisms of influence combined private and group interests. The letters sent to the Minister of Ultramar, the meetings at *Fomento*, and the intervention in Congress demonstrate that the Godó brothers worked in tight collaboration with other Catalan elites in the so-called *diputació catalana* in order to secure group interests. This demonstrates that in a political system where government was not decided through free elections, collective action became one of the strategies local elites used to exert pressure on central government.

Although the debate on economic policies became a recurring element throughout the 19th century, the growing presence of regional demands in the 1880s added a new identitary dimension to the debate. Catalanism was still a blurred and divided movement, and different tendencies existed in its interior. All this complexity however mattered little as demands for protectionism started being presented as selfish (and sometimes even as separatist) demands coming from Catalonia. The protests of *La Vanguardia* against Madrid's newspapers are particularly valuable in this respect. Despite all the efforts that this newspaper made to present protectionism as the best solution for the whole of the country, such appreciations were often overlooked once they reached Spain's capital. That *La Vanguardia* denounced the misunderstanding of Madrid's press is all the more telling given the total commitment that this newspaper showed towards Spanish identity. Indeed, if the Godó newspaper had already held the banner of Spanish patriotism during the colonial wars in Morocco (see Chapter 2), the debates on economic policy (1881) and the Cuban War of Independence (1895–1898) provided further occasions to reaffirm this commitment. If *La Vanguardia* did not see this commitment as contrary to regional identity it is because this newspaper became a revealing example of the "dual patriotism" that permeated wide segments of Catalan society.

Still, and as the following chapters of this book will demonstrate, this equilibrium would become harder to maintain in the aftermath of 1898. The shock that losing the colonies had in Spain would turn the press into an object of severe criticism, and this decisively contributed to eroding the position of liberal elites and to questioning the very idea of the Spanish nation. The devastating effects of the war on all these issues will be, precisely, the focus of Chapter 4.

4

Press, Politics and the "Disaster" of 1898

"There is the growing sensation that in a few years Spain might well break up; this danger has started being regarded as natural, and what is worse, with indifference. It is acknowledged that Catalonia might soon be absorbed by France, but what is more appalling is the answer given in the face of this possibility: after all, we can't be governed any worse than by the people in Madrid . . . ".
MANUEL DURAN I BAS TO FRANCISCO SILVELA, 5 January 1899[1]

On 1 January 1899 the Spanish flag was lowered for the last time in Santiago de Cuba. What started as a small insurrection in the Cuban town of Baire in 1895 had turned into four years of war that affected all of Spain's colonial dominions, from the Caribbean (Cuba and Puerto Rico) to South-East Asia (the Philippines). The sending of 200,000 soldiers and an expenditure of over 1,000 million *pesetas* had proved insufficient for Spain to win the war. Thus almost five hundred years of Spanish presence in the Antilles had reached an end, while the United States, in contrast, symbolically joined the group of imperial powers.

The "Disaster" of 1898, as the loss of the colonies became popularly known in Spain, was a national trauma that had long-lasting effects. In 1923, when General Primo de Rivera put an end to the Restoration and established a dictatorship, he justified the armed uprising as the result of the national decay that had begun in 1898. In the shorter term, however, the Disaster of 1898 led to a process of national introspection, which set in motion different projects aspiring to reinvigorate the country. All these projects, known as "*Regeneracionismo*", would exert a great influence in the historiography. The works of Regenerationist intellectuals like Joaquín Costa (to mention perhaps the most influential among them) decisively contributed to forging a sense of exceptionalism in the understanding of modern Spanish history.[2]

However, the intellectual paradigm that saw Spain as a history of deviance and failure (something that recalls contemporary trends in the German and the Italian historiography) has undergone a process of full revision in the last two decades. The commemoration of the centenary of the Disaster, in 1998, became an opportunity for historians and intellectuals alike to revisit prevailing paradigms of exceptionality.[3] The outcome of this centenary was a myriad of works that demystified the Disaster and framed it in the broader European context. After all, something similar to 1898 had already happened to France two decades earlier, in 1870, with the defeat of Sedan. Not by coincidence, the French case exerted a powerful influence on the response of Spanish intellectuals to the Disaster, as Vicente Cacho noted. Furthermore, Spain's loss of empire was part of the broader international context, namely that of colonial redistribution between imperial powers that took place in the late 19th century – as José María Jover noted, and Sebastian Balfour recalled. As Varela Ortega argued, even the very same crisis of legitimacy that the Restoration suffered after 1898 would not have been possible without the social, economic and political transformations that the same political system had fuelled in previous decades. Additionally, in the countries that were traditionally regarded as exemplary models of historical development (like the United Kingdom and France), the political systems did not become fully democratic until the First World War, as the same author has reminded.[4]

Therefore, the view of historians that the Disaster was a national trauma has started being replaced, in the last two decades, with an interpretation that sees it as a sign of Spain's new "drive towards modernization", to use the expression of an influential work.[5] The emergence of this new historical paradigm revealed a more confident attitude in the understanding of the recent past and was favoured by the country's belonging to the European Union.[6] Still, some historians – such as Antonio Elorza and Isabel Burdiel – have warned, without directly questioning the need for revisiting the Disaster, of the dangers of falling into an oscillating and now excessively optimistic understanding of Spain's past in relation to Europe.[7]

In my view, the historiographical revision of the Disaster of 1898 has been a fruitful and necessary attempt. That being said, the efforts of historians to stress the continuities that followed the Disaster (in opposition to the previous "dramatic" paradigm) should not lead to underestimating some of the historical changes that took place after it. In fact, there seems to be a certain tendency in emphasising that when it came to politics, little changed in the aftermath of 1898. An example of this continuity in politics would be the case of Sagasta who, despite being held responsible for the defeat, seized power again in 1903. The political failure of Regenerationist movements (like that of Joaquín Costa or José Canalejas) and the continuity of clientelistic practices would provide further evidence that when it came to everyday politics, everything remained much the same in the Restoration.

In contrast to this view, this chapter will argue that the "Disaster" of 1898 *did* mark a substantial shift in the Restoration politics, for two reasons. The first one is that the Disaster became a decisive ingredient in the growing disenchantment of Catalan elites towards the political system. This would not only represent a substantial change in the attitude of these elites, but ultimately had an impact on the entire political system. Second, the changes that started taking place in Barcelona since 1901 would be revealing of a broader European phenomenon, namely the birth of mass politics. While this was the result of longer-term structural transformations, the discredit of liberal parties in the aftermath of the Disaster provided fertile ground for new political movements to take root. Barcelona saw the rise of the first political party capable of mobilising the urban classes through new forms of discourse (namely, the Republicans of Alejandro Lerroux); as well as the creation of a Catalan nationalist party (the *"Lliga Regionalista"*), which brought together intellectuals, economic elites and the middle class. The emergence of these new parties can hardly be understood without taking into account the deep discredit that the loss of the colonies brought to the political system. And, more importantly for the aims of this book, the discredit of liberal institutions would bring direct consequences to the pre-eminence of traditional elites.

The chapter is divided into three parts. The first part will analyse the relation between the Disaster and the press. The behaviour of newspapers during the Spanish–American War resulted in public controversies where the crisis of national identity became entwined with a debate on the changes that journalism was undergoing at the time. The outcome was a prolific debate about the ideal relationship between journalists and the political system. The second part will focus on the Godós' response to the loss of empire. In the aftermath of the war a new political context emerged in Catalonia, and a substantial number of elites sought to redefine their relation with central government. This implied the political realignment of many of *La Vanguardia*'s readers, and the Godó family saw this situation aggravated by a series of internal circumstances. Hence, a new family generation arrived on the scene and faced the challenge of adapting to this incipient context of mass politics in Catalonia. The third and last part will examine the proposals the Godó family advanced through *La Vanguardia* for renewing the Restoration. These proposals will be put in contrast with those of the Gasset family, a press dynasty from Madrid, also affiliated with liberal parties, that controlled that city's *El Imparcial*. The two cases will provide a comparative perspective about the role newspaper editors played in the attempts to regenerate liberal politics.

The "Disaster" and the press

In the aftermath of the Spanish–American War (1898), the press went from supporting the patriotic discourse to searching for those responsible for the defeat. First and foremost, Sagasta and the Liberal government were blamed for the war and the humiliation the peace Treaty of Paris represented.[8] The same critique was soon extended to the whole political class and to the army.[9] Spain had not only lost its centuries-long presence in the Antilles and in South-East Asia, but it did so after an embarrassing defeat. As a result the country fell into an atmosphere of widespread pessimism where liberal elites were held responsible. Thus, while the war had been successful in uniting Spaniards against a common enemy, now its outcome was intensely felt in public debates.

Yet far from being a singularity, Spain's intellectual climate was evocative of the insecurity that pervaded European culture at the time. In contrast to the mid-19th-century confidence in progress through reason and material development, the *fin-de-siècle* was a period suffused with moral decay.[10] This pessimism was related to a conjunction of historical events, like the consequences of economic development (growth of cities, problems of alcoholism, prostitution, criminality); and a series of new controversies that raised tensions in society (like the clash between capital and labour, the rise of nationalism, and religious controversies). The new figure of the intellectual would be decisive in pervading everyday politics with this language of pessimism and decay. Hence, medical and biological terminology became part of the vocabulary that intellectuals contributed to popularise in the discourse of the nation.[11]

If pessimism was a typical feature of fin-de-siècle Europe, a series of elements further aggravated the intensity of this feeling in the Mediterranean region. The countries of this area experienced a series of setbacks in their colonial ambitions; namely: France's crisis in Fashoda (1898); Italy's defeat in Adwa (1896); the British 'ultimatum' to Portugal (1890); and Spain's loss of empire (1898). Uncertainty about their future as colonial powers became common to all these countries at a time when international relations were interpreted through the lens of Social Darwinism. Even in France, where the economic situation at the turn of the century was in a favourable condition, an atmosphere of doom pervaded. Contemporaries would often see in this situation the decadence of the Latin race.[12]

Though moral decay was a widespread feeling in the Mediterranean, national peculiarities nevertheless remained important. Besides the chronological coincidence, colonial setbacks were experienced differently in each country. In Italy, the consequence of the defeat in Adowa (1896) was the immediate resignation of Prime Minister Francesco Crispi. In Portugal the British Ultimatum (1890) had longer-term consequences in domestic politics, and became one of the factors that contributed to the discredit of the monarchy and to its toppling in 1910.[13] In the case of Spain, the Restoration survived the "Disaster" of 1898, but a new political climate resulted from it. The most important feature of this new scenario was the discredit of liberal elites and the intense criticism of the method that privileged their position: *caciquismo*.

Indeed, Spain fell into a profound process of national introspection where electoral corruption was blamed for all the nation's ills, and especially for alienating ordinary people from the political system. In an expression that gained currency, Spain was described as a body that had "lost its pulse": while liberal elites manipulated public office for their own benefit, the majority of the country remained passive. Although this type of criticism against the *caciquismo* of liberal elites was not new, the Disaster of 1898 brought it to the fore in the public debate.[14] The work of different intellectuals, like Joaquín Costa, decisively contributed to spreading this criticism. According to Costa, Spain's problem was not a parliamentary regime where corruption was widespread, but rather that corruption made up the whole political system, from which a small "oligarchy" benefited. In his view, if the denouncing of fraudulent practices had had little effect until then it was because rather than being a peculiarity, *caciquismo* constituted *the* structural feature of the political system.[15]

Costa is arguably the most quoted intellectual of *regeneracionismo*, especially in the study of *caciquismo*, and his analyses have exerted a strong influence on modern historians. However, the references Costa made to the press when studying *caciquismo* have largely gone unnoticed. In fact, of the large number of testimonies he gathered to write his work, several of them held the newspapers responsible for the persistence of fraudulent elections. The common view among these contemporaries was the impression that newspapers were misguiding the public during the Spanish–American War. Instead of alerting readers to the risks of fighting against the United States, the newspapers took advantage of the situation by fostering jingoism and selling more copies. If this behaviour of the press was regarded as a lack of honesty, the same contemporaries shared the belief that the problem stemmed from the tight links that existed between journalists and liberal elites. In their eagerness to reap the benefits of power – in the form of job recommendations, political positions and other material rewards – journalists had abandoned their neutrality and put themselves at the service of liberal politicians.[16] In so doing, journalists were contributing to sustaining the fraudulent nature of the political system and to widening the gap between the real and the legal country.[17]

The above-noted testimonies reaffirmed Costa's conviction that as well as liberal elites, another oligarchy existed: the *"oligarquía periodística"* ("press oligarchy"). This was the expression he coined to refer to a handful of influential journalists who were subject to the commands of liberal politicians, and who were ultimately responsible for building opinion.[18] The subjugation of journalists by politicians was particularly troublesome in Costa's view, because in a largely rural and backward country like Spain (which he referred to as a "semi-African country"), the people's lack of education made the influence of newspapers all the more important – and therefore more dangerous, if their power was not used in a responsible manner. Thus, in the view of this intellectual, the influence of newspapers did not stem solely from their circulation, but also from the reader's incapacity to discern news content. The problem was that journalists did not use this influence to disclose *caciquismo* in public, but rather to back the fraudulent illusion of elections. The Restoration was an utter fantasy that journalists contributed to maintain in exchange for political payoffs. As a result of this lack of sincerity among journalists, Costa concluded that Spain's recovery would never be achieved if the renewal of the political elite was not coupled with a through renewal of the press.[19]

The comments of Costa and his contemporaries are of particular value because they touch upon one of the distinctive features of the press in southern Europe: its tight links with politics. Indeed, while the transition from a partisan press model towards a commercial and independent one was a common trend to all Western countries during the 19th and 20th centuries, the pace and intensity of this historical process differed considerably between geographic areas. From the perspective of comparative media studies, Daniel Hallin and Paolo Mancini have shown that the tight links between newspapers and parties was indeed a distinctive feature of the Mediterranean.[20] Thus, and in contrast to countries like England and the United States, where the autonomy of journalists was established as an ethical code, in countries like Italy or Spain the professionalisation of journalism took longer. Yet far from being a deviance from the alleged mission that the press is supposed to play in modern democracy, these differences between countries stemmed from alternative patterns of historical development. These patterns resulted from a combination of structural features (economic development, urbanisation and education levels) with the shaping of different journalistic cultures. In contrast to countries like England and the United States, where autonomous and impartial reporting was expected of journalists, in Mediterranean ones comment and analysis of news remained an important feature of journalism.[21]

The Disaster of 1898 represents, in this respect, a valuable opportunity for the aims of this book to integrate media studies and historical analysis. The key role played by the press in popularising the war increased awareness among contemporaries about the power of the media. This awareness resulted in a rich controversy that sheds light on how the journalistic culture was being redefined, and how the case of other countries was often taken into account in this process. Indeed, Costa demonstrated his awareness about the existence of different journalist practices in other countries when he contrasted what he saw as the irresponsible behaviour of the Spanish press with England, where in his view newspapers acted according to the "general interest".[22] Moreover, the work of Costa is an illustrative example of how the redefinition of journalistic culture was entangled with the crisis of liberal politics: while contemporaries saw the new commercial press as a pernicious influence for society, at the same time they saw it as a potentially powerful agent of national recovery if it was transformed appropriately.

Furthermore, besides Costa other contemporaries devoted their attention to examining the changes in the press and how they affected society. One of them was Ramiro de Maeztu (1874–1936), one of the writers of the "*Generación del 98*".[23] Maeztu harshly criticised the press for its obsession with apportioning blame for the Disaster without assuming its own responsibility for the defeat. In response to this, Maeztu dedicated various articles to studying the changing relations between the press and politics.[24] In his view the introduction of the "factory system" – understood as the transition from a partisan model towards a commercial one – led newspapers to abandon one of their traditional duties: the duty of orienting opinion. [25]

Hence, Maeztu considered that the emphasis that newspapers now placed on providing information (which he referred to as "*menchetismo*", in reference to the first news agency established in the country) was not enough. In his view, the main limitations of the new informative press was the lack of effort it put into commenting on and balancing news; this being a limitation that the traditional partisan press supposedly did not have.[26] For Maeztu, journalists should not limit themselves to providing "facts", but also had to ponder them for their readers. In his opinion this had been the main reason for the loss of the colonies. The people had forgotten their civic duties as a result of the pernicious influence of newspapers, which accustomed them to what he called "*gobierno por la prensa*" ("government by the press"). Therefore, Maeztu concluded that:

> "To my eyes the worst crime of the press has not consisted in judging the nation as being favour to war, but has rather been *its default in fulfilling any of its duties, and especially the duty of information*. (...) where are those meticulous reports, impartial, always fair, with which the press in other countries illustrates opinion in regards to what concerns the national life?"[27]

Another intellectual who made similar observations on the changes in the press, although from Barcelona's point of view, was the journalist Teodor Baró Sureda (1843–1916). Baró was the director of *La Crónica de Cataluña* (the organ of the Liberal Party in Barcelona) and one of the most prominent journalists in this city. In contrast to the opinion of Maeztu, who considered that the new commercial press contributed to diminishing the civic culture of Spaniards,

Baró believed that commercial newspapers were the living image of the society for which they were printed. As Baró noted:

> "Everyone complains about the press, but nobody dares to turn it down [;] to the point that the press has been turned into an industry, based on profits, and which consists in publishing anything that it is easily sold in the market of curiosity and of passions, exciting them and falsifying things. Such transformation reveals that our society still leaves a great deal to be desired."[28]

Baró thus considered that in contrast to the partisan press, which had an ideal based on opinion formation, the profit-orientation of the new commercial press placed journalists at the service of their readers, whatever their taste. As a result of this change in the *raison d'être* of journalists, the press content was transformed. Journalists now focused on delivering the shallow and sensationalist news that the public was eager to read. In this regard, Baró's opinion was probably influenced by his former role as director of the *Crónica de Cataluña*, a partisan newspaper in which he defended the political function of journalism. Still, what makes the opinions of this man all the more valuable is that his comments on the commercial press were not limited to journalism but evoked the broader transformation of society. His views reflected on the rise of the new mass society, a phenomenon that was particularly acute in the city where he lived, Barcelona.

Indeed, by the time Baró examined the changes in the press Barcelona was experiencing radical transformations. The industrial tradition of the city had intensified at the turn of the new century. Attracted by the expansion of the manufacturing industry and the crisis in agriculture, regular flows of immigrants from rural Catalonia had arrived in Barcelona. Additionally, in 1897 a series of neighbouring towns were attached to Barcelona and multiplied its number of inhabitants. From 334,400 people in 1897, the population grew to 533,000 in 1900; to 587,000 in 1910; and to 710,000 in 1920. Thus the population had more than doubled between 1897 and 1920.[29] This demographic growth fostered the redefinition of the urban space. While the well-off people moved to the new avenues of *Passeig de Gràcia* and *Rambla Catalunya*, the old part of the city and the new towns attached to Barcelona in 1897 (like Gràcia and Poblenou) became the dwelling places of a growing working class. This redefinition of urban space also had an impact on the city's cultural life: *El Paralelo* emerged as the new leisure area of popular culture, while *La Rambla* lost its reputation as an affluent avenue.

The developments of new journalistic practices, like yellow journalism, and the new commercial orientation contributed to give new visibility to old urban problems, like prostitution, begging and alcoholism.[30] The press thus acted as an active agent in defining the conditions of public debate. Baró's observations reveal a negative perception about these transformations of the press, especially in the case of the commercial newspapers. The loss of the colonies provided him with the opportunity to accuse commercial newspapers of fuelling the lower passions of the people and of having a negative impact on public morality. Still, Baró absolved journalists for their new situation. After all, many of them were no longer at the service of a political community, as had traditionally been the case of the partisan press; but were now at the service of the public. In their new function, journalists were but mere servants of the "low tastes" of the masses.[31]

If the Spanish–American War increased the contemporary awareness about changes in journalism and how they affected society, the war also had a direct impact for the future of many newspapers. Their decisive contribution to spreading patriotic fervour during the war (see Chapter 3) contributed to their discredit in its aftermath. Most of newspapers suffered a loss of readers that led contemporaries and journalists alike to talk of a "crisis of public confidence". This crisis became particularly acute in Spain's capital, to the point that referring to the "crisis of Madrid's press" ("*crisis de la prensa madrileña*") became commonplace among journalists at the time.[32] As the director of *La Correspondencia de España* wrote, the "lack of public confidence" in the press was still felt intensely in Madrid as late as 1906:

> "The general opinion is completely hostile to the Press and the mistrust towards it is greater than towards any other social class. [The people] read newspapers for the need of knowing what is going on in the world, but does no longer read them in blind faith, as it was customarily. The moment has reached an end when readers "thought as their newspaper do", and this moment has been replaced by another one where readers disdain the opinion of the newspaper, or at least hold mistrust towards it, believing that their opinion is selfish or obeys to private interests. And this, no matter how sad is, is the sad truth. (...)."[33]

The situation described above reveals that the popularity the press reached during the Spanish–American War was not free from constraints. The bitter outcome became a lesson for many readers to differentiate between "printed" and "public opinion". Moreover, the above-quoted testimony challenges the view that some elites (like Joaquín Costa, Maeztu and Baró) had of readers as being vulnerable to the manipulation of editors. Indeed, the crisis of Madrid's press provides empirical evidence that communication was not a top-down process, where the people were passive consumers, but shows that readers possessed the capacity to condition the newspapers' content through their autonomy to buy one newspaper over another. The historical context certainly contributed to these change in readers' habits (e.g. the widespread feeling of moral decline resulting from losing the colonies) and to the consequences that resulted from it. Different newspapers, like *El Nacional*, *El Correo*, *El Globo*, *El Tiempo*, *La Publicidad*, *Los Debates* and *El Resumen*, were forced to close due to the fall in readers, while some other turned into *"diarios sapo"* – this being the Spanish expression used to refer to those newspapers whose financial instability led them to an erratic existence: they were published one day, only to suddenly disappear the next.[34]

The majority of the examples given above correspond to partisan newspapers. The lower number of sales they usually had (which stemmed from having an audience limited to the members of a political community) made them more vulnerable to the loss of readers. Additionally, their political orientation hindered the attempts to adopt a profit orientation based on sales revenues (even if exceptions existed). Commercial papers, in contrast, seemed to cope with the crisis better than their counterparts, even if their sales also fell considerably (by approximately one third of the total).[35] This was the case, for instance, of *El Liberal*, *La Correspondencia de España* and *El Heraldo de Madrid*, and also of *El Imparcial*, by then the top-selling newspaper in the country.[36]

La Vanguardia and the regenerationist movement

How did the press in other parts of the country experience the loss of empire? And more importantly, how was the Godó family affected by the widespread criticism of the *caciquismo* of liberal elites, and how did those elites respond in the face of it?

The Godó family confronted the Disaster of 1898 from a critical position. During the war the family's most visible members had passed away. Bartolomé Godó died in 1895 following a long disease that had confined him to his bed for three years, while his brother Carlos died in 1897 in the country house he owned in the coastal town of Teià, named *"Manso Dalmau"*. The deaths of the two brothers were recorded, as was customary at the time, in obituaries published in the press. In many of these homages the founding of *La Vanguardia* and the close links with Igualada became two recurrent elements for which the Godó brothers were remembered. Appealing to this tradition would be central to the second generation of this family, especially when the need came for them to legitimise their position in public.[37]

In the shorter term, however, the family faced more pressing needs. To start with, the negative impact the loss of the colonies had for the jute sack business. *La Vanguardia* had insistently campaigned in the past on the dangers of losing the protected market of the colonies, and these fears confirmed once the war ended. As early as July 1898 numerous factories closed and many jobs were lost (an estimated 4,000 in Barcelona alone). The Godós' factory was among those that closed down.[38] The lack of private correspondence makes it very difficult to reconstruct these events, yet there is still evidence that the closing of the factory was directly linked to the loss of Cuba and Puerto Rico. The man who made the decision to do so was Ramón Godó Lallana (Bilbao, 11/05/1864 - Barcelona, 20/09/1931). He was the only male son of Carlos and he had inherited the family textile business. The reasons he closed the factory were simple: the loss of the colonies meant the end of the tariffs protecting Spanish exports. In the face of this new situation the business was unable to compete with the new major actor in the global jute trade: the city of Calcutta (India).[39]

The case of the Godó family thus sheds light on the economic consequences of the Disaster. Between 1897 and 1898 the colonies went from representing the 30% of the total Spanish exports to only 8.3%.[40] But contrary to what these figures might suggest at first sight, the colonial loss did not result in an economic catastrophe. Economic historians have provided wide evidence that the Spanish economy overcame the end of the empire. In some aspects, it even acted as a stimulus that contributed to the economic integration of this country to European standards.[41] The Godó family were an example of those elites who managed to overcome the initial downturn. Ramón Godó started replacing the manufacturing of jute bags with the manufacturing of other fabrics made of jute, like cloth, carpets, and ropes. The lack of historical sources makes explaining this business re-orientation difficult, but, if we are to trust what little information is available, Godó seemed to have succeeded in this attempt. Hence, in 1900 – that is to say, only two years after the war – his new activity employed 1,800 workers.[42]

Besides the business in the jute industry, the deaths of both the Godó brothers also left *La Vanguardia* without an owner. The family's response to this situation was slightly different: on this occasion Carlos Godó's widow, Antonia Lallana (1836–1924), became the new owner of the newspaper. The case of Antonia Lallana was a very singular scenario: in the overwhelmingly male world of journalism, the top-selling newspaper in Barcelona was now in the hands of a woman. Even though this was a short-lived affair (her son Ramón took command of *La Vanguardia* in 1899)[43] the case of Antonia sheds light on the inner functioning of this newspaper. As Carlos' widow, she signed an agreement with the current editor (Modesto Sánchez Ortiz) in which they established the conditions under which the newspaper would operate. This contract – one of the very few documents that has survived from *La Vanguardia*'s historical archive – granted ample attributions to Sánchez Ortiz and rewarded him with a generous salary of 625 *pesetas*, plus 25% of the net profits.[44] These favourable conditions – especially if compared to the average monthly salary of journalists in Barcelona, which oscillated between 40 and 100 *pesetas* – were aimed at securing the services of the editor who had designed the successful reform plans of 1888.[45] Still, and despite the wide powers

conceded to the editor, Antonia Lallana retained for herself one single responsibility that was of paramount importance: the capacity to dictate *La
Vanguardia*'s political orientation.[46]

Indeed, the Godó family were never a dynasty of journalists *strictu sensu*.
None of their members ever signed a single article in the newspaper they
owned. The family saw journalism not as a vocation, but rather as an instrument to promote their private interests. The status of ownership is what
ultimately granted them the power to determine the editorial line. Or to put
it in other words, their influence as *political actors* stemmed from their capacity
to use the editorial line of *La Vanguardia* according to their own interests; and
this was a valuable source of public influence, since their newspaper was the
top-selling one in Barcelona.

Table 4.1. *Approximate circulation of Barcelona's main newspapers, 1898–1913*

	1898	1905	1913
La Vanguardia	14,000	18,000	58,000
Diario de Barcelona	9,000	7,000	——
El Noticiero Universal	8,000	10,000	——
Las Noticias	5,000	11,000	47,000
La Publicidad	5,000	7,000	25,000
El Correo Catalán	3,000	6,000	——

Source: María Carmen García Nieto "La Prensa diaria de Barcelona de 1895 a 1910", Barcelona,
Universitat de Barcelona, 1956 [thesis manuscript], p. 89; Francesc Espinet i Joan Manuel
Tresserras, *La gènesi de la societat de masses a Catalunya, 1888–1939,* Bellaterra, UAB, p. 77.

Indeed, and as Table 4.1 shows, the first decade of the 20th century was the
moment when *La Vanguardia* consolidated as the principal newspaper in
Barcelona. In contrast to the 1,400 copies this newspaper sold when it was first
established in 1881, it had reached a circulation of close to 20,000 copies by
1905. This represented a considerable progress, even if the sales figures of the
newspaper were still very modest – particularly if compared with other cities
in Europe. In the case of France, for instance, both *Le Petit Parisien* (1876) and
Le Matin (1883) were selling well above half a million copies by the 1890s;
while Paris' top-selling *Le Petit Journal* had passed the million copies mark by
the same date. In England, too, figures were also far higher than in Barcelona.
The London *Daily Mail*, for instance, sold an average of 700,000 copies in
1900.[47] The explanation for this huge gap between the press in Barcelona and
the above-mentioned European cities points to, once again, Spain's low development in terms of urbanisation, industrialisation and literacy levels. Still, the
contrast is also dependent on the subject of comparison. The case of Barcelona

appears to be less modest if compared with the case of Italy, where in 1900 "only a handful of newspapers sold more than 50,000 copies a day", as David Forgacs has observed.[48]

Table 4.1 also reveals that contrary to the case of Madrid, in Barcelona the press did not seem to suffer a "crisis of confidence". With the sole exception of the *Diario de Barcelona* (paradoxically, the newspaper that took the biggest stand against the war) the rest of the newspapers did not suffer a loss in readers. Their total number did not suffer significant changes either: the city had a total of 22 newspapers in 1898, and their number stood at 23 in 1899 and 24 in 1900.[49] What, then, explains the striking difference between Barcelona and Madrid? Answering this question is not easy: it has not been possible to find any clues about this in the writing of contemporaries. The scholarly literature on the topic does not make any references to this either. Still, a possible explanation for this contrast between the two cities is that press consumption patterns remained highly localised. For the most part, newspapers had a local – and at best, a regional – circulation. Only a handful of newspapers from Madrid had a national distribution.[50] This lack of integration of the press market is one hypothesis that can account for the different evolution of the press in both cities.

In fact, the persistence of local and regional patterns was something that also became present in the political consequences of the Disaster. Despite being lived as a national trauma, the loss of the colonies carried important nuances in each region. One of them was the strengthening of regional identities that pushed for the redefinition of the Spanish nation. In the case of Catalonia, this became clear in the attempt of elites to reassess their relationship with the political system. Until that time the presence of Catalan elites in the leadership of liberal parties had been, for the most part, very limited. Between 1814 and 1899, only three Spanish prime ministers came from this region, even though 115 different governments existed during this period. Similarly, there were only 22 Catalan ministers during the same time span (out of a total of 850). Therefore, the number of ministers from this region only accounted for 2% of the total during the period 1814–1899.[51]

So why was there so little involvement of the elites from the country's most industrialised region? Apart from the traditional weakness of liberal parties in Catalonia, the main reason is that Catalan elites relied on a series of mechanisms, other than the holding of public office, to secure their interests in central government and in the colonies.[52] Therefore, rather than opposing the liberal state, Catalan economic elites supported – and conditioned it – through alternative channels of influence. However, the Disaster of 1898 led a substantial part of the Catalan elites to reassess these mechanisms. The loss of the precious colonial market provided evidence of the incapacity of the political system to defend the interests of Catalan manufacturers. In response to this, on the very same day that the peace treaty of the Spanish–American War was signed in Paris (10 December 1898) the main civic and economic entities in Barcelona addressed a memorandum to the Queen Regent.[53] The main purpose of this memorandum was to express the discontent of the Catalan elites with the political system and to present a radical plan of reforms. The first of these proposals was the complete re-organisation of the Spanish state, based on the concession of autonomy to the "historical regions". Once this reform was implemented, the memorandum proposed that "The Spanish state should only keep the attributions that require the protection and promotion of the interests that are truly common to all the regions in Spain, like international relations, repression of crimes, tariffs, the navy, communications, etc. etc."[54] The second reform, of equal importance to the first one, was the reform of the universal suffrage, based on the introduction of corporate forms of representation.

The two demands expressed in the memorandum of Catalan civic entities were a direct challenge to the way the liberal state had been organised in Spain since the 1830s. Likewise, they demonstrated the discredit of liberal institutions in Europe. Hence, the arguments used in the memorandum were inspired by modern sociology and in the historicist school of law, two types of argument that were much in vogue on the Continent at the time. The memorandum evoked the medieval past as a glorious age that should be taken as a source of inspiration to reform liberal politics. In contrast to the customary uniformist model of Castile, the Crown of Aragon was presented as a historical example that recognised regional peculiarities, and therefore appeared as a suitable reference to re-organise the state-model according to a new understanding of the nation. The same historical reference applied to political representation: the corporate bodies of the medieval tradition should be used as the model to re-structure parliamentary representation according to corporate patterns.[55]

The proposal of Catalan elites thus constituted an open challenge to the liberal foundations of the state. In fact, the memorandum openly blamed "modern" influences, like the French revolution and its vindication of individual rights, as the main cause of Spain's ills. In the view of the entities that signed the memorandum there were two main conclusions that should be drawn from the current crisis: first was the failure of the liberal principles imported from France, first included in the constitution of 1812 (above all, the rights of the individual); and, secondly, the failure of "the policies the Catholic Kings started", which these entities saw as having inspired the centralised state-model of the liberals since the 1830s.[56]

The reform proposals reveal the cultural autonomy of Catalan elites. For the intellectuals in this region, the "Disaster" intensified the taking of Paris as the main point of reference, rather than Spain's capital. This manifested in many ways, like the influence French intellectuals like Ernest Renan and Hyppolite

Taine had in the Catalan historicist school. The same happened with the case of the Belgian Adolphe Prins (1845–1919), whose work on *La démocratie et le régime parlementaire* (1884) exerted great influence on the corporativist conception Catalan elites had of political representation.[57] This circulation of ideas was extended to the artistic world, and was evident in the great development *"Modernisme"* had in Barcelona; this being an artistic trend directly influenced by the French art nouveau. Moreover, the idea of "modernity" became central in the way a substantial part of Catalan elites saw the Disaster of 1898. They saw their region as the most dynamic in the country, and therefore as the most suitable to lead the national recovery. Together with Narcís Verdaguer, one of the central intellectuals of this interpretation was Joan Maragall. For him, Spain's defeat was the sign of Castille's decadence, and he saw it as a call for Catalonia to lead the task of national regeneration. As Maragall noted:

> "Everything is dying and Castile has concluded its mission. The new civilization is industrious, and Castile is not industrous; the modern spirit is analytic, and Castile is not analytic; material progress lead to cosmopolitanism, and Castile, placed in the middle of African nature, without seeing the sea, is refractory to European cosmopolitanism. (...) Castile has concluded its directive mission and has to pass over its ceptre. The Catalanist feeling, in the current agitated situation, is but the instinct in favour of this change; of this renewing. Supporting it means to give life to Spain, to rebuild a new Spain for the new century; opposing to it, directly or indirectly, implies boostening the total descomposition of the Spanish nation and to let the rejuvenation to be made outside the death Spain."[58]

For Maragall the moment had come for Castile to pass the leadership to Catalonia, with a clear objective in mind: to rejuvenate Spain. Maragall's understanding of the fin-de-siècle crisis is of particular importance, because the same cosmovision would be applied to politics, principally through the founding of the *"Lliga Regionalista"* (1901). This was to become the main party of Catalan nationalism in the Restoration, and would be one of the new political movements that fought doggedly against the political hegemony of the Godó family in Igualada. For the members of this party, regional identity was understood first and foremost as a political project aimed at modernising Spain.[59] As Piedmont had in the Italian *Risorgimento*, and Prussia in the unification of the German states, the Lliga saw Catalonia as the region that should lead the country's renovation. Political autonomy and corporate representation were the two measures Catalan nationalists advocated to put an end to the inefficiency of liberal politics (epitomised in the loss of the colonies and the widespread presence of clientelism) and to begin the "moral" conquest of Spain.

At this point we may wonder: how did the Godó family react to the changes that were taking place in the regional context? The proposals of the Catalan nationalists were a direct threat to another sector of Catalan elite who, like the Godó family, were closely involved in liberal politics and who took advantage of this political system. Worse still, a growing number of readers and group interests that *La Vanguardia* had represented in the past (like the *Fomento del Trabajo Nacional*) now started to embrace the proposals of Catalan nationalism. How did the family react to this new scenario that threatened their political hegemony, and also implied the political realignment of a part of *La Vanguardia*'s readership? To what extent was the response of this family singular, when compared with the response of liberal editors in Madrid?

Press barons and the nation: Ramón Godó (*La Vanguardia*) and Rafael Gasset (*El Imparcial*) from a comparative perspective

The proposal of reforms that the Catalan elites presented to the Queen Regent in 1898 (namely, the decentralisation of the Spanish state and the reform of the universal suffrage based on corporate representation) were two demands that eventually became the two ideological pillars of Catalan-conservative nationalists of the "*Lliga Regionalista*" (1901). The conjunction of economic elites and political Catalanism in this new party, however, was not immediate. This conjunction only started forming in 1899, following the failed attempt of economic elites to participate in the regeneration project of a General named Camilo García Polavieja.[60] This General made the first attempt at cooperation between Catalan nationalists and other Regenerationist projects from other parts of Spain. The failure of this cooperation would have important consequences – namely, the growth of Catalan nationalism and its organisation under a new party structure (the *Lliga Regionalista*, created in 1901).

General Polavieja was one of the few Generals to have escaped the discredit of the Disaster. He was a man of solid Catholic convictions, monarchic and conservative, who had been the Captain General of Cuba (1889–1890) and the Philippines (1896–1897). His military victories during war had provided him with great prestige. This popularity was evident even before the war ended, when Polavieja was received by a large crowd in Barcelona (of around 40,000 people) as part of a public welcome that the *Fomento del Trabajo Nacional* had sponsored. In fact, during the war General Polavieja established close connections with Catalan economic elites (and particularly with the *Fomento*) by paying attention to their demands for protectionism. As a result of these previous contacts, when Polavieja started preparing his entry into politics in the aftermath of the war, he requested the support of Catalan economic elites through the president of the *Fomento* (Joan Sallarès). The support for this proposal did not take long to arrive, especially after Polavieja expressed his commitment to the demands for decentralisation.

Indeed, on 1 September 1898 Polavieja made public his plan of "national reconstruction". This consisted in a reform plan aspiring to modify the traditional rotation in power between Liberals and Conservatives by creating a third party. Polavieja openly condemned liberal parties and *caciquismo* as the main reasons behind the loss of the empire. He claimed to embody a new way of doing politics, based on a series of measures to foster economic development and in a moderate proposal of administrative decentralisation.[61] Through these proposals Polavieja wished to attract the *"masas neutras"* ("neutral masses"), an expression that gained currency in the language of *regeneracionismo* to refer to the segments of society that remained alienated from the political system.

La Vanguardia positioned itself for the first time in relation to the regenerationist plan of General Polavieja on 13 September 1898, the day after it had published his manifesto (as the majority of the press did), and as the peace negotiations were still on-going. The newspaper of the Godó family applauded General Polavieja for his decision to enter politics, and welcomed the attention paid to the demands from the periphery in favour of decentralisation.[62] However, *La Vanguardia* considered the manifesto to be excessively prudent, both in its tone and in the measures it proposed. Above all, the newspaper accused Polavieja of being too cautious in his criticism of the fraudulent nature of liberal politics. As it put it:

> "These vices are the source of the pain we are suffering. Corruption in the administration and in justice, the empire of caciquismo at a local, provincial and national level sterilizes all the energies that grow in there, and *nobody shall ever count on the support of opinion* if he does not fight with resolution all these sources through explicit and concrete measures (...)."[63]

As the above-quoted paragraph shows, *La Vanguardia* adopted the language of regeneration and the criticism of corruption. The very same method that the Godó family had used to secure their own position was paradoxically criticised in their own newspaper. If the family could justify this criticism it was thanks to the division they had established between the press and politics. Editorial independence had been decisive in this strategy to separate the family's two spheres of influence. Regardless of the persistent manipulation of elections that the family had perpetrated in Igualada, Ramón Godó could afford to criticise these methods because *La Vanguardia* was no longer a partisan newspaper. The above-quoted paragraph is revealing of how this freedom of criteria made it possible to exert pressure on politicians: *La*

Vanguardia argued that Polavieja would only obtain the support of "opinion" if he condemned corruption. This reveals that editors sought to advance their own agenda by presenting it as a demand coming from the public opinion.

The cold reception *La Vanguardia* gave to Polavieja is particularly telling, especially if we take into account that this opinion was expressed when the political movement was just taking its first steps (the manifesto had only been published a day earlier). Moreover, the Godó family held close personal ties with General Polavieja. This became clear during the Spanish–American War, when before departing to the Philippines as Captain General, Polavieja had lunched with Ramón Godó and his father Carlos. The following day, the Godó family had accompanied Polavieja's wife to the monastery of Monserrat (close to Igualada) to pray for the General's safe return.[64]

This close acquaintance with General Polavieja, however, was insufficient to convince Ramón Godó to put *La Vanguardia* at his service. The main reason for this is that Polavieja wished to regenerate the country by replacing liberal parties. This was contrary to Ramón Godó's position: as *La Vanguardia* would advocate on repeated occasions, traditional parties (Conservative and Liberal) should be the ones to lead the reform of the Restoration.[65] Instead of replacing them with new ones, as Polavieja wished, *La Vanguardia* argued in favour of deeply renewing liberal parties; especially in their customary use of *caciquismo*.[66] The proposal of *La Vanguardia* to overcome the Disaster of 1898 was thus clearly defined: a need to promote a radical transformation of liberal parties (particularly regarding the widespread use of fraudulent methods), yet opposition to any plan of regeneration that attempted to sweep those parties away.

Moreover, like other contemporaries, such as Costa, Maeztu and Baró, *La Vanguardia* also argued that the reform of the political system should go hand in hand with the reform of the press. During the war the editor of this newspaper (Sánchez Ortiz) had already criticised the Spanish press for its emphasis on fostering a jingoistic discourse, while forgetting "national interests".[67] Behind this criticism was Sánchez's personal conviction that newspapers were central to public affairs because they exerted a strong influence on politicians. For Sánchez, the loss of the colonies culminated a process of decadence that was neither the sole responsibility of the government nor of a single party. Rather, it was the responsibility of what he called "*la España directiva*". With this expression Sánchez Ortiz referred to the ruling class, in which he included the press as an integral part.[68]

In this respect, the argument the director of *La Vanguardia* used to stress the importance of newspapers in the national regeneration was similar to the testimonies contained in Joaquín Costa's work. That is, contrary to liberal politicians, who were alienated from society due to their use of *caciquismo*, he considered that newspapers had a strong influence on ordinary people. The capacity to connect the political system with society is what made the press, in Sánchez's eyes, the most important political actor in the task of national regeneration.[69] Yet to be in the position to lead this mission, journalists should first assume their own culpability in the Disaster (above all, in their eagerness to increase sales), and adopt a professional code of conduct. Thus, Sánchez made a strong plea in favour of the professionalisation of journalism. This implied putting an end to the journalists' most common pitfalls: first, the perception of journalism as a pathway into public office; second, viewing sales as the only guiding principle. These two common mistakes should be replaced by two new professional ideals: "priesthood and magisterium" ("*sacerdocio y magisterio*"). That is to say, to make journalism an end in itself, rather than a route into politics; and to prioritise "truth" over profits. According to Sánchez, adhering to these professional codes would be the only way to avoid the errors of the Spanish–American War and to guide the liberal parties and society to a new age.

If the above-mentioned comments were the work of Sánchez Ortiz, the editorial position of *La Vanguardia* regarding Polavieja was dictated by Ramón Godó. Although Sánchez was the one who signed the editorials, in his position of proprietor Ramón Godó was the one who had the power to determine the newspaper's line. In this regard, what needs to be stressed about the way in which Godó positioned *La Vanguardia* in the face of Polavieja is that it differed from the attitude that Catalan economic elites adopted. If this newspaper became the distinguished organ of the "*Fomento del Trabajo Nacional*" during the War of Melilla (1893) and the Cuban War of Independence (1895), its position differed from this employer association after the Disaster took place. Thus, the *Fomento* and other economic entities rapidly supported the plans of Polavieja. This was not mere rhetoric, but rather a breakthrough in the attitude the Catalan elites traditionally adopted in relation to the political system. Thus, during the elections of March 1899, 14 of the total 44 deputies that were elected in Catalonia were members of the *Fomento* supporting Polavieja's candidacy (including the president of this entity, Joan Sallarès, and his predecessor in the post, Joan Saladrigas). This move represented the new interest of Catalan elites to actively participate in politics, and to do so through corporate action.

The attitude that Godó adopted in the face of this new political scenario, consisting in the support for the regeneration of national politics, but through the renewal of liberal parties, most surely obeyed his position as a member of the Liberal Party. Indeed, and as Chapter 5 will show in detail, Godó not only inherited the family business and the ownership of *La Vanguardia*, but also the political career of his father in the constituency of Igualada. These are important elements to understand the way he positioned his newspaper in the face of the new political scenario that was emerging in the country.

A look at Madrid, however, reveals that not all the liberal editors reacted equally to Godó. This can be seen through the case of Rafael Gasset Chinchilla (1866–1927), the owner of Madrid's newspaper *El Imparcial*. What makes the comparison between Godó and Gasset interesting is the many common points that existed between them but also their very different responses to the Disaster. Both of them descended from families that owned newspapers that were also affiliated with the Liberal Party of Sagasta. Likewise, both men were the owners of independent newspapers with a clear commercial orientation; and both inherited these newspapers shortly after the Disaster (Ramón Godó in 1899, at the age of 35; and Rafael Gasset in 1884, at the age of 23). A third similarity between the two men is that following the political careers of their respective fathers, both of them would be elected deputies in Congress; and they always did so for the same constituency, despite the fact that neither lived there.[70]

Yet regardless of these points in common, the fact is that the two liberal editors responded differently to the first regeneration attempts. In contrast to *La Vanguardia*, Gasset's *El Imparcial* did not hold the press responsible for the Disaster, but blamed liberal politicians exclusively. This became clear during the treaty negotiations in Paris. Despite the fact *El Imparcial* had been one of the newspapers that most actively promoted jingoism during the war, it opened its edition of 2 February 1898 with an article specifically addressed to Montero Ríos, who was in charge of the Spanish delegation in Paris. During the negotiations, Montero Ríos had blamed the press for the loss of the colonies. In response to this, *El Imparcial* argued that the complicity of the press to go to war had conformed to the false information that the government had provided. Consequently, when it came to establishing who was to blame for Spain's ruin, *El Imparcial* did not hesitate in pointing at "*los elementos directivos de la política*". With this expression *El Imparcial* referred to the ruling elites, but did not include the press among them. The understanding of newspapers in relation to politics thus appeared to be different to that of *La Vanguardia*: journalists did not belong to the political elites.[71]

In practice, however, Rafael Gasset was involved much more obviously in the first attempts of national regeneration than Godó. General Polavieja found in *El Imparcial* the most active supporter of his political ambitions. During the Spanish–American war Gasset criticised on several occasions the way the Liberal government had conducted the war (particularly the lack of military preparation). Disenchanted with liberal politics (in which he actively participated as deputy in Congress between 1891 and 1899) Gasset became one Polavieja's biggest supporters, encouraging him to make the jump into politics.[72] In fact, Gasset was the person who presented the manifesto of General Polavieja in Congress; and, before that, he had even participated in the writing of this document advocating for the creation of a third party.[73]

Gasset identified with the Regenerationist calls for modernising the country through economic development. To boost this programme, *El Imparcial* started to publish (in April 1899) a series of articles under the title *"Para la nueva política"* ("For the new policy"), where it stressed the need for building new infrastructures through public investment. As historian Juan Carlos Sánchez Illán has noted, this "new policy" became the new political strategy of Rafael Gasset, to which *El Imparcial* contributed on an almost daily basis.[74] Gasset's commitment to this plan of reform culminated in 1899, when his intercession became decisive to unite General Polavieja with the new leader of the Conservative Party, Francisco Silvela (who had also advocated for a Regenerationist plan). The result was the formation of a new government (on 4 March 1899) that combined the most conservative trend within the Regenerationist movements (General Polavieja) with the liberal politics represented by Francisco Silvela. For the first time in Spain, a new government seized power with an explicit political programme of national recovery. Polavieja would be appointed Minister of War, while the support of Catalan conservatives and economic elites became manifest with the appointment of Manuel Duran i Bas as Minister of Justice. Gasset was awarded for his contribution with the mayoral office of Madrid. Although he initially refused this offer, in April 1900 he joined the new government as Minister of Agriculture. His case reveals to what extent liberal editors not only promoted the war effort in 1898, but also sought to maintain their influence in this new scenario.

Summary

This chapter has demonstrated the growing mediatisation that Spanish politics was undergoing at the turn of the 19th century. Newspaper proprietors not only had influence over public opinion during the Spanish–American War, but also became decisive in the plans for the Regeneration that followed. In the new emphasis that growing voices put on the need to connect the political system with larger segments of society (the so-called *"masas neutras"*) the press appeared as the only medium capable of reaching large audiences. On some occasions newspaper editors were personally involved in this attempt to breach the gap between the real and the legal country, as the commitment of Rafael Gasset to the political project of General Polavieja illustrates. The efforts of this editor allowed Polavieja to obtain the support of one of the most influential newspapers in the country. This influence stemmed from the visibility that newspapers gave to the deeds of politicians, but also in their capacity to exert pressure during decision-making processes. In both types of influence, having *El Imparcial* on his side was particularly important for the interests of General Polavieja.

However, the aftermath of the Disaster also revealed that the action of newspapers was not free from constraints. The "crisis of Madrid's press" represents an event that clearly shows that the readers of newspapers were not a passive audience. As different contemporaries noted, the crisis of the press was, above all, a crisis of "public confidence". This crisis for newspapers in Madrid carried visible consequences: a large number of newspapers simply disappeared in the aftermath of the war; while many others suffered a considerable loss of sales. To a considerable degree, this crisis was the consequence of the very same success these newspapers had obtained during the war against the United States. These exceptional circumstances were obviously impossible to maintain in times of peace. But, still, as argued above, there are various sources that make it clear that many readers felt deeply disappointed with the attitude followed by their respective newspapers, thus providing evidence about the readers autonomy.

The Disaster also made contemporaries more aware about the power of the media in society. The opinions of intellectuals like Joaquín Costa and Ramiro de Maeztu, and of journalists like Teodoro Baró, reveal the impression that the transformations the press was undergoing had contributed to the country's decadence. By exploring the opinions of these contemporaries, this chapter has shown that the discredit of liberal politics and the re-definition of journalistic culture were deeply interwoven phenomena. The function of journalists in society was certainly not a new concern, but the defeat against the United States led contemporaries to see journalists as upholding a fraudulent system based on sham elections. The outcome was a myriad of proposals on the relations between journalists and politicians, on one hand; and on relations between journalists and society at large, on the other.

Indeed, the fin-de-siècle crisis revealed the consolidation of the new commercial press, to the detriment of the traditional partisan orientation of newspapers. The emphasis put on raw information to increase sales explains the success of commercial newspapers in the new mass society that was starting to emerge in the main European cities. Yet, paradoxically, the emphasis this commercial press placed on satisfying popular culture (and also on shaping it) was precisely what conservative men like Teodor Baró lamented. In this respect, the proposal of Catalan elites to reform universal suffrage and the criticisms of Baró of the content of commercial newspapers can be seen as two sides of the same coin, consisting in a negative perception of the "masses" and the need to confront them through new measures.

From a different perspective, Maeztu also despised the commercial press, but in his case he did not blame it on the masses. Rather, he considered that the changes brought to journalism by the factory system led newspapers to fail in their duties — such as the fostering of civic virtues. In their eagerness to provide abundant information, newspapers were abandoning their educative function in a largely rural country that, in the view of Maeztu, still had a great need of it. It must be noted, however, that despite being two contemporaries with such different views of society, Maeztu and Baró did share a subtle nostalgia towards the partisan press (which while it had certainly not disappeared was losing popularity by that time).

The consequences that stemmed from the growing influence of the press were also the concern of the director of *La Vanguardia*, Modesto Sánchez Ortiz. The incapacity of the press to accept its own responsibility for the military defeat, and the obsession of many newspapers with sales, were two elements that convinced him of the need to professionalise journalism. It should no longer be a pathway into public office, nor simply a business venture, but rather a self-sufficient occupation with a strong vocation of public service. Sánchez thus shared a common point with Joaquín Costa: both strongly criticised the behaviour of the press, but had some confidence in the contribution it could make in the task of national recovery.

The Disaster also brought important consequences in the field of politics. Even when liberal parties managed to overcome the situation (as the seizing of power by Sagasta in 1903 would demonstrate) the widespread pessimism also fostered political re-alignments. The case of the Catalan elites is particularly revealing in this respect. The reform plans that came from this region, consisting in the introduction of administrative autonomy and corporate representation, reveal to what extent the reconfiguration of the liberal state was regarded as a necessary pre-condition for Spain's recovery. In this regard, the positioning of *La Vanguardia* in relation to the new political scenario can hardly be explained without taking into account the figure of its new owner, Ramón Godó Lallana. Although his father before him had shown on many occasions his commitment to defending the economic interests of Catalan elites, particularly in the case of entities like *Fomento del Trabajo Nacional*, the distancing of *La Vanguardia* from Polavieja reveals that this newspaper did not always follow the direction of general opinion in Barcelona. Still, it also seems clear that it took care not to directly go against it. The position of this newspaper can be explained as the need to navigate between the private interests of the Godó family (linked to the Liberal Party of Sagasta) and the new political context (criticism of *caciquismo* and of liberal politics). While this reveals to what extent the editorial line was where the Godó family's power resided, putting too much emphasis on defending the family's private agenda could also have unexpected consequences. This is, precisely, what the following chapter will examine.

5

Public Image and the Mediatisation of Politics

"(...) as soon as Mr. Godó's carriage was seen coming, the bells in all the churches started ringing and all the people went to welcome him saying enthusiastically: 'Welcome to our deputy! God bless the father of the constituency! Congratulations and good health to our friend and protector of the humble! God bless Carlos Godó's son!'"[1]

By comparison to other Spanish press barons, like Luca de Tena (*ABC*), Nicolás María de Urgoiti (*El Sol*), the Brusi (*Diario de Barcelona*) and the Gasset family (*El Imparcial*), the case of Ramón Godó Lallana (1864–1931) has received surprisingly little historical attention. Books on the history of journalism often mention him as the man responsible for *La Vanguardia*'s evolution into one of Spain's main newspapers,[2] but the fact is that little is known about this man. *La Vanguardia*'s widespread image as an independent and commercial newspaper has contributed, to a considerable extent, to hiding the political career of this individual. The supposedly apolitical character of Godó would be the ultimate proof of *La Vanguardia*'s "modernity" (understood here as detachment from a partisan adscription), in contrast to other press editors who fell into the temptation of participating in politics.[3]

However, the fact is that like many other press editors at the time, Ramón Godó also held political responsibilities. During his youth he became an active member of the Liberal Party in Barcelona, and for many years represented this party in the Spanish Congress, in Madrid. But rather than being a personal vocation, his career in politics rather obeyed to a family tradition. Thus, Ramón did not only inherit from his father Carlos the ownership of *La Vanguardia* and the business in the jute industry, but also became the main responsible actor of maintaining the political stronghold the Godó family possessed in their hometown of Igualada. This local domain had allowed the family to reach national pre-eminence and to enjoy the benefits of power, and therefore it was not something that they could afford to relinquish.

The problem, however, is that when Ramón Godó replaced his father at the head of the family' political interests, the context in the country had completely changed. Spain had lost its colonies and liberal politics had fallen into deep discredit. To make things worse, in the aftermath of the Disaster some contemporaries started arguing that the crisis of the country was due, in reality, to the incapacity of the new commercial press to see beyond the private views of their proprietors.[4] This attitude, which arguably made newspapers unpredictable, was inherent to papers that were the property of liberal politicians – these were the cases, for instance, of *El Heraldo de Madrid* and *El Diario Universal*, belonging to José Canalejas and to the Count of Romanones, respectively; and of Rafael Gasset and *El Imparcial*.[5] There is evidence, in this regard, that immediately after his appointment as Minister in the Silvela–Polavieja government, in 1900, Gasset made great efforts to distinguish his entry into government from the path his newspaper would follow. This decision reveals that growing sectors of society started seeing the political affiliation of Gasset as being incompatible with a newspaper that had traditionally boasted of its political independence.[6]

The case of Rafael Gasset can thus be seen as revealing of a tension in value systems. Namely, that a certain number of readers of *El Imparcial* might see the political career of Gasset as being in conflict with the newspaper they read, especially because the identity of this newspaper was based on independence from party interference. This case highlights a change that was occurring in the public sphere, particularly from the perspective of public values. As Ivo Engels has explained, one of the main characteristics of the "long 19th century" was the establishing of sharper lines between the public and the private spheres.[7] Or to put it another way, certain practices that were regarded as being legitimate in pre-modern societies started to become problematic during the 18th and 19th centuries with the redefinition of public values. As Zygmunt Bauman and Bruno Latour have noted, one of the main characteristics of modern societies is their tendency to reduce ambiguities and to establish clear categories.[8]

From a more general perspective, historians rarely take into account the communicative nature of politics, and how changes in the media condition the nature of power, as John B. Thompson has noted.[9] In this regard, the combined study of changes in the press and in certain political behaviours, such as clientelism, can provide valuable insights about the tensions taking place between the private and the public spheres, and track the changes in the genesis of public values in modern societies. Indeed, recent research on corruption scandals has revealed that during the 19th century some places in Europe experienced changes in the perceptions of private uses of the "common good".[10] In this regard, it will be contended that since clientelism treats information as a privately-held resource, and one that is only exchanged in particularistic relationships, its disclosure in the public sphere has *the potential* of diminishing the reputation of the individuals involved.[11] This point is particularly interesting for the case of the notables, since they were a social group for whom "social esteem" was one of the pillars of their prominence as leaders of the local community, as Max Weber noted.[12]

By focusing on the case of Ramón Godó Lallana, the aim of this chapter is to analyse the reasons that led him to resign from active politics in 1906, as a result of the tensions stemming between his position of newspaper editor and that of liberal politician. In so doing, I attempt to explore how public perceptions of corruption in Restoration Spain were affected by the "Disaster" of 1898. This change was motivated, I will argue, by the emphasis the Regenerationist movement put on blaming corruption for the loss of the empire, and by the growing mobilisation that took place in Catalonia during the first decade of the 20th century. As noted before, this region was the first place where the monopoly of power by the Liberal and the Conservative party was broken in Spain. This had much to do with the emergence of two political movements (Catalanism and Republicanism) that turned the denouncing of clientelism into one of the central arguments of their political culture. This should allow further comparisons on the crisis of parliamentary politics with other European countries.

Additionally, the case of Ramón Godó will be used to study how elites transmitted power across generations. This topic should allow us to evaluate to what extent the strategies used by the first generation of the Godó family to reproduce their power were equally effective for the members of the second generation, and thus to examine how the notables reacted to the emergence of mass politics.

The generational renewal in the Godó family

Although Ramón Godó Lallana was born in Bilbao (in the Basque country), in 1864, and lived most of his life in Barcelona, he did not marry in either of these cities. Instead, he was married in Igualada, where his family had originated. His wedding was on 2 December 1893, to a local woman: Rosa Valls i Valls (1874–1922). The day after their marriage *La Vanguardia* congratulated the young couple (Ramón was 29 and Rosa 19 years old), who would go on to have numerous children in the years to come.[13] Among the celebrations that followed the wedding, there is one that is particularly revealing for the aims of this chapter. Namely, the reception that Ramón's father, Carlos Godó, gave to the members of the "*Comité Liberal Monárquico de Igualada*" to celebrate his son's marriage. This reception gathered the main members of the political network that had been contributing so decisively to the political pre-eminence the Godó family enjoyed in Igualada, by means of clientelistic practices. In fact, the Republican newspaper *El Igualadino* harshly criticised the wedding reception, likening it to the typical display of a feudal lord feeding his band of petty followers.[14]

Both the wedding and the reception were aimed at the same end, that is, the wish of connecting the second generation of the Godó family to Igualada. It was where the family had originated, and the city the brothers Carlos and Bartolomé had abandoned in the mid-19th century to search for a better living – first in the Basque Country and later on in Barcelona. But other members of the same family had remained in Igualada. This circumstance became decisive when Carlos and Bartolomé decided to run for public office at the Congress in the first years of the Restoration (1874–1923). By the turn of the century, now that Ramón Godó was making his first appearances in public life, it was time to start preparing the generational take over. In fact, family was the centrepiece in the politics of Restoration Spain. When it comes to defining the way politics operated in modern Spain, the historian Pedro Carasa has even suggested replacing the classic expression "political friends" with that of "political families". Carasa made this point after conducting a vast quantitative study on the origins of political elites in the region of Castile.[15] For the case of France, Alexandre Niess has also noted the importance of family connections and nepotism in the Third Republic (1870–1940).[16] By borrowing a concept used by medieval historians for the study of the family (the *"Sippe"*, understood as "tribe"), Niess has focused on the French department of Marne to explore "how family, matrimonial and patrimonial strategies within particular lines are explicitly constructed in order to keep up the pre-eminence of a particular social group within public affairs – including republican affairs". In this regard, what the French and the Spanish case had in common was the existence of a number of families that managed to stay afloat in politics for a long time.[17]

When Carlos Godó passed away in 1897 (four years after Ramón's wedding), the Godó family was obliged to adopt a transitional solution for the next elections. As a result of this, in the elections of 1898 the Liberal candidate for Igualada's constituency was Josep Balcells, "a rich businessman from this city [Barcelona], (...) who counts with great sympathies, not only within the Liberal party, but among all the business circles of our capital".[18] This would be the only occasion, between 1881 and 1916, when no member of the Godó family would lead the candidacy of the Liberal party in Igualada. Still, even in such an exceptional case, like the one created by Carlos' death, another member of the Godó family (Juan Godó Llucià) would be in charge of preparing the elections. Thus, Juan Godó would be responsible for introducing Balcells to the "Centro Liberal Monárquico" of Igualada, and to the leaders of the same party that came from Barcelona (Mr. Comas i Masferrer and Mr. Bosch). During this event, which took place in March 1898, frequent tributes were made to the late Carlos Godó, the "traditional" representative of Igualada's constituency. The elections finally went smoothly and Balcells was elected, thanks to the clientelistic practices of the Godó network and the low voter turnout (the war with the United States led the Government "controlling" – rigging – elections in a systematic way).

During the following year's elections, however, Ramón Godó took on the responsibility and became the official candidate in Igualada. The interval opened by Carlos Godó's death was thus rapidly put to an end when his son replaced him as the Liberal representative. The second generation of the Godó family, in the figure of Ramón, was ready to maintain the family's continuity in political affairs. It must be noted, in this regard, that Ramón followed the same strategy that his father and his uncle had traditionally used. Hence, the brothers Carlos and Bartolomé Godó (the two founders of *La Vanguardia*) had always followed the same electoral strategy: on the one hand, Carlos ran for the elections of deputy in Congress, while his brother Bartolomé, on the other hand, always ran for the elections of provincial deputy. This strategy provided valuable benefits. First, Bartolomé's position allowed him to intervene in the decisions that affected Igualada's constituency (particularly in the building of infrastructure, like roads), which in many situations depended at the time on Barcelona's Provincial Council. In parallel, the seat Carlos occupied in the Congress allowed him to extend the family's range of influence to Madrid, where economic policies and other types of infrastructure, such as the building of railway connections, were decided. This strategy of sibling cooperation allowed the family interests to be promoted more effectively in two different but complementary spaces of Spanish politics.

The strategy followed by the two brothers between 1881 and 1894 was reproduced, with minor differences, by the second generation of the family. Thus, Ramón Godó Lallana (1864–1931; the owner of *La Vanguardia*) ran for deputy in Congress, while his cousin in Igualada, Juan Godó Llucià (1851–1935), ran for deputy in Barcelona's Provincial Council.

But who was Juan Godó Llucià (1851–1935), the person with whom Ramón would base his political strategy in the future? Juan was popularly known as *"el Morrut"* (*"Morrudo"*, in Spanish) due to his bad temper, and he was the heir in the principal line of descendancy of the Godó family. This means that besides living in the family's traditional household on the *"Rambla Nova"*, he was the one who inherited *La Igualadina Cotonera* – the main business that the family traditionally ran in Igualada. By the turn of the century, *La Igualadina Cotonera* was "one of the oldest and most important textile factories in Catalonia" and employed 350 workers.[19] In an article that the journal *Ilustración catalana* dedicated to this factory in 1893, it was described as the biggest textile factory in Igualada, as well as the first one to install electric current.[20] Like his relatives in Barcelona in the jute industry, a significant number of *La Igualadina Cotonera*'s manufactures were also exported to Spain's former colonies of Cuba, Puerto Rico and the Philippines.[21] This explains why during the Spanish–American War of 1898 Juan Godó participated actively in the campaigns to raise money that his cousin Ramón had arranged through *La Vanguardia*, while his employees promised to give one day's salary every month to the war effort for as long as it lasted.[22]

The relationship between Ramón Godó and his cousin Juan went far beyond politics. As Illustration 4 shows, Ramón held strong emotional bonds with his relatives in Igualada and actively participated in the family life. Despite the fact he never lived in this city, kinship ties and the family name were two elements that grounded him in Igualada. His marriage to Rosa Valls i Valls was another aspect of this. Moreover, the links between Ramón Godó and his cousin Juan included common interests in the textile factory, which led them to establish, in 1897, a company for the production of corsets and other types of cloth made of wool, with a capital of 10,000 *pesetas*.[23] The same year the two men, together with a third cousin, established another company called "*Crédito Ygualada*", dedicated to credit and banking operations.[24] These kinds of operations ultimately reveal a tight bond between family members in which trust and cooperation were fundamental.

However, one might wonder what Ramón Godó really thought about the political pre-eminence his family had traditionally enjoyed in Igualada, especially since this pre-eminence relied heavily on clientelistic practices. All the more if Ramón's newspaper, *La Vanguardia*, presented the fight against corruption as one of the central elements necessary to 'regenerate' Spain (see Chapter 4). How did Ramón, then, deal with what might seem to be a contradiction between the discourse of *La Vanguardia* and his own position as a Liberal politician? There are some sources that shed light on Ramón's opinions about *caciquismo*. One of these sources is an open letter that a group of citizens of Sant Martí de Sesgueioles (one of the 32 small towns that formed the constituency of Igualada) addressed to Ramón Godó, in which they denounced the clientelistic practices that were dominant in the constituency. The title of the letter was already indicative of its content: "OPEN LETTER. ANOTHER ARBITRARY ACT. [LETTER] TO MR. RAMÓN GODÓ LALLANA"; and it went like this:

> "Dear Sir: For a long time, the people of your country, who do not worry about anything else but working and living this miserable life of ours (...), have been wondering for a long time... who is our Deputy? In this country, everyone thinks that the word Deputy is a synonym for *cacique*, and the *caciques* have indeed much to do with the omnipotence and despotism that prevails everywhere. This does not mean, Mr. Godó, that you are one of this kind; yet we wonder where are all the good civic customs that were the custom in this country that went beyond miserable interests, where have they gone now? All these miserable interests that unfortunately have been revived today as a result

of political struggle? Who is it that has influence in this country? Where have the tranquillity and moderate habitudes of this country, where has its perfect order and good management in public things gone now? Will you be the responsible for this, Mr. Godó? The facts do not prove it clearly; furthermore, we do not want to think so. Perhaps you don't even know that despotism and shamelessness is everywhere (...). We have not treated you well, Mr. Godó, but we believe you have honest and respectable feelings. This is why we cannot imagine you really know the state of things in this country; otherwise, how could we understand that you allowed all this without you excommunicating it? (...)."[25]

This letter, which is only partially reproduced, goes on to detail the "arbitrary acts" the mayors in their town were committing. The authors of the letter kept asking Ramón Godó rhetorically if they were "his mayors" and "whether is it really true that we're now living in the late 19th century". The fact that the letter was written in Catalan carried political connotations: Catalan was clearly the dominant language in Igualada's constituency, but not the one Godó customarily used. As explained in Chapter 1, the adoption of Spanish as the current language in the private sphere was the result of Godó's migration to the Basque Country, as well as a typical strategy of "social distinction" among the Catalan bourgeoisie. Moreover, and as the following pages will show, language would become a new issue of political debate in the new mass politics, especially as Catalan nationalists made it a sign of opposition against the liberal-state's official one (Spanish). Thus, the fact that the letter quoted above was written in Catalan is a subtle yet important element that needs to be taken into account.

The letter addressed to Godó ended with a clear warning: "He who sows the wind shall reap the whirlwind" (in Catalan, *"Qui sembra vents recull tempestats"*). Therefore, the three men that signed the letter (Tomàs Estany, Josep Pont and Joan Boria Vall, about whom nothing has been located) were clearly advising Godó to do something to remove *caciquismo*, and even left an open door in case he wanted to change things (though with a clear feeling of suspicion). Yet besides the content, this letter was clearly bad for Godó's reputation, especially if we take into account that it was published in a Barcelona newspaper, called *Diari de Catalunya*.

Godó's reply to the letter did not take long to arrive. He replied from San Sebastián, where he was on holiday, and his response was published in *La Vanguardia*. The fact that he replied in Spanish (and not in Catalan, as he had been addressed in the letter) is indicative of future political realignments of the Godó family in relation to language and identity. Ramón's letter, made it clear that he had "bothered to reply only out of social courtesy to the people who signed it", because the events the letter describes "have nothing to do with him [Ramón], as the men that signed the letter themselves admitted; and have nothing to do with his resolution as deputy, unless this public office is distorted". According to the reply given by Ramón, if he had to intervene in every small issue in his district, both the public and the private, this would foster *caciquismo* instead of fighting it. Finally, Ramón's letter made some clear statements about his own understanding of *caciquismo*:

> "In what concerns the observations made on the ills of caciquismo, whatever it takes place, Mister Godó would not hesitate to subscribe them with total sincerity. Mister Godó was granted his position of Congress as a result of the natural approval and estimation that he has in towns, and Mister Godó only wants to exert in his district the common good, as far as he is able. The doors of his house will always be open for anyone wishing to sincerely combat those ends with morality and the law. Very often, and this is not a self-defense nor a critique, but a mere observation, [people] mess caciquismo – often authentic – with what is a social state that is the result of heated confrontations. This social state, which stems from complex reasons, is not solved through authority nor the action of one single man but requires the cooperation of all the good-will men, who shall join their interests to suffocate these passions instead of fostering disharmony through prejudice."[26]

The letter quoted above is of immense value to examine the understanding that contemporaries had of *caciquismo* – especially in the case of social actors who directly exploited it for their own benefit. Thus, Ramón Godó made his opinion crystal clear: he regarded *caciquismo* as something that should be extirpated from society, thus echoing the views that *La Vanguardia* had expressed in the aftermath of the Disaster. Still, Godó noted that *caciquismo* was often mistaken as a result of the "existing tensions in society".[27] The only solution, he argued, was the "coming together of all the good men". This kind of argument, which distanced Ramón from any responsibility for clientelistic practices occurring in the district he represented in Congress, was often accompanied by a parallel discourse, consisting of stressing the excellent qualities he allegedly possessed to represent Igualada's constituency. Godó's close relation with the constituency, which stemmed from the family and material interests he had in Igualada, supposedly made him the "natural" candidate of this constituency. This kind of discourse aspired to construct a positive image of him as a deputy. The historian Manuel Marín has observed similar behaviour in the case of Pau Turull (a Catalan manufacturer from Sabadell, also involved in clientelistic practices). Marín has described this practice as the building of the image of *"el buen cacique"*.[28]

In practice, this discourse represented an investment in symbolic capital, through notions such as prestige and respectability, and served as a way to fight against defamation. In 1902, for instance, Ramón Godó made a donation of an entire building to the town of Capellades to be converted into the new town hall.[29] Capellades was one of the towns where the Godó family had traditionally faced stronger opposition. In order to combat this opposition, Godó decided to donate the building in an attempt to improve his image in Capellades, as becomes clear in his explanation for this donation.[30] In this regard, *La Vanguardia* turned out to be a particularly valuable instrument to invest in this type of symbolic capital. As had been common with Carlos Godó, when *La Vanguardia* mentioned anything about his son Ramón he was always described in especially good terms. Thus, the reception given to Ramón Godó as a result of the donation he had made to the town of Capellades was given very detailed and positive coverage in *La Vanguardia*:

> "The homage paid in honour of Mister Ramón Godó Lallana, previously announced, was celebrated amongst a level of brightness and enthusiasm superior to the most optimist estimations. (...) with great rejoice was announced the coming of Mr Ramón Godó, who came together with his friends. When they arrived they exchanged affectionate greetings with the commision (...) at the head there was the orchestra, playing patriotic songs. (...) [the commission] walked under a floral arch made in honour of Mr. Godó. (...) Before a great audience, which literally filled the whole building, a ceremony was celebrated to bless the new city hall (...) a marble inscription panel was inaugurated leaving testimony of Godó's donation. (...) all these deeds were welcomed amidsts warm cheers and shouts for Mr. Godó."[31]

Events like the one above reveal the importance that image played in the social legitimation of elites – even for those elites like Ramón Godó whose re-election was often due to clientelistic practices. In this regard, one of the limitations that can be observed in the literature is that the notion of legitimation of the elites has been too circumscribed to the sociological dimension of power. Thus, whether the aim has been to illustrate how violence was a decisive characteristic of the elites' ascendancy, or to stress the capacity of those elites to create clientelistic networks based on a patron–client basis, both accounts have failed to notice the symbolic legitimation that is, this book contends, another crucial element behind the legitimation of those elites.

In fact, the pre-eminence of the elites was not only obtained through material sources, but was also the result of a (certain) recognition from the rest of the population, based on the accumulation by those elites of social and cultural capital, as the case of Ramón Godó demonstrates. The capacity of the local members of the elite to construct an image of themselves as the representatives and defenders of local interests, as well as their prestige or attachment to the locality, were notions that reinforced their power and acted as sources of legitimation. In the case of Godó, discussed above, for instance, his reception in Capellades became a public demonstration aimed at strengthening his image in public. Thus, in addition to the public forms of gratitude that Ramón allegedly received (e.g. the crowds welcoming him, the music, the arch of triumph dedicated to him, etc.), this event became an opportunity to invest in the image of Ramón Godó as the new family leader of the Liberal Party in Igualada's constituency. Thus, a total of 16 municipalities of this constituency sent their own commission to pay tribute to Ramón, in addition to numerous social entities.[32] This kind of demonstration was good publicity and contributed to reinforcing his links with the territory. Finally, it must be noted that a substantial number of those assisting in this event were part of Ramón's own network. Among the assistants included, for instance, his cousin and provincial deputy Juan Godó Llucià.

However, despite the good relations Ramón Godó held with central government (as his sweeping electoral victories reveal), and despite his apparently solid position in Igualada's constituency, the fact is that in the years to follow his political pre-eminence would be highly contested. Or to put it in other words, the political strategy that had worked so well for the first generation of the Godó family (consisting in a combination of clientelism and the attachment to the territory through media propaganda) did not bring the same results for the second generation of the same family. This was due, for the most part, to the changed context in Barcelona in the first decade of the 20th century: namely, the emergence of mass politics.

Similar to what happened in other European cities (like Vienna, where the liberal parties were swept out of the city council in 1897),[33] in Barcelona the rise of new political forces radically changed political power in the local sphere at the turn of the century. This took place in 1901, a year that can be considered as a turning point in the Restoration. During that year, the two dynastic parties that had traditionally monopolised Barcelona's council (the Conservative and the Liberal parties, as was the case across Spain) suffered an electoral defeat against the Catalan Nationalists of *La Lliga Regionalista* and the Republicans of Alejandro Lerroux.[34] The outcome of these elections had a long-lasting effect: from 1901 onwards, Barcelona did not elect one single deputy from either the Liberal or the Conservative parties, and something similar occurred with city councillors of these parties. The system of rotation between the two parties that Cánovas and Sagasta had organised since 1885 thus started to fail in Barcelona. Hence, and as the historian Borja de Riquer has noted, after 1907 the liberal parties never managed to become again the largest political force in Catalonia. Between 1901 and 1923, the combined votes of the two liberal parties "only" amounted to 40%, compared to the *Lliga Regionalista* – 28%; the Republicans – 26%; the Catholic fundamentalists –

4%; and the other parties – 2%. In Barcelona's city council the exclusion of liberal parties became even more palpable: after 1901, not a single liberal councillor was elected.[35]

The change that occurred in Barcelona had much to do with the failure of the Silvela–Polavieja government of 1900. Despite the high expectations this government had created throughout Spain, and particularly in Catalonia (for the entry of Duran i Bas in the government as Minister of "Gracia y Justicia"), the hopes for a reform of the Restoration system rapidly vanished. This would be due to the conflicting views that existed within the Government, particularly represented by the Minister Fernández Villaverde and his attempt to raise taxes as a way to reduce the debt inherited from the Spanish–American War. Fernández Villaverde's plans were utterly opposed to the public investment defended by Rafael Gasset; and also clearly went against the economic and financial economy that Catalan elites had defended as the first step towards the decentralisation of the liberal state. The immediate outcome of Villaverde's economic policies was the resignation of Duran i Bas (he submitted his first resignation only two months after the government had started) and the emergence in Catalonia of a massive movement of opposition against paying taxes. This movement, which would popularly be known as the *"Tancament de Caixes"*, provoked the resignation of the first Catalanist mayor of Barcelona (Bartomeu Robert), the arrest of numerous people and the declaration of the state of war in this city. The outcome of the crisis would be the creation of an electoral candidacy by the main civic entities that promoted the decentralisation of the liberal state in response to the Disaster of 1898. This electoral candidacy would be known as "the candidacy of the Four Presidents" (in reference to the presidents of the four entities that formed it: the *Fomento del Trabajo Nacional*; *Societat Econòmica Barcelonesa d'Amics del País*; *Ateneu Barcelonès*; *Liga de Defensa Industrial*), who would radically break with the liberal parties' rotation in Barcelona for the first time, in 1901.

Besides their symbolic value, the elections of 1901 marked a turning point because they represented the start of mass politics in Barcelona. Hence, during that year the *"Lliga Regionalista"* was founded and, together with the Republican party of Alejandro Lerroux, came to represent a whole new way of doing politics.[36] The Republicans and the Catalanists of the *Lliga*, however, had very different political projects. On the one hand, the Republicans saw the immorality of the political system as the ultimate cause of all social ills (and this included not just the loss of the colonies, but all sorts of social problems, like prostitution, violence and alcoholism). In response to this, their new leader, a young charismatic man called Alejandro Lerroux, made use of a populist and anticlerical discourse to attract growing numbers of Barcelona's working class. In contrast to this, the *Lliga* was a party that despite officially adopting an interclassist discourse, in practice was mainly formed by the middle-upper sectors of society, including the petty bourgeoisie. This party did not call for the end of the Restoration, like the Republicans, but rather promoted its reform through transparency in elections and the decentralisation of the liberal state.

Yet despite the important differences that existed between the Republicans and the Catalanists, both in terms of discourse and social base, what they had in common is that they made use of new forms of political activity, like political rallies and mass demonstrations. A good example of this were the *"meriendas fraternales"* of Alejandro Lerroux, a gathering in the countryside that addressed the urban classes of Barcelona. On certain occasions, this kind of social event gathered more than 20,000 of Lerroux's supporters. In contrast to the liberal parties, which relied on the indifference of the population to use clientelistic practices, the Republicans and the Catalanists actively promoted the mobilisation of their supporters during elections. These two new parties made great use of newspapers to foster political mobilisation, especially at a time when the press in Spain was undergoing a process of great expansion. Thus, in comparison to the estimated 500 newspapers that existed in Spain in 1879, their number rose to 1,300 newspapers in 1900 – a growth of 240%. In this regard, this growth of the Spanish press was characterised by the great upsurge of politically oriented papers. In 1901, for instance, of Barcelona's 22 daily newspapers, half of them still had partisan orientation, while the rest defined themselves as independent.[37]

The Republicans and the Catalanists made intense use of the press to achieve their political goals. First of all, they used the press to disclose corruption in public. The aim was to provoke the reaction of their supporters as well as to educate people about their political rights. Thus, it was common that Republican and Catalanist newspapers explained the electoral laws so their readers could report any instances of misconduct during elections. Secondly, the press was also used to mobilise their partisans to assure transparency during elections. For example, in 1901, when Alejandro Lerroux gathered hundreds of his supporters in Barcelona's city council to make sure that the liberal parties did not manipulate the elections. According to some witnesses, many of Lerroux's supporters did not leave their seats despite the elections lasting the entire day. It was even said that some of the assistants would not even leave to use the lavatory because they were afraid of losing their seats, indeed some of them even relieved themselves in their seats.[38] From a more general perspective, political life increased notably in Barcelona. Thus, between 1899 and 1893 there were 38 big political demonstrations in this city; between 1899 and 1903, there were 54 (with 23 big demonstrations in 1903 alone); and between 1906 and 1909, there were 33. Therefore, there was an average of 10 "important" political events in 1890–1893; 11 in 1899–1903; and around 8 in 1907–1909.[39]

It was the use of corruption as a way to foster political mobilisation that ultimately provoked the crisis in the pre-eminence of the Godó family. Indeed, the political strategy that had worked so well for the first generation of the Godó family (that of Carlos and Bartolomé) started to be contested by the growing opposition to clientelistic practices, in which the press would play a decisive role. In contrast to the elections in which the first generation of the Godó family participated, where the opponents of liberal parties based their discourse on the fight against *caciquismo*, what started to change was the personalisation of this fight – that is to say, the fight against the *cacique*. As one of the main opponents of the Godó family explained when commenting on the elections of 1896 (the last elections in which Carlos Godó participated), "Our campaign went against caciquismo, but not against the person who, in the view of many people, would have spared the situation if it weren't for the group of people ("*camarilla*") who surrounded him".[40] The idea that clientelism was something performed by the local supporters of the Godó family, rather than by the family itself (something that, as we have just seen, was even defended by the political opponents of Carlos Godó), changed with Ramón. For he would be the one who faced the spread of mass politics from Barcelona to inland parts of the Catalan territory, like Igualada.

Indeed, Ramón Godó had won the first elections in which he participated without much difficulty. In 1899, for instance, he obtained his first victory thanks to the lack of participation of his opponents (see Table 5.1). The victory of Ramón (who apparently received this victory with "satisfaction" and "deeply felt emotion") was due to the "total indifference" of Igualada.[41] In fact, abstention would be one of the main reasons for the first victories of the Godó family's second generation. On certain occasions, such as in 1901 and 1903, Ramón simply had no opposition and obtained 99% of the votes, something that clearly indicates the use of clientelistic practices by his supporters, among the general passivity of Igualada's population.

However, there is another fact that needs to be taken into account, namely, the growing mobilisation in electoral participation. Thus, electoral turnout grew from 39.64% in 1896; to 50% between 1901 and 1906; to more than 60% in 1907; and even experienced an extraordinary turnout of 80% in 1910. This progressive change in electoral turnout is revealing, ultimately, of the growing opposition the Godó family faced in Igualada from Catalan nationalists and Republicans alike to win elections. Furthermore, the case of this city is representative of the growth these two political forces also experienced in Barcelona, where electoral turnout followed a very similar trend between 1899 and 1907. Hence, during this period electoral participation in Barcelona experienced a continued increase (10% in 1899, 20% in 1901 and 45.6% in 1903). Still, it was the year of 1907 that marked a watershed, both in Igualada (64.12%) and in Barcelona (60%).[42] This massive mobilisation

Table 5.1. *Electoral results of the Godó family between 1899 and 1915*

Year	Date of the elections	Ruling party in the Spanish Congress	Winning candidate	Other candidates	Electoral turnout	Percentage of votes obtained
1899–1900	16/04/1899	Conservative	Ramón Godó Lallana (L)	Narcís Mauri Vidal	39.64%	68.14%
1901–1902	19/05/1901	Liberal	Ramón Godó Lallana (L)	——	50.06%	99.77%
1903–1904	26/05/1903	Conservative	Ramón Godó Lallana (Liberal "Moretista")	——	59.62%	99.26%
1905–1906	10/11/1905	Liberal	Ramón Godó Lallana (L)	Ildefonso García del Corral (R)	50.68%	68.75%
1907–1909	21/04/1907	Conservative	Frederic Rahola (Lliga Regionalista)	**Juan Godó Lluchà (L)** and Josep Puig (R)	64.12%	55.70%
1910–1913	08/05/1910	Liberal	**Juan Godó Lluchà (Liberal "Canalejista")**	Frederic Rahola (Lliga Regionalista)	80.40%	50.89%
1914–1915	08/03/1914	Conservative	Manuel González Vilart (C)	**Juan Godó Lluchà (L)**	75.65%	52.97%

Source: Archivo del Congreso de los Diputados (ACD); Albert Balcells et al., *Les eleccions generals a Catalunya de 1901 a 1923. Relació dels resultats electorals de 1869 a 1899*, Barcelona, Fundació Jaume Bufill, 1982, p. 521 and p. 628; Jordi Planas i Francesc Valls-Junyent, *Cacics i rabassaires. Dinàmica associativa i conflictivitat social. Els Hostalets de Pierola (1890–1939)*, Vic, Eumo, Centre d'Estudis Comarcals d'Igualada, 2011, pp. 41–42.

would be the result of an exceptional event: the so-called *"Solidaritat Catalana"*, a political coalition that would roundly defeat liberal parties in Catalonia, including the Godó's. Yet before this occurred, this family would undergo profound internal tensions about how to respond to the rise of mass politics.

Words as weapons: Family scandals and Ramón Godó's resignation (1906)

Although *La Vanguardia* was a newspaper that fully supported the Restoration system (though advocating its full renewal), the failure of the Silvela–Polavieja Government and the *"Tancament de Caixes"* marked a substantial shift in the position this newspaper adopted in relation to Catalan nationalism. The voluntary resignation of Duran i Bas from the government provoked strong criticisms from Madrid's press, as the majority of newspapers strongly opposed the Catalan demands for decentralisation because they were regarded as a veiled attempt at separatism. This depiction of the events by the Madrid press occasionally provoked a reaction by *La Vanguardia*, as became clear on 9 May 1901 in an article entitled "Cataluña y la prensa de Madrid":

> "(...) *We are not suspicious of being Catalanists in the political sense, because we have never been in their ranks*. We love with all our heart Catalonia, and we also love with all our heart Spain, our motherland. But precisely because we pay tribute to these beloved we lament that some coleagues in Madrid miss the point of examining with serenity [the nature] of political catalanism, and they also miss, despite their intentions, in their mission, and rather contribute to confusion and to creating discomfort, when they speak of exploiters and exploited."[43]

This article illuminates the attitude *La Vanguardia* adopted in relation to Catalan nationalism. The newspaper openly admitted that "political Catalanism" had never been part of its editorial policy. Still, the fact that even a newspaper like *La Vanguardia*, which was not "suspicious" of Catalan nationalism, protested about the way the Madrid newspapers had represented this political movement, is particularly revealing of the changes that were taking place in Catalonia at the time. In fact, immediately after the Disaster of 1898, the Conservative Duran i Bas had already warned General Polavieja about the growing detachment of Catalan public opinion from the Restoration system.[44] And in 1906 this dissatisfaction resulted in the creation of the electoral coalition of the *"Solidaritat Catalana"* ("Catalan Solidarity"). As we have seen, these elections had the highest participation ever achieved in Barcelona. A similar political mobilisation also took place in Igualada, where the *Solidaritat Catalana* also ran in the elections with the specific goal of overthrowing the political domination of the Godó family.

The immediate motivation behind the creation of the *Solidaritat Catalana* was a historical event popularly known as the *"fets del Cu-Cut!"* (1905). This expression referred to the attack on the editorial offices of the satirical journal *Cu-cut!* and *La Veu de Catalunya* by the military. The first of these newspapers had ridiculed the Spanish army in a caricature and a group of young soldiers had decided to retaliate. The vast majority of Barcelona's press immediately criticised the attack and expressed its solidarity with the two newspapers affected. Like other newspapers in the city, regardless of their ideology, *La Vanguardia* condemned the assault. Yet, despite all these protests, the Liberal government of Segismundo Moret not only refused to denounce the attack but also decided to pass a new law (20/03/1906) according to which any insult against Spain or Spanish symbols (understood in a broad sense, including criticism of the army and the Crown) would be judged by martial law and military courts. The response to this law (which designated the display of the Catalan flag or the singing of the Catalan anthem as an "offence" to Spanish symbols) was a massive public demonstration in Barcelona of around 200,000 people (35% of the total population of the city). That same year, another protest gathered some 20,000 people, the biggest crowd ever achieved in a closed area.[45] All these demonstrations illustrate the growing politicisation of Barcelona's population, which culminated the following year in the creation of a wide coalition of political forces. With the sole exception of the liberal parties and the Republicans of Alejandro Lerroux (which were openly against Catalan nationalism), the rest of the political forces joined together in a coalition that would be known as the *Solidaritat Catalana* (the Carlists, the Lliga Regionalista, Centre Nacional Republicà, Unió Catalanista, federal republicans and a part of the Unión Republicana). The political programme of this coalition was based on very few points, consisting in the repealing of the abovementioned Law and a set of vague proposals (decentralisation, autonomy in education and other social services).[46]

Amidst the heated political situation of Spain, and particularly Catalonia, at the time, Ramón Godó started to become the target of the newspapers that supported the *Solidaritat Catalana*. As we saw earlier, Ramón had already been criticised in the past by other newspapers. However, what was different in 1906 was that due to the growing mobilisation of political parties in the region, the criticisms levelled at the Godó family in the press became more hostile. For instance, Ramón started to be referred to in the press as a "stranger" to his own country because of his lack of support for the cause of decentralisation and his poor knowledge of the Catalan language. Moreover, a novel strategy was used by these newspapers, consisting in the association of *La Vanguardia* with clientelistic practices. In fact, the fight against *caciquismo* would be one of the main leitmotifs of the *Solidaritat Catalana*. Thus, as *La Veu de Catalunya* claimed, in an article entitled "*La Vanguardia caciquista*":

> "*La Vanguardia* has finally removed its mask. In opposing Catalonia and the national cause, this newspaper has presented itself as it really is, namely as with

the owner of this newspaper, as the *cacique* of Igualada, the Catalan who ignores the language of his own grandparents, the *mestizo* that repudiates the traditions of the country of his own father. (...) *La Vanguardia* only keeps repeating the point of view of its *foreign* owner; this newspaper speaks in the same way as newspapers in Madrid do (...); when honourable patricians decide to start a vigorous electoral campaign, and make the effort of organising endless political rallies, *La Vanguardia* remains silent, as if nothing happened (...); it is in Igualada that elections are manipulated shamelessly; it is in Igualada that the will of the voters is manipulated, and when that is not possible, votes are bought with money or with food; it is in Igualada that elections are won at any cost, no matter who should fall to get it. The ones that rule in Barcelona want real votes; in Barcelona the Lliga Regionalista prefers losing the elections rather than winning the Republicans through illegal methods, (...) the same illegal methods that are still used in Madrid; for us it would be easy to employ such methods if we wished to. In Barcelona, if a candidate used the same methods as Godó, he would have been considered a dishonest person, and his enemy would be the one to oppose him through fair rules. (...) So please Mr. Godó don't tell us about morality... because people will laugh in your face."[47]

The article quoted above is revealing of how language and *caciquismo* were two rhetorical arguments that were used to contest the Godó's political domain. Indeed, if the members of this family had traditionally presented themselves as the *natural* representatives of Igualada, based on the deep-roots they had in this locality, now the same discourse was used against them. Thus, Ramón's supposed reluctance to use Catalan was the point that the family's political rivals sought to exploit through the press: he was not a *"native"* of Igualada, but a *"foreigner"*. He was also called *"mestizo"*, the Spanish word used in the Spanish colonies in South America to refer to the children born of Spanish and Amerindian relations. The fact that Godó's mother was Basque and his father was Catalan was probably the reason behind the use of this word. All these nicknames were used as an insult against Godó, and were aimed, above all, at discrediting him to represent local affairs. These attacks from Barcelona's press reveal the importance given in politics to the personal attachment to the constituency; as well as how the prestige of local elites was contested in the public sphere by the new political movements.

Moreover, the second persisting argument in the attacks against Ramón Godó was the link between *caciquismo* and *La Vanguardia*. The nationalist newspaper *La Veu de Catalunya* kept publishing further articles with the title *"La Vanguardia es caciquista"* (*"La Vanguardia* is the mouthpiece of *caciquismo"*, in English); while in parallel other newspapers in Barcelona accused Godó of silencing any news related to the *Lliga Regionalista*.[48] These kinds of attacks against *La Vanguardia* continued during the latter months of 1905, and not just from *La Veu de Catalunya* and *La Renaixensa*, but also from other newspapers in Barcelona, like *La Campana de Gràcia* and *El Diluvio*, as well as from the press in Igualada. *La Veu de Catalunya,* for instance, argued that "Mr. Godó is nothing more than the cacique of the district, they are all the same. And the newspaper he owns is a defender of *caciquismo* that shamefully hides behind its label as independent".[49]

The smear campaign directed at Ramón Godó demonstrates how his position as deputy was increasingly being related to his position as newspaper proprietor. This link between the two spheres of influence (politics and the press) is precisely what the Godó brothers had sought to separate with the reform plans of 1888, when *La Vanguardia* was turned into an independent newspaper. But now this strategy was starting to fail, as the family's rivals saw this double condition (proprietor of an independent newspaper as well as politician) as Ramón's Achilles' heel. These kinds of attacks contained a second aim, that of challenging the image of *La Vanguardia* as a politically neutral ("independent") newspaper.

If this string of attacks was detrimental to Godó's image as the father of the district and damaged *La Vanguardia*'s reputation as an independent newspaper, worse was still to come. A few months later, on 22 June 1906, rumours start to surface about Ramón's intention to resign as deputy of Igualada. These rumours did not stem from the attacks Ramón had received until then, but rather started when an incident that occurred in Igualada leapt onto the pages of the Barcelona press. The incident in question was the arrest of the presidents of *"El Ateneo Igualadino"* (Mr. Llansana) and of the *"Centro Autonomista"* (Mr. Mussons), two entities of Igualada that had a clear Republican and Catalanist orientation. They were arrested for having organised a meeting. This incident, for which the Godó family was blamed, was one among a number of other arbitrary acts that the followers of this family had been committing recently.[50]

The situation in Igualada reached its tipping point a few days later, in June 1906, when the second major deputy of the city was physically assaulted by an employee of Juan Godó Pelegrí – the mayor of Igualada.[51] Hence, when these events took place, the Godó family had reached its highest level of control in Igualada's political life: three members of the family were, respectively, deputy at the Congress, provincial deputy and mayor – each for Igualada's constituency. Such a monopoly over public office by members of the same family increased the feeling that despotic rule pervaded Igualada's life.

Yet what is particularly remarkable about the events that occurred in this city is that they rapidly turned into a *mediatised* scandal, capable of exceeding Igualada's local sphere and attracting the interest of newspapers in Barcelona. The event that took place in June 1906 turned into a scandal capable of generating interest not only among local readers in Igualada but also in Barcelona because it was regarded as an act of arbitrary linked to *caciquismo*. Hence, one contemporary recalled that "Almost all of Barcelona is aware of the confrontation the honourable town of Igualada is holding against a petty oligarchy, and we are all eager to follow the events". Another testimony recalled that the "majority of Barcelona's press has talked about the dispute in our city between the people and the oligarchy".[52] Furthermore, the scandal in Igualada generated an open protest by a group of deputies, who protested to the Council of Ministers in Madrid. The same deputies also visited the Civil Governor and the President of the Audience to demand an investigation for the "very serious events" that took place in Igualada, while a petition was organised to free the arrested men.[53]

As all these events took place, Ramón Godó found himself embroiled in the family scandal. In fact, Ramón was not directly responsible for the events that had occurred in Igualada. Rather, all the accusations were directed at the mayor, Joan Godó Pelegrí. But it was as a result of Ramón's *membership of a broader collective*, that is, the family, that the scandal also affected him and *La Vanguardia*. Thus, there is evidence that the day after the aggression took place (22 June 1906), Ramón arrived in Igualada to discuss what had happened with his relatives. During the following days, all sorts of rumours spread about the possibility that the three members of the Godó family would resign from public office.[54] Finally, the tension among the different members of the family was resolved on 1 July 1906, when, only one week after the "scandal" had broke, Ramón Godó decided to resign from his position as deputy. He announced this in an open letter published in *La Vanguardia*, where he stated that he would not be running for the next legislative elections. The letter stated:

"From Mr. Ramón Godó, deputie in Congress and proprietor of LA VANGUARDIA, we have received the following letter: Mr. Editor of LA VANGUARDIA. My dearest friend: on more than one occasion, I have privately confessed to my closest friends my purpose of retiring from politics. No private pleasure have I ever found in politics, and it has rather been a source of continuous annoyance and disappointment. However, since my thoughts have become public in the district of Igualada, which I am honoured to represent at the [Spanish] Congress, and have been repeatedly manipulated, I deem it necessary to announce my firm intention of not running for the next elections for deputy at the Congress, no matter the date or the party that will call these elections. Therefore, I now consider myself as retired from politics. I believe it is my duty to communicate this decision to my friends and voters in the district of Igualada, for whose affection and confidence I will always be grateful."[55]

Summary

With the above letter, Ramón Godó decided to put an end to his political career. Up to that moment, he had run in four legislative elections (spanning the years between 1899 and 1906) and had won all of them. Yet, as he confessed, he was tired of politics.

Soon after *La Vanguardia* published Ramón's letter of resignation, the traditional opponents of the Godó family celebrated the news. In the view of *El Diluvio*, the resignation of Ramón Godó was the result of the campaign in which this Barcelonan newspaper had so actively participated. [56] Other newspapers from the same city, like *La Veu de Catalunya*, reached the same conclusions as *El Diluvio*, and presented Ramón's resignation as "the victory of the good citizens of Igualada against *caciquismo*". Another newspaper insisted that "Everywhere all the newspapers talk about the same thing: articles, correspondences, telegrams and telephone calls, all these comment on and try to explain the reasons that have led him to resign."[57] Eventually, even Madrid's press made reference to Ramón Godó's letter of resignation[58]. In this regard, Ramón's decision was probably influenced by another element. Namely the fact that Spain's Superior Court had sentenced a group of Ramón's supporters to imprisonment for violently assaulting a man in Pierola (one of the towns of Igualada's constituency).[59]

In any case, regardless of what finally convinced Ramón Godó to resign from politics, his case is revealing of the growing *mediatisation* of politics. As had happened to Rafael Gasset with *El Imparcial* (explained in the introduction to this chapter) Ramón's involvement in politics started to be incompatible with his status as the proprietor of an "independent" newspaper. However, while Gasset saw the sales of his newspaper decrease as a result of his behaviour during the Disaster of 1898, in the case of Ramón the tension between the press and politics manifested itself through public accusations of corruption (clientelism). The case of the Godó family thus reveals how the fight against corruption became one of the main elements in the discourse of the Catalan nationalists and the Republicans. This chapter has shown how the fight against corruption became a new device for political mobilisation, particularly for those parties that symbolised the new mass politics.

As in the case of Vienna, where the liberal parties were swept away by a new political movement (in that case, by the anti-Semitic Catholics of Karl Lueger), something similar took place in Barcelona too. From 1901 onwards this city would not elect a single member of the Conservative or Liberal parties. Although the cases of Vienna and Barcelona obviously obey very diverse political contexts, in both cities these forces made clear a new type of *subjective* discourse, one of the characteristics of the new mass politics in Europe. That is to say, a new type of discourse emerged, based on appealing to a bourgeoning electorate through subjective elements (such as anticlericalism, nationalism, demagoguery or anti-Semitism).[60] This kind of discourse was in stark contrast to mid-19th-century politics, which showed a confidence in the progress of mankind through reason and material development. In contrast to this, the turn of the century was a moment in all of Europe (and in the Mediterranean in particular) that was dominated by pessimism and unrest about the future.

The capacity of mobilisation in the denouncing of corruption produced in Catalonia is also revealing of the changes that were taking place – arguably with less intensity – in some of Spain's major urban settings, like Valencia and Madrid.[61] Before 1898 clientelistic practices had already been criticised on many occasions. These public accusations, however, traditionally brought few consequences. The scarce interest of liberal parties in enforcing anti-corruption laws, combined with the low mobilisation of society during elections, explains why these accusations had little effect. However, the Disaster of 1898 represented a crisis of identity during which corruption and other moral issues underwent deep scrutiny in public opinion. The outcome was the strong discredit of the political system and the growing calls for the need of redefining the Restoration (or even the need of overthrowing it). Far from being monopolised by the new political movements, the calls in favour of renewing the political system were also embraced and supported – at least in public – by the same liberal parties, as the case of the Silvela–Polavieja government illustrated.

However, the case of Ramón Godó reveals to what extent the increasing mobilisation of new political parties became a serious threat for the social preeminence of liberal elites. This threat was not only evident in the calls for accountability during elections, but also in the attempts the new parties made at undermining the public legitimation of traditional elites. In this regard, the scandal that affected Ramón can be seen as part of a struggle over the sources of symbolic power. As John B. Thompson has noted, scandals have the *potential* of destroying reputation and undermining trust.[62] The same author has observed that reputation does not apply equally in all social fields. In certain fields, where confidence and trust are a crucial aspect in the legitimacy of an individual (e.g. a politician), reputation is particularly important, and therefore the consequences a scandal might entail are larger.[63]

In the case of Ramón, while he invested in his position as the heir of Carlos Godó and therefore as the "natural" representative of Igualada's interests (as became clear in his visit to Capellades), his enemies used the opposite argument. Namely, that Ramón was a "stranger" to the territory, because he was born in the Basque country and rarely used the Catalan language. Both the strategy of Ramón and that of his enemies reveal one of the characteristics historians have noted about parliamentary life in Catalonia, consisting in the general reluctance to accept "foreign candidates" (the so-called "*candidatos cuneros"*). In fact, as much as 80% of the deputies in Congress from Catalonia were born in this region, which was in contrast to the customary practice of central governments to impose their own "foreign" candidates in given constituencies.[64] In other Spanish regions this reluctance was not so evident as it was in the case of Catalonia.

In this struggle for the symbolic sources of legitimation, public opinion became the target sought by the different actors involved. Since 1881, the Godó family had seen the establishing of *La Vanguardia* as an opportunity to gain public visibility and as a way to promote their private agenda more effectively. The resignation of Ramón Godó, however, reveals the unexpected consequences of Godó's strategy to expand their influence to new publics. The role of newspaper editor exposed Ramón in public (even when he did not use the press in the same self-oriented way as Gasset did with *El Imparcial*) and meant being subject to criticism from a wider range of political actors. Especially since the passing of the new press freedom law of 1883, and the expansion of both the number of newspapers and the reader market (mentioned earlier), public opinion became an alternative channel to elections for a growing number of political actors.[65] The outcome was a new space for political participation that was more plural and depersonalised, and therefore harder for the Godó family to control.

As a man who based the popularity of his newspaper on the commitment to providing neutral information, Ramón Godó probably decided to resign from politics to save *La Vanguardia* from the bad publicity caused by the family scandal.[66] Ramón's resignation, however, can hardly be justified if we do not take into account the very special historical context in which it took place (the highly politicised moment of post-1898, the crisis of legitimation of the Restoration system and the creation of the *Solidaritat Catalana*), and the expansion of the reading market and its pluralistic characteristics. The conclusion that can be drawn from this is that for social actors, controlling the legitimate discourse became a much more difficult goal to achieve in the increasingly plural market of readers.

Finally, it must be noted that in his attempt to save the prestige of *La Vanguardia*, Ramón Godó disrupted the strategies of his relatives in Igualada. His resignation meant that the Godó family, which had monopolised public office in this constituency for years, now suddenly disappeared from the politcal map. However, the family did not give up its position in the Congress without a fight. According to this determination to resist, the family would redesign its traditional strategies to face the challenge of the *Solidaritat Catalana*. Ramón Godó himself would participate in this attempt, though by using more subtle forms of exerting influence. This redefining of strategies will be the focus of Chapter 6.

6

Two Different Reactions to the Challenge of Mass Politics

"¡Long life to Catalonia! ¡Long live to Spain! For Catalonia and Spain, please vote who loves both equally; and this is Mr. Godó."

La Vanguardia, 2 May 1910, p. 10

The aim of this chapter is to analyse the way the Godó family responded to the crisis of liberal politics, as part of the rise of the new mass society in Europe. The years prior to the First World War (1914–1918) were a period of drastic transformations across the entire Continent. One of the features that characterised this moment of change was the broadening of the political spectrum, spurred by a double process: the widening of the franchise and the politicisation of larger segments of society, on the one hand; and the advent of a new class of professional politicians and large-scale organisations, on the other. A series of heated controversies galvanized these transformations and divided European societies profoundly. Disputes over the role of religion, tensions over social reforms and challenged understandings of the nation pervaded public debate during this period. None of these controversies were new, but intensified as a result of structural transformations (such as urbanisation and industrialisation) and the arrival on the scene of a new social actor: the "masses".

These were all transformations that put liberal institutions and the elites who traditionally benefited from them in dire straits. Historian John Garrard has identified two different patterns of response among Europe's liberal elites to this new situation, divided by the Rhine. According to Garrard, while elites on the west side of the Rhine (e.g. England and France) accepted the widening of the franchise, after previous periods of initial resistance, elites located on the east of the Rhine, in contrast, accepted the widening of the social bases of their regimes, but arguably "did so within political frameworks intended to remain basically autocratic". This would be the case, for instance, of Italy.[1] The dividing line that Garrard establishes with the Rhine constitutes an attempt to provide an overview of a phenomenon that is difficult to classify at a European scale.

Still, the geographic division made by this author seems to draw on the same perspective that dominated the debate in the 1990s about the role of the "bourgeoisie" in the crisis of liberalism. Hence, in the case of southern Europe, historians have long debated the capacity – and above all, the willingness – of traditional elites to promote the democratisation of the political system; as well as how these attitudes contributed or not to the rise of new authoritarian regimes in the 1920s. Nowadays the breakdown of parliamentary representation continues to be an important topic of debate, where emphasis is still put on examining electoral legislation, the deeds of statesman and the evolution of liberal parties, among other topics.[2]

This chapter will adopt an alternative perspective, where the focus is put on local elites and the strategies they designed to cope with the new mass politics. One of the reasons for doing so is because in countries like Italy and Spain the crumbling of liberal institutions primarily began at a local level, rather than at a national scale.[3] It was in big cities like Bologna, for the Italian case, and Barcelona, Valencia and Madrid, for that of Spain, where the political hegemony of liberal parties was first challenged.[4] The first part of this chapter will examine how the Godós reacted to the threat of mass politics, as the crisis of liberal parties spread from Barcelona to the stronghold family in their hometown of Igualada.

The second part of this chapter will focus on a second member of the same family, who lived in Barcelona: Ramón Godó, proprietor of *La Vanguardia*. As explained in the previous chapter, in 1906 Ramón resigned from politics to protect the prestige of his newspaper. In contrast to his relatives in Igualada, he had broken his ties with the Liberal Party and with clientelistic practices. However, this abandoning of public office did not imply his dissatisfaction with politics, but rather the adoption of an alternative channel to participate in political life, by supporting the plans of national regeneration of a politician named Antonio Maura. Therefore, this chapter will examine the different responses that were given, even within the same family, to the rise of mass politics. Moreover, and similarly to other countries in Europe, national identity and anticlericalism became two central topics in the realignment of political debate, and therefore conditioned the notables' strategies of adaptation. In this way, the case of the family will shed light on how the crisis of liberal politics created tension in the relations between family members, but also unveil the new possibilities that the press opened up for the notables in the new political scenario.

Juan Godó: The search for new forms of legitimising power

Historians have seen in the general elections of 1907 a sign of the transition to the new mass politics in Restoration Spain.[5] Next to the traditional fraudulent practices, like the purchase of votes and the intervention of state officials, these elections evidenced important changes in political behaviour. In contrast to the customary apathy, liberal parties faced the growing competition of alternative political movements. Of the total 155 constituencies in which the country's electoral map was divided, in 62 of them the emerging political forces (Republicans, Democrats and Carlists) presented their candidates.[6] In parallel, these elections became tainted by a strong ideological controversy. In 1905 France established the separation between the state and the church and this decision was echoed in Spain, where anticlericalism became central to the political agenda of the Liberal Party and especially of the Republicans. This propaganda resulted in the mobilisation of Catholics – through demonstrations, protests and the active use of the press – and in their increasing involvement in elections to defend religion.[7] All these elements revealed the growing competition in elections and the politicisation of wider segments of society, two elements that were traditionally absent in the Restoration.

Catalonia arguably became the place where changes in politics became more evident. The broad electoral coalition named the "*Solidaritat Catalana*" had gathered, since 1906, all the parties in this region, with the sole exception of the two liberal parties and the Republicans of Lerroux. The threat this coalition represented to the status quo became evident in the elections of 1907, when the *Solidaritat Catalana* won in 41 of the 44 districts. This overwhelming majority exposed the decay of the liberal parties in Catalonia and indicated an unprecedented – yet to some extent, conjectural – mobilisation of society.

The Godó family became an example of those local elites whose social pre-eminence was threatened by the new competitive politics embodied by the *Solidaritat Catalana*. As Table 5.1 showed, before the elections of 1907 this family had achieved a solid political hegemony. Regardless of the party in power (Conservative or Liberal), the owner of *La Vanguardia*, Ramón Godó, won four elections in a row. Moreover, he won them without much difficulty: on two occasions he faced no competition and electoral turnout was low. These two elements, combined with clientelism, allowed him to secure ample victories (sometimes with 99% of the vote). However, and as a result of the broader changes taking place in Catalonia, the elections of 1907 marked a turning point in the Godó family's trajectory. As Chapter 5 showed, the creation of *Solidaritat Catalana* resulted in a smear campaign against Ramón Godó, who decided to resign in order to save the reputation of *La Vanguardia*.

Furthermore, the decision of this man to abandon politics would have direct consequences for the whole of the Godó family. In the next years, this family started suffering a series of electoral defeats that culminated in 1914 – which would be the last time a member of the Godó family would run in an election (see Table 5.1, page 129). Yet far from resignedly accepting the end of their political hegemony, before these defeats took place the Godós' made various attempts to adapt to the new mass politics. These attempts will be used as a case study to examine, from a micro-perspective, the ways in which liberal elites sought to cope with the new mass politics, as part of the debate about the end of the notables in Europe.

As soon as the resignation of Ramón Godó became public, in late 1906, rumours began to spread that his relatives in Igualada would follow suit and abandon politics too.[8] The decision of the owner of *La Vanguardia* put the family's traditional strategy in crisis: while Ramón ran for Congress, his cousin in Igualada (Juan Godó Llucià) ran for Provincial Council. But now this strategy based on kinship cooperation was no longer feasible as a result of Ramón Godó's resignation. The end of this strategy implied the risk of losing access to Congress, the position from which the family traditionally expanded its influence to Madrid. From a broader perspective, the same challenge was extended to other liberal elites in Catalonia. With the exception of the Conservatives (who expected to win the elections with the support of their party, now in government) the majority of liberal elites in this territory decided not to run for elections in 1907.[9] The broad party coalition the *Solidaritat Catalana* represented made it difficult for liberal elites to win.

Yet contrary to the majority position, the Godó family decided to stand for election: Juan Godó Llucià (1851–1935) became the new family candidate for Congress. As explained before, Juan was the heir of the Godó family's branch in Igualada, as well as a prominent textile manufacturer. Still, the decision of standing for election did not seem to be his own, rather it obeyed the pressures from the family's supporters in the 32 towns that formed Igualada's constituency.[10] The resignation of the owner of *La Vanguardia* in 1906 had already generated great unease among these family supporters (or "clients"), for it implied the risk of losing their access to public office.[11] Given this possibility, the mayors of different towns mobilised and pressured Juan Godó to stand for election; they even announced his candidacy in public, despite his promise of not running for elections.[12] This case illustrates to what extent clientelism implied a whole set of close and long-lasting relations of personal dependence. The Godó family could not abandon politics because it meant leaving behind the people who had been supporting the family for 30 years.

Still, all these efforts became insufficient for the family to win the elections of 1907. The constituency of Igualada witnessed the early expansion of mass politics in Catalonia and demonstrated the negative consequences this represented for traditional elites. Electoral turnout increased substantially (see

Table 5.1) and echoed the structural transformations Igualada was undergoing at the time. Indeed, the economic downturn this city suffered in the mid-19th century did not prevent it from maintaining a strong industrial character.[13] The textile and leather industries remained the leading economic sectors of this city with a population of 10,000 inhabitants at the beginning of the 20th century – including a large working class.[14] These economic transformations in Igualada were accompanied by the mushrooming of spaces of sociability and political activism. New party headquarters were established at the turn of the century, comprising Republicans, Catalan nationalists, Catholics and Anarchists.[15] Among them, the Republicans consolidated as the new leading force. This varied range of political movements managed to expand their influence over Igualada's population based on two pillars: first, the proliferation of different social spaces (like social centres and "*ateneos*") where the working people and the petty bourgeoisie gathered. These centres promoted all sorts of leisure and educative activities (like choral groups and public libraries) and provided a fertile ground for new currents of thought to spread, such as rational education, antimilitarism and masonry.[16]

The second element that most contributed to the growth of new political movements in Igualada was a modest yet still very active press. Thus, at the beginning of the 20th century the press experienced a major growth in this city: the number of newspapers increased from 2, in 1900, to 12 in 1910. Thanks to some valuable local studies, the common features of these newspapers can be delineated.[17] Most of them had a partisan orientation, and their sales did not surpass a few hundred copies. The majority of them followed an erratic existence and usually did not last for more than a few years. Yet even under such modest circumstances, the press became one of the most valuable instruments for the opponents of the Godó family.

This expanding civil society is where the new emerging forces, like the *Lliga Regionalista* and above all the Republicans, widened their social bases and used it to fight the Godó's domination. The elections of 1907 became an example of the vital function of the press in mobilising society against *caciquismo*. In the days prior to elections, the newspaper of the Catalan nationalists (*Pàtria*) gave much publicity to the candidate of the *Solidaritat Catalana* (Frederic Rahola) and published different articles specifically addressed to workers, and to women, as well. Although the electoral law of 1890 did not allow women to vote, the press encouraged them to participate in the demonstrations and thus contribute to the victory of the *Solidaritat Catalana* against *caciquismo*.[18] This reveals that in contrast to liberal politics, which were the concern of a social minority, the new political movements sought to politicise wider segments of society. Moreover, the articles published during these days demonstrate that Republicans and Catalan nationalists used the press to educate people about their political rights and instructed them on how to prevent the rigging of elections. Hence, readers were advised to be at the electoral college by seven o'clock in the morning and to bring with them "any friends, relatives or people you may know". The press also encouraged them to report any wrongdoing they might witness, like vote shopping, and told them not to fear intimidation.[19] These recommendations exemplify how the press became a central device in mobilising broader segments of society.

Still, the new practices of the emerging parties sometimes ran parallel to more traditional ones, like clientelism. One of the leaders of the *Lliga Regionalista* (Francesc Cambó) made arrangements addressed at winning the support of local bosses who traditionally supported the Godó family.[20] This case illustrates that although the fight against *caciquismo* was a central point in the programme of the *Solidaritat Catalana*, on some occasions their candidates used it to their own advantage. These dubious practices, also noticed in other constituencies in Catalonia,[21] were morally justified by the challenge of removing the Godó's long-established roots from the territory. The scale at which the new political movements made use of *caciquismo* seemed to be considerably lower, yet still the leaders of the *Lliga Regionalista* justified these measures for the great importance they gave to winning in Igualada.[22]

But the Godó family did not watch the exploits of their enemies with their arms folded; they mobilised their supporters too. One of the ways they did so consisted in monitoring the electoral roll, which became one of the most important features of the new competitive politics. On polling day the chamber of notaries in Igualada was flooded with petitions to appoint legal assistants to monitor the vote counting. This was a strategy aimed at manipulating the census, and in the worst case preventing political rivals from doing so.[23] Among the people who made these requests were various relatives of the Godó family; mayors of neighbouring towns; and the very same owner of *La Vanguardia*, Ramón Godó.[24] The intervention of this man revealed that his retirement from politics did not mean leaving his cousin in the lurch. Moreover, in the days prior to the elections Ramón Godó visited the constituency in his car, almost certainly to encourage the family's supporters in the different towns of the constituency to rig the elections.[25] His actions show to what extent the kinship ties with his cousin Juan remained strong, even when he had retired from politics. In the fierce competition against the new political rivals, the family stood together to maintain their political stronghold.

Still, the efforts that the Godó supporters expended in counteracting the mobilisation of the *Solidaritat Catalana* were insufficient and they lost the elections. Of the total 31,819 people with the right to vote in 1907, Juan Godó only obtained 2,898 votes; in contrast to his competitor, who obtained 3,571.[26] An important segment of the electorate did not participate (3,507 voters) but these elections registered the highest electoral turnout in the history of Igualada's constituency (64%). This growth in participation went in line with the broader situation in Catalonia, where the politicised atmosphere increased electoral turnout to similar levels.[27] The case of Igualada consequently shows that the crisis of liberal parties was not exclusive to big cities like Barcelona – as the literature has often assumed[28] – but was expanding to inland and medium-sized cities of the Catalan territory too.

The Godó's case demonstrates nevertheless that this was a long and uneven process. The growing mobilisation of society did not imply the immediate disappearance of the family, but forced them to develop new strategies to adapt to the new mass politics. Despite the fact Juan Godó lost the elections in 1907, in the 1910 elections he reversed the situation and managed to win them. And, most importantly for the aims of this book, he did so in a context of spectacular mobilisation: in 1910, voter turnout in Igualada reached 80%. That percentage revealed a highly politicised local context, where the traditional oligarchy and the emerging political forces fiercely competed to mobilise the population. These elections presented further novelties: a new electoral law now existed; and Godó's opponents were no longer united in the *Solidaritat Catalana*. The wide ideological spectrum of this coalition proved to be too strong to survive, and by 1909 the *Solidaritat Catalana* ceased to exist.[29] These changes in the regional context were echoed in the local sphere, and the coalition also ceased to exist in Igualada.

In this now fragmented yet highly mobilised political panorama, the Godós made an attempt to adapt to the new mass politics and professionalize their sources of authority. Hence, Juan Godó did not seek to limit the rigging of elections, as was customary in the family, but actively sought to attract new supporters. To this end he began an electoral campaign and with a long caravan of cars and other vehicles he visited all the towns in the constituency. This strategy reveals two important novelties in his strategy (e.g. the launch of an electoral campaign and the use of cars to do so) and reveals that besides the rigging of elections he was now interested in addressing the voters too. In this attempt, Juan Godó also displayed a new discourse based on identity issues: all the cars of his caravan hoisted Spanish flags. This was a subtle but not meaningless detail, for it revealed how the liberal elites' strategies of adaptation were tightly interwoven to the new political context.

Indeed, the first decade of the 20th century was a moment when identity issues became a heated issue in most of Europe. Although nationalism was not a new phenomenon, in this period it presented some distinctive features if compared to previous decades. In contrast to the democratic revolutions of the mid-19th century, when nationalism carried progressive and even emancipatory connotations, the picture was different at the beginning of the 20th century. Nationalism now highlighted the difficulties of the liberal's nation-building project to integrate the whole of society.[30] These difficulties manifested differently, according to each country. In central Europe, for instance, nationalism took a reactionary shape and revealed the tensions of multi-ethnic entities, as in the case of the Habsburg Empire.[31] In the Spanish case, in contrast, nationalism took the form of alternative voices from the periphery that challenged the liberal's centralist understanding of the "nation", and held it responsible for the country's state of decay (intensified in the Disaster of 1898).[32]

Indeed, the victory of the *Solidaritat Catalana* in 1907 gave new visibility to identity issues at a national level. Together with the Republicans, the nationalists of the *Lliga Regionalista* were now the leading force in Catalonia and proposed to regenerate Spain by means of a decentralised administration.[33] These demands for autonomy, however, were often regarded in the rest of Spain as a selfish demand containing a hidden separatist agenda.[34] In this context, the Godó family saw in Spanish identity the opportunity to mobilise the segment of society that did not identify with the growing influence of the *Lliga Regionalista*. Juan Godó thus tried to make identity a new element of his candidacy, and in that attempt he relied on the precious support of his cousin and thus also of his cousin's newspaper, *La Vanguardia*. The paper gave positive coverage of Godó's electoral campaign and stressed his defence of Spanish identity. In the meantime, it also criticised his rivals from the *Lliga Regionalista*. As this newspaper stated:

> "In few constituencies of this region the electoral contest appears to be so tight as in Igualada. The Regionalist candidate multiplies its efforts to recover the simpathies of voters, which was severly damaged during his time as deputie (...). This hard to be achieved aim seems to give no fruits by now, as it could be observed in the meeting celebrated yesterday [in the town] of La Torre de Claramunt, where the Liberal candidate Mister Juan Godó received clear indications of support from the local people and from people coming from other towns, this being something that allows predicting his victory in the next elections. The Regionalist candidate and his friends arrived with their coaches hoisting Catalan flags, and were received with few applause; [in contrast] to the arrival of Mr. Godó, who arrived in a caravan where all the cars were hoisting Spanish flags. (...) Around two thousand people attended the meeting, and who showed throgh their applause their clear commitment to Mr. Godó."[35]

This article reveals the importance the press played in the new mass politics. Despite the fact the electoral rally of Juan Godó was held in a very small town (Torre de Claramunt) the rally was turned into a media event that thousands of readers learned about thanks to the intermediary role of *La Vanguardia*. The newspaper, by then Catalonia's top-selling paper, contributed to publicising the image of Juan in highly positive terms: emphasis was put on the warm welcome he received from the local population (*"the crowds received him with enthusiasm"*); while the presence of Spanish flags in his caravan was implicitly contrasted with the Catalan flags of his opponent. This double-identity discourse was repeated in subsequent rallies, and *La Vanguardia* actively contributed to giving it the maximum publicity possible:

> "The electoral contest will be very disputed in Igualada's constituency; both sides battle with determination and candidates do not stop for a moment in their rallies of propaganda around the differen towns in the constituency (...) the adversaries carry in their vehicles the Catalan flag (...) We – he added – carry both the Catalan and the Spanish flag. *¡Long life to Catalonia! ¡Long live to Spain! For Catalonia and Spain, please vote who loves both equally; and this is Mr. Godó.*"[36]

Articles similar to the one quoted above provide evidence of Juan Godó's attempts to take advantage of the new political scenario. At a time when the Catalan nationalists were challenging the hegemony of liberal parties, identity issues appeared as a new element for the notables to re-define their position in public. Hence, and in contrast to the Catalan flags that the *Lliga*'s candidates usually hoisted, Juan Godó sought to embody a new image based on a dual understanding of identity. This language of "dual patriotism", which understood Catalan and Spanish as two sides of the same coin, rather than as opposed, had already been somehow present – though in a more subtle manner – in the pages of *La Vanguardia*, especially during the debates on economic policies of the 1880s.[37] But in the new 20th century, and as quarrels over identity arose passionate debates throughout the Continent, identity also spilled out into the contest between the new mass parties and their liberal opponents. In this regard, the aim of Juan Godó was to exploit the discontent of those segments of population that felt concerned with the discourse of the *Lliga*, and to turn it to his favour. In this way, Godó was trying to combine the traditional discourse based on acting as the "father of the district" with a new ingredient, based on the defence of a unitary understanding of the Spanish nation.

As part of these self-fashioning strategies, the ownership of *La Vanguardia* became a precious instrument. Hence, the audience that was susceptible of receiving the message that Godó was trying to publicize was not limited to the towns he visited with his electoral team, but reached a massive audience thanks to the help from his cousin at *La Vanguardia*. The numerous articles that the newspaper devoted to commenting on the electoral campaign in Igualada were a clear move aimed at supporting the family's interests through the press. Moreover, in the pages of *La Vanguardia* the candidate of the *Lliga* frequently received a bad treatment; it was highlighted for instance that he did not enjoy the same support from the people that Godó did.[38] All this provides empirical evidence for one of the arguments of this book. That is, that the influence of journalists as *political actors* consisted in their capacity to select which events were given public visibility, and to choose the nature of this publicity (positive or negative), depending on the owner's interests. Instead of rigging the elections, Ramón Godó was now supporting his cousin in Igualada through a subtler – yet equally valuable – manner consisting in using *La Vanguardia* to support his cousin's political campaign.

The lengths to which Ramón Godó would go to maintain the family hegemony in Igualada were laid bare when it became evident that the above-quoted article of *La Vanguardia* was a fantasy. As copies of the edition with this article about the glorious reception that Juan Godó received in the town of Torre de Claramunt were distributed, various voices started questioning that version of events. Apparently, the strong animosity Juan Godó faced in this town had ultimately led him to stay away and instead to send one of his delegates. These last-minute changes, however, were ignored in *La Vanguardia*, and a fake report of the events was made up instead. Barcelona's press rapidly noticed the false article in *La Vanguardia* and criticised the editorial independence that this newspaper liked to boast about.[39] Ramón Godó's attempts to support his relatives in Igualada had thus tarnished the image of the newspaper, and not for the first time.[40] This anecdote reveals the importance traditional elites gave to public opinion to redefine their sources of authority; yet at the same time demonstrates that public opinion was hard to control and open to contest from other actors. In such a disputed field, not even the editorial independence of *La Vanguardia* was a safeguard.

In the end, and despite this small controversy, Juan Godó won the elections of 1910. Apart from the new methods he started implementing in these elections, there is evidence that he made an intense use of clientelism too. Hence, Godó mobilised as many as 286 assistants and six notaries to monitor (and manipulate) the electoral roll. The opposition denounced these fraudulent practices, but once more the liberal institutions showed their disinterest in promoting accountability, and the protests were disregarded once he was in Congress.[41] These elections illustrate, in consequence, that even when a high mobilisation of the electorate took place (voter turnout reached 80% on this occasion) the use of clientelist practices did not disappear but coexisted with the new methods of competitive politics. Traditional elites like the Godó family consequently demonstrated that while relying on the traditional practices based on clientelism, they also sought to adopt some of the methods of the new professional politics. The electoral campaign, the organisation of caravans of cars, the use of a discourse based on identity, and the use of the press as an instrument of propaganda, are all evidence of this.

All these new methods, however, became insufficient to maintain the family stronghold in Igualada. In a chronology very similar to other notables in Europe, the political careers of the Godó family suffered an abrupt end in the years around the First World War (1914–1918). But what were the specific reasons for the end of the Godós' political career? At least three elements can be identified, the first of which is the active mobilisation of the opposition. Republicans and Catalan nationalists learned a bitter lesson from the elections of 1910: when they ran separately they were incapable of defeating the Godó family. They managed to do so in 1907, when they ran together in the *Solidaritat Catalana*, but failed when they ran alone. All this explains why in the next elections, in 1914, the political opposition (the Republicans, the Catalanists and even the Catholics) united again. On this occasion they did not do so by forming a coalition, but through supporting the Conservative candidate (see Table 5.1). This shows that in Igualada political struggle did not consist in liberal parties versus new emerging ones, but in a fight between all the parties and one single family. This polarisation of local politics explains why a Republican journal like *El Igualadino* presented the elections of 1914 as a "war of liberation" against *caciquismo*, even though the candidate this newspaper now supported belonged to the Conservative party.[42]

The second cause of the demise of the Godós' hegemony is that the family started suffering from the same government intervention in elections that it had traditionally benefited from. The strong position this family built in Igualada on behalf of the Liberal Party traditionally led the other liberal party (the Conservatives) not to present their candidate in this constituency. This situation started to change in 1914, when the Conservatives started competing against the family. This decision echoed the growing confrontation between liberal parties on a national scale,[43] and the growing difficulties they faced to impose their will in elections. As a result, the Conservative Party attempted to retrieve the constituency in Igualada from the Godós' hands. This became evident in the methods the Conservative government of Eduardo Dato used in 1914, when a classic repertoire was used to rig the elections (including physical intimidation, intervention of state officials and coercion of voters). Ironically, the Godós were now the ones who denounced, via the ever-supportive *La Vanguardia*, the coercion the government exerted on voters.[44] Indeed, although Juan Godó kept participating in public events to reinforce his image as the "father of the district" (see Illustration 5) such efforts proved to be in vain. The government's pressure on the Godó family became so strong that it reached a point where the supporters of this family in the city council (eight councillors in total, including Juan Godó Pelegrí) resigned en masse. This was a move aimed at denouncing the Conservatives' new decision to meddle in Igualada's affairs, and reveals to what extent the state's intervention remained an important element in local politics.[45]

The third and most important reason for the Godó's downfall was the resignation of Juan Godó in March 1916. On previous occasions Juan had considered abandoning public office. His continuous hesitation led the family's supporters to pressure him not to resign. The last evidence of this was in 1914, when an event was organised to thank both Juan Godó and his son Juan Godó Pelegrí for their years of public service as deputy and mayor, respectively (see Illustration 6). As many as 600 people attended this event, including representatives from all 32 towns in the constituency, and it sheds light on the pyramid of patron–client relations that stemmed from Godó's leadership, and on the large number of people who were interested in maintaining the family's hegemony.

All these attempts from supporters (or "clients"), however, were insufficient to convince a man that was tired of the disquiet and squabbles of local politics. The aggressive attacks from the press, combined with some rather more prosaic reasons, finally led Juan Godó to abandon politics. And like his cousin Ramón before him, he also announced his retirement from politics through an open letter in *La Vanguardia*:

> "We have been kindly asked to publish the following letter: Mr. Editor of LA VANGUARDIA. My dearest friend: Due to the smear campaign I have been suffering lately and having not recovered yet from my last automovile accident, I have decided to stay appart from political struggle and to withdraw my candidacy for deputie in Congress in representation of Igualada's constituency. I also ask you, Mr. Editor, when making this announcement public through your newspaper, to express my gratitude to the goodfriends I have in this constituency, for the loyalty they have shown to me in all times, and I promise to all of them my most loyal frienship and help in whatever concerns the private sphere. (...) *Juan Godó Llucià*."[46]

Ramón Godó: Building the charisma of Antonio Maura

The letter Juan Godó Llucià sent to *La Vanguardia* in 1916 put an end to the Godós' long political hegemony, achieved by two successive generations of the same family. This letter was published in the same newspaper that had already been of invaluable support to his electoral campaign in the past. Yet contrary to what might be expected, *La Vanguardia* did not lament Juan Godó's decision to resign from politics, but welcomed it in favourable terms. In the view of this newspaper, noble interests no longer inspired politics in Igualada, and consequently Juan's decision was praised as being the right one.[47]

The attitude of *La Vanguardia* might seem surprising at first glance. After all, the resignation of Godó implied the end of the family's long political career. However, the attitude of this newspaper was not that surprising if we focus on the trajectory of its owner, Ramón Godó Lallana (1864–1931). As Chapter 5 explained, Ramón had retired from politics in 1906, in response to the smear campaign he had received from the *Solidaritat Catalana*. However, and as the following pages will show, this resignation from politics also followed his new will to embrace the cause of a politician called Antonio Maura. The attitude that he showed towards this conservative politician, who embodied one of the most ambitious plans to renovate liberal politics, will reveal that Ramón Godó was still firmly committed to political action – yet not through public office, but through his position as newspaper proprietor!

In February 1911, a letter addressed to Ramón Godó had accidentally arrived in the hands of his cousin living in Igualada, Juan Godó Llucià. This letter was written by one of the leading figures in Spanish politics, Antonio Maura, who wished to thank the owner of *La Vanguardia* for the support he received from this newspaper. Ramón Godó took advantage of this letter to introduce himself to this politician and express the great admiration he felt for him:

> "Dear Mr. Antonio Maura. My illustrious and respectable friend; (...) I would like to take advantage of this confusion to let you know that few years ago I retired from active politics and broke my family commitment with the Liberal Party, due to the unpatriotic behaviour of this party, as well as for the positive admiration I feel for your person and your political aims. I have thus ceased in being deputie to Congress and have concentrated in expanding the influence and circulation of my newspaper "La Vanguardia" with the final aim of turning it into a powerful instrument of conservative opinion in Catalonia from where I can support more efficiently the noble ideals that your person embodies, and which represent the only possible salvation for our country. I can assure you that I will contribute with all my efforts to such task, and the letter you sent to me has brought me great joy, and has reasserted me in my determination (...)."[48]

This letter illustrates the deep change in Ramón Godó's political views. As he made clear, both his political career in Igualada's constituency and his affiliation to the Liberal Party obeyed a family tradition. This confession demonstrates to what extent politics was a family enterprise, where the different members cooperated to reach collective aims. Yet as Godó himself explained, he had ended this family tradition in 1906 for two reasons: "the antipatriotic attitude of the Liberal Party" and the "admiration" he felt for the politics of Maura. The following pages will examine these two reasons, because they were two elements that decisively contributed to the crisis of the Restoration. This will provide the historical context in which to frame the agency of Ramón Godó as a newspaper proprietor, and to explain his declared objective of "turning *La Vanguardia* into an important instrument of conservative opinion in Catalonia"; a task to which he promised to dedicate "all my efforts".

Who was Antonio Maura? What was the political programme of this politician, to which Godó referred as "the only salvation for our country"? Maura had started his political career in the ranks of the Liberal Party of Sagasta, but later abandoned it to join the Conservatives.[49] In his view, Spain's state of decay resulted from the great distance that existed between society and the liberal-state project. For a large number of Spaniards the state was a detached entity whose presence in the local sphere was mostly perceived in negative terms (in the form of taxes and interventions in elections). To counteract this situation, Maura designed a programme of national regeneration based on two pillars. The first one was the eradication of *caciquismo*. In the view of this politician, the rigging of elections had decisively contributed to widening the distance between society and liberal institutions, and led him to argue in favour of "dignifying" and "moralising" public life (in his words). During his time as Prime Minister (1907–1909) Maura sought to materialise this philosophy through a triple legislative reform, consisting in the reform of local government, a new electoral law, and the reform of municipal justice.

The second pillar in the programme of this politician consisted in broadening the social basis of the Restoration, in a progressive way and within the framework of the political system. To do so he sought to attract those conservative elements of society that were alienated from politics, and to whom Maura referred as the *"clases neutras"* ("neutral classes", in English). In contrast to other supporters of the renewing politics, Maura had an optimistic outlook on society and believed that the majority of the people were conservative. The problem, however, was that the liberal parties had paid little attention to integrating broader segments of society into the political system, as clientelism had demonstrated. Through the legislative measures he proposed to moralise public life, and in combination with a moderate plan of social reforms, Maura aspired to begin a "revolution from above" that would integrate the "conservative classes" into the political system. Total support of the Monarchy, as well as of Catholicism and social order, were other elements in the regenerationist programme of this liberal conservative politician.

The emphasis Maura placed on appealing to the *neutral masses* is what made the support of Ramón Godó particularly valuable for the plans of this politician. If it is taken into account that Maura lacked an official mouthpiece, and that he paid little attention to propaganda activities,[50] it can be argued that *La Vanguardia* became Maura's most influential organ in Barcelona. This support became manifest when an unexpected event put an end to Maura's government (1907–1909) and to his plans of regeneration. This event was the "Tragic Week", as the popular insurrection that took place in Barcelona during the last week of July 1909 became known. A new military intervention in Morocco promoted a series of protests that eventually turned into a general and anticlerical revolt. As many as 12 churches and 40 convents were burned in the space of a week, and the corpses of nuns were paraded through the streets of Barcelona. This city remained stranded as the events unfolded and the authorities utterly failed to control the situation, creating an acute sense of insecurity among the well-off citizens and revealing the rise of a new social actor (the masses).[51]

Indeed, the black columns of smoke rising from the convents lingered for a long time in the city's memory. In the years that followed, some people regarded the Tragic Week as a plot aimed at social revolution, while others saw it as a spontaneous upheaval against the church. For some of the progressive movements, like the Republicans of Lerroux, the Tragic Week became part of their political imaginary based on anticlericalism, and they referred to it as "the Glorious" or the "Red" week. The most conservative and religious elements in society, in contrast, referred to it as the "Bloody" or "Black" week. In the short term, the Tragic Week resulted in a harsh repression from the conservative government of Antonio Maura. More than 3,000 people were arrested and more than 150 worker unions and secular schools were shut down, accused of having promoted anticlericalism. In August the first five death sentences were pronounced, but one single man was blamed as the sole intellectual instigator. This man was Francesc Ferrer i Guàrdia (1859–1909), a renowned educator who promoted a network of state-independent schools based on secular and rationalist education.

The prosecution and execution of Ferrer, however, unleashed an extraordinary campaign throughout Europe that greatly discredited Maura's public image. Thousands of people mobilised across the Continent, in what became a pan-European mobilisation with some resemblance to the Dreyfus affair (1895). Paris became the first focus of the protest campaigns and more than 10,000 protested in front of the Spanish embassy. Demonstrations also spread to literally all the corners of the French territory (incidents were recorded in 52 departments and 82 cities) and the number of people who demonstrated was the largest since the days of the Paris Commune.[52] In Italy too, demonstrations mobilised a great number of people across the country. As many as 10,000 people rallied in Rome, while 3,000 people did the same in Naples and Turin. In the city of Forli, a young socialist called Benito Mussolini participated in Ferrer's solidarity campaign and held him as an example to follow in the fight against the church's tyranny.[53] Demonstrations also took place in the United Kingdom, Germany and Russia, and different national parliaments held plenary sessions to discuss the events in Barcelona.[54]

This extraordinary mobilisation in support of Ferrer shows the prominent place religious controversies had in Europe at the time. While the Church traditionally had uneasy relations with the liberal state, the first decade of the 20th century saw an unprecedented mobilisation of Catholics and their involvement in political struggle through new organisations. In opposition to this, liberal progressive parties started making secularisation a new central element of their political agenda. This was a common trend in most European countries, which historians often explained as an attempt of liberal parties to address the new expanding franchise, and to distract voters from labour disputes. More recently, however, it has been argued that anticlericalism was much more than a tactical move from liberal parties. In reality, it was a phenomenon that epitomised the strong polarisation of European societies around religion.[55]

The Tragic Week exemplified how popular anticlericalism was among Barcelona's working class, and also showed the vital function of the press in creating an unprecedented – though ephemeral – "European public opinion".[56] Newspapers became the main channel through which news about Ferrer circulated between countries, and contributed to disseminating imaginaries that were re-adapted to local contexts. In Italy, for instance, the doors of some churches were burned for the first time as a symbolic act of anticlericalism borrowed from Barcelona's Tragic Week.[57] Additionally, newspapers contributed to popularising the name of Ferrer and to transforming him into a major icon among the intelligentsia and the progressive minds of all Europe. The dubious evidence used by the authorities to sentence and execute Ferrer turned him into a martyr of rationalism and freethinking who transcended national boundaries.[58] In blunt contrast, Antonio Maura was held responsible for the execution and was harshly criticised by the same protestors. The editorials of newspapers all over the Continent emphasised the numerous irregularities of the trial and generally condemned the execution. The French newspapers *L'Humanité* and *La guerre sociale*, for instance, portrayed Maura as the archetypical politician of a backward country dominated by intolerance and religious fanaticism. Moderate newspapers, like the *The Times* of England, also noted the bad impression the execution made for the international image of Maura's government; while the Italian *Il Corriere della Sera* denounced the repression of the Spanish government in strong terms.[59]

The case of *La Vanguardia* revealed the unease this supra-national campaign in support of Ferrer had started generating among the conservative segments of Spanish society. Godó's newspaper deemed the attacks against Maura as a smear campaign against Spain ("*campaña anti-patriótica*"), and complained about the recurring stereotypes published in the European press. In fact, in most countries the progressive forces spoke of Maura's government through a limited yet highly evocative repertoire of images (like the Inquisition and religious fanaticism) that had a long history and were inspired by the country's "black legend".[60] The most conservative segments of Spanish society mobilised against these attacks and set up different initiatives to protest against what they saw as an internationally orchestrated campaign supporting the deeds of the Tragic Week.[61] Ramón Godó actively contributed to this conservative reaction through the press. *La Vanguardia* supported the idea of creating a group of journalists in charge of counteracting foreign news, and made an open call to foreigners living in Barcelona to contradict the image the foreign press gave of this city.[62]

Moreover, the international campaign in support of Ferrer carried destabilising effects in domestic politics. Until that time, and in sharp contrast to the rest of Europe, the indictment of Ferrer had provoked few protests in Spain. However, once the international outcry started, the Spanish left saw it as an opportunity to revive the animosity it traditionally felt towards Maura. Before the Tragic Week the left had already had strong confrontations with this politician. These confrontations were mostly related to Maura's sympathies with the Church and with his strict measures to combat terrorism. The outcome was the union of the left in a new coalition called the "*Bloque de Izquierdas*" ("Left Bloc") in 1908. This coalition was a novelty in the Restoration, as it brought one of the liberal parties (the Liberal Party) together with parties that opposed the political system (the Republicans and the Democrats). This coalition revealed the efforts of the Liberal Party to renew the political agenda by putting an emphasis on the primacy of civil institutions over the church. This new policy based on secularisation, coupled with the anticlerical discourse, went in line with the realignment other liberal progressive parties adopted in Europe.[63]

What makes the Spanish Liberal Party interesting, in this regard, is that in its eagerness to replace Maura in power the party relied upon the support of a new media holding called the "Trust". This English term was how the "*Sociedad Editorial de España*" was commonly known, and it was the first media holding ever created in Spain. The Trust consisted in an alliance of progressive-oriented newspapers aimed at sharing production costs and counteracting the loss of sales the press suffered after the Disaster of 1898.[64] With a capital of 10 million *pesetas*, the Trust brought together nine different newspapers. Some of them were top-selling papers like *El Imparcial* and *El Heraldo de Madrid*, while others were created with the aim of extending the Trust's influence to other cities (like *El Liberal*, which started to be published in Barcelona, Seville and Bilbao). The newspapers of the Trust covered a wide geographic area and a broad range of opinion (especially on the centre-left) and gave, above all, great capacity of influence to their editors. In fact, all the Trust's editors were also deputies in Congress, a feature that reveals the intertwined relations between the press and politics at the time.[65]

The capacity of the Trust to influence policy-making became manifest when Maura's government was toppled shortly after the Tragic Week. As the international campaign started protesting against Ferrer's indictment, the Trust mobilised all their efforts into an aggressive campaign under the slogan "*Maura no!*". Day after day, the various newspapers belonging to this media holding attacked Maura, and blamed him for Spain's discredit in the international arena. At the peak of this campaign, the Trust's standard bearer – Madrid's *El Imparcial* – addressed an article to the King with a clear warning: the Liberal Party could hardly support the Monarchy in the future if Maura's government was to remain in power for much longer. This article was published one day before King Alfonso XIII suddenly decided to remove Maura from power.[66] As the King would recognise later on, his decision was motivated by the heated atmosphere that had followed Ferrer's execution, as well as by the need to distance the crown from Maura's negative public image.[67] This incident reveals the considerable influence editors had over policy-making. They were not simple recorders of events, but actively sought to shape them as political actors.

The fall of Maura's government in October 1909 decisively contributed to the crisis of the Restoration. The change of government put an end to Maura's plans of national regeneration and, above all, revealed a new way to reach power. Instead of resulting from an agreement between the two liberal parties, the Liberal Party reached power through the pressure the Trust exerted on the King. As the leader of the Conservative Party, Maura was deeply disappointed with this strategy and considered that it broke the consensus Liberals and Conservatives had established since 1885 to rotate in power. Maura saw the attitude of the Liberal Party as a stab in the back, and after that time refused any form of agreement with this party. Thus the traditional consensus between liberal parties, upon which the Restoration stood, started to tremble.

La Vanguardia became the way through which Godó expressed his dissatisfaction with the new political situation. The newspaper put in very clear terms the discontent about the Tragic Week and the following political crisis. Such a bold statement was not very common for a newspaper that was independent and therefore preferred to avoid political confrontation. However, the crisis of October 1909 led Godó to express in clear terms the social model he supported, and announced the attitude it would hold in relation to the Liberal Party led by Segismundo Moret:

> "(...) LA VANGUARDIA does not need to hide that it saw with discontent the unfolding of the last crisis, as well as the aggressive campaign launched against the previous government [Maura]. We have also deplored that the Liberal Party has not been capable of adopting a clear position in relation to the events of July, nor against the critiques Spain received from abroad. (...).

LA VANGUARDIA sympathises with the ideas of social conservation, but it does not exclude any development that is done with order; nor any legitimate conquest of the modern law; this is a conservative newspaper, but will never be the mouthpiece of any political party. (...) The fact that we supported Mr. Maura in the recent past did not mean that we were the organ of his government; what it really meant was to support Spain, since national interests were at stake. In this respect, we will also support Mr. Moret (...) when the same national interests are at stake, even if this does not mean giving up our own judgement [;] we only wish that the new government will not be incompatible with the supreme national interests to which we have referred."[68]

The above-quoted article was published as an editorial that positioned *La Vanguardia* in relation to the Tragic Week and to the new political situation. The newspaper defined itself as conservative, yet open to change as long as this took place within the political system's framework. This position revealed the fear of social revolution, as evidenced in the Tragic Week, but also showed a clear awareness of the need to promote reforms. Additionally, the above-cited editorial contained a clear criticism of the attitudes of the Liberal Party and of the Trust for taking advantage of the international campaign to attack Maura. On repeated occasions *La Vanguardia* criticised this press holding for having an irresponsible attitude, similar to the one that led to the Disaster of 1898, and for preventing the renewal of the Liberal Party. Thus, whereas the Conservatives adopted a plan of national regeneration based on Maura's policies, *La Vanguardia* criticised the Trust for acting as a boa constrictor that was coiled around its prey (the Liberal Party). This media holding impeded the movements of the party and risked the peril of crushing it to death.[69] Evidence of this was the Liberals' strategy of criticising Maura and its anticlerical propaganda. This was, in sum, the *"antipatriotic behaviour of the Liberal Party"* that Ramón Godó criticised in his correspondence with Maura.

The importance of the press in the new mass society became evident as the crisis of liberal politics intensified. In 1913, Maura began suffering the opposition of his own party. The boycott policy that he had adopted against the Liberal Party created unease within the Conservatives, who started deeming this position as too radical. The boycott exerted against the Liberals precluded the Conservatives from the support of the government in elections; and therefore from the benefits of holding public office. This situation eventually provoked the crisis of Maura's leadership within the Conservative Party and the splitting of this organisation into two factions: the supporters of restoring the consensus with the Liberals (named *"idóneos"*, in Spanish), and the supporters of Maura, who were still reluctant about the situation that had developed. The climax of this intra-party crisis occurred in October 1913, when King Alfonso XIII called the leader of the *"idóneos"* into power (Eduardo

Dato) to Maura's detriment. This decision demonstrated the consequences that the Tragic Week was still producing on domestic politics, and symbolised the crumbling of the Restoration due to the division between the liberal elites.

Paradoxically, the tensions Maura encountered within his own party greatly increased his popularity, to the point that a new charismatic movement known as *"Maurismo"* emerged. A historian who has studied this movement in detail has stressed how difficult *Maurismo* is to define.[70] *Maurismo* was not a political party, but rather a body of opinion that eventually aspired to transform itself into a stable political organisation. It was not a class movement, although the majority of its members were conservative, Catholic, and mostly of a middle-class background. The people who formed it belonged to the segment of society who deeply disliked the anticlerical agenda of the Liberal Party and listened in horror to stories about the burning of convents in Barcelona. They all identified with the regeneration ideals Maura embodied, and sympathised with the marginalisation he had suffered – to the point of creating a cult of celebrity around this politician.[71] Such veneration stemmed from the effective communicative skills of this politician, like his brilliant oratorical skills or the pomposity of his gestures; as well as the numerous attacks he was victim to. The vociferous campaigns of the Trust under the slogan *"Maura, no!"*, and the decision of the King to remove him from power, contributed to Maura's image of martyrdom. The more Maura was attacked, the more supporters he gained. Yet, and surprisingly, this politician never nurtured this movement nor looked for its support. In fact, it can be said that *Maurismo* existed *in spite of* Maura.[72] The movement saw the politician as more of a hero that embodied a noble ideal of regeneration, than as a liberal politician.

The case of Ramón Godó is evocative of the social and political context that gave birth to *Maurismo*. Godó became the archetypical person who saw in the exclusion of Maura the same obstacles that prevented Spain's salvation. *La Vanguardia* had already expressed solidarity with this politician during Ferrer's international campaign, but the exclusion Maura suffered in the Conservative Party in 1913 intensified even further the admiration that Godó felt for this politician. The correspondence between the two men reveals that Godó's admiration eventually developed into open worship:

"Dear Mr. Antonio Maura. My illustrious and respectable friend; (...) I cannot resist the temptation of asking for a portrait of your person, bearing your signature, so I can hold it in my office in <u>La Vanguardia</u>. I believe that this newspaper deserves such honour and that shall correspond to this honour in the future (...) I must tell you that I follow with great interest the unravelling of national affairs, and especially the confrontation between the conservatives. Needless to say it, I am looking forward to hearing from you, and I am ready to breaking the silence and start the campaing when you order it. You have the power to decide when the moment has come to do so, and we shall all respect your prudence; but our restlesness is natural, for it is born from the great admiration that both the cause and the leader inspires us (...)".[73]

Antonio Maura did not disappoint Godó and rewarded him with a portrait of himself. The fact that Maura's brother painted the portrait illustrates how close the relation between the two men had become. Moreover, Godó was not content with merely hanging the portrait in his office at *La Vanguardia*, but decided to publish a full-page reproduction of the painting in his newspaper, including the personal dedication it contained (see Illustration 7). This gesture, and the letter quoted above, provide clear evidence of the great interest Godó still had in politics. Yet more importantly, his case reveals that besides public office, alternative channels of political action existed, like contributing to build the charisma of a politician through the mass press.

Summary

This chapter has shown how an episode in European history, like the responses of the elites to the birth of mass politics, becomes particularly complex and nuanced if studied from a micro-perspective. The reactions of the Godó family to the challenges of mass politics were far from being the same. On behalf of the Liberal Party, and based on a combination of clientelism and a new repertory of political action, Juan Godó Lluçià fought to maintain the family's local dominion in Igualada. In contrast, his cousin Ramón Godó embraced, through the pages of *La Vanguardia*, a project of national regeneration that sought the eradication of *caciquismo*. The case of these two men illustrates to what extent traditional elites gave different responses to the same challenge. These different attitudes illustrate the impact that the crisis of liberalism had at a micro-scale, which challenged the solidarity between family members. Yet, in the end, kinship ties proved to be stronger than personal views, as shown in the cooperation the Godó family sustained. The conclusion that can be drawn is that the family continued to play a central role in the social cohesion of elites, even though the crisis of liberalism (sometimes) posed a serious threat to the status quo.

The full mobilisation of the family's members, however, became insufficient to save the Godó family's political domain in Igualada. This case study provides an alternative view about the transition from the liberal's monopoly of power to the new mass politics. While historians have mostly explained this transition through the case of big cities, this chapter has examined the transition through the case of a smaller city. Igualada was an industrial location immersed in a rural constituency of 32 small towns. In each and every one of these towns the Godós had a branch of local supporters. As the family crisis intensified, this network of "clients" became more visible as they mobilised to uphold the family's hegemony, which they themselves benefited from. In the meantime, an alternative segment of society – those who did not benefit from this privileged access to public benefits, based on patron–client relationships – started participating in politics and challenged the supremacy of the family.

The outcome was a new political scenario where local society became deeply polarised with respect to the Godó family. In contrast to the confrontation that existed at a national level between traditional and new political parties, in local politics this confrontation took place around the position of one single family. Yet, and contrary to what is often assumed, the new competitive and plural character of elections neither removed clientelism nor led the traditional elites to respond exclusively through autocratic methods. Instead, clientelism took a new form where the two confronting camps competed for the influence of local bosses, while at the same time the local elite sought to redefine (or "professionalise") its sources of authority.

The strategies the family developed to redefine their legitimacy can be compared with the strategies of other European elites. For the case of Italy, for instance, Anthony Cardoza has demonstrated that the Piedmontese nobility progressively abandoned its leadership in liberal parties, but kept its sway in public life by "investing" in informal channels of influence.[74] These channels consisted in those social fields where aristocratic values remained predominant (e.g. diplomacy and the army); but also in the developing new spaces of sociability (like mutual aid societies and religious associations) that allowed noblemen to reassert their role as community leaders. The case of the Godó family highlights an alternative strategy, where elites sought to maintain their influence through public office. The new competitive and plural character of elections, however, implied that clientelism was no longer sufficient to control this position. The case of Juan Godó Llucià reveals different attempts to adapt to the new situation, and it is what allowed him to win in highly competitive scenarios (like the elections of 1910, with an 80% electoral turnout). If all these attempts to renovate the sources of authority finally failed it was, in part, due to the changing relations between this family and the central government. Local politics, therefore, was highly autonomous and yet not totally alienated from outside interference.

Public opinion became an alternative dimension where traditional elites sought to build a new legitimation. If Ramón Godó Lallana achieved a privileged position in society it was not thanks to the combined use of press and public office, but stemmed solely from the former. This reveals a substantial transformation in the Godó's traditional sources of influence, consisting in the growing differentiation between two spheres (press and politics). It was in their capacity to address an audience of thousands of readers that the political power of editors now stood. The case of the Trust illustrates this point, and reveals the growing importance that contemporaries were giving to public space, despite the importance clientelism still had. The emergence of an – ephemeral – European public opinion, and the advantage the Trust took from this to topple Maura from power, exemplify how important public opinion was becoming in political decision-making.

Contrary to the Trust, Ramón Godó could no longer base his influence on acting as the representative of a political party. Yet rather than an inconvenience, editorial independence allowed him room for a range of manoeuvres, and concentrated *La Vanguardia*'s influence in his sole hands. This freedom of criteria allowed Godó to continue exerting an influence in politics according to his particularistic views, as the absolute support he gave to Maura reveals. This instrumentalization of the press to support a private agenda, however, also made editors highly dependent on this blurred and diffused power that public opinion represented. Now that he could no longer rely on either party affiliation or public office, Godó's influence was directly subject to his capacity to appeal to the widest number of readers possible. The strategies he designed to do so will be the focus of the final chapter of this book.

7

The Golden Age of *La Vanguardia* and the Crumbling of the Liberal Order

"It would be hard to find a city in the world with as many sources of disturbance and social unrest as Barcelona."

MANUEL DE BURGOS, Spanish Minister of Interior (1919)[1]

Between 1914 and 1918, Europe and large parts of the world were subsumed into the bloodiest war ever seen. For the scale of tragedy it entailed (an estimated 17 million deaths and 20 million wounded) and the geography of the countries it involved, the First World War represented a truly global event.[2] In Europe, the deep social and economic distress that resulted from the war, including the changes in the political map (four empires and three dynasties fell) have led historians to see the First World War as the symbolic demarcation between two eras. That is, a war that put an end to the so-called "Long 19th century" and heralded the birth of a new era, increasingly regarded as a "European civil conflict", lasting up to the Second World War (1939–1945).[3] Historians have traditionally considered that all these changes deepened the transformation that European elected representatives started to act after the 1880s: the "decline" of the notables and its substitution by the new mass parties and the professional politicians.[4] The case of Ramón Godó, however, will provide an opportunity to examine how some elites resorted to alternative mechanisms besides official politics to maintain their influence in society, at a time when the war shook the liberal regimes to its core all over the Continent.

In order to examine the elites' strategies of adaptation in depth, this chapter is divided in two parts. The first part will examine the reasons behind the exponential growth that *La Vanguardia* experienced since the second decade of the 20th century, and which turned it into Spain's top-selling newspaper, only equalled by Madrid's *ABC*. Central to this success was the ambitious programme of reforms that Godó designed in order to broaden the newspaper's readership. At a time when he could no longer rely on political office, the adoption of a more professionalised form of journalism, based on continuous investment in technology and communication services, became an alternative platform to hold sway in society.

However, the golden age of *La Vanguardia* also coincided with the crisis of the Restoration regime. In line with the rest of Europe, Spain's liberal institutions entered a profound crisis in the aftermath of the Great War. The massive economic dislocation and the social distress resulting from the conflict intensified ideological militancy and increased the crisis of parliamentarism. In parallel, the triumph of the Bolshevik Revolution in 1919 had a profound echo and intensified class struggle. As Spain's most industrialized region, Catalonia is where all these elements behind the crisis of liberalism were lived out with more intensity.[5] On one hand, Catalan nationalism sponsored one of the more serious attempts to transform the liberal state-model from within. On the other, between 1918 and 1919 Barcelona fell into a semi-revolutionary climate that threatened to overthrow the whole system from the outside. In the aftermath of the First World War Spanish politics thus became engulfed in a double process whose origins lay in Barcelona: that is, the "Catalan quagmire and the red spectre".[6] The second part of this chapter will examine how Godó manouevered in the face of these two elements that not only posed a threat to the Restoration system, but were also a direct menace to his position as proprietor of Catalonia's leading paper.

The specialisation of *La Vanguardia* in informative journalism

As Table 7.1 shows, during the First World War (1914–1918) the newspaper of Ramón Godó practically doubled its circulation. The rest of Barcelona's big dailies, in contrast, experienced few changes, as in the case of *Las Noticias* and *La Publicidad*; or even suffered a drastic loss of readers, such as in the case of *La Veu de Catalunya*. What were the reasons, we may then wonder, behind *La Vanguardia*'s singular growth during this period? What made this newspaper different from the other ones in Barcelona, so as to achieve such a spectacular expansion? To what degree did the European conflagration contribute to this expansion?

It was in the early 20th century that Godó planted the seeds of the growth that *La Vanguardia* would experience in the next two decades. On 25 October 1903, this newspaper devoted seven pages to explaining a new plan of reforms. Among other things, these reforms included moving *La Vanguardia*'s headquarters to a new building, located at number 28 on Pelai, an excellent location in the centre of Barcelona.[7] The building was designed

Table 7.1. *Circulation of the main newspapers in Barcelona between 1905 and 1920*

	1905	1913	1918	1920
La Vanguardia	18,000	58,000	90–100,000	100,000
Las Noticias	11,000	47,000	45–50,000	60,000
La Publicidad	7,000	25,000	25–30,000	85,000
El Noticiero Universal	10,000	——	20–25,000	30,000
El Diluvio	10,000	——	15–17,000	40,000
La Veu de Catalunya	4,000	20,000	6–8,000	——

Source: Josep Lluís Gómez Mompart, *La gènesi de la premsa de masses a Catalunya (1902–1923)*, Barcelona, editorial Pòrtic, 1992, p.133.

in Modernist style, containing a floral decoration and a series of stone reliefs in its interior that were recognised with an honorary mention in Barcelona's historical-artistic buildings awards of 1904. The dimensions of the new headquarters, built on purpose, were considerable: two five-story buildings, one facing Tallers Street and the other facing Pelai. The building's construction amounted to 335,000 *pesetas* and contained a total surface of 26,479 palms.[8] The mere fact that a newspaper owned a building constituted a whole novelty at the time: as late as the 1920s only two newspapers in Barcelona did – *La Vanguardia* and *Las Noticias*.[9]

The first floor of *La Vanguardia*'s new building contained a series of decorative figures that symbolised the journalistic model that the newspaper wished to champion. These decorative figures consisted of three different elements – "*Science and the Arts*", the "*Telephone*" and the "*Printing Press*" – and were sculpted as allegorical figures to which the newspaper wished to pay tribute. This type of decoration reveals a cult of modernity based on the progress that technological innovation (in the form of communication and speed) had brought to journalism. In fact, the same admiration for technology was present in the description *La Vanguardia* made of a new printing machinery it had recently purchased. The characteristics of the new machinery was described in an almost poetic manner:

"Downstairs there is the wide room, at the centre of which lies the machine with its complicate organism, in a calm state as we are writing these lines, but waiting for the moment when the engine shall bring it into life, puting in motion its cogwheels, its cilinders, its fingers made of wood, all this labryinth of gears, where every part fits each place and obeys one purpose."[10]

In this way, the new rotary press was referred to as a living thing – "organism", "life", "fingers" were some of the words used to describe it – that was perfectly designed and ready to show its full potential. This admiration mainly originated in the new opportunities it offered for journalism. The new rotary press, bought from the German company Koenig and Bauer, was indeed an example of the practical opportunities technology opened for the journalistic profession: it would allow *La Vanguardia* to publish twice as many pages, and to do so quickly.[11] If these examples reveal that technology was seen in *La Vanguardia* as a tool of progress, the way this newspaper justified the need for investing were the changing needs of Barcelona's audience. And this audience, it must be noted, was not a uniform body, but was integrated by a multiple and diverse number of readers, each of them having their own political preferences. In contrast to the biased character of the partisan press, *La Vanguardia* described its target readership as a public holding a diversity of opinions. Hence, this newspaper presented itself as a newspaper that "has come to enjoy the favour of the public, to the point of having extended its presence to all the social classes". The support from such a plural audience, the newspaper argued, is what ultimately imposed the duty of introducing new reforms.[12]

The plan of reforms of October 1903 was an idea of *La Vanguardia*'s new owner, Ramón Godó Lallana (1864–1931). As explained in previous chapters, this takeover was the result of a generational renewal prompted by the death of the founding brothers Bartolomé (in 1894) and Carlos Godó (in 1897), and entailed not only the transmission of the family business in the jute industry, but also the leadership in the family's political career. As the new owner, Ramón wished to give the newspaper a new impulse, and to this end he was responsible behind *La Vanguardia*'s move to the new headquarters in Pelai Street. The move became an opportunity that he used to portray himself as the heir of a rich journalist tradition. Thus, when *La Vanguardia* announced the inauguration of the new building, it printed a portrait of the two founding brothers (Carlos and Bartolomé Godó) on its front page.[13] The faces of the two brothers were also sculpted onto the façade of the new company building. Besides being a mark of respect that Ramón wished to pay to his father and uncle (whose portraits he displayed in his office), these gestures contained a symbolic dimension. Publishing the portraits of the founding brothers was a way of reinforcing the family tradition in public. Linking the name of *La Vanguardia* to that of the Godó family constituted a way of reasserting his control over the newspaper, and to proclaim that he was now responsible for its conduct.

Next to reassuring his control over *La Vanguardia*, Ramón Godó also wished to give it a renewed impetus. He summarised this aspiration with a new motto: it was necessary "to keep up with the times and avoid crystallising" ("*hay que marchar al compás del tiempo, rehuyendo de cristalizarse*").[14] This motto reveals that Godó did not conceive of the press as a self-sufficient element, but rather as one that was highly dependent on the social context in which it was published. This line of reasoning, which was publicised on further occasions, implied a clear premise: if the newspaper was to survive, it should be capable of matching the broader changes in society. If there was an area where Godó considered that La Vanguardia was not staying sufficiently abreast with the times, it was in the area "concerning information".[15] This statement reveals that the owner of La Vanguardia had the impression that Barcelona's public opinion was demanding a different, more informative-oriented newspaper. The crisis the press suffered in Spain, in the aftermath of 1898, might have acted as a stimulus in this regard.

In fact, during the first quarter of the 20th century the deep transformations taking place in Barcelona had the effect of changing the needs and tastes of newspaper consumers. Between 1887 and 1910, the city grew from 400,000 to 587,000 inhabitants.[16] The majority of this population growth came from the inner parts of Catalonia, and were people attracted by the employment opportunities of a city that was abandoning its traditional dependence on the textile industry. Triggered by the broadening of Barcelona's borders (in 1897 the city absorbed six of its neighbouring towns) the building industry stood at the helm of a process of industrial diversification, while the metallurgical and chemical sectors gained a new presence too.[17] These were also the years of improvement in the literacy levels (between 1900 and 1910, illiteracy dropped from 54% to 41%; by 1930, it had decreased to less than 15%). In the field of culture, "*Modernisme*" kept expanding its presence in Barcelona's intellectual life and architecture (of which the headquarters of La Vanguardia were an example), while a series of technological innovations – like the electric light, the telephone, the automobile, the radio and the airplane – intensified a feeling of rapid transformation that contemporaries repeatedly noticed. Moreover, the general improvement in living conditions was expressed in new forms of leisure that gained weight in the following decades, like cinema, sports and eventually even jazz.[18]

It was in the context of some of these transformations taking place in Barcelona that the Godós sought to specialize La Vanguardia in informative journalism. This line of reasoning, summarised in the motto referred to above, was explained in further detail in an article entitled "*El periódico moderno*" ("the modern newspaper"). For the type of reflections it contained, this article constituted a roadmap summarising the journalistic ideal to which La Vanguardia wished to subscribe in the future. The argument of the article was presented in clear terms and according to a Darwinist standpoint: the newspaper should be regarded as a "living organism". As such, if it was to survive it should be capable of "adapting quickly" to changing environments. One of the main reasons behind this change, La Vanguardia claimed, was the "development of industry, commerce and banking", which required "vast amounts of information". When nations lived in a system of autarchy, the article reasoned, reading about foreign events constituted a mere "amusement". Now, by contrast, "a war taking place in America or in the Far East touches on the commercial transactions of the entire world; (...) likewise, if England persists in its free trade policies or decides to move into protectionism it might provoke a cataclysm in some businesses, like the agricultural and manufacturing indus- tries. It is clear, then, why all the news is of great importance for the public, no matter how insignificant they may seem".[19]

The world *La Vanguardia* was describing in this article of 1903 was one undergoing a rapid process of economic integration. If this newspaper was to satisfy the needs of the public, it could not afford to lose its grip on the changes taking place in society. In this regard, the case of *La Vanguardia* is illustrative of how newspapers were seeking to adapt to the globalisation process that took place in the 19th century. Indeed, as Jürgen Osterhammel has explained, global communications provided the means for newspapers to gather the news from literally every corner of the world. For the leading newspapers, reporting on worldwide events simply became a must.[20] Together with foreign corre- spondents, the press based the task of newsgathering on the service a few agencies provided, like Reuters and Havas. These agencies were the most important actors in the global distribution of news, thanks to the vast network of correspondents they possessed. Equally as important as the growing depend- ence newspapers had on agencies is *how* this dependence transformed the content of newspapers. Hence, and according to Osterhammel, agencies distributed the news without modifying its content, thus contributing to fostering a "uniform kind of journalism" that epitomised "the ideology of objectivity".[21]

What makes the case of *La Vanguardia* interesting, in this regard, is that it constitutes an empirical case study through which studying how the growing interest to learn about distant parts of the world ("being informed") altered the way of presenting the news, as part of the broader changes in the journal- istic field.[22] According to the self-perception of *La Vanguardia*, the wish to provide greater quantities of news obliged newspapers to restructure their content. *La Vanguardia* strongly criticised the Spanish newspaper's traditional tendency of publishing long and complicated articles that only a select audi- ence was capable of understanding. In contrast to this, the Godós' newspaper considered that articles should be shorter and written with clarity and conci- sion, so as to make them accessible to the average reader. The news provided by news agencies also contributed in such attempts to popularise the press. According to *La Vanguardia*'s estimates, this news format multiplied its pres- ence in newspapers by ten times, to the point of appropriating some of the space traditionally devoted to the articles written by journalists.

All these changes in the content and format of news represented an attempt to broaden the newspaper readership. As *La Vanguardia* argued, "the modern newspaper must provide room for all the events taking place (...) because it has thousands and thousands of subscribers, and each of them devotes himself to a different profession and has his own understanding of things". Thus, having the capacity to fit more news into less space, thanks to the advantages provided by news agencies and the telegraph represented an advantage. Additionally, addressing a wider audience also required presenting the news in a different language: the tone used in the articles should be as moderate as possible, so as to avoid upsetting the views of any potential reader. This moderate tone in news, *La Vanguardia* concluded, is what explained the "death of the partisan press" and justified, ultimately, the huge circulation foreign newspapers (deemed by *La Vanguardia* as being "very neutral" in their coverage) had achieved.[23]

From this testimony it can be deduced that writing news with a moderate tone was still a rare practice among the majority of the Spanish press, which was still driven by partisan ethics. One of the longest-serving journalists at *La Vanguardia*, named José Escofet (1884–1939), expressed his dissatisfaction with the work of journalists in Spain, and with those in Madrid in particular. According to Escofet, the Spanish capital was still dominated by an old journalistic ideal, where the newspapers focused on three topics: theatre, bullfighting, and politics.[24] The reason these three topics, which Escofet considered as mere "gossip" ("*chismorreo*"), were given such preference in Madrid's press was related to the characteristics of the journalistic profession: the majority of journalists were still self-educated men who, after having "wasted their time writing poetry, novels and comedies", decided to enter in the world of journalism to make a living. It was no surprise, then, that this passion for literature went to the detriment of news. Inspired by the larger circulation achieved by foreign newspapers, in contrast *La Vanguardia* considered that adopting a more informative orientation was the key to success.

The strongest proof of Godó's intention to turn *La Vanguardia* into an informative newspaper was his new massive investment in international news, through the French news agency Havas. While Spanish newspapers usually relied on the work of journalists when it came to reporting on local and national events, their coverage of international affairs heavily depended on the services of news agencies. As in most of Europe, in Spain too different news agencies were founded in the 19th century to supply foreign news to newspapers. This was the case, for instance, of the agencies Fabra (1865) and *Mencheta* (1876).[25] However, during the first decade of the 20th century the global information market experienced a process of integration that eventually resulted in the oligopoly of three big agencies: the French Havas, the English Reuters and the German Wolff. These three agencies partitioned the world in three respective areas of influence, according to which Spain fell into Havas' area. The outcome was that Havas came to monopolise the information flow between Spain and the rest of Europe. Such dependence on this French news agency is what led historian María de la Paz Rebollo to refer to Spain's dependence on Havas as a type of "information colonialism".[26]

The following pages will argue that the aim of turning *La Vanguardia* into the best-informed newspaper in Barcelona, as stated in the reform plans of 1903, is what led Ramón Godó to make Havas a central part of his strategy for increased readership. A close look at Havas' historical records, located in the French National Archives (Paris), reveals that the newspaper of the Godó family had become the best customer the French agency had in Barcelona by the outbreak of the First World War. The reason for this was *La Vanguardia*'s continuous increase in the pace of demand. Hence, while all the newspapers started demanding from Havas a similar quantity of information (around 12,000 words per month), *La Vanguardia* distinguished itself from the rest of the pack in the contract it negotiated. In contrast for instance to the "*Asociación de Prensa de Barcelona*" (an association that gathered some of the most important newspapers in the city), which set strict limits on the consumption of words by sticking to a fixed monthly instalment (400 *pesetas* in 1908; around 800 in 1913), *La Vanguardia* requested a mode of payment that left the door open to increase its demand in the foreseeable future.[27] This method of payment was based on economy of scale: the more words the newspaper requested, the cheaper the cost (e.g. under 15,000 words - 6 *ptas* per 100 words; over 15,000 words – 5 *ptas* per 100 words).

The difference in the fees agreed between Havas and *La Vanguardia* and its competitors in Barcelona eventually marked a massive difference in the pace of demand. Whereas the number of words that the *Asociación de Prensa de Barcelona* consumed grew very gradually over the years (12,000 words in 1908; 16,000 in 1913); in the case of *La Vanguardia* this demand rocketed: 15,000 words (1909); around 75,000 (1911); 81,000 (1913), 100,000 (mid-October 1913 onwards).[28] Therefore, in barely five years the newspaper of the Godó family had multiplied the number of words it bought from Havas by six times, and had reached 100,000 words per month just before the war started. The service of the rest of Barcelona's newspapers, in contrast, experienced minor changes and halted at 16,000 words by the same period.[29] This great divergence in the pace of consumption had a direct impact in the newspaper's content: whereas the pages of *La Vanguardia* started being filled with news about the whole the world that Havas provided, the rest of its competitors in Barcelona had a more parochial character.

Further evidence of *La Vanguardia*'s pioneer role in adopting an informative model is that it became the first newspaper in Spain to install a telegraphic station in a newsroom. This took place in 1909, when a station was established at the newspaper headquarters. The station consisted of one Hughes and one Morse receiver, as well as a cable that connected the headquarters of *La*

Vanguardia with Barcelona's telegraphic network. This meant that the newspaper was capable of transmitting and receiving information from all the Spanish and international telegraph stations that were connected to Barcelona's station.

New channels of influence in the age of mass politics

Spain was part of the small group of European countries that did not enter the First World War. As early as 30 October 1914, the Conservative government of Eduardo Dato proclaimed the country's official neutrality. The vast majority of the political class immediately supported the government's decision. Such consensus among liberal politicians was based on the shared perception, which the Disaster of 1898 and the subsequent calls for national regeneration were a painful reminder of, that Spain had very limited room for manoeuvre in international relations. Ironically, once the war started to reveal its full horror, Spain's neutral position appeared to have saved the country from its worst consequences.

However, in recent years scholars have challenged the myth that Spain's official neutrality saved it from being engulfed by the war. The new works published on the occasion of the First World War centenary have provided further evidence that Spain was, in reality, another piece in the complicated European chessboard of 1914–1918 – certainly not the most important one, but one whose fate was still tightly intertwined to that of the Continent.[30] An example of this was propaganda. Some of Spain's characteristics (like its geostrategic position in the Mediterranean, its condition as market supplier to the warring countries, as well as its potential entry into the war) made both the Allies and the Central Powers aware of the importance of getting the public opinion of this country on their respective sides.

Initially, when the First World War started *La Vanguardia* took a neutral standpoint. This position went in line with *La Vanguardia*'s self-proclaimed desire, in the reforms of 1903, to be as neutral as possible when reporting events. Hence, the editorials of *La Vanguardia* referred to the war as the "failure of a whole civilization" and praised the liberal politicians for having defended a neutral alignment for Spain.[31] However, as the illusion of a hasty war faded and the conflict deteriorated into trench warfare in late 1914, Spanish society started to take sides. The country's official neutrality began to be contested by the creation of two opposing camps, which saw in the war the opening of new perspectives for Spain's future recovery.

On one hand, there were the "Germanophiles", who saw in the Central Powers the model of order, tradition and discipline they considered Spain needed. This side was formed by the most traditional and conservative ranks of Spanish society, like the church, the army, the catholic fundamentalists and the aristocracy, but also contained many admirers of Germany's technology and culture. Overall they were the majority in Spanish public opinion (in contrast to the majority of non-aligned countries in Europe) and argued for Spain's most absolute neutrality in relation to the conflict. In practice, the Germanophiles' advocacy for "absolute neutrality" benefited the interests of the Central Powers, since Spain's international commitments were with the Allies (Treaty of Algeciras, 1906). On the other hand, there was the pro-Allied side, which identified France and the United Kingdom with liberty and democracy. The pro-allies also considered that Spain's decay was the result of the country's historical detachment from Europe. For this reason, and now that the fate of the Continent was being decided on the battlefield, the pro-Allies felt that Spain should not remain detached. Consequently, Spanish pro-Allies were the fiercest detractors of the country's official neutrality, and pressured for an open alliance with France and the UK, if necessary by joining them in the war. The supporters of this trend were mostly the Republicans, the socialists (who would abandon their initial neutralism) and progressive intellectuals. The pro-Allies had a strong presence in the most dynamic regions of the country, like Catalonia, Valencia, Vizcaya and Asturias.

Between these two confronting camps (supporters of the Allies and supporters of the Central Powers) there remained only a small heterogeneous group who advocated for alternative views: the liberal politicians, most of whom stood for neutralism; the Anarchists, who argued in favour of internationalism but also experienced important divisions; and a small group of intellectuals, led by Eugeni d'Ors, who deplored the conflict as a European civil war. The vast majority of Spain's public opinion, however, passionately took sides in the face of the conflict. The testimonies of contemporaries evoke the heated discussions that took place at every moment – in coffee shops, at the tramway, or on the corner of the street, the Great War provoked heated discussions between old friends and family members.[32] It was amidst this highly polarised public opinion that *La Vanguardia* gained popularity thanks to its informative character. In contrast to the biased opinions that most newspapers provided, the Godó newspaper put an emphasis in raw information that attracted the interest of both Allies and Germanophiles. Thus, as one witness (Claudi Amettla) commented in his memoirs:

> "The passion that this event [the First World War] has arisen is so enormous that you should not be surprised to see that every citizen follows it with great interest. In so doing, one learns about tactics and strategy, international politics and geography. [As a result of this] newspapers see their circulations increase, especially in the case of '*La Vanguardia*', which due to the wider information it provided, started to stand out in relation to the rest of

these newspapers, in such measure that this newspaper never lost its principal position."[33]

"In all the material respects, [*La Vanguardia*] stood out among the rest of newspapers. It was better informed than any other, and counted on its own exclusive means (...). It reached the point were it became indispensable, even for those who supported a political cause and were loyal to a partisan newspaper."[34]

The above-quoted testimony demonstrates that providing greater quantities of information was not a minor aspect for newspapers; especially if we take into account the great interest the First World War awoke in Spain. This interest, as the testimony quoted above reveals, was not limited to the harsh confrontation between Germanophiles and pro-Allies. In many ways, the war also represented a media spectacle in itself. In fact, the war was the first moment when a series of technological innovations were implemented in modern warfare, like the airplane, the tank and the Zeppelin. Likewise, the war was also singular for the wide range of countries and geographies it involved. For thousands of readers in Barcelona, all these novelties turned the war into a spectacle they followed eagerly in the newspapers. It was precisely in this field of competition, consisting in the abundance and novelty of news, that *La Vanguardia* stood out from its competitors and reached its peak of circulation – to the point of practically doubling the sales of its immediate competitor (*Las Noticias*).[35]

Still, *La Vanguardia*'s emphasis on information did not imply that its sources of information were always more neutral or reliable than the news of its competitors. Havas' service certainly allowed *La Vanguardia* to have faster access to more news, but this did not assure impartiality. The reason for this is because during the Great War, news agencies were turned into the loudspeakers of state propaganda. In the case of the English agency Reuters, for instance, the German origins of its owner (Baron Herbert) brought about many concerns in England about its reliability. These concerns only stopped when Reuters gave public proof of its "Britishness".[36] In France too, the government repeatedly used Havas' influence to spread propaganda messages throughout Europe.

All this reveals that contrary to what some scholars like Jurgen Osterhammel have suggested, the growing investment in news agencies was not a guarantee of "objectivity".[37] Moreover, the case of Ramón Godó provides a micro-perspective that reveals how the informative character of a newspaper also left ample room for its owner to promote his own political agenda. Indeed, since 1914 Godó started considering that defending neutrality in *La Vanguardia* was not sufficient. The reason for this is because Catalan society was becoming divided in the face of the conflict. As the owner of a newspaper published in Barcelona, this polarization of opinion was something that deeply troubled Godó, as it became evident in the letter he wrote to the Conservative politician Antonio Maura. In this letter, written on 25 October 1914, Godó asked Maura to advise him on how to position *La Vanguardia* in relation to the war, but also took the opportunity to put forward his own opinion:

> "Dear Mr. Antonio Maura. My illustrious and respectable friend; (...) At the newspaper of my property La Vanguardia, we have adopted a passive attitude until now, in what concerns the international events. Yet still, I believe that the circumstances impose that we should be very concerned. Mr. Oliver [the editor of *La Vanguardia*] has his own and particular criteria. Mine, and not just my own, but that of a newspaper proprietor, is different in certain aspects. I don't think that La Vanguardia should start an active campaign, in any sense (...) But I do believe that a prudent collaboration could serve as guidance for the right-oriented people and keep them animated. I don't argue in favour of immediate mobilization, which would ruin us, but I do argue in favour of getting ready in case mobilization is necessary. I believe we have too many troops in Morocco and that they should be transferred [to the Peninsula]. I think we cannot go against England, as long as she keeps her fleet, but also not to much in favour of the Allies, for history reminds us that all the ills have always originated beyond the Pyrenees. To sum up, I believe that without being passionate, for all the news service comes from France, and sometimes, it does with an irritating partiality, that things need to be contrasted with prudent articles. We should not forget that all the neutral masses in the country have positioned in one side. They shall have their reasons for doing so. All this I explain to you for the great steem I have for your opinion, for it is for me the most urgent necessity to adopt a position. (...) Ramon Godó, Barcelona, 26 October 1914".[38]

The letter that Godó wrote to Maura needs to be framed in the proper historical context. Godó wrote this letter barely one month after the Battle of Marne (5–12 September 1914), which represented the first great victory of the Allies and marked a turning point in the course of the war. The consequences of this victory had a strong impact in Spain, where it produced the first great upsurge of pro-Allied sentiment and even led the Socialists to abandon their previous neutralism and to embrace the cause of France and England.[39] This pro-Allies euphoria was felt with particular intensity in Catalonia, the region where the Allied cause traditionally enjoyed more sympathies. Thus, the moment when Godó wrote to Maura was characterised by the growing mobilisation of Catalan public opinion in favour of the Allies.

This context explains why Godó felt troubled about the need of "orienting the conservative masses", which he regarded as "the healthiest" segment of opinion in the country ("*la más sana del país*"). Godó's concern about the ideological stance of Catalan society demonstrates that as a newspaper proprietor, he was deeply attentive to politics. In fact, and as he had already explained to Maura in 1911, he had a precise political mission for *La Vanguardia*: to be the lighthouse of the political right in Catalonia.[40] This reveals to what extent Godó had a clear idea of the kind of reader *La Vanguardia* should target. The problem with Godó's political preferences, however, was that a significant part of the Catalan public opinion sympathised with the Allied cause. This situation was worrying from the sales point of view since many of these people were part of Barcelona's educated upper-middle class male readership, which *La Vanguardia* was targeting.

Moreover, for Godó the situation was all the more difficult given that the editor of his newspaper, Miquel dels Sants Oliver, sympathised with the Allies. Oliver (1864–1920) was a Majorcan journalist who had consolidated his career in the *Diario de Barcelona*. In 1906, and following a personal confrontation with the Brusi family, who owned the *Diario*, he left this newspaper and decided to join *La Vanguardia*.[41] For Godó, this came as a great opportunity: at a stroke, he incorporated one of the most reputed journalists in Barcelona and harmed the image of his competitor at the *Diario*. In the next years, the influence of Oliver in *La Vanguardia* would increase enormously, especially as a result of his literacy skills and intellectual stature.[42] The coming of the First World War, however, put a challenge to the relationship between the editor and the owner of *La Vangaurdia*. As Godó explained to Maura in the above-mentioned letter, Oliver had "his own and particular criteria [in relation to the war] which differs from mine in certain points".

The difference of criteria that Godó and Oliver had regarding the war is confirmed by the testimony of two journalists who worked for *La Vanguardia*: "Gaziel" (the nickname of Agustí Calvet) and Joan Puig i Ferreter (1882–1952). According to the testimony of the former, the division arose out of the different ideological views the two men had about the war, regardless of the common admiration that they felt for Maura. On the one hand, Godó is described as a "fervent supporter of the German cause", who loved reading the Germanophile articles of Madrid's newspaper *ABC* and wished to adopt a similar stance in *La Vanguardia*. On the other hand, Oliver is depicted in the same memoirs as a "sincere and disinterested pro-Ally" who deplored the war as a civil European conflict, and who was determined to keep *La Vanguardia* absolutely neutral. According to same testimony, the main consequence of the different positions that Godó and Oliver had about the war was the worsening of their relationship.[43] Every time the course of the war changed, Godó was tempted to adopt a more favourable stance towards the Central Powers. Additionally, numerous Germanophiles who saw *La Vanguardia* as a potentially valuable mouthpiece for their cause repeatedly pressured Godó to abandon this neutrality.[44] According to Gaziel, only Oliver's resistance prevented Godó from turning *La Vanguardia* into the mouthpiece of the Central Powers' interests in Barcelona. The outcome of this difference of criteria was the worsening of the relations between the two men; to the point that Oliver, tired of the daily struggle he held with Godó, handed in his resignation (which was not ultimately accepted).[45]

Moreover, Godó's correspondence with Maura shows that his distaste with France was not a kneejerk reaction, but rather a judgement that he had formed from the past. As he himself asserted, "history tells us that all our troubles have always come from beyond the Pyrenees". It was in accordance with this way of reasoning that Godó suggested to Maura nothing less than sending the entire Spanish army from its current posting in Morocco to the French border in the Pyrenees. Although Maura rapidly tempered this warlike attitude,[46] Godó's opinion reveals the animosity that notorious segments of the Spanish right felt towards France. Although various elements help to explain the distaste of Spanish conservatives for their neighbouring country – like the secular and Republican nature of the French state model, or the tight constraints that France imposed over Spain's colonial ambitions in Morocco – there was one cause that was of primary importance. This cause was the mass demonstrations that took place in France in reaction to Ferrer i Guàrdia's indictment and execution, in the aftermath of the Tragic Week (1909). For right-wing oriented people like Godó, these mobilisations were seen as an attack against Spain's honour (see Chapter 6).

This resentment proved to be alive by the time of the Great War, when in his correspondence with Maura Godó noted the partisan character of French news and "the need to counterweight them". Godó's determination to make his opinions correspond with those of his newspaper was made evident on repeated occasions. In 1913, for instance, he sent a letter to Paris in which he directly required Havas to "abstain from providing comments and to confine itself to providing information".[47] Likewise, when in October 1913 Godó discussed expanding *La Vanguardia*'s contract with Havas he made it conditional upon receiving more news from Germany, Austria and England. The reason for this, Godó argued, was that "many readers of *La Vanguardia* are of Saxon nationality (sic) and they have protested, not without reason, about the scarcity of information concerning their countries."[48]

Still, Ramón Godó's boldest move to break France's monopoly of information took place in the run-up to the war. Thus, in March 1914, before the First World War started, Godó secretly contacted the German consulate in Barcelona to explore the possibility of obtaining news directly from the country. According to the historical documents of this operation that have been preserved, and which are held in the German Foreign Ministry Archives, in Berlin, Godó's self-confessed attempt was to "free his newspaper from the excessive dependence on Havas" and to "seek new information sources, prefer-ably from German origins".[49] These two statements, reported by the German representative in Barcelona, reveal to what extent Godó sought to make the opinions of *La Vanguardia* reflect his own. The adoption of an informative model had been decisive in boosting the readership of his newspaper, and explains its transformation into Barcelona's leading paper. But as the evidence above-quoted reveals, the intense use of news agencies and new technologies was not an obstacle for press barons to instrumentalise newspapers according to their own views.

The debate on Catalan autonomy and the politics of identity

The impact of the First World War on Spain was not only visible in the sharp division of opinion, but also in the deep disruption it caused in the social, economic and political fields. To begin with, the war ravaging Europe opened unprecedented opportunities for Spanish exports. The country experienced a wave of economic prosperity that allowed for the amassing of large fortunes in a short period of time. In Catalonia, as much as 95% of wool manufactures and 70% of cotton were destined for the warring countries, while in the Basque Country the steel industry doubled its sales and the banking sector expanded enormously.[50] The economic boom, however, was unevenly distributed between regions and sectors and provoked great material distress among wide segments of society. Living costs rose by 78% between 1914 and 1917 but wages lagged behind, the result being an inflationary spiral that set off numerous mutinies and riots. Deterioration of living standards also raised class-consciousness and gave unprecedented strength to the labour movement. Membership of the anarcho-syndicalist CNT and of the Socialist PSOE-UGT increased enormously during these years and turned them into mass organisa-tions. Combined with the passionate disputes between pro-Allies and Germanophiles, the social question became another issue dividing the country, as well as another major challenge to the political system.

The two liberal parties that traditionally acted as the backbone of the Restoration were in a poor state to cope with all these challenges.[51] Since 1913 both the Conservative and the Liberal Party had been locked in internal quar-rels over leadership and had become divided into numerous factions.[52] Unable to reach consensus, the division of liberal parties hardened the functioning of the two-party rotation (the so-called *turno dinástico*) and left the burden of deciding government make-up on the Crown's shoulders. King Alfonso XIII consequently became the arbiter of an extremely delicate situation in which successive cabinets lacked sufficient majority and fell at short notice. Such weakness of liberal parties did not only prevent governmental action in the most basic areas (for instance, no budget was approved between 1914 and 1920) but even paralysed national politics. Besieged liberal governments often resorted to the practice of closing Parliament to cope with the perennial situation of crisis.[53]

Amidst this context of instability, the Catalanists of the *Lliga Regionalista* emerged as a central player in Spanish politics. In 1914 this party had achieved one of its major goals for regional decentralisation, consisting in the pooling of the four Catalan provincial councils in one single entity called *Mancomunitat*. Although this measure did not entail the concession of new administrative powers, it recognised Catalonia's territorial unity under one single governing body. This became a landmark victory for the *Lliga*, which experienced an ongoing growth that consolidated it as the hegemonic force in Catalonia. But far from confining its ambitions to this region, in the next years the *Lliga* designed an ambitious programme that aspired to modernise the entire country. Under the new motto "*Per Catalunya i l'Espanya Gran*" (For Catalonia and a Greater Spain), coined on the occasion of the 1916 elections, the Regionalists set a new agenda that coupled the fight for Catalonia's home rule with the bid for a federal understanding of the state. In the view of this party, Spain had to regain awareness of its internal diversity and to draw energy from the most dynamic regions to recover from its current state of decline. As the most industrialised region, Catalonia was to lead this process of national regeneration whose ultimate goal was to recover Spain's position in the international arena.[54]

The *Lliga*'s new positioning resulted in a bold move to intervene in Restoration politics with the aim of putting an end to the monopoly of power by liberal parties and to transform the centralist organisation of the state. In practice, however, this agenda became extremely hard to fulfil and led the *Lliga* to adopt a changing strategy that would oscillate between opposition and collaboration with the liberal parties.[55] The relations between Catalanist parties and liberal parties eventually reached a new, critical phase as a result of the changes taking place in Europe and the world. The end of the Great War in 1918 coincided with the end of Spain's last government of national unity and opened the doors to a novel situation. Thrilled by the Allied victory and the US President Wilson's declaration of the Fourteen Points for the postwar period, Catalan nationalists thought that a historic opportunity had opened for their interests. As their leader Francesc Cambó put it, "The time for Catalonia's autonomy has come". The world was entering a new phase in which the demands for home rule were seemingly going to receive a more favourable treatment in the international arena. Although President Wilson's principle of self-determination was, in reality, a measure addressed to the situation in Central Europe and the colonies, the consequences of such a declaration went far beyond this conception. As the British ambassador in Madrid confessed in private, the government of her Majesty would now look more favourably at demands coming from nationalist movements.[56] King Alfonso XIII himself encouraged Catalan demands for autonomy. During a private talk he held with Cambó, he apparently described the Catalan issue as a good way of diverting the country from other pressing issues, above all the fear of social revolution.[57] This favourable context, both in Spain and in Europe, encouraged the *Lliga Regionalista* to go a step further in their political demands and, in late November 1918, a group of Catalan deputies handed Prime Minister García Prieto a proposed statute of political autonomy. For the first time in Spain's history, a proposal for the concession of home rule was going to be discussed in Parliament.

This unprecedented episode in the country's history did not take Ramón Godó by surprise. Although he had resigned as deputy for the Liberal Party in 1907, he remained deeply committed to public affairs. The strong support he had given to Antonio Maura's programme of national regeneration (see Chapter 6) provided evidence of this, and revealed that Godó was not just a mere observer of events, but rather a political actor who actively tried to shape them. The only thing that had changed were the strategies he used in order to exert his influence in politics: he no longer sought to do so from public office, but through his more subtle yet equally effective position as owner of Barcelona's top-selling paper. In this respect, *La Vanguardia*'s great expansion during the First World War considerably increased Godó's scope for action. The audience that was susceptible to being influenced by his opinions had grown to approximately 100,000 daily readers, this being a number that was almost double the amount of the nearest competitor in Barcelona. All this capacity for influence of public opinion, however, had been of little use to save Godó's candidate from falling into disgrace. In 1913 Maura had been politically ostracised and the numerous editorials that *La Vanguardia* published supporting *maurismo* had been futile and unable to reverse the situation. But worse still, and to Godó's despair, in the following years the charismatic leader resigned himself to this secondary position in Spanish politics and only abandoned this lethargy to preside over cabinets of national unity.

For Godó, the discussions on Catalan autonomy (November-December 1918) came as a double threat. The *Lliga Regionalista* had not only contributed to Maura's fall in 1913, but was also the main reason for the crumbling of the Godó family's long political career. Indeed, and as shown in previous chapters, the *Lliga* played a crucial part in the downfall of the Godó's political stronghold in Igualada. This family debacle was a profoundly bitter disappointment for the owner of *La Vanguardia*. The destruction of the family political fiefdom became "a poisoned thorn in Godó's heart" and made him hold a deep animosity against Catalan nationalists throughout his life. The inconvenience for this man, however, was that his sworn enemies were at the peak of their political influence. To make things worse for Godó, the *Lliga* was also the party with which a considerable part of *La Vanguardia*'s readership identified. The investment in communication technologies, such as the telegraph and the news agencies, implied adopting a quality press model that targeted the Catalan middle and upper classes, precisely the *Lliga*'s main grassroots base.[58] The uncomfortable situation in which Godó was trapped, between his personal inclinations and those of his readers, may be one of the reasons behind the moderate reception that his newspaper initially gave to the *Lliga*'s bid for home rule. Hence, in an article entitled "*Se impondrá la templanza*" (Temperance shall prevail), the newspaper warned readers about the very delicate issue the Congress was about to start discussing. In its view, the most important thing was to prevent evil passions from boiling over and to deal with the forthcoming debate through mutual respect and compromise. *La Vanguardia* considered that it was entitled to make such demand "in the name of the thousands of readers who share the same attitude, which is not a neutral nor a passive one, but essentially a patriotic one".[59] But patriotism, for *La Vanguardia*, was not a vague expression, but contained a very precise meaning:

> "To put it shortly: the majority of Catalans, while feeling deeply conscious of their own personality, also feel deeply Spanish, regardless of all the quarrels and discrepancies they might hold against the official State, that is to say, against the political oligarchies which so often mishandle and misrepresent this State."[60]

Statements such as this reveal that the Godó newspaper was not content with acting as "the mirror of reality", as it asserted – on repeated occasions – but also aspired to behave as the spokesman for Catalan society. Hence, the large number of copies it sold was the rhetorical argument that *La Vanguardia* invoked to speak on behalf of its readers in the face of identity issues. Hence, the newspaper considered that national confraternity, based on the idea that Catalonia and Spain were part of the same nation, should prevail. The newspaper's standing for the principle of "dual patriotism" (Catalan and Spanish) thus explains the journal's initial call for moderation and mutual understanding.[61]

The soothing words of *La Vanguardia*, however, soon proved to be in vain. The debate that took place in the Spanish Congress between November 1918 and February 1919 to discuss the petition of Catalan autonomy descended into a bitter confrontation over identity issues. With the exception of the Count of Romanones, who showed some sympathy towards the *Lliga*'s demands, the other factions within the liberal parties (such as the "democrats" of García Prieto and the leaders of other minority groups, like Niceto Alcalá-Zamora and Rafael Gasset) bluntly opposed them as an attack on Spain's unity. Only on the margins of the political spectrum did the plea of the Catalanists arouse some support, especially among the Left Republican sectors, and to a lesser extent among the Traditionalists. But the bulk of forces that were present in Congress, with the "Izquierda Liberal" of Santiago Alba at their head, felt extremely annoyed by the *Lliga*'s demands and vociferously rejected them as a separatist initiative.

Moreover, opposition to the autonomist demands did not remain limited to the halls of Congress but eventually spilled out onto the streets. Hence, a sudden outburst of Spanish patriotism came on the scene and showed a remarkable capacity for mobilisation.[62] In Madrid, civic entities such as the *Círculo de la Unión Mercantil* called for the closing of shops and set up a demonstration that gathered a massive number of participants (the estimates range from between 40,000 and 100,000 people, depending on the source) in the streets of Spain's capital. The rally ended in front of the King's palace, where the crowds chanted Alfonso XIII's name as the symbol of Spanish unity.[63] In parallel, the Provincial Deputations in Castile united to reject the Catalanist project, considering it a selfish demand, and even called for a boycott of Catalan products. Amidst such a strenuous campaign, to which pro-Spanish newspapers such as *El Imparcial* and *El Eco de Castilla* contributed actively, the position of the *Lliga* started to lose steam. The final blow came when Maura, who had previously shared many synergies with the Regionalists, and who held a close acquaintance with Cambó, also railed against the *Lliga*'s proposal. As the Majorcan politician put it, somewhat sentimentally, "No one can choose his mother, or brothers, or household, hometown or fatherland". Catalanist deputies were also Spanish ones, Maura concluded, whether they liked it or not.[64] Discouraged by the massive opposition, on 13 December 1918 Francesc Cambó and the rest of the Catalanist deputies threw in the towel and abandoned the Congress to express their unease with the situation. What had begun as a proposal to reform the organisation of the state had thus ended in a passionate debate on the very essence of Spanish identity and the *Lliga*'s abandoning of Parliament. A new wave of Spanish patriotism, which often did not spare anti-Catalanist tones, had made its appearance, revealing how sensitive identity issues were in the political debate.

La Vanguardia felt deeply disappointed at the way events had turned out. The newspaper lamented the most caustic expressions of anti-Catalanism that had taken place during Madrid's rally and explicitly criticised *El Imparcial* for this. Fortunately, though, the Godó's newspaper considered that such excesses had been corrected in time and that Madrid's demonstration had unfolded in a peaceful and convivial atmosphere.[65] In the view of this newspaper, the real culprit for the situation was the *Lliga*. Cambó's decision to abandon Parliament had been a reckless move – the kind of imprudent decisions to which *La Vanguardia* had warned against. Bothered by such behaviour, the newspaper published a hostile editorial entitled "The need for reflection", in which it accused the *Lliga* of embracing an extra-parliamentarian positioning. With the decision of abandoning Congress, *La Vanguardia* considered that Catalan nationalists were fuelling the danger of social revolution. The newspaper wondered what the reaction would be, in the face of such peril, of the "great mass of regionalism, which is precisely that of orderly work, of production, of trade, of intelligence, of all that it feels now more than ever, see this longing for peace and stability with kindness and approval?".[66] This question served as a direct warning: with such imprudent behaviour, the *Lliga* was risking losing the support of the better-off segments of Catalan society.

The author behind the editorial was none other than Ramón Godó himself. The Catalanists' behaviour had bothered him so much that he had ordered the writing of the above-mentioned editorial criticising them.[67] Fearing that this positioning was too strong for a moderate newspaper published in Barcelona, *La Vanguardia*'s editor Oliver refused to sign the editorial. But Godó's anger with the Catalanists was such that he went ahead with his decision and the editorial condemning the *Lliga* was finally published, despite the editor's opposition.[68] The consequences of such a bold move did not take long to arrive. The day after the editorial criticising the *Lliga* was released, a group of demonstrators gathered in front of *La Vanguardia*'s headquarters, in Pelai Street, to express their anger. The number of demonstrators was considerable, to the point that traffic was interrupted and the doors to the building were locked to prevent damage. Stones where thrown and some windows were broken. Amidst this moment of increasing tension Godó, who was working in his office on the building's first floor, became aware of the protests and was furious.

"It was in that moment when Godó, beside himself with rage, wanted to leave in any way he could, pushing and standing up against those that stood in his way to the outside balcony. And it was upon viewing the hostile demonstration, the stopped traffic, the queuing trams, and the masses gesticulating furiously and the continued stone throwing against "*La Vanguardia*", that Godó – in a fit of rage – took a small revolver that he always carried with him out of his pocket and pointed it at the crowd. It was a miracle that nobody out in the street realised; the fear of those around him was such that they snatched the weapon from him and forced him into the building again. Godó locked himself inside of his office, not wishing to see anybody and shouting and cursing as if he were a small, bratty child; and the protestors, after blowing off their own steam as well and upon seeing a group of police officers arrive, slowly dispersed. Meanwhile, "*La Vanguardia*" would again continue to open its doors for business."[69]

The incident at the newspaper's headquarters revealed how enraged Godó was with the Catalan nationalists, to the point of mania and paranoia. His sudden decision to draw his gun is the most visible sign of a temperamental man who felt deeply resentful towards the party that had destroyed his family's political ambitions. As could be expected, news of this tragicomic incident spread rapidly across Barcelona. The following day, various newspapers reported on the events, despite Godó's personal efforts to prevent this from occurring.[70] On a different level, the incident revealed a new episode in the confrontation between the editor and the proprietor on how to position *La Vanguardia*. After repeated attempts to convince Godó of the need to hold a moderate position, Oliver had retreated to his office at the Ateneu Barcelonès. It was the day after, whilst at home, that Oliver read with surprise *La Vanguardia*'s editorial criticising the *Lliga*. Godó had not listened to his advice and had gone ahead and published the editorial. All the efforts that the editor had made until then to keep *La Vanguardia* neutral in the face of identity issues had thus been in vain. The owner was so upset at the deeds of Catalan nationalists that he had completely ignored Oliver's advice and had changed the newspaper's positioning on his own initiative. According to a contemporary witness, Godó's actions had profound emotional consequences for Oliver. He did not return to work for a few days, and shortly after he suffered an attack that left him with general paresis.[71] The debate over identity issues was so passionate that it broke the relationship between the two men controlling *La Vanguardia* and revealed, once again, two opposing forces that struggled to determine the newspaper's editorial line.

From a different angle, the incidents at Pelai Street were also revealing of the great influence *La Vanguardia* had attained in Barcelona. At a time of mass politics and growing political polarisation, the publishing of an editorial in the city's top-selling newspaper had stirred a reaction on the streets. The press was no longer the kind of medium that had existed at the beginning of the Restoration, when it had a low readership that was limited to the members of a political party. Barcelona was now a big city with a large literate population that turned to newspapers to learn about the latest political events. The existence of such a wide audience was not only an opportunity for press barons to exert their influence in society, but was also a subject to be contested from below. The crowd that protested against the editorial of *La Vanguardia* is a telling example of how news consumption was not a passive activity, but was capable of stirring opposition against the very newspaper that published the news.

Moreover, Godó's reaction to the protests is revealing of a wider segment of Catalan society who started feeling troubled with the *Lliga*'s behaviour. Although the deputies from this party received a warm welcome on their arrival from Madrid, their decision to abandon Congress also raised concern among other parts of Catalan society. Godó's reaction to protestors was probably the most humorous example of this reaction, but he was not alone in this. Growing sectors of the Catalan business community started seeing with unease the polarisation of the *Lliga* and the pernicious consequences that this entailed for the social stability. The King himself also revealed how disappointed he felt about the actions of Catalan nationalists. This concern only grew in intensity as Cambó declared, during a meeting held in mid December 1918, that the quest for autonomy should no longer be subject to the form of government. The *Lliga* was ready to continue to seek its agenda in a new political system, no matter if it was a monarchy or a republic.

Such radicalisation of the *Lliga* became one of the key reasons behind the birth of a new political movement in Barcelona, in which Godó was to play a decisive role. Under the name *"Unión Monárquica Nacional"* (National Monarchist Union), a new party arose in the first months of 1919 in direct response to the debate on Catalonia's autonomy and the intensifying of the labour conflict. Worried by the country's delicate situation, a group of distinguished men jumped into the political arena in defence of Spain and the King. They did so through a public call published in *La Vanguardia*, in which they asked all the citizens of Barcelona to express their support of the Crown.[72] As the announcement published in Godó's newspaper declared, the commitment to the monarchy was based on the belief that the Crown was the supreme emblem of the social order, fatherland and religion. These three principles were to become the slogan of a force that, rather than a political party, presented itself as a spontaneous movement coming from the civil society.[73] Godó contributed to this new political endeavour through an active campaign made through the pages of *La Vanguardia*. On repeated occasions, he made an instrumental use of the newspaper to give the maximum visibility to the new political movement.[74] Godó was thus abandoning the moderate standing that the editor had recommended for the newspaper, and instead decided to put it to the service of a new political movement that aspired to challenge the hegemony of Catalan nationalists. The call achieved considerable success, and around 40,000 people gathered in Barcelona's General Captaincy to sign a manifesto in support of the King.[75]

Still, the creation of the *Unión Monárquica Nacional* (UMN) was not such as spontaneous movement as their supporters liked to boast. In reality, it proved to be a carefully planned strategy aimed at breaking with the *Lliga's* dominant position in Catalonia. The ascendancy of Regionalists and of Republicans had left liberal parties in this region as a weakened and divided force, unable to implement the *turno dinástico*. Only a few local party bosses or *caciques* had managed to stay afloat, especially in the Catalan provinces of Lleida and Tarragona, where the growth of the *Lliga* had been more limited. The UMN was designed to reverse this situation, and to unite the scattered remnants of liberal parties in one single force. King Alfonso XIII contributed to that endeavour directly. Through his personal correspondence, he encouraged many Catalan aristocrats to join forces and form a new party that would bring voters of the *Lliga* to the cause of the monarchy.[76] Not surprisingly, many of the men who released the manifesto supporting the Crown were also aristocrats, such as the Marquis of Sentmenat, the Count of Güell, the Marquis of San Román or the Marquis of Castelldosrius.[77] The UMN thus appeared as a new political force composed of a mixture of liberal politicians and noblemen, and sought to attract the middle and upper middle-class sectors that were uneasy about the *Lliga*'s latest moves. To that end the UMN defended an ultra-conservative agenda, according to which the Catholic religion and the armed forces were the two pillars of the social order, and at the same time displayed a bellicose Spanish nationalist discourse. The UMN despised Catalanism as a parochial sentiment and considered that it was necessary "to stay above the local passions which, although they must be respected, degenerate into poor exaggerations".[78] In contrast to the Catalanist demand for home rule, the UMN stood for municipal autonomy. It was through the defence of "prudent local liberties", to be combined with the supreme defence of national unity, that the new party considered that Catalans would contribute to "the great and holy task of rebuilding Spain".[79]

That Ramón Godó decided to join the ranks of the UMN should not come as a surprise. In fact, he can even be regarded as a prototype of this new political force. He was a fervent Spanish patriot who had viewed with concern the growth of Catalanism, and had also acted as a liberal politician for many years. On the top of that, since 1916 he also possessed a noble title. The main reason behind his new title as "Count of Godó" had been his "long and varied services to Spain", and especially in his role as newspaper proprietor.[80] Although the information available makes it hard to ascertain if there were political interests behind the concession of this noble title, it is nevertheless an example of the wide influence Ramón Godó had achieved in society – regardless of his retirement from active politics.

The fear of social revolution and the resort to force

The recognition of Godó's new social status, however, did not spare him from a new, dangerous issue. That is, the threat of social revolution. The most worrying sign of this came in February 1919, when a strike was called at the Anglo-Canadian hydroelectric Ebro Irrigation and Power Company, popularly known as '*La Canadenca*' – by then Barcelona's principal energy supplier. A group of workers affiliated to the anarcho-syndicalist CNT were fired for their attempts to form a union. Other workers at the company protested and were also dismissed, eventually triggering a massive wave of solidarity that expanded to other city sectors, such as the gas, electricity and water companies. In the blink of an eye, Barcelona was left completely paralysed. The city was plunged into darkness, public transport stopped working and the most basic services were suspended; even cleaners and those in charge of burying the dead stopped work.[81] The suspension of activity extended to the press: the Union of Workers of Graphic Arts imposed a "red censorship", according to which it forbade of any news running against the interests of strikers. With the exception of three newspapers, which were duly fined, the rest of the press in Barcelona (*La Vanguardia* included) had no other choice but to obey the order.[82] During the long forty-four days that the *La Canadenca* strike lasted (5 February-17 March 1919), Barcelona was left at a standstill. Following a failed attempt from the authorities to bring the strike to an end through coercive measures (hundreds of employees were imprisoned, martial law was implemented and the work force was militarised), the Liberal Government of Romanones finally opted for a more conciliatory strategy. Imprisoned workers were freed, salaries were raised and the eight-hour day was granted – Spain being the first country in Europe where this measure was passed.

The end of *La Canadenca* strike became a landmark victory for the working movement in general, and for the anarcho-syndicalist CNT in particular. This organisation had displayed an enormous capacity for mobilisation, gathering thousands of their supporters. Such strength was not casual, but evidenced the organisational changes that its Catalan branch (the so-called *Confederación Regional del Trabajo*) had adopted half a year earlier in the Congress of Sants (28 June-1 July 1918). This congress marked the adoption of a new organisation structure, according to which the workers were no longer unionised according to their craft, but were now enrolled in single trade unions (*Sindicat Únic*).[83] *La Canadenca* strike was the most telling example of this measure that sought to unite forces in the face of labour disputes, and revealed the strong support that the CNT had among the Catalan workers. In 1919 its membership went beyond the 250,000 affiliates in Barcelona alone, making this one of the largest unionised cities in Europe.[84]

For Catalan industrialists like Godó, *La Canadenca* strike was a dreadful experience. The anarcho-syndicalist movement had displayed an unparalleled capacity for organisation and self-discipline. In fact, what employers feared the most was not the violence of those days, for there was little of this, but rather the extraordinary capacity that the CNT had shown to run the strike quietly. In the words of an industrialist, it had been a "strike of staggering tranquillity".[85] If Catalan employers were stunned at the anarcho-syndicalist's capacity for organisation, their anger was addressed against the Liberal government for having intervened in the labour dispute. Most employers had a paternalistic understanding of labour relations and considered the factory as an extension of their own house. Accordingly, they rejected any interference from the state and argued, in contrast, for a corporatist solution consisting in the compulsory merging of workers and employers in the same trade unions (*sindicalización forzosa*).[86]

Such animosity against state intervention in labour issues ran parallel with the impression that liberal politicians were unable to maintain order. The main employer, *Fomento del Trabajo Nacional*, protested to Prime Minister Romanones that they had felt "totally defenceless". The events in Barcelona convinced Catalan industrialists of the need for taking their own measures to stop the revolutionary threat. To this end, employers designed a massive counter-offensive through the establishing of corporate organisations and the use of coercive methods. The first example of this was the creation, in March 1919, of the *Federación Patronal de Cataluña* (Catalonia's Employer's Federation) as an entity designed to unite all the employers in their fight against the CNT. To this end it promoted the creation of a single labour contract, sponsored the creation of blacklists and even hired armed gangs to intimidate workers.[87] In parallel, Catalan employers restored an old civil militia known as *Sometent*. Its origins went back to medieval times, when it operated as a group of armed volunteers that protected rural areas against foreign attacks. In the aftermath of the Great War, however, the *Sometent* took a different shape, and was reorganised as an urban and bourgeois paramilitary force, in charge of defending the social order.[88]

The first test for the *Sometent* came on 24 March, when a new general strike was called in Barcelona. Both the military and the Catalan employers wanted revenge and, to such end, General Milans del Bosch refused to free the workers arrested during *La Canadenca* strike. This decision, which implied disobeying the orders received from central government, left the CNT with no other choice but to call another strike. On this occasion, however, the employers and the military were ready to respond. Milans del Bosch imposed martial law and the *Sometent* was rapidly displayed: 8,000 armed men rushed onto the streets of Barcelona and collaborated with the armed forces in arresting trade unionists and sealing off the main working-class quarters. In parallel, measures were taken to prevent the city services from disruption and collapse again. Members of the *Sometent* kept the tramways running and collaborated in all sorts of everyday measures, such as delivering mail and forcing shops to remain open. Some of the wealthiest men in the city, such as the Baron of Güell and Eusebi Bertrán, were seen driving cars carrying food and fish.[89] The reaction of the military and the *Sometent* proved to be a great success. In contrast to *La Canadenca* strike, on this occasion the joint efforts between the military and the industrialists had rapidly crushed the workers' protests. By 7 April the CNT agreed to return to work, having been unable to continue the struggle.[90]

Ramón Godó stood among the men of the *Sometent* who patrolled the streets of Barcelona with rifles on their shoulders. Apparently, the owner of *La Vanguardia* did so with great determination. Indeed, as some gunshots were heard and the *Sometenistas* looked for refuge, Godó apparently remained motionless in the middle of the street, as if nothing had happened. Motionless, although, according to witnesses, this was not so much a sign of courage but was rather a consequence of the serious hearing impediment the owner of *La Vanguardia* suffered – apparently he was so deaf that he couldn't even hear the gunfire (!).[91] This anecdote is evocative of Godó's strong involvement in the employer's counter-offensive. The owner of *La Vanguardia* became one of the main donors to the armed militia, together with other distinguished wealthy men, like the Marquis of Comillas, Milá i Camps and Bertrán i Musitu. The attitude evidenced the employers' determination to combat syndicalism with their own means, this being an attitude that even surpassed political affiliation. Indeed, some of the main leaders behind the *Sometent* belonged, like Godó, to the newly created Monarchic Union, but Catalan nationalists were predominant. The worsening of social conflict had eclipsed demands for autonomy and brought the *Lliga* members to put class interests first. The social crisis was so intense that the ranks of the *Sometent* contained men of different political adscription (Catalanists, Monarchists, Carlists, etc.) and its social spectrum widened.[92]

It was in this context that Godó took advantage of his personal acquaintance with the Conservative politician Antonio Maura and wrote him a letter. As in other times of urgency, Maura had been appointed as Prime Minister of a new cabinet (April 1919), and Godó sought to exploit this. As the letter went:

"(...) Permit me to fix your attention on the Sometent formed during this strike that has not yet ended, and that has lent a marked service to the cause of order. My judgement, which is shared by others, is that the Sometent should continue, even when the state of war is lifted, and that it should be placed under miliary jurisdiction as a gaurantee of its preservation (...). When we return to normality, the personal attacks will again be repeated due to the lack of civic courage of the jurors. However, if the unions – or whoever they may be – know that all attacks against a member of the Sometent would be tried by a military tribunal, it is most likely, if not certain, that those attacks will cease or at least diminish by a notable proportion since there would be no immunity that has remained with them until now. Also, the functions of civil guards could also be entrusted to the Sometent.

Barcelona is not yet pacified and I am very much afraid that in the near future we will see the return of the disturbance of public order. Acts of sabotage are committed daily and trade unionism operates with the same powers and abuses as usual. Finally, it seems to me that there is not enough energy on the part of those in charge of ensuring the control of order and destruction of certain agitatory elements."[93]

The above letter is a valuable testimony of the feeling of insecurity that pervaded the Catalan upper classes in the days of 1919. Godó was convinced that the semi-revolutionary atmosphere that pervaded Barcelona would endure, even once the strike had ended. For this reason his main petition to Maura was the concession of military status to the *Sometent*. Until that moment this civic guard had operated with no official legal status, and in fact it even required permission from the Captain General to enter the city of Barcelona. Godó wanted to change this situation, convinced that the *Sometent* had offered a great service, and that its new status as a military force would offer wider protection to their members. Godó was evoking, in reality, the concerns of broader corporate interests. Hence, the petition for the militarisation of the *Sometent* was not new, but had already been made to the previous government of Romanones, and received the support of Barcelona's main civic organisations. But like his predecessor before him, Maura refused to agree to the measure. Catalan employers were determined to combat the CNT at all costs (Godó's letter clearly demonstrated the employers' distrust towards the security forces), but accepting the measure implied the risk of losing the state's monopoly of force.

However, the prudence of liberal politicians like Maura and Romanones to contain the intransigent position of Catalan employers proved to be futile. Between 1919 and 1922, industrialists in this region systematically boycotted all Government attempts to introduce conciliatory policies and instead resorted to aggressive measures. One of the most repeated measures consisted in the closing of factories. The direst example of this strategy took place in November 1919, when a lockout left a quarter of a million workers jobless and contributed to toppling the liberal cabinet.[94] In parallel, Barcelona slipped into an open social warfare, and its streets became the setting for continuous shootings between the employer's armed gangs and the *cenetistas*. A new trade union called *Sindicatos Libres* (Free Trade Unions) took the lead in the assault and murder of numerous workers. It is estimated that between 1919 and 1923 as many as ninety-eight CNT members were killed, and thirty-three were injured.[95] The action groups of the regional confederation responded to this through spectacular attacks, such as that on the FTN's president Félix Graupera (5 January 1920) and the assassination of Conservative Prime Minister Eduardo Dato (8 March 1921). Still, the working movement bore the worst brunt of the conflict. In addition to the attacks of the *Libres*, a succession of hard-line military governors unleashed a total offensive against the labour movement. Not only were all unions closed and many labour leaders jailed, but all sorts of drastic measures were deployed. The worst of these were implemented during the period of Martínez Anido, a former colonial officer who designed the practice of shooting prisoners under the false pretext of trying to escape (*Ley de Fugas*). During these years of brutal violence, Catalan employers and military authorities signed an alliance that openly challenged the decisions of liberal governments. When in June 1921 a liberal cabinet ordered the dismissal of Martínez Anido, the board of *Fomento* reacted by proposing the concession of a noble title to the general and the granting of the honorary title of Barcelona's adoptive son.[96] All this reveals to what extent the alliance between industrialists and military officers increasingly functioned as an alternative power that challenged the liberal order.

Summary: The road to dictatorship

On 13 September 1923 the captain general of Catalonia Miguel Primo de Rivera weathered a coup d'état and installed a military dictatorship. In line with other constitutional regimes in Europe, the Restoration was finally brought to an end in the aftermath of the Great War. The instalment of a dictatorship in Spain must be seen, in this regard, as part of a broader European process; and more precisely, as a regional example of the first wave of fascist regimes that seized power on the Continent in the 1920s. Still, it is also true that the immediate reasons behind the coup obeyed a strictly national logic. Hence, when Primo de Rivera rose in arms he did so with the declared purpose of ending the state of decay into which Spain had fallen since the Disaster of 1898. In an open letter, he declared that his main motivation was to release the motherland from the liberal politicians who had brought it to perdition twenty-five years earlier.[97]

If Catalonia had been one the main headaches for the military, it was also in this region where the insurrection was prepared. On the crucial night of 13 September, the future dictator received the support of conspicuous members of Barcelona's bourgeoisie, such as the Count Güell, Alfonso Sala and the Marquis of Comillas, among others.[98] The day after, the main Catalan business associations expressed their total support for the insurrection. In a similar vein, *La Vanguardia* did not hide its enthusiasm about the new situation, and welcomed it as an "attempt at national regeneration".[99] With their lack of determination, the newspaper considered that liberal politicians had brought the country to a state of lawlessness. Against this background, *La Vanguardia* considered that "it can be asserted, without a fear of being mistaken, that by raising against this state of things (...), the Army is acting as the representative of public opinion and counts with the sympathies of all the sane elements in the nation."[100] The support that this newspaper had given to reformist attempts that fitted within the official channels of liberal politics until then, such as *Maurismo*, was thus finally abandoned. *La Vanguardia*'s loss of belief in the prospect of successful reconciliation through civil means echoed the sentiment of the well-off classes and their profound discontent with the Restoration. For this social group, bringing in a 'sword-wielding surgeon' appeared to be the only possible solution to prevent social revolution.

Epilogue

Press, Politics and National Identities in the Crisis of Liberalism

On 21 September 1931 Barcelona witnessed the burial of one of its most prominent men. The funeral procession began at number 115 on Pau Claris, the home of the deceased, where large numbers of relatives and friends had gathered to pay their last respects. According to the reports, the assembled crowd amounted to hundreds of people, to the point that the horse-drawn carriage carrying the coffin struggled to make its way out of the street. The large procession then continued down the Gran Vía Diagonal in the direction of Gràcia, where psalms were sung in the Church of Santa María de Jesús, and then processed through Barcelona's famous avenue, the Passeig de Gràcia. The multitude comprising this cortège contained some of the most important people in the city. Following the bereaved family, there were numerous aristocrats (including the Marquis of Olèrdola, the Marquis of Alfarràs and the baron of Bonet), trailed by a delegation of the Catalan employer *Fomento del Trabajo Nacional* (Luis Bosch Labrús, Gual Villalbí, Marcelino Graell and José Pellicer), and several public officials, including deputies and senators. Next in line were the proprietors of different Barcelonan newspapers, such as *El Noticiero Universal*, *Las Noticias* and *El Siglo Futuro*; and a representation from the city of Igualada. Finally, and among the hundreds of people, the funeral procession included workers from a jute factory, and *La Vanguardia*'s entire newsroom.[1]

The person who gathered this multitude was Ramón Godó Lallana, First Count of Godó. He had died at the age of 64, having suffered from a painful disease that lasted a few months. He did so after a lifetime devoted to his position as proprietor of *La Vanguardia*. In fact, and as the obituary of this newspaper recalled, Godó was not the kind of person to take much pleasure in the rituals of high society. At the weekends he would feel desperately bored, impatient for Monday's arrival and for the return to the newsroom. As his obituary confirmed, Godó's devotion to his newspaper was such that it could be considered that "the life of the Count of Godó and of that of *LA VANGUARDIA* developed as two parallel lines".[2]

Before passing away, Ramón Godó still had the opportunity to steer his newspaper through the latest change of regime in Spain. Following almost seven years of authoritarian rule, Primo de Rivera's dictatorship (1923–1930) was followed by a period of political instability that culminated in the proclamation of the Second Spanish Republic (1931–1939). This new democratic and republican regime, which was born from the municipal elections of 12 April, marked a radical watershed in Spain's recent history. Despite it being a tumultuous and short-lived period, which tragically ended with the Spanish Civil War (1936–1939), it came to embody the hopes for change and modernity of the most progressive sectors in society. Barcelona would remain at the centre of this period. In fact, it was the first place where the new political situation was proclaimed, amidst an explosion of joy and elation. It seems reasonable to believe, in this regard, that Godó did not join in with the general euphoria. Although there are no sources available to support this point, his behaviour during the last years of his life provides ample evidence to believe that this was the case. As a strongly conservative man, who had joined the National Monarchic Union and who was granted a noble title, Godó most likely viewed the exile of King Alfonso XIII with deep concern, if not horror. In fact, a little earlier, when the dictator Primo de Rivera was forced to resign amidst widespread discredit, *La Vanguardia* did not hesitate to thank the general "for his memorable service to the Spanish nation".[3] It is more likely to believe, therefore, that Godó felt deeply troubled about the new road the country had just taken.

Yet at the same time, as a newspaper proprietor Godó was well aware of the perils of running against the mainstream of opinion. If *La Vanguardia* had succeeded in achieving one of the highest circulations in Spain, it was certainly not by behaving as a radical newspaper. Rather, the secret behind its success stood in its capacity to adopt a moderate editorial line and its continuous efforts to meet the changing tastes of a plural audience. Based on this idea, and besides the bitter feeling that this probably left in Godó, on 23 May 1931 *La Vanguardia* publically accepted the Second Republic. It was already a bit late to do so, for five weeks had already passed since the municipal elections of 12 April, and the newspaper announced it without much enthusiasm. Still, the newspaper proclaimed that it would remain faithful to the principle that a newspaper's "only obligation [...] is to faithfully follow the way that the public conscience and the majority have shown".[4]

This delicate balance, between the private opinions of the owner and those of the mainstream of opinion, was the game in which *La Vanguardia* had been trapped since its first owners, the brothers Carlos and Bartolomé Godó Pié, decided to turn it into a commercial newspaper. Their decision had not been casual, but rather part of the brothers' strategy to widen their influence beyond the Constitutional Party that *La Vanguardia* was originally established to promote. Under a heading that had lost its political meaning, the second generation continued in the wish of turning the newspaper into the best example of quality journalism in Barcelona. When Ramón Godó passed away, shortly after the Second Republic was proclaimed, he had largely succeeded in this ambition. By 1931 *La Vanguardia* was the top-selling newspaper in Catalonia, and its circulation of 200,000 copies was amongst the highest in Spain, with only the Madrid newspapers *ABC* and *El Heraldo* enjoying similar figures.[5] As important as its circulation was the reputation this newspaper had come to enjoy, to the point of representing "essential reading for elites across Spain, and even abroad".[6]

The man that would continue the family tradition of running *La Vanguardia* was Carlos Godó Valls (1899–1987), the first son of Ramón Godó Lallana. Born in Barcelona and educated in the *Escuelas Pías* of the well-off neighbourhood of Sarrià, Carlos studied industrial engineering.[7] From an early age he showed great interest in public affairs, and his political leanings ran parallel to those of his father. Hence, during his youth he was affiliated to the *Juventudes Mauristas* (Maura's Youth movement) and later on to the Spanish nationalist *Unión Patriótica*.[8] He also remained a loyal Monarchist and inherited the title of Count of Godó. But besides the well-ensconced position he inherited from his family, Carlos Godó Valls would also face the great challenge of directing *La Vanguardia* through Spain's most turbulent years. The most delicate moment was definitely the Spanish Civil War (1936–1939). Like many other Catalan conservative men who feared for their lives, Godó fled to the Italian city of Genoa, and only returned when the war was over.[9] He did so with the aim of recovering ownership of his newspaper, expropriated during the conflict by the Republican authorities, and to put it at the service of Spain's new dictatorship. To remove any uncertainty about his support for the new political situation, Godó changed the name of his newspaper to that of "*La Vanguardia Española*". In this way, and 58 years after it was established, the heading of the newspaper recovered political meaning: now it wished to serve at the *vanguard* of General Franco's new dictatorship.[10]

By unveiling the trajectory of '*the most important newspaper in Catalonia and one of the most influential in modern Spanish history*' the main contribution of this book has been to take a novel approach to the crisis of the liberal state in Europe. This has been done through an interdisciplinary perspective that brings politics and the press together. The analysis of two generations of the same family has made it possible to examine this process over a long span, and to show how elites took advantage of the press to advance their position in society. From being the mouthpiece of the Constitutional Party in Barcelona and having a circulation of 1,400 copies, by 1931 *La Vanguardia* had attained a circulation of 200,000 copies and was one of the benchmarks of modern journalism in Spain. This transformation was neither casual nor unique. Rather, it evokes a broader historical process that took place across Europe and the United States during the second half of the 19th and the beginning of the 20th centuries, consisting in the transition from an advocacy press model towards an independent and commercial one.

Media scholars have often described this transition as a history of progress. They have done so influenced by the liberal tradition, according to which the press has a public mission in democratic societies. This mission is often referred to acting as "the fourth state" or as the "watchdog of democracy", and is considered to have profound consequences for the work of journalists. Hence, in their aim to fulfil this democratic mission, journalists are expected to be as neutral as possible when reporting events, for their duty is to provide an "objective" account of reality. The problem with this approach, however, is that scholars have often confused the emergence of a new professional ethics in journalism (the birth of the so-called "news paradigm") with a normative ideal against which to judge press history.[11] As a result, the specific characteristics that the press presented in Southern Europe, such as its strong partisan character, the low levels of circulation or the scarce professionalisation of journalists, have resulted in the countries in this area being seen as a *failure* in historical development.

The case of *La Vanguardia* has been used to argue against this understanding of press history based on *ideal types*, and to demonstrate the epistemological value of empirical analysis in revealing the limitations of normative approaches. Likewise, the case of this newspaper has served to challenge economic perspectives, which tend to identify the growing commercialisation of newspapers with the depoliticisation of news. Although the Godó family managed to turn *La Vanguardia* into one of the finest models of independent journalism in Spain, they were never afraid to use their newspaper to publicise their political agenda. Therefore, and in contrast to the two mentioned narratives (liberal and economic), the case of *La Vanguardia* shows that the birth of the new mass press was a more complex and contradictory process, which requires taking into account the broader changes in the political culture and the historical context; as well as reflecting on the intimate circumstances of historical actors.

The long presence of the Godó family in Catalan and Spanish politics (in fact up to this very day) has provided an opportunity to draw on the work of early sociologists, such as Gaetano Mosca and Vilfredo Pareto, and examine the power that a reduced number of elites exerted over society. Furthermore, our emphasis has been placed on examining the elites' *strategies of adaptation* during the birth of democratisation and of mass politics through a micro-perspective. The long trajectory of the Godó family can be seen, in this respect, as an example of what the Italian micro-historian Edoardo Grendi called the "exceptional normal".[12] In other words, the apparently extraordinary capacity of adaptation of this family has served to unveil what might have been, this book suggests, a more widespread phenomenon in Europe's transition to mass society.[13]

Along two generations the Godós managed to build a solid political career based on the combined use of politics and the press. At a time when liberal politics in Europe was organised according to cadre parties, the foundation of *La Vanguardia* allowed the members of this family to insert themselves in the patron–client networks of the Restoration (1874–1923) and to expand their range of influence. From an initially modest position in the ranks of Barcelona's Constitutional Party, the press allowed the Godó family to gain public notoriety and to improve their position within the party hierarchy. What followed, afterwards, was the *cursus honorum* typical of liberal elites, consisting in the ascension through the ladders of public office (councilman, provincial deputy and deputy in Congress). Crucial to this process of upward mobility was the decision of Carlos and Bartolomé Godó to abandon the partisan adscription of *La Vanguardia*, and to turn it into a commercial and politically independent newspaper.

The fact that they took *The Times* as a model to carry out these reforms, as the Italian *Il Corriere della Sera* also did, reveals the importance of moving beyond national perspectives when explaining the birth of modern journalism in Europe. The structural differences that existed between the different countries – still important in so many ways – were not an impediment for the circulation of journalistic practices across national boundaries. The situation was actually the opposite: the wish to imitate what was regarded as a more modern type of journalism is what stimulated these cultural transfers. *The Times* perhaps was no longer the successful newspaper it had once been, but for editors in Barcelona and Milan it remained the best symbol of quality journalism. By importing some of its features to Barcelona's atmosphere, and broadcasting the fact, the Godós' aim was to extend their influence beyond the Liberal Party and reach broader segments of society. Therefore, the reform plans of 1888 are central to understand the sudden growth that *La Vanguardia* experienced from that point onwards, as well as to comprehend the importance that elites gave to the public sphere as a means of advancing their position in society.

Another decisive element behind the Godós' success in rising to national pre-eminence was their collective action. This means that instead of focusing on the agency of single individuals, emphasis has been placed on examining the collaboration between family members and also on the tensions these produced between them. Thus, while one family member would run for Congress, another would run for Provincial Government. This collective

strategy, which was reproduced by both generations, provided multiple benefits. On the one hand, it allowed the family to obtain access to key
decision-making positions (providing, for example, information on elections
and infrastructures), and on the other hand it meant they could expand the
family's range of influence to Madrid, where the main political decisions
affecting the family business in the colonies were taken. Kinship cooperation
thus proved to be decisive to expand the family's range of influence to different
levels of governance.

This family strategy, however, would fall into a deep crisis after Spain's loss
of empire. The so-called Disaster of 1898 was, it has been argued, the regional
manifestation of Europe's fin-de-siècle crisis. Pessimism and lack of confidence
in progress became widespread throughout the Continent, but in
Mediterranean countries the feeling of national decline was felt with particular
intensity. At first sight, liberal politicians in Spain seemed better able to overcome their particular colonial drawback when compared, for example, with
Italy or Portugal. In practice, however, the Disaster of 1898 *did* mark a turning
point, for it contributed – among other things – to intensifying the discredit
of the Restoration and to the birth of new political forces that sought to challenge the liberal order. This book has shown how the growing criticism of
caciquismo became entangled in a rich controversy over the function that journalism ought to play in society. The feeling of national degeneration is what
led contemporaries, like Joaquín Costa and other witnesses examined in this
book, to criticise the collusion between the press and politicians, and to implicitly argue in favour of the professionalisation of journalism (even if none of
them ever explicitly used this expression). Still, other contemporaries held the
opposite view, and argued that the new commercial orientation of the press is
what had ultimately led to the loss of the colonies – thus exposing a hidden
nostalgia for the partisan press.

Yet paradoxically, and despite the different views held by these contemporaries, they all evoked the sense of unease that resulted from the emergence of
a new mass society. Regardless of their opinion, they all shared the conviction
that the press exerted a strong influence over society. This perception might
seem incongruous for a country as rural as Spain, where a considerable part of
the population was still illiterate and lived in small villages. Still, it was
precisely this lack of development that ultimately led contemporaries to see the
press as a power with great ascendancy over the population; and therefore an
indispensable force in any attempt to rejuvenate the country. It is interesting
to note, in this regard, that the growing prominence of press barons in public
life was not a Spanish singularity, but rather a European trait.

In the case of Germany, for instance, historian Bernhard Fulda has observed
a similar pattern of behaviour in the Berlin of the Weimar Republic (1919–
1933).[14] Contemporaries tended to regard the press as having great power of

persuasion among their fellows. This *perception* that contemporaries had about the press – a phenomenon media scholars refer to as the "Third Person Effect" – was particularly pronounced among the elites, like politicians and intellectuals. According to Fulda, this was because politicians were still not used to handling the number of new audiences produced by the advent of mass politics. As a result, they tended to assign great power of manipulation to the press, reflecting a perception that implicitly assumed that media consumers were passive. In this regard, what makes the examples of Germany and Spain interesting is that despite their obvious differences, contemporaries in each became increasingly aware of the growing *mediatisation* of society. This perception, it has been argued, was the result of the newspapers' transformation into the new main form of mass communication.

In their double condition as politicians and press barons, the Godó family became trapped in the crisis of liberal institutions. The initial response that this family gave to the threat that mass politics posed to their position consisted in separating the two spheres (press and politics) that had traditionally been so closely entwined in their power strategies. Hence, the owner of *La Vanguardia* (Ramón Godó Lallana) broke with the family tradition and resigned from active politics. From that moment onwards, he decided to concentrate exclusively on his role as newspaper proprietor. In contrast, his cousin in Igualada (Juan Godó Llucià) reacted very differently to the threat of mass politics: he continued with the family's traditional affiliation to the Liberal Party, and continued to see clientelism as the best way to maintain the family's political domain. The case of this family thus reveals that, when studied from a micro-perspective, the responses of traditional elites to the birth of mass politics was a complex and nuanced episode, and that different responses were given – even in the same family.

Moreover, and contrary to the narrative focusing on the "end of the notables", the case of Juan Godó Llucià (studied in Chapter 6) demonstrates that even in the case of those notables who stuck to clientelist methods, seeing them as simply opposed to democratisation is incomplete. Drawing on the line of research that historians Jean Briquet and Renato Camurri have opened for the case of France and Italy, this book has provided new insights about the notables' *strategies of adaptation*.[15] The launching of an electoral campaign, where public meetings were organised and a caravan of cars visited all the villages in the constituency, reflected a new attempt to win the vote through legal means – albeit in combination with clientelism. Another novelty was the introduction of a new discourse based on identity issues. Thus, Juan Godó did not only present himself as the community leader, but also started championing a dual conception of identity (Spanish and Catalan) in the local sphere – this being an image that his cousin contributed to publicise through the pages of *La Vanguardia*. These self-fashioning strategies reveal the importance that the public sphere played for the social reproduction of elites. Because elections were manipulated on a systematic basis, in the case of Italy, Portugal and Spain, it is often assumed that controlling the mechanisms of favour assured the dominant position of elites. The family examined in this book challenges these assumptions, and demonstrates that even in those societies where wide segments of the population were de-mobilised and clientelism was a persisting feature, the symbolic dimension was a crucial element in the legitimation of elites.

As in other parts of Europe, national identity was an element that featured prominently in the realignment of political debate, and therefore conditioned the notables' strategies of adaptation. In their condition as newspaper proprietors, the Godó family became tightly involved in all these debates. Examples of these were the discussion of economic policies, the colonial wars in Morocco and Cuba, the consequences of the Tragic Week (1909) and the debate on Catalan autonomy (1918–1919). In all of them, and without relinquishing their private interests, the Godós sought to use *La Vanguardia* as a bridge between Barcelona and Madrid. Moreover, on repeated occasions they would use the press as an instrument to promote Spanish feelings in Catalonia – or, to put it in more precise terms, to promote a Catalan understanding of the Spanish nation.[16] This is an aspect that has received scarce attention in the literature, in part because historians have often adopted a centre-periphery perspective, where the rise of Catalan nationalism is seen as a challenge to the liberal state-model. Likewise, the role of the state has been placed at the centre when studying Spain's nation-building process and its alleged "weakness" compared to other countries in Europe.[17]

This book, in contrast, has adopted an alternative viewpoint, in which the attention has been placed on civil society, and on how Spanish identity was lived in Catalonia. This has revealed that the state was not the only protagonist in the task of building the nation, but that socio-political actors were also decisive in this process.[18] Since its foundation, *La Vanguardia* consistently portrayed Catalan and Spanish identity as multiple and shared. On repeated occasions its pages would voice the unease of regional elites with the decisions of central government, but none of this undermined the commitment of the newspaper to the liberal national project. Moreover, the fact that thousands of readers chose to buy *La Vanguardia* every day over its competitors suggests that a similar understanding was shared – or at least was not regarded as offensive – by wide segments of Catalan society. The case of this newspaper thus reveals that contemporaries did not always see differing identities as contradictory, nor in black and white terms, but often as overlapping lived experiences.[19]

Nevertheless, this shared identity underwent reconsideration in the aftermath of the Disaster of 1898. The loss of the colonies intensified the discrediting of liberal institutions and gave fuel to a series of political forces that put forward alternative political imaginaries. In this respect, the rise of

Catalan nationalism not only posed a challenge to the Restoration parties, but was also seen as a threat by a group of Catalan elites, inducing them to react. The case of the First Count of Godó is particularly telling in this respect. As noted in his obituary, "He was a spirited and fervent Spaniard, to the point that patriotism became one of the more distinguishing features of his character [;]. Even during the difficult period that Catalonia and Spain have traversed, he maintained his faith in the country's destiny, and was not drawn for adverse events."[20] Godó initially saw *Maurismo* as a third-way between the outmoded plans of liberal politicians and the – for him overly radical – Catalanism of the *Lliga Regionalista*. Later on, however, and worried by the heated debate on Catalan home rule (1918–1919), he radicalised his position and embraced the ultraconservative project of the Monarchic Union. As a result, the discourse of shared identities in *La Vanguardia* was gradually replaced by a bolder, openly promoted Spanish conservative nationalism.

The worsening of social conflict also influenced the owner of *La Vanguardia*. Together with the "Bolshevik Triennium" that shook the Andalusia country-side between 1918 and 1920, Catalonia was the other region where social violence reached the harshest extremes. The decision of Godó to join the *Sometent* and march through the streets of Barcelona with a rifle on his shoulder evokes the fear that pervaded conservative elites throughout inter-war Europe and their resolution to resort to violent means to fight against the labour movement. In fact, the case of Godó provides further evidence of the decisive role that the "Catalan counter-revolutionary coalition" had in setting the ground for the arrival of Primo de Rivera's dictatorship.[21]

However, and as Spain entered a new democratic phase in the 1930s, the ownership of a newspaper proved to be a priceless instrument to cling to power. Hence, and as Ramón Godó once confessed to Antonio Maura, his main goal was "expanding the influence and circulation of my newspaper *"La Vanguardia"* with the final aim of turning it into a powerful instrument of conservative opinion in Catalonia".[22] The case of Ramón Godó reveals that next to Parliaments and other elected bodies, alternative spaces existed for European notables to uphold their position once the liberal order had vanished. The thousands of readers that bought newspapers every day became one of these alternative and more subtler channels that elites used to advance their position. The case of the Godó family thus neatly encapsulates the main argument of this book with regards the role of the press in relation to the crisis of liberal politics in Europe. That is, that the transformation of the press not only fostered democratisation (in so far as it contributed to making the corrupt practices of liberal elites more visible) but opened new channels for traditional elites to maintain and transfer their influence in the new mass society.

Notes

Introduction

1   Joaquín Costa, *Oligarquía y caciquismo como la forma actual de gobierno en España: urgencia y modo de cambiarla*, Madrid, Biblioteca Nueva, 1998 [1st ed. 1901], p. 217. Originally written in Spanish.

2   Joaquín Costa, *op. cit.*, pp. 218–219.

3   As Alan S. Kahan has observed, "the traditional political explanation for the decline of liberalism, sometimes given in tandem with arguments about the decline of the middle classes and sometimes independent of them, is based on the decline of "the politics of the notables", and its replacement by "mass politics". Alan S. Kahan, *Liberalism in Nineteenth-century Europe: The Political Culture of Limited Suffrage*, Basingstoke–New York, Palgrave Macmillan, 2003, p. x.

4   Heinrich Best and Maurizio Cotta, "Elite Transformation and Modes of Representation since the Mid-Nineteenth Century: Some Theoretical Considerations", in: H. Best and M. Cotta (eds.), *Parliamentary Representatives in Europe 1848–2000: Legislative Recruitment and Careers in Eleven European Countries*, Oxford, New York, Oxford University Press, 2000, pp. 1–28.

5   *Ibidem*, p. 21.

6   Arno J. Mayer, *The Persistence of the Old Regime: Europe to the Great War*, New York, Pantheon Books, 1981.

7   Olivier Dard, Jens Ivo Engels, Andreas Fahrmeir et Frédéric Monier (eds.), *Scandales et corruption à l'époque contemporaine*, Paris, Armand Colin, 2014; Jean Garrigues, *La république des hommes d'affaires: 1870–1900*, Paris, Aubier, 1997.

8   See, for instance, Edmond Demolins, *A quoi tient la supériorité des Anglo-Saxons?* 1899; Giuseppe Sergi, *Origine e diffusione della stirpe mediterranea*, 1895. On the alleged decay of Mediterranean countries: Lily Litvak, *Latinos y anglosajones: orígenes de una polémica*, Barcelona, Puvill, 1980; and Paul Aubert (ed.), *Crise espagnole et renouveau idéologique et culturel en Méditerranée. Fin XIXe–début XX siècle*, Aix-en-Provence, Publications de l'Université de Provence, 2006.

9   "Journalists as Political Actors. Introduction", Frank Bösch and Dominik Geppert (eds.), *Journalists as Political Actors. Transfers and Interactions between Britain and Germany since the late 19th Century*, Augsburg, Wißner, 2008, pp. 7–15. A similar observation for the cases of Italy and Spain, in: Javier Moreno Luzón, "La historiografía sobre las elites de la España liberal" and Renato Camurri, "Las *elites* italianas: estado de los estudios y perspectivas de investigación", both in: Rafael Zurita, Renato Camurri (eds.), p. 32 and p. 22, respectively. Some valuable exceptions to this lack of studies are: Juan Carlos Sánchez Illán, *Prensa y política*

en la España de la Restauración. Rafael Gasset y El Imparcial, Madrid, Biblioteca Nueva, 1999; Paul Aubert et Jean-Michel Desvois, *Les Élites et la presse en Espagne et en Amérique latine: des Lumières à la seconde guerre mundiale*, Madrid, Casa Velázquez, 2001. A different, though widely extended practice, has been the depiction of press barons as exceptional and clairvoyant figures. For a critique of this "great men" narrative, see: Jean K. Chalaby, "No ordinary press owners: press barons as a Weberian ideal type", *Media, Culture & Society*, 1997, Vol. 19, pp. 621–641.

10   Asa Briggs & Peter Burke, *A Social History of the Media: From Gutenberg to the Internet*, Cambridge, Polity, 2002, p. 2. Elizabeth L. Eisenstein, *The Printing Press as an Agent of Change: Communications and cultural transformations in early modern Europe*, Cambridge-New York, Cambridge University Press, 1979; Sabrina Alcorn Baron, Eric N. Lindquist (eds.), *Agent of Change:. Print Culture Studies after Elizabeth L. Eisenstein*, Amherst, University of Massachusetts Press, 2007.

11   Jaume Guillamet, La significació històrica de "La Vanguardia", *L'Avenç*, num. 313, May 2006, pp. 42–49.

12   Gaziel, *Una història de La Vanguardia, 1884–1936*, París, Edicions catalanes de París, 1971, p. 72.

13   Further insights on this subject, in: Isabel Burdiel, Myths of Failure, Myths of Success: New Perspectives on Nineteenth-Century Spanish Liberalism, *The Journal of Modern History*, 70 (December 1998), pp. 892–912. More recently: María Cruz Romeo & María Sierra (eds.), *La España Liberal, 1833–1874*, Madrid, Marcial Pons – Zaragoza, Prensas de la Universidad de Zaragoza, 2014.

14   Pollard, *Peaceful conquest*, p. 206; quoted in J.K.J. Thomson, Explaining the 'take-off' of the Catalan cotton industry, *Economic History Review*, LVIII, 4 (2005): 701; Albert Carreras, "Cataluña, primera región industrial de España", in: J. Nadal, and A. Carreras (eds.), Pautas regionales de la industrialización española (siglos XIX y XX), Barcelona, 1990, pp. 259–295.

15   Jesús Cruz, "The Moderate ascendancy, 1843–1868", in: José Alvarez Junco & Adrian Shubert (eds.), *Spanish History since 1808*, London: Arnold, 2000, pp. 33–47; Salvador Calatayud, Jesús Millán, Mª Cruz Romeo (eds.), *Estado y periferias en la España del siglo XIX. Nuevos enfoques*, València, Publicacions de la Universitat de València, 2009; Angel Smith, *The Origins of Catalan Nationalism, 1770–1898*, Basingstoke, Palgrave Macmillan, 2014, esp. chapters 2 and 5.

16   A. Smith, *op. cit.*, pp. 2–3.

17   "*La Vanguardia* is a basic enterprise which the Catalans should have created and protected with more effort than the textile or metallurgical industry, if they were to have a clear vision of reality and of what was of interest to maintain its very essence. (...) *La Vanguardia* has gained more influence than the *Foment*, the *Cambra de Comerç* and the *Institut Català de Sant Isidre*, and continues to have it to this day". Gaziel, *op. cit.*, p. 36.

18   *The Times*, 20/05/1916, p. 5.

19   There are, however, some very valuable works that have been dedicated to examining this newspaper in recent periods of Catalan and Spanish history. See: Rafael Aracil, Andreu Mayayo, Antoni Segura (eds.), *Diari d'una postguerra. La*

Vanguardia Española (1939–1946), Catarroja-Barcelona, Afers, 2010; Anna Nogué, Carlos Barrera, *La Vanguardia. Del franquismo a la democracia*, Madrid, Fragua, 2006; Francesc Vilanova, *La guerra particular de Gaziel i el comte de Godó (1940–1945)*, Barcelona, Ploion, 2004.

20 Daniel E. Jones, Llibre sobre els Godó i "La Vanguardia", *Talaia*, 2006, n° 18, pp. 225–229.

21 The few authors that have dealt with this topic are: Pedro Voltes Bou, "Vida y obra de don Ramon Godó y Lallana, primer conde de Godó", Universitat Autònoma de Barcelona, "Tesina de licenciatura", 1980; and "Historia de La Vanguardia" [manuscript]. Josep Maria Huertas, *Una història de «La Vanguardia»*, Barcelona, Angle Editorial, 2006; Vis Molina, *Los Godó. Los últimos 125 años de Barcelona*, Madrid, Martínez Roca, 2005. The book of Molina was written on the occasion of *La Vanguardia*'s 125 anniversary and can be considered the official (indeed commissioned) history of the Godó family. In practice, it is a book that consists of a description of various family members, mostly based on personal anecdotes, but does not contain any feasible explanation, for instance, on the trajectory of their political careers nor on the reasons – still largely unknown – that led them to establish *La Vanguardia*.

22 For a detailed list of the primary sources used for this book, see the Bibliography.

23 Jean-Ives Mollier, Jean-François Sirinelli et François Vallotton (eds.), *Culture de masse et culture médiatique en Europe et dans les Amériques. 1860–1940*, Paris, Presses universitaires de France, 2006; Marcel Broersma (ed.), *Form and Style in Journalism. European Newspapers and the Representation of News, 1880–2005*, Leuven, Peeters, 2007; Richard L. Kaplan, *Politics and the American Press: The Rise of Objectivity, 1865–1920*, Cambridge-New York, CUP, 2002.

24 Geoffrey Crossick and Gerhard Haupt, *The Petite Bourgeoisie in Europe, 1780–1914. Enterprise, family, and independence*, London-New York, Routledge, 1995; Ralf Roth and Robert Beachy, *Who Ran the Cities? City Elites and Urban Power Structures in Europe and North America, 1750–1940*, Aldershot, Ashgate, 2007. It is not our aim here to enter into the historiographical debate about the controversial "bourgeois" character of the liberal revolution. For a recent state of the art, see: Jorge Luengo, *Una sociedad conyugal. Las élites de Valladolid en el espejo de Magdeburgo en el siglo XIX*, València, PUV, 2014, pp. 17–20.

25 *"Partido Conservador"* and *"Partido Liberal"*, in Spain; *"Destra"* and *"Sinistra"*, in Italy; *"Partido Regenerador"* and *"Partido do Progresso"*, in Portugal.

26 Javier Tusell, "Dos formas de liberalismo oligárquico: rotativismo y turnismo", DDAA, *Los 98 Ibéricos y el mar*, Lisboa, Sociedad estatal Lisboa, Fundación Tabacalera 1998, vol. III, pp. 57–77; Pedro Tavares de Almeida & Javier Moreno Luzón (ed.), *Das urnas ao hemiciclo: eleições e parlamento em Portugal (1878–1926) e Espanha (1875–1923)*, Lisboa, Assembleia da República, 2012 [the Spanish edition, 2015].

27 In the Italian case, the political system proved to be more open to integrating other parties, and the government intervention in elections was less widespread than in Spain; and manifested with particular intensity in the *Mezzogiorno*. Renato Camurri, "La Italia liberal y la España de la Restauración: una perspectiva compa-

rada", Rosa Ana Gutiérrez, Rafael Zurita y Renato Camurri (eds.), *Elecciones y cultura política en España e Italia (1890–1923)*, València, Publicacions de la Universitat de València, 2003, p. 21. For comparisons between the Italian and Spanish case, see: Gabriele Ranzato, La forja de la soberanía nacional: las elecciones en los sistemas liberales italiano y español, *Ayer*, 3, 1991, pp. 115–138; and Manuel Suárez Cortina, "*Trasformismo y Turno*: dos versiones latinas de la política liberal europea de la Belle Epoque", Silvana Casmirri y Manuel Suárez Cortina (eds.), *La Europa del sur en la época liberal: España, Italia y Portugal. Una perspectiva comparada*, Universidad de Cantabria-Università di Cassino, 1998, pp. 225–249.

28   Maurizio Ridolfi, "Republicanos y socialistas en la Italia y en la España liberal (1890–1923)", R. A. Gutiérrez, R. Zurita y R. Camurri (eds.), *op. cit.*, pp. 49–69.

29   For an overview of this literature for the Italian case, see: Alberto Mario Banti, Retoriche e idiomi. L'antiparlamentarismo nell'Italia di fine Ottocento, *Storica*, 1995, n° 3, pp. 7–41; Jean Louis Briquet, "Les infortunes de la vertu. La critique des moeurs parlementaires en Italie (1860–1890)", Jean-Louis Briquet and Frédéric Sawicki (eds.), *op. cit.*, pp. 251–276.

30   *Diccionario de la Lengua Española*, Madrid, RAE, p. 219. In Portuguese the "cacique" was also popularly known in the 19th century as "*o influente*" ("the one who has influence").

31   Eugene Weber, for instance, referred to the personalized character of notable politics as "evidence of a primitive mentality". Eugene Weber, *Peasants into Frenchmen: The Modernization of Rural France, 1870–1914*, Stanford, Stanford University Press, 1976, p. 256.

32   Paul Corner, The Road to Fascism: an Italian *Sonderweg? Contemporary European History*, Volume 11, Issue 2, May 2002, pp. 273–295; Nick Carter, Rethinking the Italian Liberal State, *Bulletin of Italian Politics*, Vol. 3, No. 2, 2011, pp. 225–245. For the Spanish case, examples of this interpretation were: Antonio Ramos Oliveira, *Historia de España*, México, Compañía General de Ediciones, 1952, 3 vol.; Manuel Tuñón de Lara, *La España del siglo XIX (1808–1914)*, París, Librería Española, 1961; Richard Herr, "La élite terrateniente española en el siglo XIX", *Cuadernos de Investigación Histórica*, Madrid, Fundación Universitaria Española, Seminario Cisneros, 1978, n° 2.

33   Raffaele Romanelli (Ed.), *How did they become voters? The History of Franchise in Modern European Representation*, The Hague, Boston, Kluwer Law International, 1998, p. 5. See also: Isabel Burdiel, Myths of Failure, Myths of Success: New Perspectives on Nineteenth-Century Spanish Liberalism, *Journal of Modern History*, Vol. 70, No. 4 (December 1998), pp. 892–912.

34   Raffaele Romanelli, "Introducción", Salvador Forner Muñoz (ed.), *Democracia, elecciones y modernización en Europa: siglos XIX y XX*, Madrid, Cátedra, 1997, pp. 25–26. Jürgen Kocka and Allen Mitchell (eds.), *Bourgeois society in Nineteenth-century Europe*, Oxford, Providence, Berg, 1993.

35   In this respect, Javier Tusell's theory of the "encasillado" deserves special mention. Focusing on the case of Andalusia, Tusell provided a detailed analysis of how the central parties in Madrid and the local "caciques" agreed the results

of elections, explaining how the *encasillado* (as the executive's candidate was referred) repeatedly succeeded in winning elections. Javier Tusell, *Oligarquía y caciquismo en Andalucía (1890–1923)*, Barcelona, Planeta, 1976.

36 In the case of Spain, at the forefront of this interpretation there was a group of historians, like José Varela Ortega and Joaquín Romero Maura, who were influenced by the work of British anthropologists such as Ernest Gellner and the teachings of Raymond Carr at Oxford. Additionally, the works José María Jover had great influence, for instance in the crucial work of Javier Tusell. See: *Revista de Occidente*, n° 127, February 1973; José Varela Ortega, *Los amigos políticos: partidos, elecciones y caciquismo en la Restauración, 1875–1900*, Madrid, Marcial Pons, Junta de Castilla y León, 2001 [first ed. 1977]. Javier Tusell, *op. cit.*

37 As Javier Moreno Luzón has observed, in the case of Spain the work of Manuel Tuñón de Lara became decisive in spreading the use of this term. Inspired in the work of US sociologists like Charles Wright Mills, Tuñón defined "elite" [in Spanish] as: *"un grupo reducido de hombres que ejercen el Poder o que tienen influencia directa o indirecta sobre . . . "*. Quoted in: Javier Moreno Luzón, "La historiografía sobre las elites de la España liberal", Rafael Zurita, Renato Camurri (eds.), *op. cit.*, p. 28. Still, and as the same author has observed, the term "elite" was not introduced in Spain's dictionary of the Royal Academy until 1984. For the Italian case, Renato Camurri, "Las *elites* italianas: estado de los estudios y perspectivas de investigación", *Ibidem*, pp. 15–16.

38 Above all, the works of Vilfredo Pareto and Gaetano Mosca. See: Pedro Carasa, De la burguesía a las élites, entre la ambigüedad y la renovación conceptual, *Ayer*, 42, 2001, pp. 213–214.

39 Daniel Halévy, *La fin des notables*, Paris, Bernard Grasset, 1972 [1st ed. 1930].

40 Max Weber, *El político y el científico*, Madrid, Alianza editorial, 2005 [1st ed. 1919].

41 Ewald Frie & Jörg Neuheiser, Introduction: Noble Ways and Democratic Means, *European Journal of Modern History*, Volume 11, November 2013, pp. 433–453 (p. 441).

42 H. Best and M. Cotta (eds.), *Parliamentary Representatives in Europe 1848–2000*, *op. cit.*. See also: H. Best and Ulrike Becker, *Elites in Transition: Elite Research in Central and Eastern Europe*, Opladen, Leske-Budrich, 1997.

43 Like Juan José Linz, among others. JJ. Linz, "Continuidad y discontinuidad en la elite política española: de la Restauración al régimen actual", C. Ollero (ed.), *Estudios de ciencias política y sociología. Homenaje al profesor Carlos Ollero*, Madrid, Gráficas Carlavilla, 1972, pp. 361–472

44 H. Best and M. Cotta (eds.), *op. cit.*, p. 514.

45 In Germany "nobility fell from 35% to less than 5%" between 1880 and 1920. In the case of Italy there was a "decline" of traditional elites (like landowners and nobility) and the growing importance of lawyers. *Ibidem*, p. 513, p. 514, respectively. Arno J. Mayer, *The Persistence of the Old Regime: Europe to the Great War*, New York, Pantheon Books, 1981. Still, and as noted before, European aristocracy was not a fixed group, but its internal composition had been throughly redefined since the 18th century. See: Ewald Frie & Jörg Neuheiser, *op. cit.* For the case of Spain, Miguel Artola Blanco has viewed the Second Republic as a turning

point in the aristocracy's decline. See: Miguel Artola Blanco, *El fin de la clase ociosa. De Romanones al estraperlo, 1900–1950*, Madrid, Alianza editorial, 2015, p. 271.

46   Ellis Wasson, *Aristocracy and the Modern World*, Basingstoke, Palgrave Macmillan, 2006, p. 3; Michael Rush, "The Decline of the Nobility", in M. Cotta and H. Best, *op. cit.*, pp. 29–50.

47   We will set to examine, therefore, what the French sociologist Pierre Bourdieu called the *"strategies of social reproduction"* of elites. These strategies can be defined as [in Spanish] "las estrategias, conscientes o no, que en diferentes campos procuran la reproducción de una clase o de una fracción de clase, es decir, la conservación o la mejora de sus condiciones de vida y de su posición respecto de otros grupos". Pierre Bourdieu, *Las estrategias de la reproducción social*, Madrid, Siglo XXI, 2011. The reference made to liberal elites as reacting through "autocratic means", in: John Garrard, "The Democratic Experience", S. Berger (ed.), *A Companion to Nineteenth-century Europe, 1789–1914*, Oxford, Blackwell, 2006, p. 149.

48   This book will preferently use the term *elite* rather than *notable*. According to the classic definition of André-Jean Tudésq, the notables in Europe can be defined according to the three characteristics they shared: an affluent position, a prominent role as members of the ruling class, and an adscription to the family *milieu*. A.J. Tudésq (1964), *Les Grands Notables en France (1840–1849). Étude historique d'une psychologie sociale*, Presses Universitaire de France, Paris, 1964, p. 10. On the different connotations the term historically had in Italy, France, Spain and Germany, and their use in the historiography, see the monograph edited by Renato Camurri, Notabili e sistemi notabiliari nell'Europa liberale, *Ricerche di storia politica*, Nuova Serie, December 2012, vol. 3.

49   According to John B. Thompson, "reputation" is a form of symbolic capital that can be defined as "the relative estimation or esteem accorded to an individual or institution by others". John B. Thompson, *Political Scandal: Power and Visibility in the Media Age*, Cambridge, Polity, 2000, p. 246.

50   This can be defined as "(...) the social-historical conditions which have established a particular set of linguistic practices as dominant and legitimate". John B. Thompson, "Editor's Introduction", Pierre Bourdieu, *Language and Symbolic power*, Oxford, Polity Press, 1991 [1st ed. in French, 1982], p. 5.

51   Hilda Sábato, *The Many and the Few: Political Participation in Republican Buenos Aires*, Stanford University Press, 2001. See also: Borja de Riquer, "Los límites de la modernización política. El caso de Barcelona, 1890–1923", José Luis García Delgado (ed.), *Las ciudades en la modernización de España. Los decenios interseculares*, Madrid, Siglo XXI, 1992, p. 23.

52   Craig Calhoun, *Habermas and the Public Sphere*, Cambridge, MA, MIT Press, 1992; François Bastien et Erik Neveu (eds.), *Espaces publiques mosaïques. Acteurs, arènes et rhétoriques des débats publics contemporains*, Rennes, Presses Universitaires de Rennes, 1999.

53   *"Eccezionale normale"* being the expression coined by the Italian micro-historian Edoardo Grendi. E. Grendi, "Micro-analisi e storia sociale", *Quaderni Storici*, N° 35, pp. 506–520.

Chapter 1

1 Gaziel, *Història de "La Vanguardia" (1884–1936)*, Barcelona, Edicions Catalanes de París, 1971, pp. 28–29; *De París a Monastir*, Barcelona, Libros del Asteroide, 2014, pp. 143–152.

2 *Ibid.*

3 Joan Torrent and Rafael Tasis, *Història de la premsa catalana*, Barcelona, Bruguera, 1966, vol. I, p. 141.

4 Jean-Ives Mollier, Jean-François Sirinelli et François Vallotton (eds.), *Culture de masse et culture médiatique en Europe et dans les Amériques. 1860–1940*, Paris, Presses universitaires de France, 2006; Richard L. Kaplan, *Politics and the American Press: The Rise of Objectivity, 1865–1920*, Cambridge-New York, CUP, 2002.

5 Arxiu Històric Comarcal d'Igualada (AHCI), Llibre de matrimonis (1684–1726), any 1716, fol. 181.

6 Montserrat Duran Pujol (ed.), *Llibre de la confraria y offici de perayres de la vila de Igualada, en lo qual estan continuadas las ordinacions y determinacions de dit offici, tretas del llibre de la confraria de perayres de la ciutat de Barcelona (1614–1887)*, Barcelona, Fundació Noguera, 2011, vol. I, 12 June 1718, pp. 345–346.

7 Jordi Maluquer de Motes, "The industrial revolution in Catalonia", in: N. Sánchez-Albornoz (ed.), *Economic modernization of Spain, 1830–1930*, New York, 1987, pp. 169–190; J.K.J. Thomson, Explaining the 'take-off' of the Catalan cotton industry, *Economic History Review*, LVIII, 4 (2005), p. 701.

8 It is not my intention here to provide a detailed account of the industrialization process. For a thorough analysis, see: Julie Marfany, *Land, proto-industry and population in Catalonia, c. 1680–1829: An Alternative Transition to Capitalism?* Farnham, Ashgate, 2012; J.K.J. Thomson, *A distinctive Industrialization: Cotton in Barcelona, 1728–1832*, Cambridge, Cambridge University Press, 2002; Jaume Torras, *Fabricants sense fàbrica. Els Torelló, d'Igualada (1691–1794)*, Vic, Eumo, 2007.

9 J.M. Torras i Ribé, "Trajectòria d'un procés d'industrialització frustrat", *Miscellanea Aqualatensia*, n° 2, 1974, p. 181.

10 Arxiu Notarial d'Igualada (ANI), Notary Vicenç Perramon Solans, vol. 1819–1820, pp. 72–73.

11 Pere Pascual i Domènech, *Els Torelló . . .* , vol. 1, p. 67.

12 Even if he was only ranked 28th on Igualada's taxpayers list. P. Pascual i Domènech, *op. cit.*, vol. I, p. 67 and pp. 132–3, respectively.

13 Arxiu Municipal d'Igualada (AMI), Padró municipal d'habitants, n° 2070.

14 For a comparison between the partible and impartible systems of inheritance in Spain: Llorenç Ferrer, *Hereus, pubilles i cabalers. El sistema d'hereu a Catalunya*, Catarroja, Afers, 2007, pp. 359–398.

15 Vis Molina, *op. cit.*, p. 26.

16 Will of Ramón Godó Llucià (21st June 1851), ANI, Testaments, 1851, expedient 278.

17 Josep Fontana, "La época del liberalismo", in J. Fontana and R. Villares (dirs.), *Historia de España*, Barcelona-Madrid, Crítica-Marcial Pons, 2007, vol. 6, pp. 267–277.

18 Francisco Olaya Morales, *Historia del Movimiento Obrero Español . . .* , p. 189, n. 38.

19   J. Ferrer Farriol, *op. cit.*, p. 13.

20   *La Época*, 06/07/1855, p. 3.

21   Baltasar Porcel, *La revuelta permanente*, Barcelona, Planeta, 1978; Joan Ferrer Farriol, *op. cit.*, pp. 14–15; F. Olaya Morales, *op. cit.*

22   Between 1868 and 1881 salaries in Igualada's textile industry were lowered by 25%. Jorge Pablo Martínez de Presno, *Moviments socials a Igualada al segle XIX: anys 1854–1890*, Barcelona, Publicacions de l'Abadia de Montserrat, 1993, p. 18; Josep Maria Torras i Ribé, Trajectòria d'un procés d'industrialització frustrat, *Miscellanea Aqualatensia*, n° 2, 1974, p. 181.

23   *Ibid*; *La Nación*, 20/07/1855, p. 1; *La España*, 22/07/1855, p. 3; *El Clamor público*, 07/07/1855, p. 3. In the case of Barcelona, *La Crónica de Cataluña* provided a similar account.

24   "That narrow-minded attitude was personified by the Godós of Igualada, who became the *caciques,* or bosses. (...) For years and years they were the most hated of all bosses, and that came about as a result of the very hard strike of 1854 (sic)." Baltasar Porcel, *op. cit.*

25   Stéphane Gerson, *The Pride of Place. Local Memories and Political Culture in Nineteenth-Century France*, London–Ithaca, Cornell University Press, 2003; David Blackbourn and James Retallack (eds.), *Localism, Landscape, and the Ambiguities of Place: German-speaking Central Europe, 1860–1930*, Toronto, University of Toronto Press, 2007.

26   "Porque D. Carlos Godó, que en su juventud fué simple obrero, llegó, gracias á sus extraordinarias condiciones de actividad y de talento, á poseer un capital de los primeros de Barcelona". *La Correspondencia de España*, 10/07/1897, p. 1.

27   *El Liberal*, 14/02/1900, p. 2.

28   LV, 28/01/1894, p. 2.

29   Cemeteries and mausoleums were another example of the construction of these values. See: Gary Wray McDonogh, *Good Families of Barcelona: A Social History of Power in the Industrial Era*, Princeton University Press, 1986.

30   Laurence Fontaine, Kinship and Mobility, in David Warren Sabean, Simon Teuscher and Jon Mathieu (eds.), *Kinship in Europe. Approaches to long-term development (1300–1900)*, New York–Oxford, Berghan, 2007, p. 194.

31   David W. Sabean, S. Teuscher and J. Mathieu, *op. cit.*, p. 20.

32   *Ibidem*, AHFB, Archivo Municipal de Bilbao, c. 259, leg. 1; and c. 254, leg. 5.

33   This can be defined as "that movement in which prospective migrants learn of opportunities, are provided with transportation, and have initial accommodation and employment arranged by means of primary social relationships with previous migrants." John S. MacDonald and Leatrice D. MacDonald, "Chain Migration Ethnic Neighborhood Formation and Social Networks", *The Milbank Memorial Fund Quarterly*, Vol. 42, No. 1 (Jan., 1964), p. 82.

34   "Ronda, 25 y 27, *Godó Hermanos*. – Almacén al por mayor de géneros nacionales y extranjeros en tejidos de seda, lana, hilo, algodon, tapicerías, alfombras y pañolería.   Casa de comision de compra y venta y transportes. – Géneros de punto. Sres. Godó hermanos." Luis Marty Caballero, *Anuario General del Comercio . . . ,* Madrid, Imprenta Oficinas del Anuario, 1863, p. 46 ("Bilbao").

35   AHFB, Sección Bilbao primera, c. 73, l. 77.

36   M. T. Pérez, A. Segura and Ll. Ferrer (eds.), *Els catalans a Espanya, 1760–1914*, Centre d'Història Contemporània de Catalunya, 1996, pp. 135–138.

37   Felipa Belaunzaran Hormaza (Bilbao, 1839–?); Dolors Brunet Cucurull (La Habana,? – Barcelona, 1871); and Gloria Eguía de Muruaga (Bilbao, 1842– Barcelona, 1908). The marriages took place in 07/11/1860; in 1870(?) and in 16/11/1872, respectively. AHEB, Registro de Matrimonios, p. 257; pp. 144– 145. Bartolomé's second wife was descendant of the Brunet's, a Catalan family who had migrated to San Sebastián in the 18th century. See: Montserrat Gárate Ojanguren, "De los catalanes en Gipuzkoa (siglos XVIII-XIX)", in M. T. Pérez, A. Segura and Ll. Ferrer (ed.), *op. cit.*, pp. 139–147.

38   AHPB, Notari Josep Ferrer Bernadas, vol. 5, 23/11/1897, fols. 5254–5257.

39   AHEB, Registro de matrimonios, p. 250.

40   Agustí Calvet, *Història de «La Vanguardia» (1881–1936) i nou articles sobre periodisme*, Barcelona, Empúries, 1994 [1st ed. Paris, 1976], p. 42.

41   Further evidence of this change of language is provided by a recent interview to *La Vanguardia*'s current owner, Javier Godó Muntañola: "Familia Godó, empresarios del textil de Igualada, ¿cuándo perdieron el idioma como lengua familiar? "Quizás con el bisabuelo Carlos, que se casó con una vasca con gran personalidad, y cambió el idioma". *"El ADN de 'La Vanguardia' es catalán"*. LV, 01/05/2011.

42   Pierre Bourdieu, *Language and Symbolic Power*, Oxford, Polity Press, 1991.

43   AHPB, Notari F. Moragas Ubac, Vol. 1, 01/02/1870, fols. 219–222.

44   AHFB, Archivo del Corregimiento, Legajo 2108, n° 7.

45   For a renewed outlook on this period, see: Rafael Serrano García (dir.), *España, 1868–1874. Nuevos enfoques sobre el Sexenio Democrático*, Valladolid, Junta de Castilla y León, 2002; and Rafael Serrano (ed.), El Sexenio Democrático, *Ayer*, 44 (2001).

46   Isabel María Pascual Sastre, *La Italia del Risorgimento y la España del Sexenio Democrático (1868–1874)*, Madrid, CSIC, Biblioteca Historia, 2001, esp. pp. 51–92.

47   Even if these measures became temporary. Marició Janué, *Els polítics en temps de revolució. La vida política a Barcelona durant el Sexenni Revolucionari*, Vic, Eumo, 2002, pp. 88–92 and pp. 111–117.

48   *Ibidem*, p. 14, p. 221 and pp. 232–233, respectively.

49   *"Políticamente, el Sr. Godó militó constantemente en el partido liberal. De arraigadas convicciones, y carácter intependiente, nunca rindió vasallaje sino á los dictados de su recta conciencia (…)"*. J. Roca i Roca, LV, 28/01/1894, p. 2.

50   Jorge Vilches, *Progreso y libertad. El Partido Progresista en la revolución liberal española*, Madrid, Alianza, 2001, pp. 170–1; and Ángel Bahamonde, *Historia de España: siglo XIX*, Madrid, Cátedra, 2007, pp. 547–549.

51   "Bourgeois conquérant" ("the conquering bourgeois") became a common expression among Marxist historians (though not only) to refer to the assault of power by one single class ("the bourgeoisie") after the French Revolution (1789). See: Charles Morazé, *The Triumph of the Middle Classes*, New York, Anchor Books,

1968 [original edition in French: *Bourgeois conquérants*]; Eric Hobsbawm, *The Age of Capital, 1848–1875*, London, Weidenfeld and Nicolson, 1975, p. 2. This interpretation has been deeply challenged in the last two decades. See: Jerrold Seigel, *Modernity and Bourgeois Life: Society, Politics and Culture in England, France and Germany since 1750*, Cambridge, CUP, 2012, pp. 2–4.

52 As evidenced, for instance, by the difficulties of the Italian state to meet the different needs of local elites. Raffaele Romanelli, *Il commando impossible. Stato e società nell'Italia liberale*, Bologna, Il Mulino, 1988. See also Chapter 3.

53 María Sierra, Rafael Zurita & María Antonia Peña, *La representación política en el discurso del liberalismo español (1845–1874)*, Ayer, 61, 2006, pp. 30–31.

54 Gregorio L. de la Fuente Monge, "Élite política y clientelismo durante el Sexenio Democrático (1868–1874)", A. Robles Egea (ed.), *Política en penumbra. Patronazgo y clientelismo políticos en la España contemporánea*, Madrid, Siglo XXI, 1996, pp. 133–168.

55 Namely: Parliamentary monarchy between 1871–1873; Federal Republic in 1873; and a "conservative" Republic in 1874.

56 Alan S. Kahan, *Liberalism in Nineteenth-Century Europe. The Political Culture of Limited Suffrage*, Basingstoke-New York, Palgrave Macmillan, 2002, pp. 21–171; and Raffaele Romanelli, *How did they become voters? The history of franchise in modern European representation*, The Hague, Boston, Kluwer, 1998.

57 Raymond Huard, "Las prácticas del sufragio universal en Francia entre 1848 y 1914. Avances pioneros, novedades provisionales, proyectos inacabados", in Salvador Forner (coord.), *Democracia, elecciones y modernización en Europa. Siglos XIX y XX*, Madrid, Cátedra, 1997, pp. 47–72; and Gilles Le Béguec, "Il caso francese", Maria Serena Piretti (ed.), *I sistemi elettorali in Europa tra Otto e Novecento*, Bari, Laterza, 1997, pp. 81–129; Margaret Lavinia Anderson, *Practicing Democracy. Elections and Political Culture in Imperial Germany*, Princeton University Press, 2000.

58 M. Kreuzer, "Democratisation and changing methods of electoral corruption in France from 1815 to 1914", in Eduardo Posada Carbó, *Political Corruption in Europe and Latin America*, Basingstoke, Macmillan Press, 1996, p. 98. Alain Garrigou, *Le vote et la vertu. Comment les français sont devenus électeurs*, Paris, Presses de la Fondation National des Sciences Politiques, 1992.

59 This point will be examined in further detail in Chapter 3.

60 Maricló Janué et al. (eds.), *La diputació revolucionària: 1868–1874*, Barcelona, Diputació de Barcelona, 2003.

61 Geoffrey Crossick and Gerhard Haupt, *The Petite Bourgeoisie in Europe, 1780–1914: Enterprise, Family, and Independence*, London-New York, Routledge, 1995, p. 132.

62 A valuable comparative analysis between the different attributions that municipal governments had in Prussia and in Spain, in Jorge Luengo, *Una sociedad conyugal. Las élites de Valladolid en el espejo de Magdeburgo en el siglo XIX*, València, PUV, 2014, pp. 97–109.

63 Quoted in Jesús Cruz, "The Moderate ascendancy, 1843–1868", in J. Álvarez Junco and A. Shubert, *op. cit.*, pp. 33–47 (p. 43).

64 *Ibidem.*

65 AHDB, Llibre de registre de diputats (1812–1890), fols. 247–249.

66 AHDB, *op. cit.*, p. 247; and *El Eco del Noya*, 08/09/1878, p. 3.

67 The best study on Balaguer is: Joan Palomas Moncholí, *Víctor Balaguer. Renaixença, Revolució i Progrés*, Vilanova i la Geltrú, El Cep i la Nansa, 2004.

68 ABMVB, Vilanova i la Geltrú, Private correspondence of Víctor Balaguer (1842–1876), letter n°. 7103131.

69 J. Vilches, *op. cit.*, pp. 170–180.

70 The division between the Constitutionals of Barcelona, in: M. Janué, *op. cit.*, pp. 61–82.

71 Maurice Duverger, *Los Partidos Políticos*, México, Fondo de Cultura Económica, 1979, and Angelo Panebianco, *Modelos de partido: organización y poder en los partidos políticos*, Madrid, Alianza Editorial, 1990; Michel Offerlé, *La profession politique. XIXe–XXe siècles*, Paris, Berlin, 1999.

72 Max Weber, *Política y ciencia*, Buenos Aires, La Pleyade, Editorial Elaleph, pp. 19–22.

73 AHDB, Libro de Actas 1871, 8 April, fol. 169; and 14 April, fol. 203–204.

74 B. Riquer (ed.), *Història de la Diputació de Barcelona: 1812–2005*, Barcelona: Diputació de Barcelona, 2007, vol. I, p. 249.

75 J. Varela Ortega, *op. cit.*, pp. 25–93.

76 María Sierra, "El espejo inglés de la modernidad española: el modelo británico y su influencia en el concepto de representación liberal", *Historia y Política*, n° 21, 2009, pp. 139–167.

77 This was particularly the case of the Constitution of 1876. The majority of the articles were inspired by the Moderate constitution of 1845. Remedios Sánchez Ferriz, Génesis del proyecto constitucional: la comisión de los notables, *Revista de Derecho Político*, n° 8, 1981, pp. 33–54.

78 J. Varela Ortega, *op. cit.*, pp. 121–128.

79 Joan Palomas Moncholí, *op. cit.*, pp. 456–457.

80 ABMVB, Epistolari Víctor Balaguer (1842–1876). N°. 7500896, 24/09/1875.

81 ABMVB, Epistolari, N° 7500909. 26/11/1875.

82 Prior to the elections the state provincial officer (Mr. Villalba) removed the city mayors of Igualada's constituency and replaced them with new mayors that were favourable to the government's candidate. *La Iberia*, 07/01/1876, p. 2.

83 Maria Gemma Rubí Casals, "El món de la política en la Catalunya urbana de la Restauració. El cas d'una ciutat industrial. Manresa: 1875–1923", Universitat Autònoma de Barcelona – École des Hautes Études en Sciences Sociales, 2003 [Thesis manuscript], p. 176.

84 "LA VANGUARDIA", LV, 01/02/1881, p. 2.

85 J. Torrent and R. Tasis, *Història de la premsa catalana*, Barcelona, Bruguera, 1966, vol. I, p. 140.

86 At the time, permission was needed from the "Gobierno Civil" to establish a newspaper. According to Joan Givanel, Bartolomé Godó received such permission. Unfortunately, Givanel's claim is difficult to substantiate as no evidence attesting to this has been found. Joan Givanel Mas, *Materials per a la*

bibliografía de la premsa barcelonesa (1881–1890). Barcelona, Altés, 1933, pp. 15–16.

87 *La Época*, 13/11/1880, p. 2. This newspaper quoted the news published by *La Correspondencia*.

88 "Este periódico debe su fundación a Bartolomé Godó. Periódico de lucha en un principio, para defender á un partido (...)". Jordi Roca Roca, LV, 28/01/1894, p. 2.

89 *Semanario de Igualada*, 26/10/1884, p. 1 and 04/04/1886, p. 1, respectively.

90 Pierre Bourdieu, *Language and Symbolic Power . . .* , *op. cit.*

91 *Diario de Barcelona*, 26/01/1871 (Morning ed.), p. 933.

92 P. Bourdieu, *op. cit.*, pp. 107–116 ("the social institution of symbolic power").

93 Daniel C. Hallin and Paolo Mancini, *Comparing Media Systems. Three Models of Media and Politics*, Cambridge-New York, CUP, 2004, p. 67; Valerio Castronovo, *La stampa italiana nell'età liberale*, Bari, Laterza, 1979, pp. 15–69; Ana Cabrera (ed.), *op. cit.*.

94 Agustí Calvet, *op. cit.*, p. 29 and p. 63.

95 *Semanario de Igualada*, 26/10/1884, p. 1 and 04/04/1886, p. 1, respectively.

96 *La Correspondencia de España*, 20/02/1881, p. 3. *La Vanguardia* did not lose the opportunity to reproduce the news of *La Correspondencia*. LV, 22/02/1881, p. 2.

97 On this character, see: Josep Mª Vallès i Martí, *De l'idealisme a l'oblit. Poesia i teatre de Pere Antoni Torres Jordi,* Valls, Cossetània, 2007.

98 Named "La Prensa", "La Prensa Libre" and "La Nueva Prensa". *Ibidem*, p. 17.

99 The first four directors were: Pere Antoni Torres Jordi (1844–1901); Alfredo García López (?-1906), who had been the director of the Madrid newspaper *La Mañana* (the mouthpiece of Víctor Balaguer in Madrid) and was a Liberal; Josep Roger i Miquel (1829–1892), who was the former director of the Liberal Barcelona newspaper *La Bomba*; and Modesto Sánchez Ortiz (1857–1937), who had worked at *El Correo de Madrid*.

100 José Alvarez Junco, "Lerroux, El País y el periodismo de izquierdas", *op. cit.*, pp. 51–54 (for the street cleaner's anecdote see p. 51); and Jesús Timoteo Álvarez, *Restauración y prensa de masas. Los engranajes de un sistema, 1875–1883*, Pamplona, Ediciones Universidad de Navarra, 1981.

101 Adolfo Scotto di Luzio, "Tra campo letterario e politica: i giornalisti in età liberale", G. Mellis (ed.), *Le élites nella storia dell'Italia unita*, Napoli, Cuen, 2003, pp. 195–211; Valerio Castronovo, *La stampa italiana nell'età liberale*, Bari, Laterza, 1979, pp. 62–68; Ana Cabrera (ed.), *Jornais, jornalistas e jornalismo: séculos XIX–XX*, Lisboa, Livros Horizonte, 2011; Marie-Ève Thérenty et Alain Vaillant (dir), *Presse et plumes. Journalisme et littérature au XIXe siècle*, Paris, Nouveau Monde Éditions, 2004.

102 *"General Director of Health and Wellness"*. J. M. Vallès i Martí, *op. cit.*, p. 16. Torres acted as deputy in the Congress for the constituencies of Tarragona-Reus-Falset (1879 and 1886), Gandesa (1888 and 1886), Puigcerdà (1893) and Valls (1896). Maria Gemma Rubí Casals y Josep Armengol Segú, "Cataluña", in J. Varela Ortega, *op. cit.*, p. 267.

103 LV, 02/02/1881, p. 3 and 14/03/1881, p. 2.

104 Evidence of the state's support to Godó was that the Civil Governor of Barcelona forced the mayors of Igualada's constituency to support his candidacy. J. Palomas i Moncholí, *op. cit.*, pp. 894–895.

105 The agreement was a way of assuring the stability of the political system after the death of King Alfonso XII (November 1885), and with a civil war ("Tercera Guerra Carlista", 1872–1876) and a separatist insurrection in Cuba ("Ten Years War", 1868–1878) going on.

106 All the electoral results, in: José Varela Ortega (dir.), *El poder de la influencia. Geografía del caciquismo en España, 1875–1923*, Madrid, Marcial Pons, Centro de Estudios Políticos y Constitucionales, 2001.

107 Quoted in Georgina Blakeley, "Clientelism in the Building of State and Civil Society in Spain", in S. Piattoni, *Clientelism, op. cit.*, p. 83.

108 See: Gabriele Ranzato, La forja de la soberanía nacional: las elecciones en los sistemas liberales italiano y español, *Ayer*, 3, 1991, pp. 115–138; Silvana Casmirri y Manuel Suárez Cortina (eds.), *La Europa del sur en la época liberal: España, Italia y Portugal. Una perspectiva comparada*, Universidad de Cantabria-Università di Cassino, 1998; and Javier Moreno Luzón y Pedro Tavares de Almeida (eds.), *De las Urnas al Hemiciclo. Elecciones y parlamentarismo en la Península Ibérica (1875–1926)*, Madrid, Marcial Pons, 2015.

109 "A nuestros lectores", LV, 01/01/1888, p. 1.

110 "Impresiones", *La Dinastía*, 10/01/1888, p. 1.

111 LV, 14/03/1885, pp. 7–8.

112 *El Barcelonés*, 13/06/1885, p. 1.

113 Ramon Grau (ed.), *Exposició Universal de Barcelona. Llibre del Centenari, 1888–1988*, Barcelona, L'Avenç, 1988. On World Fairs, see: Alexander Geppert, *Fleeting Cities: Imperial Expositions in Fin-de-Siècle Europe*, New York, Palgrave Macmillan, 2010.

114 Jordi Maluquer, *Història econòmica de Catalunya. Segles XIX i XX*, UOC-Proa, 1998, p. 139.

115 Joan Ramon Resina, *Barcelona's Vocation of Modernity. Rise and Decline of an Urban Image*, Stanford University Press, 2008; and Rosa Cabré, *La Barcelona de Narcís Oller. Realitat i somni de la ciutat*, Valls, Cossetània, 2004.

116 This event granted Rius great prestige. See, for instance: "El gran alcalde barceloní", in: Rosa Cabré, *op. cit.*, pp. 193–196.

117 "El Señor Sánchez Ortiz", LV, 11/12/1901. Sánchez' appointment was announced in late December 1887. *La Vanguardia*, 29/12/1887, p. 3.

118 J. T. Álvarez, *op. cit.*; and "El retraso español", in: Josep Francesc Valls, *Prensa y burguesía en el XIX español*, Madrid, Anthropos, 1987, pp. 160–170; and more recently, Jaume Guillamet, "Por una historia comparada del periodismo. Factores de progreso y atraso", *Doxa Comunicación*, nº 1, 2003, pp. 35–56. On the limitations of modernisation theories, see: Isabel Burdiel, Myths of Failure, Myths of Success: New Perspectives on Nineteenth-Century Spanish Liberalism, *The Journal of Modern History*, Vol. 70, No. 4 (December 1998), pp. 892–912. On cultural tranfers, see: Michel Espagne, *Les transferts culturels franco-allemands*, Paris, Presses Universitaires de France, 1999; Michael Werner

and Bénédicte Zimmermann, Beyond Comparison: *Histoire Croisée* and the Challenge of Reflectivity, *History and Theory* 45 (2006), pp. 30–50; Wolfgang Schmale, "Cultural Transfer". *European History Online* (EGO). Mainz, 2012-12-05. URN: urn:nbn:de:0159-2012120501.

119 There are different accounts on the history of this newspaper. The ones used here are: Oliver Woods & James Bishop, *The Story of the Time: Bicentenary Edition, 1785–1985*, London, Michael Joseph, 1985; and especially Stanley Morison, *The History of The Times*, London, Office The Times, 1935–1952, 5 vols.

120 S. Morison, *op. cit.*, vol. 1, pp. 20–25 (esp. p. 24).

121 LV, 01/02/1888, p. 1.

122 "Las reformas de La Vanguardia", LV, 21/02/1890, p. 1.

123 Josep Maria Fradera, *Cultura nacional en una societat dividida: patriotisme i cultura a Catalunya (1838–1868)*, Barcelona, Curial, 1992; Stephen Jacobson, *Catalonia's Advocates: Lawyers, Society and Politics in Barcelona, 1759–1900*, Chapell Hill, University of North Carolina Press, 2009, pp. 198–238; Eric Storm, *The Culture of Regionalism. Art, Architecture and International Exhibitions in France, Germany and Spain, 1890–1913*, Manchester, Manchester University Press, 2010.

124 Maiken Umbach, "A Tale of Second Cities": Autonomy, Culture, and the Law in Hamburg and Barcelona in the Late Nineteenth Century, *American Historical Review*, June 2005, pp. 659–692.

125 See: Juan Valero de Tornos, *Barcelona tal cual es. Por un madrileño*, Barcelona, Sucesores de N. Ramírez y Cᵃ, 1888, p. 40 (chapter "La ciudad moderna").

126 The so-called "Penya de La Vanguardia". LV, 25/10/1903, p. 9.

127 The full list of collaborators was: "José Zulueta, José Coroleu, José Ixart, Juan Sardá, Narciso Oller, Melitón González, Ramón D. Perés, Francisco Virella, Emilio Blanchet, Josefa Pujol de Collado, E. Suñol, Rafael Puig y Valls, J. Vergés y Almar, José Passos, Doctor Xercavins, Santiago Rusiñol, Ramón Casas, José Luis Pellicer, Felipe Pedrell." LV, 21/02/1890, p. 2.

128 This issue has been analysed in: Elena Cueto Asín & David R. George, Jr., Looking to France from Barcelona: correspondence and travel writing in La Vanguardia (1890–1900), *Journal of Spanish Cultural Studies*, Vol. 9, No. 3 November 2008, pp. 265–283. See also: LV, 28/02/1890, p. 2.

129 LV, 05/05/1889, p. 1.

130 LV, 01/01/1888, p. 1. Italics added.

131 "In this apparently simple but very complex formula is where all the modern journalism is condensed: to serve the public, instead of the party or the faction. The newspaper can no longer be, as it has been for many years, a dispersed number of articles based on the fantasy of the writer. (...) Today's press requires, as in reflecting civilization, to be made by providing *facts, facts and facts*; but has to be as complex as civilization." LV, 21/02/1890, p. 1. Italics added.

132 As the London newspaper proclaimed: "(...) and we, the TIMES, being the PUBLIC'S most humble and most obedient Servants (...)". S. Morison, *op. cit.*, vol. 1, p. 30.

133 Quoted in: J. Chapman, *op. cit.*, p. 48.

134 J. M. Casasús Gurí, "Estudio introductorio", in: Modesto Sánchez Ortiz / El Periodismo, Barcelona, Fundación Conde de Barcelona, La Vanguardia [Facsímil de la edición de 1903]; introducción de J. M. Casasús Gurí], 1990, p. ix.

135 M. Sánchez Ortiz, *El Periodismo . . .*, *op. cit.*, p. 9.

136 *Ibidem*, p. 53.

137 J. Chapman, *op. cit.*, p. 78.

138 Marcel Broersma (ed.), *Form and Style in Journalism. European Newspapers and the Representation of News, 1880–2005*, Leuven, Peeters, 2007; Svennik Høyer and Horst Pöttker (eds.), *Diffusion of the News Paradigm, 1850–2000*, Goteborg, Nordicom, 2014.

139 J. Lee Thompson, *Northcliffe. Press Baron in Politics, 1865–1922*, London, John Murray, 2000, pp. 140–159.

140 Svennik Høyer "Old and New Journalism in The London Press. The 1880s and 1890s", in: S. Høyer and H. Pöttker (eds.), *Diffusion of the News Paradigm 1850–2000*, Goteborg, Nordicom, 2014, pp. 65–74; and Dean de la Motte & Jeannene M. Przyblyski (eds.), *Making the News: Modernity & the Mass Press in Nineteenth-Century France*, University of Massachusetts Press, 1999.

141 British historians hold different opinions about the levels of continuity and rupture between the Old and the New Journalism in the 1880s. For a brief outline of this debate, see: Mark Hampton, "Newspapers in Victorian Britain", *History Compass* 2 (2004), 101, pp. 1–8.

142 J. F. Valls, *op. cit.*, p. 207.

143 Joaquín Romero Maura, *"La rosa de fuego". El obrerismo barcelonés de 1899 a 1909*, Madrid, Alianza, 1989, p. 572 and p. 573.

144 *El Diluvio*, 17/08/1901, p. 12.

145 David Forgacs, *Italian Culture in the Industrial Era: Cultural Industries, Politics, and the Public*, Manchester–New York, Manchester University Press, 1990, p. 36.

146 Valerio Castronovo, *La stampa italiana nell'età liberale*, Bari, Laterza, 1979, pp. 157–162 (p. 159).

147 *Ibidem* (esp. p. 161).

148 The first serial novel published in *La Vanguardia* was Edward Bulwer-Lytton's *The Last of the Barons* (1st ed. 1843). "El Último Barón. Novela inglesa.", in: LV, 21/02/1890, p. 5.

149 Maria Adamowicz-Hariasz, "The Roman-Feuilleton and the Transformation of the Nineteenth-Century French Press", in: Dean de la Motte & Jeannene M. Przyblyski, *Making the News: Modernity & the Mass Press in Nineteenth-Century France*, University of Massachusetts Press, 1999, pp. 160–184 (p. 160).

150 Jane Chapman, *Gender, Citizenship and Newspapers: Historical and Transnational Perspectives*, Basingstoke, Palgrave Macmillan, 2013, esp. Chapter 2, "France. Pioneering the Popular Newspaper Brand and the Female Market", pp. 25–61.

151 In 1887 53% of Catalan men were literate, but only 28% of women. J. M. Tresserras, *op. cit.*, p. 69.

152 Joan Ramon Resina, *op. cit.*

153 See, for instance, the advertisement published on the left side of the front-page the first day *La Vanguardia* started implementing the reforms. LV, 01/02/1881, p. 1. This advertisement was for corsets for pregnant women: "Corsé higiénico. El verdadero Corsé higiénico privilegiado por la M. Iltre. Academia de Medicina y Cirujía de esta ciudad hecho expresamente para el periodo del embarazo y para señoras delicadas, únicamente lo encontrarán en esa casa, Escudillers Blanchs, 8, La Emperatriz."

154 LV, 28/03/1888, p. 3.

155 M. Sánchez Ortiz, *El Periodismo . . .* , *op. cit.*, p. 21.

Chapter 2

1 Henri L. Wesseling, *Divide and Rule: The Partition of Africa, 1880–1914*, London, Praeger, 1996.

2 John M. Mackenzie, *Propaganda and Empire*, Manchester, Manchester University Press, 1984; and *Imperialism and Popular Culture*, Manchester, Manchester University Press, 1986.

3 Catherine Hall and Sonya O. Rose, *At Home With the Empire: Metropolitan Culture and the Imperial World*, Cambridge, New York, Cambridge University Press, 2006; Tony Chafer and Amanda Sackur, *Promoting the Colonial Idea: Propaganda and Visions of Empire in France*, Palgrave Macmillan, 2002; John M. Mackenzie (ed.), *European Empires and the People: Popular Responses to Imperialism in France, Britain, the Netherlands, Belgium, Germany and Italy*, Manchester, New York, Manchester University Press, 2011. A sceptical view about the presence of the Empire in British identity, in: Bernard Porter, *The Absent-Minded Imperialists: Empire, Society and Culture in Britain*, Oxford University Press, 2004.

4 Edward Berenson, *Heroes of Empire: Five Charismatic Men and the Conquest of Africa*, Berkeley, University of California Press, 2010; Robert Aldrich, *Vestiges of the Colonial Empire in France: Monuments, Museums, and Colonial Memories*, New York, Palgrave Macmillan, 2005; Alda Blanco, *Cultura y conciencia imperial en la España del siglo XIX*, València, PUV, 2012.

5 Benedict Anderson, *Imagined Communities*, New York, Verso, 2006 [1st ed. 1983], pp. 33–65.

6 Richard Pennell, *Morocco since 1830: A History*, London, Hurst & Company, 2000; Luis Miège, *Le Maroc et l'Europe*, Paris, Presses Universitaires de France, 1961, 4 vol.

7 Azucena Pedraz Marcos, *Quimeras de África. La Sociedad Española de Africanistas y colonialistas. El colonialismo español de finales del siglo XIX*, Madrid, Ediciones Polifemo, 2000, pp. 139–142; the so-called "*Doctrina de la comodidad*", in: Josep Pich i Mitjana, *Francesc Pi i Margall i la crisi de Melilla de 1893–1894*, Barcelona, Bellaterra, 2008, pp. 58–63. See also: Elena Hernández Sandoica, *Pensamiento burgués y problemas coloniales en la España de la Restauración, 1875–1887*, Madrid, Universidad Complutense, 1982; Manuel Fernández Rodríguez, *España y Marruecos en los primeros años de la Restauración, 1875–1894*, Madrid, CSIC, 1985.

8 Sebastian Balfour, *España, Marruecos y las grandes potencias, 1898–1914*, in: Guadalupe Gómez-Ferrer y Raquel Sánchez, eds, *Modernizar España. Proyectos de reforma y apertura internacional (1898–1914)*, Madrid, Biblioteca Nueva, Colección Historia, 2007, pp. 143–173; J. Pich i Mitjana, *op. cit.*, p. 42.

9 Further thoughts on the Spanish Africanist lobby, in: Azucena Pedraz Marcos, *op. cit.*; Víctor Morales Lezcano, *Africanismo y orientalismo español en el siglo XIX*, Madrid, UNED, 1988.

10 José Antonio González Alcantud & Eloy Martín Corrales (eds.), *La Conferencia de Algeciras en 1906: un banquete colonial*, Barcelona, edicions Bellaterra, 2007, p. 20, n. 7.

11 Jean Louis Miège, "Les efforts de pénétration de l'Espagne", *Le Maroc et l'Europe*, Paris, Presses Universitaires de France, 1961, vol. 3, pp. 207–231.

12 M. Marín, Un encuentro colonial: viajeros españoles en Marruecos (1860–1912), *Hispania*, vol. LVI-192 (1996), pp. 93–114; L. Litvak, *Viajeros españoles del siglo XIX por países exóticos (1800–1913)*, Barcelona, 1984. For the Catalan case, see: M. D. García Ramon, Joan Nogué i Perla Zusman (eds.), *Una mirada catalana a l'Àfrica. Viatgers i viatgeres dels segles XIX i XX (1859–1936)*, Lleida, Pagès editors, 2008; and Eloy Martín Corrales, Un siglo de viajes y viajeros catalanes por tierras del norte de África y Próximo Oriente (1833–1939): peregrinos, nostálgicos y colonialistas, *Illes i Imperis*, 8, 2006, pp. 83–111.

13 Dominique Barjot et Jacques Fémeaux (eds.), *Les sociétés coloniales à l'âge des empires. Des années 1850 aux années 1950*, Paris, SEDES, 2012; José Antonio Rodríguez Esteban, "Las Sociedades Geográficas y el proceso colonial", A. R. Díez Torre (ed.), *Ciencia y Memoria de África. Actas de las III Jornadas sobre Expediciones científicas y africanismo español, 1898–1998*, Madrid, Universidad de Alcalá, 2002, p. 163.

14 A. Pedraz Marcos, *op. cit*; and José Luis Villanova Valero, Las sociedades geográficas españolas como impulsoras del colonialismo español en Marruecos, *Transfretana. Revista del Instituto de Estudios Ceutíes*, n. 5, 1999, pp. 133–148.

15 A. Pedraz Marcos, *op. cit.*, pp. 155–164.

16 *Revista de Geografía Comercial*, 31/10/1885, p. 1.

17 "Nuevos mercados para la industria española", *Revista de Geografía Comercial*, 08/1889, p. 3.

18 See Chapter 1.

19 Josep Boada Romeu, *Allende el Estrecho. Viajes por Marruecos. (1889–1894)*, Melilla, Ciudad Autónoma de Melilla, 2009 [1ˢᵗ ed 1895]. On Boada's book, see: J. A. Gonzálzez Alcantud, *El orientalismo desde el sur*, Barcelona, Anthropos editorial-Junta de Andalucía, Col. Pensamiento Crítico, Pensamiento Utópico, 2006; M. D. Garcia Ramon, J. Nogué and P. Zusman (eds.), *op. cit.*; and C. García Romeral Pérez, *Bio-bibliografia de viajeros españoles (siglo XIX)*, Madrid, Ollero y Ramos Ed., 1995.

20 "El jueves último salió en expedicion comercial para Fez, el propietario del periodico La Vanguardia, D. Carlos Godó, socio de la casa fabril Godó Hermanos de Barcelona. Le acompañan el ex diputado Sr. Collaso, el periodista Sr. Boada, otro Sr. representante de la prensa de la ciudad condal [Reig], y el

intérprete D. Bernardo Blanco". *Al-moghreb al-Aksa*, Instituto Cervantes en Tánger (Morocco), 10/03/1889, p. 3.

21 J. Boada, *op. cit.*, p. 122.

22 "Fundación de la Compañía Hispano-Marroquí", AHPM, Notary Francisco Lozano Muñoz ("Cónsul de España en la Ciudad de Tanger, Marruecos"), vol. 36486, pp. 338–341.

23 Louis Miège gives the example of a piece of land that cost 32 pesetas in 1860, 500 ptas. in 1876 and 1,000 ptas. in 1890. Louis Miège, "La propriété immobilière à Tanger d'après un plan du XIXè siècle", *Revue Maroc Europe*, I, 1991, pp. 84–90 (p. 86).

24 Bernabé López García, "Los españoles en Tánger", *Awraq*, n° 5–6, 2012, p. 10 and p. 8, respectively.

25 Juan Bautista Vilar, *Los españoles en la Argelia francesa (1830–1914)*, Madrid-Murcia, Centro de Estudios Históricos CSIC, Universidad de Murcia, 1989; and Eloy Martín Corrales, "La emigración española en Argelia", *Awraq*, n° 5–6, 2012, pp. 47–63.

26 "Problemas marroquíes. La emigración española", LV, 28/09/1889, p. 1. Italics added.

27 The National Archives (NA), FO 99/269, Edward E. Meakin to Lord Salisbury (Letter of 18/09/1889). Further information on this diplomat, in: S. E. Fryer, 'Meakin, James Edward Budgett (1866–1906)', rev. Mark Pottle, *Oxford Dictionary of National Biography*, Oxford University Press, 2004.

28 "Spain and Morocco", *Western Morning News*, September 1899. Clipping of the newspaper added in Meakin's letter to Lord Salisbury. NA, FO 99/269.

29 AHPM, Tánger, 17/04/1899, AHPM, Notary Francisco Lozano Muñoz ("Cónsul de España en la Ciudad de Tanger, Marruecos"), vol. 37568, pp. 57–58.

30 A wide literature exists on the Franciscan Missions in Morocco, mostly written by members of the same order. José Mª Álvarez Infante, *La Misión Franciscana de Marruecos: desde su restablecimiento en 1856 hasta nuestros días*, Barcelona, Tip. Católica, 1911; Juan Menéndez Pidal, *Album hispano-marroquí. Misiones católicas de Marruecos*, Barcelona, Asociación de Señoras Españolas bajo los auspicios de María Inmaculada, 1897. An exception to this trend is: Ricardo Castillo Larriba, "Los franciscanos y el colonialismo español en Marruecos. José María Lerchundi y Francisco María Cervera (1877–1926)", Universidad de Alcalá, Doctoral thesis, 2014.

31 José María López, *El P. José Lerchundi. Biografía documentada*, Imp. Clásica Española, 1927; Ramón Lourido Díaz (ed.), *Marruecos y el Padre Lerchundi*, Madrid, Mapfre, 1996.

32 Martín Rodrigo Alharilla, "Una avanzadilla española en África: el grupo empresarial Comillas", in Eloy Martín Corrales (ed.), *op. cit.*, pp. 133–166; and M. Rodrigo Alharilla, *Marqueses de Comillas. Antonio y Claudio López, 1817–1925*, Madrid, LID, 2000.

33 Archivo General de Palacio (AGP), Reinado Alfonso XIII, Caja 8730, exp. 2.

34 "Bautizo de una mora" ("Baptizing of a Moor girl"), LV, 28/10/1893, p. 5.

35 M.P. Corresp. de la Legación de España en Marruecos, Solla, 198–8, Letter of the Spanish Consulate in Tangier (Mr. Figuera) to the Foreign Minister (Marquis Vega de Armijo), Tangier, 21/04/1889.

36 "En resumen el Padre Lerchundi cuya influencia sobre el Sultan seria un poderoso elemento para nosotros si pudieramos utilizarlo, pero por lo que voy viendo es ya *mas Romano que español* y en la actualidad espera mas del Santo Padre que del Gobierno de SM. *Todo ello nos crea una situación delicadísima (...)*." *Ibidem*, Letter of Figuera to Vega de Armijo (Tangier, 06/04/1889). Italics added.

37 L. Miège, *Le Maroc et l'Europe . . . , op. cit.*; Richard Pennell, *Morocco since 1830: A History*, London, Hurst & Company, 2000.

38 "Melilla", LV, 03/10/1893, p. 5.

39 The War of Melilla would also be referred to as "la Guerra de Margallo" or simply as "la Guerra Chica", as it only lasted three months (October-December 1893).

40 The most recent examples of this enthusiasm were the African War of 1859–1860 and the Cuban War of 1868–1878. Albert García Balañà, "Patria, plebe y política en la España isabelina: la guerra de África en Cataluña (1859–1860)", E. Martín Corrales, *op. cit.*, pp. 13–78; Martín Rodrigo Alharilla, "Cataluña y el colonialismo español (1868–1899)", in: Salvador Calatayud, Jesús Millán, María Cruz Romeo (eds.), *Estado y periferias en la España del siglo XIX. Nuevos enfoques*, València, Publicacions de la Universitat de València, 2009, pp. 315–356. Some sporadic outbursts of patriotism also took place in 1883 (during the visit of King Alfonso XII to Paris) and in 1885 (resulting from a diplomatic incident with Germany over the Carolinas Islands).

41 These exceptions were the socialist Pablo Iglesias and the republican federalist Francesc Pi i Margall. See: J. Pich i Mitjana, *op. cit.*

42 "Entusiasmo patriótico", LV, 06/10/1893, p. 6; "Doscientos contra seis mil", LV, 05/10/1893, pp. 5–6.

43 "Manifestación en Valencia", "Otra manifestación en Granada", "otra manifestación", "En Sevilla", "Manifestaciones", LV, 13–17, 19, 22, 26, 29–31 October 1893, pp. 3–6.

44 Like the city councils of Gràcia, Manresa and Barcelona. LV, 05/11/1893, p. 2; 06/10/1893, p. 6.

45 LV, 07-14 October 1893, pp. 1–5; and 05/11/1893, p.2; 07/10/1893, p. 5.

46 Jordi Llorens i Vila, *La Unió Catalanista i els orígens del catalanisme polític*, Barcelona, Publicacions de l'Abadia de Montserrat, 1992; and Borja de Riquer, *La Lliga Regionalista: la burgesia catalana i el nacionalisme (1898–1904)*, Barcelona, Edicions 62, p. 48; and Stephen Jacobson, *Catalonia's Advocates: Lawyers, Society, and Politics in Barcelona, 1759–1900*, Chapel Hill, University of North Carolina Press, 2009, pp. 198–238 (esp. 203).

47 "Movimiento saludable", *El Imparcial,* 06/10/1893, editorial.

48 Eloy Martín Corrales, "El "moro", decano de los enemigos exteriores de España. Una larga enemistad (siglos VIII–XXI)", in: Xosé M. Núñez Seixas, Francisco Sevillano Calero (eds.), *Los enemigos de España. Imagen del otro, conflictos bélicos y*

disputas nacionales (siglos XVI–XX), Madrid, Centro de Estudios Políticos y Constitucionales, 2010, pp. 165–182.

49 Albert Garcia Balañà, "Patria, plebe y política en la España isabelina: la Guerra de África en Cataluña (1859–1860)", in Eloy Martín Corrales (ed.), *op. cit.*, pp. 13–77. The theatre play "Verdaderos Voluntarios Catalanes de la guerra de África", in "Los Aucellets", LV, 27 and 28/10/93, p. 6. The proposal to recover the corps was made by the general Francisco Mª de Borbón to the "Diputaciones provinciales", LV, 19/10/1893, p. 2.

50 LV, 19/10/93, pp. 1–2.

51 *El Imparcial*, 06/10/1893, p. 1. Similar views were expressed in: LV 17/10/1893, p. 5.

52 See: "¡Comeremos moros!", *El Imparcial*, 6th October 1893, p. 1. This article was later transcribed in *La Vanguardia*, 8th October 1893, p. 5.

53 "L'única solució nacional", *Almanach de la Campana de Gracia*, 1894; "Contra 'l moro", *L'Esquella de la Torratxa*, 13th October 1893, p. 5.

54 Xavier Garcia Olivé, "'Moros de dos menas'. Republicanismes barcelonins i la 'guerra de Margallo'" [Master thesis, Universtitat Pompeu Fabra, 2008, unpublished manuscript, 57 pages.]. The following quotations are indebted to the work of this author.

55 As *La Campana de Gracia* put it: *"not all the Moroccans live beneath the Strait* [of Gibraltar], *but we also have them in Spain"*.

56 [originally published in Catalan as: "Lector, pénsathi una mica / y digasme si ets servit: / ¿Ahónt son *los verdaders moros:* / á Melilla o á Madrit?"]. *La Campana de Gràcia*, 28/10/1893, p. 4.

57 *El Diluvio*, 10/10/1893, p. 2, *Ibidem*, p. 24.

58 Rafael Núñez Florencio, *Militarismo y antimilitarismo en España (1888–1906)*, Madrid, CSIC, 1990, pp. 115–145.

59 *Diluvio*, 13/10/1893, p. 3.

60 Albert García Balañà, "Patria, plebe y política en la España isabelina . . . ", *op. cit.*

61 *El Diluvio*, 09/12/1893, p. 5, X. Garcia Olivé, *op. cit.*, p. 30.

62 LV, 03/10/1893, p. 5. This is an approximate translation.

63 "Lo de Melilla en Barcelona", LV, 08/10/1893, p. 5.

64 *Ibidem.*

65 "Para las tropas de Melilla. La suscripción de "La Vanguardia", LV, 01/11/1893, p. 4.

66 "Nuestra misión en Marruecos", LV, 14/10/1893, p. 4. Italics added.

67 "Lo de Melilla", LV, 31/10/1893, p. 2.

68 Javier Moreno, José Ricart y Giralt (1847–1930). Una vida dedicada a la cultura marítima, *Drassana: revista del Museu Marítim*, n° 14, 2006, pp. 63–83; Eloy Martín Corrales, *El nacionalismo catalán . . .* , *op. cit.*

69 "Nuestra misión en Marruecos", LV, 14/10/1893, p. 4. José Carlos Ferrero Cuesta, *Segismundo Moret. Una biografía política*, Madrid, Universidad Autònoma de Madrid, 2002.

70 Edward Said, *Orientalism. Western Conceptions of the Orient*. London, Penguin, 1995 (1st ed. 1978).

71 M. Marín, Un encuentro colonial: viajeros españoles en Marruecos (1860–1912), *Hispania*, vol. LVI-192 (1996), pp. 93–114; L. Litvak, *op. cit.*; and H. Driessen, Images of Spanish colonialism in the Rif. An essay in Historical Anthropology and Photography, *Critique of Anthropology*, 7, 1 (1988), pp. 53–66; Luis Riudor, "Entre la curiositat i el plaer: del viatger al turista o la mutació d'una espècie", in: M. D. Garcia Ramon, J. Nogué and P. Zusman (eds.), *op. cit.*, pp. 137–171.

72 Juan Carlos Sánchez Illán, *Prensa y política en la España de la Restauración: Rafael Gasset y El Imparcial*, Madrid, Biblioteca Nueva, 1999, p. 89.

73 Gerald J. Baldasty, *The Commercialization of News in the Nineteenth Century*, Wisconsin, University of Wisconsin Press, 1992, pp. 139–146.

74 María Dolores Sáiz y María Cruz Seoane, *Historia del periodismo en España*, Madrid, Alianza ed., Vol. 2: "El siglo XIX: 1898–1936", p. 296.

75 LV, 12/10/1893, p. 1.

76 Susan Martin-Márquez, *Disorientations. Spanish Colonialism in Africa and the Performance of Identity*, New Haven, Yale University, 2008.

77 LV, 10/10/1893, p. 4.

78 Josep Boada, *Allende el Estrecho . . .* , p. 611; and Josep Boada, LV, 10/03/1894, p. 4.

79 Unfortunately, it has been impossible to find further evidence about Godó's plans to build a neighbourhood in Tangier. This suggests that for one reason or another, his plans were not realised. The lack of sources, however, makes it hard to explain the reasons for this.

80 As will be examined in the following chapter.

Chapter 3

1 Pier Luigi Ballini, "Las leyes electorales italianas (1900–1923)", R. A. Gutiérrez, R. Zurita, R. Camurri (eds.), *Elecciones y cultura política en España e Italia (1890–1923)*, València, PUV, 2003, pp. 73–74; Pier Luigi Ballini, *Le elezioni nella storia d'Italia dall'Unità al fascismo*, Bologna, Il Mulino, 1988; and Raffaele Romanelli, Le Regole del gioco. Note sull'impianto del sistema elettorale in Italia (1848–1895), *Quaderni Storici*, Nuova Serie, 69, 1988, 3, pp. 685–725. Pedro Tavares Almeida, "Reformas electorales y dinámica política en el Portugal liberal (1851–1910)", in: Salvador Forner (ed.), *Democracia, elecciones y modernización en Europa. Siglos XIX y XX*, Madrid, Cátedra, 1997, p. 103.

2 Aurora Garrido Martín, "La reforma electoral de 1890", in: Carlos Malamud (ed.), *Legitimidad, representación y alternancia en España y América Latina. Las reformas electorales (1880–1930)*, México, Fondo de Cultura Económica, 2000, pp. 41–61. On the liberals' little interest to promote accountability: M. Teresa Carnero Arbat, "Ciudadanía política y democratización. Un paso adelante, dos pasos atrás", in: Manuel Pérez Ledesma (ed.), *De súbditos a ciudadanos. Una historia de la ciudadanía de España*, Madrid, Centro de Estudios Políticos y Constitucionales, 2007, pp. 230–231. A more positive assessment, in: Alicia Yanini, La manipulación electoral en España: sufragio universal y participación ciudadana (1891–1923), *Ayer*, n. 3, 1991 ("El sufragio universal"), p. 104.

3   S. Berger (ed.), *L'organizzazione degli interessi nell'Europa Occidentale*, Il Mulino, Bologna, 1983; Jean Garrigues, *La république des hommes d'affaires, 1870–1900*, Paris, Aubier, 1997; Juan Pan-Montojo (ed.), Poderes privados y recursos públicos, *Ayer*, N° 66, 2007; Mercedes Cabrera and Fernando del Rey Reguillo, *The Power of Entrepreneurs: Politics and Economy in Contemporary Spain*, New York, Berghahn Books, 2007 [1ˢᵗ ed. in Spanish, 2002]; Salvador Calatayud, Jesús Millán, Mª Cruz Romeo (eds.), *Estado y periferias en la España del siglo XIX. Nuevos enfoques*, València, Publicacions de la Universitat de València, 2009.

4   Dipesh Chakrabarty, *Rethinking Working-Class History: Bengal 1890–1940*, Princeton University Press, 2000 [first ed.1989], p. 17. The academic literature is mostly concerned with the two cities that controlled jute trade at a global scale (Dundee, in Scotland; and Calcutta, in British India). See: Anthony Cox, *Empire, Industry and Class: The Imperial Nexus of Jute, 1840–1940*, Abingdon, Routledge, 2013; Gordon T. Steward, *Jute and Empire: The Calcutta Jute Wallahs and the Landscapes of Empire*, Manchester, Manchester University Press, 1998.

5   Carles Enrech, *Indústria i ofici: conflicte social i jerarquies obreres a la Catalunya tèxtil (1881–1923)*, Bellaterra, Servei de Publicacions de la UAB, 2005, p. 110 and p. 103.

6   AHPB, Manuel Borras i de Palau, 1897, vol. 3, 09/09/1897, pp. 2911–2936. J. Nadal and Xavier Tafunell, *Sant Martí de Provençals, pulmó industrial de Barcelona (1847–1992)*, Barcelona, Columna, 1996, p. 302.

7   "Cataluña en la Exposición . . . ", *El Liberal*, 14/02/1900, p. 2.

8   Kevin H. O' Rourke and Jeffrey G. Williamson, *Globalization and history: The Evolution of a Nineteenth-century Atlantic Economy*, MIT Press, Cambridge, MA, 1999, p. 93.

9   Esther Calzada del Amo, *Germán Gamazo, 1840–1901. Poder político y redes sociales en la Restauración*, Madrid, Marcial Pons Historia, 2011. José María Serrano Sanz, *El viraje proteccionista en la Restauración. La política comercial española, 1875–1895*, Madrid, Siglo Veintiuno editores, 1989.

10 On the "diputació catalana", see: Joan Palomas and Montserrat Bravo, Víctor Balaguer, la diputació catalana i la lluita pel proteccionisme (1881–1890), *Recerques*, 1992, Núm. 25, pp. 31–52. On this form of corporate politics during the "Trienio", see: Ernest Lluch, *El pensament econòmic a Catalunya (1760–1840). Els orígens ideològics del proteccionisme i la presa de consciència de la burgesia catalana*, Barcelona, edicions 62, 2009 [1ˢᵗ ed. 1973].

11 Jaume Vicens Vives, *Noticia de Cataluña*, Barcelona, Destino, 1954.

12 Ramón Casteràs, *Actitudes de los sectores catalanes en la coyuntura de los años 1880*, Barcelona, Antrhopos, 1985; Carles Enrech, *El Pla contra la Muntanya. La crisi de la indústria tèxtil del pla i la colonització fabril de la muntanya (1874–1904)*, Lleida, Edicions de la Unviersitat de Lleida, 2003, pp. 108–111. This attitude was in direct contrast to the interclassist politics that were promoted during the 1840s and 1850s. See: Albert Garcia Balañà, *La fabricació de la fàbrica. Treball i política a la Catalunya cotonera, 1784–1884*, Barcelona, Abadia de Montserrat, 2004; and Genís Barnosell, *Orígens del sindicalisme català*, Vic, Eumo, 1999.

13 ABMVB, Private Correspondence between Víctor Balaguer and Bartolomé Godó. Letter n°. 7000524 (20 May 1874).

14 ABMVB, Letter n°. 7400359 (15 January 1874).

15 AHFTN, *Foment de la Producció Nacional. Llibre d'Actes. Juntes Generals (09-01-1869/06-07-1879)*, p. 2. This employer association was the result of the merging of two entities in 1889: the *"Fomento de la Producción Nacional"* (established in 1869, Godó was involved in its foundation) and the *"Instituto del Trabajo Nacional"* (1879). Guillem Graell, *Historia del Fomento del Trabajo Nacional*, Barcelona, Imp. de la viuda de Luis Tasso, 1910.

16 *"Clase 5ª. Delmiro de Caralt, José Casals, Pedro Alier, Vda. De José Borrull, Fabra y Portabella, Maristany M., Agustin Serdañons, Bartolomé Godó, Hijos de J. Vives Bonamusa, José de Caralt, Lluis Garriga, Brunet y Serrat, C. Mitjans y Cª, Camins y Cª"*. AHFTN, *Actas Junta Directiva (28-04-1889/10-6-1891)*, p. 50.

17 Besides the case of Sagasta, another Liberal politician who became a renowned supporter of free-trade policies was Segismundo Moret. Carlos Ferrera, *La frontera democrática del liberalismo. Segismundo Moret (1838–1913)*, Madrid, Biblioteca Nueva, 2002.

18 "LA VANGUARDIA", LV, 01/02/1881, p. 2. In another article of the same edition, entitled *"Nuestro criterio económico"* ("Our criteria in economy"), the newspaper reinforced the commitment to protectionism.

19 José Luis Ollero Valdés, *Sagasta: de conspirador a gobernante*, Madrid, Marcial Pons, 2006, pp. 171–193; and pp. 242–245.

20 "ALERTA", LV, 05/03/1881, pp. 4–5.

21 See: Enrique Fuentes Quintana (ed.), *Economía y economistas españoles*, Madrid, Galaxia Gutenberg, 1999, vol. 4.

22 "Catalanismo", LV, 25/03/1881, p. 5.

23 For an in-depth analysis about the development of regionalist consciousness in Catalonia, see: Angel Smith, *The Origins of Catalan Nationalism, 1770–1898*, Basingstoke, Palgrave Macmillan, 2014, esp. Chapter 3.

24 Almirall made the call through the pages of the *Diari Català* (1879), the first newspaper to be published entirely in Catalan. Josep M. Figueres (ed.), *El Primer Congrés Catalanista i Valentí Almirall. Materials per a l'estudi dels orígens del catalanisme*, Barcelona, Generalitat de Catalunya, p. 65. Josep Pich i Mitjana, *Almirall i el Diari Català (1879–1881). L'inici del projecte politicoideològic del catalanisme progressista*, Vic, Eumo, 2003.

25 "Catalanismo", LV, 25/03/1881, p. 5.

26 "A una provocación", LV, 10/04/1882, p. 7. Italics added.

27 Josep Maria Fradera, *Cultura nacional en una societat dividida: patriotisme i cultura a Catalunya (1838–1868)*, Barcelona, Curial, 1992; and from the same author, "The Empire, the Nation and the Homelands: Nineteenth-Century Spain's National Idea", in: Joost Augusteijn & Eric Storm (eds.), *Region and State in Nineteenth-century Europe: Nation-building, Regional Identities and Separatism*, Basingstoke, Palgrave Macmillan, 2012, pp. 131–148.

28 "Catalanismo", LV, 25/03/1881, p. 2.

29 On this term, see the explanation above.

30   The *Fomento* addressed a letter to Godó and to other Catalan deputies asking
     them to attend the voting in Congress. AHFTN, Comunicaciones, n° 5, letter
     4 April 1882; J. Palomas i M. Bravo, *op. cit.*, p. 34. With the exception of one
     deputy, all the deputies attended the votation (including Godó). LV,
     10/04/1882, pp. 15–16.

31   LV, 02/06/1882, p. 18; and 10/04/1882, p. 9.

32   Ferran Soldevila, *El Año Político, 1895*, Madrid, Imp. E. Fernández de Rojas,
     1896, p. 71; Antonio Elorza and Elena Hernández Sandoica, *La Guerra de Cuba
     (1895–1898)*, Madrid, Alianza ed., 1998, pp. 186–188.

33   Inés Roldán de Montaud, *La Restauración en Cuba. El fracaso de un proceso
     reformista*, Madrid, CSIC, 2000, pp. 573–601.

34   "Reunión importante", LV, 24/02/1895, p. 5.

35   Jordi Maluquer de Motes, "El mercado colonial antillano en el siglo XIX", in
     Jordi Nadal and Gabriel Tortella (eds.), *Agricultura, comercio colonial y crecimiento
     económico en la España contemporánea*, Barcelona, Ariel, 1972, pp. 322–357; César
     Yáñez, "El perfil ultramarí de l'economia catalana", in Josep Mª Fradera (ed.),
     Catalunya i Ultramar. Poder i negoci a les colònies espanyoles (1750–1914),
     Barcelona, Museu Marítim-Ambit, 1995, pp. 53–76; José A. Piqueras, *Cuba,
     emporio y colonia. La disputa de un mercado interferido (1878–1895)*, Madrid,
     Fondo de Cultura Económica, 2003.

36   Further statistics can be found in: Borja de Riquer, *Lliga Regionalista:
     la burgesia catalana i el nacionalisme (1898–1904)*, Barcelona, Edicions 62, 1977,
     pp. 63–65.

37   "Gran fábrica de hilados y tejidos de yute, la más importante de España. Utiliza
     procedimientos privilegiados y produce entre otros artículos una enorme
     cantidad de saquería, en su mayor parte destinada á la exportación á América.".
     Josep Roca i Roca, *Barcelona en la mano. Guía de Barcelona y sus alrededores*,
     Barcelona, Enrique López, 1895, p. 347.

38   In addition to the meeting at *Fomento*, Carlos also attended the meeting held by
     another employer's association named "Liga de Productores". LV, 03/04/1895,
     p. 2. On this employer association, see: Jordi Planas i Maresma, La Lliga de
     Productors de Catalunya i els interessos agraris (1894–1898), *Recerques, 47–48*,
     2003–2004, pp. 155–186.

39   "La agitación en Cuba", LV, 28/02/1895, pp. 1–2.

40   "Información cubana. Ropa hecha. Antecedentes", LV, 05/03/1895, p. 5. Italics
     added.

41   "Información cubana. Camisería", LV, 10/03/1895, p. 1.

42   *Ibidem.*

43   "Información cubana. Corbatería", LV, 12/03/1895, p. 5. Italics added.

44   M. Vilanova Ribas y X. Moreno Julià, *Atlas de la evolución del analfabetismo en
     España de 1887 a 1981*, Madrid, MEC, 1992, p. 166; Francesc Espinet i Joan
     Manuel Tresserras, *La gènesi de la societat de masses a Catalunya, 1888–1939*,
     Barcelona, UAB, 1999, p. 69, n. 127.

45   Fernando Soldevila, *El Año Político 1895*, Madrid, Imprenta de Enrique
     Fernández de Rojas, 1896, pp. 83–87.

46 Christopher Schmidt-Nowara, 'La España Ultramarina': Colonialism and Nation-Building in Nineteenth-Century Spain, *European History Quarterly*, 2004, Vol. 34 (2), pp. 191–214.

47 "La semana en Barcelona", LV, 10/03/1895, p. 4. Italics added.

48 Carlos Serrano, Prófugos y desertores en la guerra de Cuba, *Estudios de Historia Social*, nº 22–23, 1982, pp. 253–278; Núria Sales, *Sobre esclavos, reclutas y mercaderes de quintos*, Esplugues de Llobregat, Ariel, 1974.

49 Borja de Riquer, *op. cit.*, p. 66.

50 As a result of military operations, sugar production fell abruptly from more than a million tonnes in 1894, to only 286,000 tonnes in 1896. Carlos Serrano, *Final del imperio. España, 1895–1989*, Madrid, Siglo Veintiuno Editores, 1984, p. 23; US Department of State. United States-Division of Insular Affairs, "Industrial conditions in Spain", *Monthly summary of commerce of the island of Cuba*, 1901, p. 217.

51 "Un donativo", *El Imparcial*, 27/08/1895, p. 3.

52 "Donativos", *El Liberal*, 24/11/1893, p. 3. "También se entregó dos pesetas á los sargentos, seis reales á los cabos y una peseta á los soldados, dinero procedente del donativo de Don Carlos Godó. (...) Debiera imitarse el proceder del señor Godó. Es lo menos que pueden dar los ricos á los soldados que van á defender la honra y los intereses nacionales". Rafael Guerrero, *Crónica de la Guerra de Cuba (1895–96)*, Barcelona, Librería ed. M. Maucci, 1896, vol. 1, 2ª part, p. 120.

53 LV, 22/04/1896, p. 2; 11/06/1896, p. 5.

54 An example is: "La actitud de los Estados Unidos con relación á España y Cuba", LV, 11/10/1895, p. 4.

55 *El Imparcial*, 01/03/1896. Quoted in A. Elorza & E. Hernández, *op. cit.*, p. 365.

56 *La Correspondencia de España*, 01/03/1896, p. 1.

57 LV, "Ecos de la política", 28/02/1897, p. 5.

58 LV, 24/04/1898, p. 1.

59 "Entusiasmo en Igualada", *La Dinastía*, 26/04/1898, p. 3.

60 José Andrés Gallego, *Un 98 distinto. Restauración, Desastre, Regeneracionismo*, Madrid, Encuentro, 1998, p. 140.

61 Núria Sales, *op. cit.*; Carlos Serrano, *op. cit.*. The best in-depth analysis of the attitudes of society in the face of the war is: Manuel Pérez Ledesma, "La sociedad española, la guerra y la derrota", Juan Luis Pan-Montojo (ed.), *Más se perdió en Cuba. España, 1898 y la crisis de fin de siglo*, Madrid, Alianza editorial, 1998, pp. 91–150.

62 *El Imparcial*, 26/04/1898, p. 1; *La Época*, 26/04/1898, p. 4.

63 LV, 24/04/1898, p. 1.

64 Juan Carlos Sánchez Illán, *Prensa y Política en la España de la Restauración. Rafael Gasset y El Imparcial*, Madrid, Biblioteca Nueva, 1999, p. 111; Rosario Sevilla Soler, *La Guerra de Cuba y la memoria colectiva. La crisis del 98 en la prensa sevillana*, CSIC, Sevilla, 1996, pp. 39–40; Fernando San Agustín Farlete, "El desencadenamiento de la guerra de Cuba en la prensa de Barcelona", Barcelona, Escuela Oficial de Periodismo, 1975 [unpublished Master thesis].

65 J. C. Sánchez Illán, *op. cit.*, p. 103.

66 Carola Duran Tort, *Pere Aldavert: una vida al servei de l'ideal*, Barcelona, Publicacions de l'Abadia de Montserrat, 2006, p. 168.

67 *Ibidem.*

68 The attitude of the *Diario de Barcelona* has been examined in: M. C. García Nieto, *op. cit.*

69 An example of this, in: Álvaro de Figueroa y Torres, Conde de Romanones, *Notas de una vida*, Madrid–Barcelona, Marcial Pons, 1999, [1st edition 1934], vol. 1, p. 103.

70 *Ibidem*, p. 138.

71 LV, 11/07/1897, p. 2; *La Renaixensa*, 10/07/1897, p. 1336.

72 Martín Rodrigo Alharilla, "Cataluña y el colonialismo español", S. Calatayud, J. Millán, M. Cruz Romeo (eds.), *op. cit.*, pp. 315–356.

73 E. Calzada del Amo, *op. cit.*; M. del P. Calvo Caballero, "Defensa de intereses y cultura de la patronal castellano-leonesa . . . ", *op. cit.*

Chapter 4

1 Borja de Riquer (ed.), *Epistolari polític de Manuel Duran i Bas (correspondència entre 1866 i 1904)*, Barcelona, Publicacions de l'Abadia de Montserrat, 1990, p. 489.

2 Santos Juliá, Anomalía, dolor y fracaso de España, *Claves de la Razón Práctica*, 66 (octubre 1996), pp. 10–21; Isabel Burdiel, Morir de éxito: el péndulo liberal y la revolución española del siglo XIX, *Historia y Política*, 1999, 1, pp. 181–203.

3 Vicente Cacho Viu, *Repensar el 98*, Madrid, Biblioteca Nueva, 1997; Juan Pablo Fusi, *España, 1808–1996. El desafío de la modernidad*, Madrid, Espasa Calpe, 1997; Juan Pan-Montojo (ed.), *Más se perdió en Cuba. España, 1898 y la crisis de fin de siglo*, Madrid, Alianza, 1998. An overview of the literature, in: María Dolores Elizalde Pérez-Grueso, El 98 desde una perspectiva normalizadora. Reflexión historiográfica de un centenario, *Hispania*, XCI/2, n° 208, 2001, pp. 207–236.

4 María Dolores Elizalde et al., *1898: ¿Desastre nacional o impulso modernizador?*, *Revista de Occidente*, n° 202–203, 1998.

5 *Ibidem.*

6 Rafael Núñez Florencio, *El peso del pesimismo. Del 98 al desencanto*, Madrid, Marcial Pons, 2010, pp. 400–411 (esp. 406).

7 *Ibidem*, pp. 410–411; Isabel Burdiel, *op. cit.*, p. 182.

8 José Luis Ollero Vallés, De "Viejo Pastor" a "chivo expiatorio": Sagasta y el 98, *Berceo*, N° 135, 1998, pp. 25–38.

9 Sara Núñez de Prado y Clavell, "La prensa y la opinión pública española en torno al "Desastre"", Juan Pablo Fusi y Antonio Niño (eds.), *Antes del "Desastre": Orígenes y antecedentes de la crisis del 98*, Madrid, UCM, 1996, p. 458.

10 Mikulas Teich & Roy Porter (eds.), *Fin de Siècle and its Legacy*, Cambridge, CUP, 1990; Daniel Pick, *Faces of Degeneration: A European disorder, c. 1848–1918*, Cambridge–New York, CUP, 1989; Luisa Mangoni, *Una crisi fine secolo: la cultura italiana e la Francia fra Otto e Novecento*, Torino, Einaudi, 1985.

11 *Ibidem*; Robert A. Nye, *Crime, Madness and Politics in Modern France: The Medical Concept of National Decline*, Princeton, Princeton University Press, p. 330.

12 Eugene Weber, *France, Fin de Siècle*, Cambridge University Press, 1986, p. 3; Lily Litvak, *Latinos y anglosajones: orígenes de una polémica*, Barcelona, Puvill, 1980.

13 Hipólito de la Torre, *op. cit.*; Joâo Medina, A crise colonial dos anos novemta em Portugal e Espanha e as suas consecuencias para os dos paises ibericos (1890–1898), Estudo de historia comparada, Hipólito de la Torre (ed.), *Portugal, España y África en los últimos cien años*, Madrid, UNED, 1992, pp. 17–27.

14 An example of early criticism towards caciquismo is: Valentí Almirall, entitled *España tal como es*, Barcelona, Anthropos, 1983 [1ˢᵗ edition printed in Paris, in 1886].

15 Joaquín Costa, *Oligarquía y caciquismo como la forma actual de gobierno en España: urgencia y modo de cambiarla*, Madrid, Biblioteca Nueva, 2011 [first ed. 1902], pp. 72–73. Emphasis added.

16 *Ibidem*, p. 216.

17 *Ibid.*, p. 217.

18 *Ibid.*, pp. 217–218.

19 *Ibid.*, pp. 218–219.

20 Daniel Hallin and Paolo Mancini, *Comparing Media Systems: Three Models of Media and Politics*, Cambridge–New York, Cambridge University Press, 2004, p. 98.

21 *Ibidem*, p. 29 and p. 67.

22 Joaquín Costa, *op. cit.*, p. 218.

23 Name given to an intellectual movement that emerged in Spain in response to the loss of the colonies. Maeztu would be one of its most conspicuous representatives, together with other names like Azorín, Miguel de Unamuno and Pío Baroja. See: Pedro Laín Entralgo, *La generación del 98*, Madrid, Espasa Calpe, 1997.

24 "Responsabilidades", Ramiro de Maeztu, *Hacia otra España*, Barcelona, Editorial Planeta DeAgostini, 2011 [1ˢᵗ ed. in 1899], p. 141. Maeztu had a good knowledge of the Spanish-American War, both from his experience as a soldier (posted in Mallorca) and knowledge of Cuba, where he had spent part of his childhood.

25 It must be noted that Maeztu used the English expression "factory system".

26 *Ibidem*, p. 154.

27 Ramiro de Maeztu, *op. cit.*, p. 155. Italics in the original.

28 Teodoro Baró, *Discursos leídos en la Real Academia de Buenas Letras de Barcelona en la recepción pública de D. Teodoro Baró el día 23 de noviembre de 1902*, Barcelona, Casa Provincial de Caridad, 1902, p. 7.

29 Pere Gabriel, "Espacio urbano y articulación política popular en Barcelona, 1890–1923", in: José Luis García Delgado (ed.), *Las ciudades en la modernización de España. Los decenios interseculares*, Madrid, Siglo XXI, 1992, p. 61.

30 Rafael Alcaide González, Inmigración y marginación: prostitución y mendicidad en la ciudad de Barcelona a finales del siglo XIX. Una

comparación con la actualidad, *Scripta Nova: Revista electrónica de geografía y ciencias sociales*, N° 94 (103), 2001.

31 *Ibidem*, pp. 9–10.
32 *El Mundo*, 08/06/1905.
33 *La Correspondencia de España*, 07/05/1906. Quoted in Pedro Pedro Gómez Aparicio, *Historia del periodismo español*, Madrid, Editora Nacional, 1974, p. 72.
34 "Sapo" means "toad" in English. *Ibidem*, p. 79.
35 *Ibidem*. Some newspapers even made a more pessimistic analysis, and estimated the fall of sales in the 40% of the total: Manuel Ortega Gasset, *El Imparcial. Biografía de un gran periódico español*, Zaragoza, Librería General, 1956, p. 167. Quoted in: Juan Carlos Sánchez Illán, *Prensa y política en la España de la Restauración*, Madrid, Biblioteca Nueva, 1999, p. 137.
36 J. Sánchez Illán, *op. cit.*, p. 137; and María Cruz Seoane & María Dolores Sáiz, *op. cit.*, p. 72. To a certain extent this fall in the figures was also the flipside of the same growth newspapers experienced during the war (*El Imparcial*, for instance, saw its sales increase to 140,000 thanks to the jingoist wave).
37 See Chapter 7.
38 *La Época*, 15/07/1898, p. 3; Dórico, "Cierre de fábricas", *El País*, 28/07/1898, p. 2.
39 *El Liberal*, 14/02/1900, p. 2.
40 "El atraso económico y la regeneración", Juan Pan-Montojo (ed.), *Más se perdió en Cuba. España, 1898 y la crisis de fin de siglo*, Madrid, Alianza, 1998, p. 285.
41 Historians have put forward various arguments to support this statement: the war provoked the repatriation of a large number of capitals; the end of the war effort (which had annually consumed the equivalent of two years of Spain's GDP) relieved public expenditure; while alternative markets were found to compensate the loss of the colonies (especially in South America). See: *Ibidem*, esp. pp. 286–288.
42 *El Liberal*, 14/02/1900, p. 2.
43 On 8 October 1897 Carlos Godó's widow and his son divided the inheritance between them. Initially Ramón assumed the textile business, while his mother (Antonia Lallana) temporarily took charge of *La Vanguardia* (which by then had an estimated value of 100,000 pesetas). Arxiu Històric de Protocols de Barcelona (AHPB), Manuel Borràs i de Palau, 1897, vol. 4, 8 d'octubre de 1897, pp. 3183–3204.
44 Pedro Voltes Bou, "Historia de La Vanguardia", [unpublished manuscript], chapter 10, p. 63.
45 M. C. García Nieto, *op. cit.*, p. 187.
46 "Convenio entre Doña Antonia Lallana, viuda de Godó, propietaria del periódico". Voltes, *op. cit.*
47 Carlos Barrera (ed.), *Historia del Periodismo Universal*, Barcelona, Ariel, 2007, pp. 114–117.
48 David Forgacs, *Italian Culture in the Industrial Era, 1880–1890. Cultural Industries, Politics and the Publics*, Manchester-New York, Manchester University Press, 1990, p. 34.

49   M. C. García Nieto, *op. cit.*, p. 88.

50   Something similar happened with the case of Italy. Valerio Castronovo, *La stampa italiana nell'età liberale*, Bari, Laterza, 1979, p. 15.

51   Borja de Riquer i Permanyer, El surgimiento de las nuevas identidades contemporáneas: propuestas para una discusión, *Ayer*, Nº 35, 1999, p. 37.

52   An in-depth analysis of these strategies to influence central-government, in Chapter 3.

53   These entities were the "Societat Econòmica Barcelonesa d'Amics del País"; "Fomento del Trabajo Nacional"; "Instituto Agrícola de San Isidro"; "Ateneu Barcelonès"; "Liga de Defensa Industrial y Comercial". A reproduction of this referendum can be found in: LV, 10/12/1898, p. 3.

54   LV, 10/12/1898, p. 3. Italics in the original.

55   *Ibidem.*

56   *Ibid.*

57   Jordi Casassas, *Els intel·lectuals i el poder a Catalunya*; and Giovanni Cattini, *Prat de la Riba i la historiografia catalana. Intel·lectuals i crisi política a la fi del segle XIX*, Catarroja–Barcelona, Afers, 2008, esp. p. 189. The influence of French intellectuals in other countries, like Italy, in: Luisa Mangoni, *op. cit.*

58   Quoted in: Carlos Serrano, "Conciencia de la crisis, conciencias en crisis", Juan Pan-Montojo (ed.), *Más se perdió en Cuba. España, 1898 y la crisis de fin de siglo*, Madrid, Alianza, 2006, p. 390.

59   Vicente Cacho Viu, *El nacionalismo catalán como factor de modernización*, Barcelona, Quaderns Crema, 1998.

60   Borja de Riquer, *op. cit.*, p. 305.

61   "El manifiesto del General Polavieja", LV, 12/09/1898, p. 1.

62   Especially when a Catalan (Mr. Manuel Duran i Bas) was appointed Minister of Justice. "Ecos de la política", LV, 05/03/1899, p. 4.

63   "Ecos de la política. El manifiesto del General Polavieja", LV, 13/09/1898, p. 4. Similar statements in relation to caciquismo, in: "Ecos de la política", LV, 06/03/1898, p. 5.

64   "El general Polavieja en Barcelona", *La Dinastía*, 07/11/1896, pp. 1–2.

65   "El manifiesto del general Polavieja", LV, *op. cit.* Emphasis added.

66   *Ibidem.*

67   "La prensa española, lo decimos con el respeto y con el amor que nos inspira nuestra madre, pero convencidos, no ha estado en medio de tantos azares como ha producido el problema cubano á la altura que podía esperarse (...). En cuanto ha sido sentimiento de patriotismo, de abnegación (...) ha dado toda ella un ejemplo que nos enorgullece (...) Pero en nuestra humildísima opinión, por punto general y sin excluirnos nosotros, le ha faltado serenidad de juicio y previsión en cuanto ha sido obra de análisis para conocer aquel problema y para guiar á la opinión en los momentos supremos. En ninguna nación, pero singularmente en las meridionales (...) existe un poder superior de hecho, al que la prensa en su conjunto ejerce. En cada acto de Gobierno tiene la prensa una parte principalísima (...). Esta ventaja ha de tenerse como una carga antes que como un beneficio, porque entraña una responsabilidad, y la mayor prueba de

patriotismo que puede dar la prensa es recabar esa responsabilidad cuando encierra la amargura del error (...)." LV, 01/01/1897, p. 3. Emphasis added.

68 Modesto Sánchez Ortiz, "La política en 1898", LV, 01/01/1899, p. 4.

69 Modesto Sánchez Ortiz, *El periodismo*, Barcelona, Fundación Conde de Barcelona, 1990 [1st ed. 1903], pp. 89–96.

70 Ramón Godó was deputy for Igualada between 1899 and 1906, while Rafael Gasset was deputy for the constituency of Noya, in the region of Galicia, between 1896 and 1910. Both of them also had relatives who would hold other political positions. See the Chapter 5.

71 "Contra una iniquidad. Para el Sr. Montero Ríos", *El Imparcial*, 08/02/1899, p. 1.

72 Further information on Gasset's political career, in: J. C. Sánchez Illán, *op. cit.*, p. 379.

73 The manifesto of Polavieja was written by a close friend of Gasset (Augusto Suárez de Figueroa, the director of *El Heraldo de Madrid*). J. Sánchez Illán, *ibid.*, p. 117.

74 *Ibid.*, p. 124.

Chapter 5

1 LV, 19/05/1901, p. 6.

2 According to Henry F. Schulte, "the Godó family started La Vanguardia, which was begun as a small, partisan organ, favoring the policies of Sagasta. However, under the direction of Ramón Godó Lallana, who took charge in 1897 after the death of his father, the newspaper's founder, *La Vanguardia* grew into a national newspaper, a role it fills today (...)". Henry F. Schulte, *The Spanish Press, 1470–1966: Print, Power and Politics*, University of Illinois Press, 1968, p. 214. A similar statement, in: Manuel Goméz Aparicio, *Historia del periodismo español*, Madrid, Editora Nacional, 1971, vol. 3, p. 646.

3 Jaume Guillamet, Las élites catalanas y la prensa, in: Paul Aubert et Jean Michel Desvois (eds.), *Les élites et la press en Espagne et en Amerique latine des Lumières à la seconde guerre mondiale*, Casa de Velázquez-Maison des Pays Ibériques, 2002, p. 132.

4 "La crisis de la prensa madrileña", *El Nuevo Mundo*, 08/06/1905, p. 1.

5 *Ibidem.*

6 J.C. Sánchez Illán, *Prensa y política en la España de la Restauración. Rafael Gasset y El Imparcial*, Madrid, Biblioteca Nueva, 1999, p. 137.

7 Jens Ivo Engels, Corruption as a Political Issue in Modern Societies: France, Great Britain and the United States in the Long 19th Century, *Public Voices* X, N° 2, 2008, pp. 68–86.

8 Cited in J. Ivo Engels, *ibid.*

9 John B. Thompson, *The Media and Modernity: A Social Theory of the Media*, Polity, 1995.

10 Olivier Dard, Jens Ivo Engels, Andreas Fahrmeir et Frédéric Monier (eds.), *Scandales et corruption à l'époque contemporaine*, Paris, Armand Colin-Recherches, 2015.

11   J. Ivo Engels, *ibid.*

12   Max Weber, *Economía y sociedad*, México DF, Fondo de Cultura Económica, 2014 [1st ed. in German, 1922], pp. 1080–1081.

13   The marriage produced seven children: Rosa (married to Pere Bonet); Antònia (Pasqual Girona); Merçè (Marcel·lí Coll), Ramón (Carme Mir); Roser (Josep Bravo), Maria and Glòria. ACAN, Llibre de Matrimonis (1879–1893), 1893, fol. 285 (52). The comments that *La Vanguardia* dedicated to the wedding, in: LV, 03/12/1893, p. 2.

14   Juan del Noya, "¡QUÉ ASCO!", *El Igualadino. Semanario político*, 10/12/1893, nº 32, p. 2.

15   Pedro Carasa (ed.), *Élites castellanas de la Restauración*, Valladolid, Junta de Castilla y León, Consejería de Educación y Cultura, 1997, p. 71. The book of the historian José Varela Ortega popularised the expression "political friends": *Los Amigos políticos. Partidos, elecciones y caciquismo en la Restauración, 1875–1900*, Madrid, Marcial Pons, 2001 (1st ed. 1977).

16   Alexandre Niess, Nepotism and family confiscation in the electoral system of the Third Republic, *French History*, vol. 26, No. 3, 2012, pp. 325–343. See also: Christophe Charle, *Les élites de la République, 1880–1900*, Paris, Fayard, 1987, pp. 327–366.

17   Heinrich Best and Daniel Gaxie, "Detours to Modernity: Long Term Trends of Parliamentary Recruitment in Republican France 1848–1999", H. Best and M. Cotta (eds.), *op. cit.*, p. 109.

18   LV, 11/03/1898, p. 3.

19   M. A. Bisbal & T. Miret, *Diccionari biogràfic . . .* , p. 97; Pere Pascual Domènech: *La Igualadina. Símbol de la Revolució Industrial a Catalunya*, Igualada, Ajuntament d'Igualada, Institut Municipal de Cultura, 2014.

20   *La Ilustració catalana*, 31/07/1893, p. 14.

21   *Ibidem.*

22   The amount of money donated by Ramón was the highest in all of Barcelona's provinces, and Juan's was the second. All these donations were commented on in different Spanish newspapers: "Entusiasmo en Igualada", *La Dinastía*, 26/04/1898; and *El Imparcial* and *La Época* on 26/04/1898.

23   The society, called Baldomero Camps y Compañía was established with a third partner (Baldomero Camps Blaví). Ramón and Juan provided the capital in equal parts (5,000 ptas each) while Baldomero Camps was in charge of the management. *Diario de Oficial de Avisos de Madrid*, 17/11/1897, p. 1.

24   AHPB, Notari Josep Ferrer i Bernadas, 1897, vol 6è, 3 November 1897, fols. 5406–5411.

25   Tomás Estany, Joseph Pont, Joan Boria y Vall, "Carta desclosa. Sobre un altre cas arbitrari. A D. Ramón Godó Lallana". *La Renaixensa. Diari de Catalunya*, 30/08/1900 Letter written in Sant Martí de Sesgueioles, 23th August 1900, p. 1. Original version in Catalan.

26   "NOTAS LOCALES", LV, 07/09/1900, p. 2.

27   *Ibidem.*

28   Manuel Marín, "El buen cacique", *Historia Social*, nº 36, 2000, pp. 21–34.

29   The new town hall was established in a pre-existing building that Ramón had originally bought from Jaume Prats Casañas on 2 November 1900. ANI, Notari Martí Gual, any 1902, fols. 742–743.

30   *Ibidem.*

31   LV, 29/07/1902, p. 3.

32   The municipalities that sent their comissions were: Monbui, Montmaneu, Bruch, Carme, Copons, Vilanova del Camí, Prat del Rey, Collbató, Miralles, Tous, Pobla de Claramunt, Castellolí, Castellfollit de Riubregós, Calonge de Calaf, Sant Martí de Sesgueioles and La Llacuna. The social entities were the Liga Comercial, Industrial y Agrícola, Centro Moral é Industrial, Junta de Socorros Domiciliarios, Círculo Popular, Círculo de la Esperanza.

33   For the case of Vienna, see the classic book: Carl E. Schorske, *Fin-De-Siecle Vienna: Politics and Culture*, London, Weidenfeld and Nicolson, 1980.

34   José Álvarez Junco, *The Emergence of Mass Politics in Spain: Populist Demagoguery and Republican Culture, 1890–1910*, Brighton, Sussex Academic Press, 2003 [1st ed. in Spanish, 1990].

35   Borja de Riquer, "Los límites de la modernización. El caso de Barcelona, 1890–1923", in: J.L. García Delgado (ed.), *Las ciudades en la modernización de España. Los decenios interseculares*, Madrid, Siglo XXI, 1992, p. 57, n. 57; "Les eleccions de la Solidaritat Catalana a Barcelona", *Recerques*, 1972, núm. 2, pp. 93–140. A general overview, in: Maria Gemma Rubí Casals & Josep Armengol Segú, *Vots, electors i corrupció. Una reflexió sobre l'apatia a Catalunya (1869–1923)*, Barcelona, Publicacions de l'Abadia de Montserrat, 2012.

36   José Alvarez Junco, *op. cit.*; Joan B. Culla and Joaquín Romero Maura. On the Catalan nationalism of the *Lliga Regionalista*: Borja de Riquer, *Lliga Regionalista. La burgesia catalana i el nacionalisme, 1898–1904*, Barcelona, Edicions 62, 1977; Charles E. Ehrlic, *Lliga Regionalista. Lliga Catalana, 1901–1936*, Barcelona, Institut Cambó, 2004.

37   Ideological orientation of Barcelona's partisan press: Republicans (2), Catalan Nationalists (3), Carlists (2), Conservatives (1), Liberal Conservatives (1), Democrats (2). María Carmen García Nieto "La Prensa diaria de Barcelona de 1895 a 1910", Barcelona, Universitat de Barcelona, 1956 [thesis manuscript], p. 88.

38   Joaquín Romero Maura, *"La Rosa de Fuego". El obrerismo barcelonés de 1899 a 1909*, Madrid, Alianza, 1989, p. 124.

39   Pere Gabriel, "Espacio urbano y articulación política popular en Barcelona, 1890–1920", in: José Luis García Delgado (ed.), *Las ciudades en la modernización de España: los decenios interseculares*, Madrid, Siglo XXI, 1992, pp. 61–94.

40   *La Semana de Igualada*, 23/04/1899, p. 1.

41   As one Republican newspaper lamented, "while all the Liberals fought with great efforts to win the position of deputy, the majority of people have remained indifferent in these elections which unfortunately have given the victory to Mr. Godó". *El Semanario de Igualada*, 23/04/1899, p. 4.

42   In the case of Barcelona a similar turnout would not be achieved again until the 1930s. The electoral results (which correspond to general elections), in: Albert

Balcells, Joan B. Culla, Conxita Mir, *Eleccions generals a Catalunya* de 1901 a 1923, Barcelona, Fundació Jaume Bofill, p. 628.

43 "Cataluña y la prensa de Madrid", LV, 09/05/1901, p. 5. Italics added.

44 See the quotation opening Chapter 4.

45 Pere Gabriel, *op. cit.*, pp. 71–72.

46 On this coalition, see: Gemma Rubí i Francesc Espinet, *Solidaritat catalana i Espanya (1905–1909)*, Barcelona, Base, 2008.

47 ""La Vanguardia" es caciquista", *La Veu de Catalunya*, 28/09/1905, p. 2. Night edition.

48 "Mentidas del 'Ciero' y 'La Vanguardia'," *La Veu de Catalunya*, 16/09/1905, p. 1, Night edition.

49 The original text stressed in italics "the newspaper he owns". *Ibidem.*

50 The newspaper *El Igualadino* would make a detailed account of events. "Dietario de Igualada", *El Igualadino*, 30/06/1906, p. 1.

51 Juan Godó Pelegrí (1876–1957), popularly known as *"Juanito"*, was the son of Juan Godó Llucià. He was appointed mayor of Igualada by royal decree on January 1st 1906, a position he held until 1914.

52 Numerous newspapers of Barcelona (like *La Campana de Gràcia*, *La Renaixensa*, *El Poble Català* and *El Diluvio*) referred to the events and used the opportunity to criticise, once again, the Godó family. See, for instance, *El Diluvio*, 26/06/1908, p. 14.

53 "Gacetilla", *El Diluvio*, dissabte 30 de juny 1906, pp. 9–10.

54 "Dietario de Igualada", *El Igualadino*, 30/06/06/1901, p. 1.

55 LV, 01/07/1906, p. 2.

56 "Gacetilla", *El Diluvio*, 03/06/1906, pp. 8–9.

57 R. Romesquet Picantó, "¡¡¡Quin desastre!!!", *El Igualadino*, 08/07/1906, p. 2.

58 "Retirada de Godó", *ABC*, 03/07/1906, p. 10.

59 "Regionales", *El Diluvio*, 03/07/1906, p. 10.

60 Carl E. Schorske *Fin-De-Siecle Vienna . . .* , *op. cit.*

61 In the case Valencia, the Republicans broke the monopoly of power of liberal parties and gained control of the city council in 1891. In Madrid the Republicans (and to a lesser extent, the Socialists) considerably improved their results, especially in 1893 and 1903; but they did not manage to transform the electoral map. Alicia Yanini y Rafael Zurita Aldeguer, "Comunidad Valenciana"; and Rogelio López Blanco, "Madrid", both in: Joaquín Varela Ortega (ed.), *El poder de la influencia. Geografía y caciquismo en España (1875–1923)*, Madrid, Marcial Pons, Centro de Estudios Políticos y Constitucionales, 2001, pp. 383–419; and pp. 283–324, respectively.

62 John B. Thompson, *Political Scandal: Power and Visibility in the Media Age*, Cambridge, Polity, 2000, p. 247.

63 *Ibidem*, p. 249.

64 Maria Gemma Rubí y Josep Armengol Segú, "Cataluña", Joaquín Varela Ortega (ed.), *El poder de la influencia. Geografía del caciquismo en España (1875–1923)*, Madrid, Marcial Pons, 2001, p. 257.

65 See the remarks of Hilda Sábato quoted in the Introduction of this book.

66 As the Republican newspaper *El Igualadino* commented: "The advice of family and friends . . . and the serious damage that Godó feared in *La Vanguardia*, led him to take the decision [to resign] (...) Everywhere the press is full of it". R. Romesquet Picantó, "¡¡¡Quin desastre!!!", *El Igualadino*, 29/09/1906, p. 2.

Chapter 6

1 These considerations do not imply that the democratisation of politics was a top-down process controlled by elites, but rather an uneven and often erratic process. John Garrard, "The Democratic Experience", Stefan Berger (ed.), *A Companion to Nineteenth-century Europe, 1789–1914*, Malden, Blackwell, 2006, pp. 149–163; John Garrard, Vera Tolz, Ralph White (eds.), *European Democratization since 1800*, Hampshire, Macmillan, 1999; Raffaelle Romanelli (ed.), *How Did They Become voters? The History of Franchise in Modern European Representation*, The Hague–Boston, Kluwer, 1998.

2 Nick Carter, Rethinking the Italian Liberal State, *Bulletin of Italian Politics*, Vol. 3, No. 2, 2011, pp. 225–245; Ángeles Barrio (ed.), La crisis del régimen liberal en España, 1917–1923, *Ayer*, Num. 63, 2006; Edward Acton, Ismael Saz (eds.), *La transición a la política de masas*, València, Universitat de València, 2001; Salvador Forner Muñoz (ed.), *Democracia, elecciones y modernización en Europa. Siglos XIX y XX*, Madrid, Cátedra, 1997; Marcela Alejandra García Sebastiani, Fernando del Rey Reguillo (eds.), *Los desafíos de la libertad. Transformación y crisis del liberalismo en Europa y América Latina*, Madrid, Biblioteca Nueva, 2008; Manuel Suárez Cortina (Ed.), *La crisis del Estado liberal en la Europa del Sur*, Santander, Sociedad Menéndez Pelayo, 2000.

3 John Davis, "Liberal elites and Mass politics in Italy 1860–1914", I. Saz, E. Acton, *op. cit.*, p. 17.

4 Axel Körner, *Politics of Culture in Liberal Italy: From Unification to Fascism*, New York, Routledge, 2009; José Luis García Delgado (ed.), *Las ciudades en la modernización de España. Los decenios interseculares*, Madrid, Siglo XXI, 1992; José Varela Ortega (ed.), *El poder de la influencia. Geografía del caciquismo en España (1875–1923)*, Madrid, Marcial Pons, 2001.

5 Rosa Ana Gutiérrez & Rafael Zurita, "España en la campaña electoral de 1907: entre la vieja y la nueva cultura política", R.A. Gutiérrez, R. Zurita, R. Camurri (eds.), *Elecciones y cultura política en España e Italia (1890–1923)*, València, Publicacions de la Universitat de València, 2003, pp. 121–142 (esp. p. 139).

6 *Ibidem*, pp. 139–140.

7 Julio de la Cueva Merino, Católicos en la calle: la movilización de los católicos españoles, 1899–1923, *Historia y Política*, 3, 2000, pp. 55–80; Rafael Cruz (ed.), "El anticlericalismo", *Ayer*, 27, 1997 (monograph).

8 *"El Igualadino*, 30/06/1906, p. 1.

9 Gemma Rubí, *op. cit.*, p. 87.

10 *El Igualadino*, 20/04/1907, pp. 2–3. The historians Jordi Planas and Francesc Valls have written an excellent analysis of one of the rural towns (Pierola) where the Godó family had wide support. J. Planas and F. Valls, *Cacics i*

rabassaires. Dinàmica associativa i conflictivitat social. Els Hostalets de Pierola, 1890–1939, Vic, Eumo, 2011.

11 R. Romesquet Picantó, "¡¡¡Quin desastre!!!", *El Igualadino*, 08/07/1906, p. 2.

12 LV, 01/04/1907, p. 3. Juan Godó Llucià personally assured the members of the *Solidaritat Catalana* that he would not run for the next elections: Pilar Martínez-Carné Ascaso, *Els inicis del catalanisme polític i Leonci Soler i March: 1858–1932*, Barcelona, Publicacions de l'Abadia de Montserrat, 1999, pp. 523–524.

13 Pere Pascual Domènech, *Fàbrica i treball a la Igualada de la primera meitat del segle XX*, Barcelona, Abadia de Montserrat, Ajuntament d'Igualada, 1991.

14 The main working association was the *"Federación local de Sociedades Obreras"*, established at the end of the 19th century. Antoni Carner, *Els moviments obrers a Igualada durant el segle XIX*, Igualada, Centre d'Estudis Comarcals, 1971, p. 33.

15 The new party headquarters of the Republicans were: the *"Centre Republicà Històric"* (1886), *"Centre de la Unió Republicana d'Igualada"* (1893), *"Cercle Republicà d'Igualada"* (1904). The Carlists gathered in the *"Centro Tradicionalista de Igualada"* (1889) and the Anarchists in the *"Federación Igualadina"* (1883–1885). *Ibidem.*

16 Jorge Pablo Martínez de Presno, *Moviments socials a Igualada al segle XIX (anys 1854–1890)*, Barcelona, Publicacions de l'Abadia de Montserrat, 1993; Soledad Bengoechea, *Les dècades convulses. Igualada com a exemple. Mobilització patronal i obrera entre principis del segle XX i la dictadura de Primo de Rivera*, Igualada, Publicacions de l'Abadia de Montserrat, 2002.

17 Maria Teresa Miret, *La premsa a Igualada (1808?-1982)*, Barcelona, Departament de Cultura de la Generalitat de Catalunya, 1983, 2 vol.

18 "It is time that women abandon certain concerns and besides being good wives and exemplary mothers they also work for their land (...). Wives, mothers, sisters, fiancées and girlfriends, work for the victory of this candidacy; and support those men who shall defend our [national] rights in Congress." It must be noted that this article (written originally in Catalan) was authored by a women, Maria Dolors Cortades. "D'eleccions. A les dones", *Pàtria*, 20/04/1907, p. 1; "Als obrers", *Pàtria*, 13/04/1907, p. 1.

19 "¡Electors!", *El Igualadino*, 20/04/1907, p. 1.

20 Cambó urged the need of winning the favour of a local boss in the town of Calaf to rig the elections: "[Mister] Ferrer Carulla, from Calaf, can contribute decisively to our victory. It is of central importance for the Lliga that Rahola wins the elections. I am aware you have influence on Ferrer. It is necessary that you make the greatest use of it. Yours faithfully, Francesch Cambó". Pilar Martínez-Carné Ascaso, *Els inicis del catalanisme polític i Leonci Soler i March: 1858–1932*, Barcelona, Publicacions de l'Abadia de Montserrat, 1999, p. 524.

21 Gemma Rubí, *Els catalans i la política en temps del caciquisme. Manresa, 1875–1923*, Vic, Eumo, 2006.

22 Pilar Martínez-Carné Ascaso, *op. cit.*

23 The Article 32 of the electoral law of 1890 allowed candidates to appoint legal

assistants to monitor the elections. José Carlos Rueda (ed.), *Legislación electoral española (1808–1977)*, Madrid, Ariel, 1998, p. 160.

24 Such as Hermenegildo Godó Llucià (brother of the candidate); Antoni Llansana Soler, who was the examining judge ("juez de instrucción") and brother-in-law of Juan Godó Llucià; Baldomero Camps Blaví, who was a business partner of Juan and Ramón Godó; and Josep Ferrer Carulla, the mayor of the neighbouring town of Calaf. Arxiu Notarial d'Igualada (ANI), Notari Martí Gual, 1907, pp. 291–292.

25 *El Igualadino*, 20/04/1907, p. 2.

26 Modesto Sánchez de los Santos, *Las Cortes españolas: las de 1907*, Madrid, Antonio Marzo, 1908, p. 245.

27 Electoral turnout in the four Catalan provinces: Barcelona (55.93%), Girona (58.46%), Lleida (66.73%), Tarragona (68.27%). G. Rubí (2008), *op. cit.*, p. 91.

28 G. Rubí (1995), *op. cit.*, p. 60.

29 Among the novelties included in the new electoral law, there was the introduction of compulsory voting; and different measures aimed at counteracting *caciquismo*. The most problematic of these measures was Article 29, according to which in those constituencies where there was only one candidate standing for election, he would be elected automatically. In practice, rather than preventing caciquismo this article (which was proposed by the Republican Gumersindo Azcárate) was exploited by local elites for their own benefit. See: María Jesús González Hernández, *El universo conservador de Antonio Maura. Biografía y proyecto de estado*, Madrid, Biblioteca Nueva, 1997, pp. 145–150. On the breaking of the *Solidaritat Catalana*, see: G. Rubí & F. Espinet, *op. cit.*

30 Marteen Van Ginderachter and Marnix Beyen (eds.), *Nationhood from Below: Europe in the Long Nineteenth Century*, Basingstoke, Palgrave Macmillan, 2012.

31 Pieter M. Judson, *Exclusive Revolutionaries: Liberal Politics, Social Experience, and National Identity in the Austrian Empire, 1848–1914*, Ann Arbor, University of Michigan Press, 1996.

32 It is impossible to mention here the vast bibliography on this topic, however some valuable references are: José Alvarez Junco, *Mater Dolorosa: la idea de España en el siglo XIX*, Madrid, Taurus, 2001; Clare Mar-Molinero and Angel Smith (eds.), *Nationalism and the Nation in the Iberian Peninsula: Competing and Conflicting Identities*, Oxford–Washington, Berg, 1996.

33 Borja de Riquer, *Lliga Regionalista. La burgesia catalana i el nacionalisme, 1898–1904*, Barcelona, Edicions 62, 1977; Charles E. Ehrlic, *Lliga Regionalista. Lliga Catalana, 1901–1936*, Barcelona, Institut Cambó, 2004.

34 On the receptions of the demands of Catalan autonomy: Borja de Riquer, *Escolta, Espanya: la cuestión catalana en la época liberal*, Madrid, Marcial Pons, 2001.

35 "Movimiento electoral", LV, 25/04/1910, p. 3. Emphasis added.

36 LV, 02/05/1910, p. 10. Emphasis added. The same strategy was used in the elections of 1914. LV, 03/03/1914, p. 6.

37 See Chapter 3.

38 Examples of this bad publicity, in: LV, 02/05/1910, p. 10; 25/04/1910, p. 3.

39 "El famós meeting de Torra de Claramunt", *La Veu de Catalunya*, 29/04/1910, p. 2; "Lo que n'ha dit la premsa", *La Veu de Catalunya*, 26/04/1910, p. 3.

40 See Chapter 5. As one newspaper rightly put it: "Bien puede estarle agradecido el Godó de Igualada al Godó de Barcelona, puesto que en obsequio del primero sacrifica don Ramón hasta la seriedad y el buen nombre de 'La Vanguardia'". *Ibidem*.

41 Further details on the protests for the numerous irregularities, in: Modesto Sánchez de los Santos, *Las Cortes Españolas: las de 1910*, Madrid, Establecimiento Tipográfico de A. Marzo, 1910, pp. 341–342.

42 "Redempció", *L'Igualadí. Setmanari Republicá Autonomista*, 01/03/1914, p. 2.

43 The divisions between liberal parties will be studied in the second part of this chapter.

44 "Igualada", LV, 09/03/1914, p. 5.

45 *ABC*, 13/03/1914, p. 10.

46 LV, 31/03/1916, p. 3.

47 LV, 31/03/1916, p. 3.

48 AFAM, l. 266, c. 2. Letter written on 08/02/1911.

49 His affiliation to the Liberal Party had personal motives, for Maura married the daughter of a prominent liberal politician named Germán Gamazo. See: Esther Calzada del Amo, *Germán Gamazo, 1840–1901. Poder político y redes sociales en la Restauración*, Madrid, Marcial Pons Historia, 2011.

50 M. J. Hernández González (1997), *op. cit.*, pp. 61–64; 117.

51 Joan Connoly Ullman, *The Tragic Week: A Study of Anticlericalism in Spain, 1875–1912*, Cambridge, MA, Harvard University Press, 1968. A detailed state of the art, held on the centenary commemoration of the Tragic Week: Eloy Martín Corrales (ed.), *Semana Trágica. Entre las barricadas de Barcelona y el Barranco del Lobo*, Barcelona, Bellaterra, 2011. An overview of the events: Antoni Dalmau, *Siete días de furia. Barcelona y la Semana Trágica (julio de 1909)*, Barcelona, Destino, 2009.

52 Vincent Robert, La protesta universal contra la ejecución de Ferrer: las manifestaciones de octubre de 1909, *Historia Social*, 1992, 14, pp. 61–82.

53 Quoted in: Wolfram Kaiser, "'Clericalism – that is our enemy!': European anticlericalism and the culture wars", in: Christopher Clark & Wolfram Kaiser (eds.), *Culture Wars. Secular-Catholic Conflict in Nineteenth-Century Europe*, Cambridge, CUP, 2003, p. 74.

54 A general view of Ferrer's international impact, in: Juan Avilés, *Francisco Ferrer y Guardia. Pedagogo, anarquista y mártir*, Madrid, Marcial Pons, 2006, pp. 247–258; Maurizio Antonioli (ed.), *Contro la chiesa. I moti pro Ferrer del 1909 in Italia*, Pisa, BFS, Edizioni, 2009.

55 C. Clark and W. Kaiser (eds.), *op. cit.*, esp. chapters 1 and 2.

56 *Ibidem*, pp. 64–74; Lisa Dittrich, Die Hinrichtung Francisco Ferrers. Ein Fall für die europäische Öffentlichkeit im frühen 20. Jahrhundert?, ["The execution of Francisco Ferrer. A case for the European public in the early 20th century?"], *Themenportal Europäische Geschichte* (2008), Accessed online: http://www.europa.clio-online.de/2008/Article=325.

57 Adrian Lyttleton, An Old Church and a New State: Italian Anticlericalism, 1876–1915, *European History Quarterly*, 1983, 13, pp. 225–248.
58 Daniel Laqua, Freethinkers, anarchists and Francisco Ferrer: The making of a transnational solidarity campaign, *European Review of History: Revue européenne d'histoire*, 2014, 21, 4, pp. 467–484.
59 Luis Simarro, *El proceso Ferrer y la opinión europea*, Madrid, Imp. Eduardo Arias, 1910, pp. 281–284.
60 Frierich Edelmayer, The "Leyenda Negra" and the Circulation of Anti-Catholic and Anti-Spanish Prejudices, *European History Online* (EGO), 2011. Accessed online: .
61 Juan Avilés, "L'image de Ferrer dans la presse conservatrice espagnole", in: Anne Morelli and Jacques Lemaire (eds.), *Francisco Ferrer, cent ans après son exécution. Les avatars d'une image*, Brussels, La Pensée et les Hommes, 2011, pp. 53–70.
62 Alfredo Opisso, "Nueva Hermandad", LV, 01/09/1909, p. 4; "BARCELONA", 15/09/1909, p. 4.
63 W. Kaiser, *op. cit.*, pp. 47–48.
64 See Chapter 5.
65 Miguel Moya, José Ortega Munilla, José Gasset Chinchilla (owner of the newspaper *El Imparcial*) and Antonio Sacristán. They were all journalists and deputies. Pedro Gómez Aparicio, *Historia del periodismo español*, Madrid, Editora Nacional, vol. 3, p. 250.
66 Juan Carlos Sánchez Illán, *Prensa y política en la España de la Restauración. Rafael Gasset y El Imparcial*, Madrid, Biblioteca Nueva, p. 246.
67 J. Avilés (2006), *op. cit.*, pp. 260–261.
68 "BARCELONA", LV, 06/11/1909, p. 6.
69 "LAOCONTE DE LA POLÍTICA", LV, 25/09/1909, p. 4.
70 M. J. Hernández González, *Ciudadanía y Acción . . . , op. cit.*
71 A deeper insight than the one provided here about the characteristics of charisma, in: Edward Berenson and Eva Giloi (eds.), *Constructing Charisma: Celebrity, Fame, and Power in Nineteenth-Century Europe*, New York–Oxford, Berghan, 2012; Lucy Riall, *Garibaldi. Invention of a Hero*, New Haven–London, Yale University Press, 2007.
72 *Ibidem*, p. 396.
73 AFAM, l. 45, c. 29.
74 Anthony L. Cardoza, *Aristocrats in Bourgeois Italy: The Piedmontese Nobility, 1861–1930*, Cambridge, Cambridge University Press, 2002.

Chapter 7

1 Burgos y Mazo, *El verano de 1919 en Gobernación*, p. 449, quoted in Charles E. Ehrlich, *Lliga Regionalista: Lliga Catalana, 1901–1936, op. cit.*, p. 306.
2 Jay Winter (ed.), *The Cambridge History of the First World War*, Cambridge–New York, CUP, 2013, Volume 1 "Global War".
3 Julián Casanova, *Europa contra Europa, 1914–1945*, Barcelona, Crítica, 2011.

4   Heinrich Best and Maurizio Cotta, "Transformations of the Original Parliamentary Establishment between the 1880s and 1920s", in: H. Best and M. Cotta (eds.), *op. cit.*, p. 513.

5   See: Angel Smith, The Catalan Counter-revolutionary Coalition and the Primo de Rivera Coup, 1917–23, *European History Quarterly*, Vol. 37(1), pp. 7–8.

6   Francisco J. Romero Salvadó, Between the Catalan quagmire and the red spectre. Spain, November 1918 - April 1919, *The Historical Journal*, 2017.

7   "Á NUESTROS LECTORES", LV, 24/10/1903, p. 2.

8   Pere Voltes, "Análisis empresarial y contable del auge del diario "La Vanguardia" en el periodo comprendido entre 1881 y 1939", Barcelona, Colección "Cuadernos de Investigación, N° 19, p. 5. The total surface of the two buildings, in "La casa de La Vanguardia", LV, 25/10/1893, p. 4.

9   Víctor Alba, *Sísif i el seu temps*, vol I "Costa avall", Barcelona Laertes, 1990, p. 92.

10 "Á NUESTROS LECTORES", LV, 24/10/1903, p. 2.

11 *Ibid.*

12 "La casa de La Vanguardia", LV, 25/10/1893, p. 4.

13 For instance on 24 December 1911, when the newspaper inaugurated a new rotary press.

14 LV, *op. cit.*

15 *Ibid.*

16 F. Espinet & J.M. Tresserras, *op. cit.*, p. 11.

17 *Ibid.*, p. 22.

18 "The telegraph, the telephone, electricity, the automobile, the cinematograph, the phonograph, these are all novelties which have not arrived here yet [in his hometown of Sarral] [but] that characterise this fecund age and are the subject of passionate debate (....). Perhaps someone will come from Barcelona who has already seen all these devices!." Claudi Ametilla, *Memòries polítiques*, Barcelona, Pòrtic, 1963, vol. 1, p. 86.

19 A. Riera, "El periodismo moderno", LV, 25/10/1903, pp. 10–11.

20 "The major newspapers felt they had a responsibility to print news from all over the world – indeed, only if they were capable of providing international coverage could they "hit the big time". Jürgen Osterhammel, *The Transformation of the World: A Global History of the Nineteenth-century*, Princeton University Press, 2014, p. 37.

21 J. Osterhammel, *op. cit.*, p. 38.

22 Roland Wenzlhuemer, *Connecting the Nineteenth Century World: The Telegraph and Globalization*, Cambridge, CUP, 2013, esp. pp. 91–92.

23 A. Riera, "El periodismo moderno", LV, 25/10/1903. Emphasis added.

24 José Escofet, "Costumbres viejas. La prensa y los teatros", LV, 29/09/1917, p. 8.

25 Pedro Gómez Aparicio, *Historia del periodismo español*, Madrid, Editora Nacional, 1971, vol. 2, p. 256 and pp. 648–649, respectively.

26 María Antonia Paz Rebollo, "El Colonialismo informativo de la Agencia Havas en España, 1870–1940", Madrid, Universidad Complutense de Madrid, 1988 [unpublished thesis].

27 ANF, 5 AR/424. The *Asociación de Prensa Barcelonesa* (Barcelona's Press

Association) was integrated by *La Veu de Catalunya*, *Las Noticias* and *El Diluvio*. The newspaper *La Publicidad* joined this service temporarily (between 15/08/1908 and 01/08/1910).

28   The only exception to this progression was the year of 1912, when *La Vanguardia* set a limit of 55,000 words per month. In October 1913 this limit was removed. This parenthesis might have had something to do with the newspaper's temporary lack of liquidity. ANF, 5 AR/95, "La Vanguardia", 22/03/1912, 02/08/1912 and 20/10/1913.

29   ANF, 5 AR/424.

30   Eduardo González Calleja and Paul Aubert, *Nido de espías. España, Francia y la Primera Guerra Mundial, 1914–1919*, Madrid, Alianza, 2014; Fernando García Sanz, *España en la Gran Guerra. Espías, diplomáticos y traficantes*, Madrid, Galaxia Gutenberg, 2014; and Maximiliano Fuentes Codera, *España en la Primera Guerra Mundial. Una movilización cultural*, Madrid, Akal, 2014.

31   Alfredo Opisso, "La semana en el extranjero", LV, 07/08/1914, p. 7.

32   Josep Maria de Sagarra, *Memorias*, Barcelona, Editorial Noguer, 1957, p. 553.

33   Claudi Ametilla, *Memòries polítiques, 1890–1917*, Barcelona, editorial Pòrtic, 1963, pp. 338–339.

34   *Ibidem*, pp. 216–217.

35   For the circulation of Barcelona' newspapers, see the table at the beginning of this chapter.

36   As the agency rapidly proclaimed, "Reuter's Agency has always ben recognised as a British institution representing the English point of view". See: Donald Read, *The Power of News: The History of Reuters, 1849–1989*, New York, Oxford University Press, 1992, pp. 111–112.

37   "The agencies contributed to the globalized production and dissemination of news, passing it along without additional comment in a powerful expression of the ideology of 'objectivity'. On the other hand, their standardized reports promoted a uniform kind of journalism, now that all print media were more or less in the same boat." J. Osterhammel, *op. cit.*, p. 38.

38   AFAM, l. 45, c. 29.

39   Gerald H. Meaker, *op. cit.*, pp. 22–23.

40   Chapter 6.

41   J.M. Desvois, *La prensa en España (1900–1931)*, Madrid, Siglo XXI, 1977, p. 17.

42   There is an excellent biography on this figure: Gregori Mir, *Miquel dels Sants Oliver. Nacionalisme i síntesi liberal-conservadora, 1898–1919*, Palma de Mallorca, Miquel Font, 1993, 2 vol.

43   Agustí Calvert ("Gaziel"), *Història de La Vanguardia (1884–1936)*, París, Edicions catalanes de París, 1971, p. 83.

44   *Ibid.*, pp. 83–84.

45   *Ibidem*.

46   Maura advised the owner of *La Vanguardia* to keep this newspaper in the field of strict neutrality. AFAM, l. 45, c. 29. Letter of A. Maura to R. Godó, Madrid, 27/10/1914.

47   "La Vanguardia" nous prie de nous abstenir dans les dépêches de tous commentaires et de nous limiter exclusivement aux information". ANF, 5 AR/95, "La Vanguardia", p. 5.

48 ANF, 5 AR/424, p. 42, letter of Ramón Godó to the Director of Havas, 09/10/1913.

49 Luis Álvarez Guitiérrez, "Intentos alemanes para contrarrestar la influencia francesa sobre la opinión pública española en los años precedentes a la Primera Guerra Mundial", in: VVAA, *Españoles y franceses en la primera mitad del siglo XX*, Madrid, CSIC, 1986, pp. 1–22; and "Proyectos alemanes para crear un servicio permanente de noticias en España durante los primeros lustros del siglo XX", *Cuadernos de Historia Moderna y Contemporánea*, nº 4, Ed. Univ. Compl. Madrid, 1983, pp. 141–174.

50 Ramón Villares y Javier Moreno Luzón, "Restauración y Dictadura", in: Josep Fontana y Ramón Villares (dirs.), *Historia de España*, vol. 7, pp. 435–436.

51 For a detailed analysis of this central element, which historians often neglect, see: Javier Moreno Luzón, "The Government, Parties and the Kig, 1913–23", in A. Smith and F. J. Romero Salvadó, *The Agony of Spanish Liberalism . . .* , pp. 32–61.

52 Further details in: *Ibid.*

53 Javier Moreno Luzón, The Government, Parties, and the King, 1913–23, in: Francisco J. Romero Salvadó & Angel Smith (eds.), *The Agony of Spanish Liberalism . . .* , p. 41 and p. 44.

54 Enric Ucelay Da Cal, *El imperialismo catalán. Prat de la Riba, Cambó, D'Ors y la conquista moral de España*, Barcelona, Edhasa, 2003; Charles Ehrlich, Per Catalunya i l'Espanya Gran: Catalan Regionalism on the Offensive, 1911–19, *European History Quarterly*, Vol. 28 (2), pp. 189–217.

55 Thus, in a first phase, the Regionalists became the frontrunners of a wide coalition of opposing forces (the Assembly of Parliamentarians of 1917) that sought to bring down the *turno dinástico* and implement a constitutional reform. Unable to topple the political system and concerned by the call for a worker's general strike in August 1917, the Lliga abandoned this strategy and opted for a new, more moderate one, which sought to combine the bid for democratic reform with the preservation of the social order.

56 Carlos Seco Serrano, *Una gran dama catalana en la corte de Alfonso XIII . . .* , p. 15, quoted in Riquer, *op. cit.*, p. 112, n. 3.

57 Riquer, *op. cit.*, pp. 113–115.

58 Still, and contrary to what is often assumed, the social profile of Lliga went beyond the Catalan upper classes. See: Charles E. Ehrlich, Per Catalunya i l'Espanya Gran . . . , *op. cit.*

59 "Se impondrá la templanza", LV, 03/12/1918, p. 10.

60 LV, 03/12/1918, p. 10.

61 *Ibid.* See also chapter 3.

62 Javier Moreno Luzón, De agravios, pactos y símbolos. El nacionalismo español ante la autonomía de Cataluña, *Ayer*, n. 63, 2006, pp. 119–151.

63 "La manifestación de hoy", LV, 10/12/1918, p. 9.

64 Quoted in: Borja de Riquer, *Alfonso XIII y Cambó . . .* , p. 118.

65 *La Vanguardia* also criticised the *Círculo de la Unión Mercantil* for giving a too rabid character to the demonstrations. "Las estridencias", LV, 10/12/1918, p. 6.

66 "Reflexión necesaria", LV, 14/12/1918, p. 8.

67   As acknowledged by one of newspaper's journalists (Agustí Calvet). For further
      details, see: Gaziel, *Història de La Vanguardia*, p. 10.

68   Gaziel, *Història de La Vanguardia*, p. 10.

69   *Ibid*, pp. 91–92.

70   The Republican newspaper *El Diluvio* provided an almost exact description of
      the same events, including the detail of Godó's pistol. "Un capítulo de historia
      barcelonesa", *El Diluvio*, 19/01/1919, p. x.

71   Gaziel, *Història de La Vanguardia . . .* , p. 92.

72   "Día de afirmación monárquica", LV, 05/01/1919, p. 4.

73   *Op. cit.*

74   *La Vanguardia* devoted an entire page to give the maximum visibility to the
      call in support of the King. Moreover, a note was added below the call, stating
      that *La Vanguardia* fully endorsed the homage to the King. "Notas locales",
      LV, 06/01/1919, p. 4.

75   "En la Capitanía General. Día de afirmación monárquica", LV, 07/01/1919, p. 3.

76   Borja de Riquer, *Alfonso XIII y Cambó . . .* , pp. 129–130.

77   Día de afirmación monárquica", LV, 05/01/1919, p. 4.

78   Josep Puy i Juanicó, La Unión Monárquica Nacional frente al catalanismo de la
      Lliga, 1918–1923, *Estudios de Historia Social*, n° 28–29, 1984, p. 468.

79   *Ibid.*

80   The concession of the noble title was made official in the Royal Decree of 18
      September 1916. Among the reasons that were put forward to justify the
      concession of the title was Ramón's position as newspaper proprietor:
      "Propietario del importante diario *La Vanguardia*. Ha consagrado á esta
      publicación todas sus energías é invertido en ella cuantiosas sumas, hasta
      convertirla en uno de los principales periódicos de España. Cuenta *La
      Vanguardia* con edificio propio, gabinete telegráfico, linotipias, cajas,
      estereotipia y rotativas." *Gaceta de Madrid*, 15/11/1916, p. 598.

81   Pedro Gual Villalbí, *Memorias de un industrial de nuestro tiempo*, Barcelona,
      Sociedad General de Publicaciones, 1922, pp. 161–162.

82   The three newspapers that stood against the "red censorship" were the *Diario de
      Barcelona*, the *Gaceta de Cataluña* and *El Progreso*. Each of them was charged with
      a fine of 1,000 *pesetas*. Gómez Aparicio, *Historia del periodismo*, vol. 3, p. 602.

83   For a more detailed examination, see: Angel Smith, *Anarchism, Revolution and
      Reaction: Catalan Labour and the Crisis of the Spanish State, 1898–1923*, New
      York, Berghahn, 2007, pp. 225–254. For a broader context on Barcelona's class
      conflicts, see the book edited by the same author: *Red Barcelona: Social Protest
      and Labour Mobilization in the Twentieth Century*, Routledge, London and New
      York, 2002.

84   Chris Ealham, *Anarchism and the City: Revolution and Counter-revolution in
      Barcelona, 1898–1937*, Edinburgh, AK Press, 2010, p. 40.

85   Pedro Gual Villalbí, *Memorias de un industrial de nuestro tiempo . . .* , p. 163.

86   McDonough, *The Good Families . . .* ; A. Smith, Anarchism, *Revolution and
      Reaction . . .* , p. 231.

87   Soledad Bengoechea, *Organització patronal i conflictivitat social a Catalunya.*

Tradició i corporativisme entre finals de segle i la dictadura de Primo de Rivera, Barcelona, Publicacions de l'Abadia de Montserrat, 1994, pp. 191–195 and pp. 207–213.

88   Eduardo González Calleja & Fernando del Rey Reguillo, *La defensa armada contra la revolución*, Madrid, CSIC–Biblioteca de Historia, 1995, p. 72. Still, and as the two authors observe, in the days after the Sometent was created it comprised a mix of social classes.

89   LV, 15/04/1919, p. 9.

90   *Ibid*.

91   Joaquim Maria de Nadal, *Memòries. Vuitanta anys de sinceritats i de silencis*, Barcelona, editorial Aedos, 1965, p. 303.

92   E. González Calleja & F. del Rey Reguillo, *La defensa armada . . .* , p. 91.

93   AFAM, l. 219, c. 16.

94   Bengoechea, *El Locaut . . .*

95   Pere Gabriel, Red Barcelona in the Europe of war and revolution, 1914–30, in: A. Smith (ed.), *Red Barcelona . . .* , p. 59.

96   Francisco J. Romero Salvadó, The Catalan employer's dirty war, in: F. J. Romero Salvadó and Angel Smith (eds.), *The Agony of Spanish Liberalism . . .* , p. 188.

97   For the full manifiesto, see: "Al país y al Ejército", LV, 13/09/1923, p. 18.

98   F. J. Romero Salvadó, The Catalan Employer's Dirty War . . . , pp. 191–192; Fernando del Rey, El capitalismo catalán y Primo de Rivera: en torno a un golpe de estado, *Hispania*, XLVIII/168, January–April 1988, pp. 294–307.

99   "Tentativa de regeneración nacional", LV, 14/09/1923, p. 3.

100   *Ibid*.

Epilogue

1   All the information on the events described, in: "EL ENTIERRO", LV, 22/09/1931, p. 8.

2   "LOS QUE MUEREN", LV, 22/09/1931, p. 8.

3   "Una crisis histórica", LV, 30/01/1930, p. 6.

4   "Nuestra posición", LV, 23/05/1931, p. 4. On the little enthusiasm the newspaper showed about the way the Second Republic was proclaimed, see: "La demagogia en el Ayuntamiento", *op. cit.*

5   Gaziel, *Una història de La Vanguardia, 1884–1936*, París, Edicions catalanes de París, 1971, p. 111; María Cruz Seoane & María Dolores Sáiz, *Historia del periodismo en España*, Madrid, Alianza editorial, 1996, vol. 3 "El siglo XX: 1898–1936", pp. 428–430.

6   Moreover, it is estimated that as much as the 20% of the newspaper' total circulation was sold outside Catalonia. Daniel E. Jones, Perspectiva econòmica de la premsa diària durant la II República, *Gazeta. Actes de les primeres jornades d'història de la premsa*, vol. 1, 1994, p. 238.

7   LV, 23/12/1987, p. 2.

8   Francesc Vilanova, *La guerra particular de Gaziel i el comte de Godó (1940–1945)*, Barcelona, Ploion, 2004, p. 88.

9 A detailed explanation of these events, in: Agustí Calvet, *Història de La Vanguardia, 1884–1936*, París, Edicions catalanes, 1971, pp. 115–121; and F. Vilanova, *op. cit.*

10 Further insights on this period, in: Rafael Aracil, Andreu Mayayo, Antoni Segura (eds.), *Diari d'una postguerra. La Vanguardia Española (1939–1946)*, Catarroja-Barcelona, Afers, 2010; and F. Vilanova, *Ibid.*

11 Michael Schudson, *Discovering the News: A Social History of American Newspapers*, New York, Basic Books, 1978; Høyer, Svennik and Pötkker, Horst (eds.), *Diffusion of the News Paradigm 1850–2000*, Goteborg, Nordicom, 2014; Marcel Broersma (ed.), *Form and Style in Journalism. European Newspapers and the Representation of News, 1880–2005*, Leuven, Peeters, 2007.

12 E. Grendi, Micro-analisi e storia sociale, *Quaderni Storici*, N° 35, pp. 506–520.

13 Further insights on this subject, in: Ellis Wasson, *Aristocracy and the Modern World*, Basingstoke, Palgrave Macmillan, 2006, p. 43.

14 Bernhard Fulda, *Press and Politics in the Weimar Republic*, Oxford, Oxford University Press, 2009; W. Phillips Davison, The Third Person Effect in Communication, *Public Opinion Quarterly*, (1983) 47 (1), pp. 1–15.

15 Renato Camurri, I tuttori della nazione: i «grandi notabili» e l'organizzazione della politica nell'Italia liberale; Jean-Louis Briquet, Notabili e processi di notabilizzazione nella Francia del diciannovesimo e ventesimo secolo, *Ricerche di storia politica*, Nuova Serie, December 2012, vol. 3, pp. 261–278 and pp. 279–294, respectively.

16 On the region as one of the multiple paths into Spanish nationalism, see: Xosé-Manoel Núñez Seixas, The Region as Essence of the Fatherland: Regionalist Variants of Spanish nationalism (1840–1936), *European History Quarterly*, vol. 31, issue 4, 2001, pp. 483–518; Joost Augusteijn & Eric Storm (eds.), *Region and state in Nineteenth-century Europe: Nation-building, Regional Identities and Separatism*, Basingstoke: Palgrave Macmillan, 2012.

17 Borja de Riquer, La débil nacionalización española del siglo XIX, *Historia Social*, 20, 1994, pp. 97–114; Juan Pablo Fusi, "Centre and periphery 1898–1936: National Integration and Regional Nationalisms Reconsidered", in Frances Lannon & Paul Preston (eds.), *Elites and Power in Twentieth-Century Spain*, Oxford, Oxford University Press, 1990, pp. 3–40; José Alvarez Junco, 'The nation-building process in nineteenth-century Spain', in Clare Mar-Molinero & Angel Smith (eds.), *Nationalism and the Nation in the Iberian Peninsula: Competing and Conflicting Identities*, Oxford, Berg, 1996, pp. 89–107.

18 Further insights on the links between civil society and the nation-building process, in: Alejandro Quiroga & Ferran Archilés (eds.), La nacionalización en España, *Ayer*, 90, 2013 (2); and Jorge Luengo, "La formación de la sociedad civil en la España del siglo XIX", in: Bartolomé Yun-Casalilla and Jorge Luengo (eds.), *Pensar el poder: Liber Amicorum de Pedro Carasa*, València, PUV, forthcoming. I am grateful to the author for giving me access to the manuscript.

19 Anthony D. Smith, *National Identity*, London, Penguin Books, 1991, pp. 1–42. As noted before, the present volume is indebted to the work that Josep Maria

Fradera has developped for an earlier period. See: *Cultura nacional en una societat dividida: patriotisme i cultura a Catalunya (1838–1868)*, Barcelona, Curial, 1992. This book went to press before the publication of Joan Lluís Marfany' new study, *Nacionalisme espanyol i catalanitat (1789–1859): cap a una revisió de la Renaixença*, Barcelona, Edicions 62, 2017. This author provides stimulating ideas for future rdiscussion.

20 "LOS QUE MUEREN", LV, 22/09/1931, p. 8.
21 Angel Smith, The Catalan Counter-revolutionary Coalition, 1917–1923, *European History Quarterly*, vol. 37(1), pp. 7–34.
22 See Chapter 6.

Index

NOTE ON STYLE: Catalan names and places have been kept in their original form, except in cases of individuals and institutions for which there is clear evidence that they preferred to use Castilian (Spanish). For example, in the case of Godó Lallana, the Castilian forename Ramón has been used rather than the Catalan Ramon, reflecting his customary use of Spanish as an important element of social distinction. The criteria adopted thus reflects the coexistence and uneven use of two languages in the same territory (Catalan and Castilian), which varied according to the social and political purpose given to language by different actors.

Page numbers in italics refer to tables; *plate/plates* refer to the illustrations (see page 000).